# War, Guilt, and World Politics after World War II

When do states choose to adopt a penitent stance toward the past? When do they choose to offer apologies for historical misdeeds, offer compensation to their victims, and incorporate the darker sides of history into their textbooks, public monuments, and museums? When do they choose not to do so? And what are the political consequences of how states portray the past?

This book pursues these questions by examining how governments in post-1945 Austria, Germany, and Japan have wrestled with the difficult legacy of World War II and the impact of their policies on regional politics in Europe and Asia. The book argues that states can reconcile over historical issues, but to do so requires greater political will and imposes greater costs than is commonly realized. At the same time, in an increasingly interdependent world, failure to do so can have a profoundly disruptive effect on regional relations and feed dangerous geopolitical tensions.

Thomas U. Berger is an Associate Professor in the Department of International Relations at Boston University. He is the author of *Cultures of Antimilitarism: National Security in Germany and Japan* and of *Redefining Japan and the U.S.-Japan Alliance* and coeditor of *Japan in International Politics: Beyond the Reactive State*. He has published extensively on issues relating to East Asian and European international relations, including essays that have appeared in *International Security*, *Review of International Studies*, *German Politics*, and *Asian Security*. His primary research areas include international security, international migration, and the politics of memory and historical representation. Prior to joining the faculty at Boston University in 2001, he was an Associate Professor at Johns Hopkins University. He has held a number of postdoctoral and research fellowships, including the Harvard Academy Junior Researcher Fellowship, the Olin Postdoctoral Fellowship in International Security Studies, and Fulbright, Japan Foundation, MacArthur, and DAAD doctoral research fellowships. He received his PhD in Political Science from MIT and his BA from Columbia College.

# War, Guilt, and World Politics after World War II

THOMAS U. BERGER

*Boston University*

CAMBRIDGE
UNIVERSITY PRESS

CAMBRIDGE UNIVERSITY PRESS
Cambridge, New York, Melbourne, Madrid, Cape Town,
Singapore, São Paulo, Delhi, Mexico City

Cambridge University Press
32 Avenue of the Americas, New York, NY 10013-2473, USA

www.cambridge.org
Information on this title: www.cambridge.org/9781107674950

First published 2012

Printed in the United States of America

A catalog record for this publication is available from the British Library.

Library of Congress Cataloging in Publication Data
Berger, Thomas U.
War, guilt, and world politics after World War II / Thomas U. Berger.
  pages  cm
Includes bibliographical references and index.
ISBN 978-1-107-02160-0 (hardback) – ISBN 978-1-107-67495-0 (paperback)    1. World War,
1939–1945 – Reparations.    2. World War, 1939–1945 – Historiography.    3. Restitution –
Europe.    4. Reparations for historical injustices – Europe.    5. Cultural property – Repatriation –
Europe.    6. World War, 1939–1945 – Confiscations and contributions – Europe.    7. Guilt –
Political aspects.    8. World War, 1939–1945 – Psychological aspects.    9. War victims.    I. Title.
D818.B47   2012
940.53'14–dc23        2011051170

ISBN 978-1-107-02160-0 Hardback
ISBN 978-1-107-67495-0 Paperback

# Contents

# Tables

# Introduction

This book is about the effects of historical memory on the political affairs of nations. It is based on a detailed analysis of three countries who have struggled to face up to their morally troubling past in the wake of World War II – Germany,[1] Austria, and Japan. The central objective of the book is to explain why these states have promoted particular official historical narratives and to identify the domestic and international consequences of their doing so. Why, for instance, did the Federal Republic of Germany early on adopt a relatively penitent stance regarding the crimes of the Nazi period, whereas Austria and Japan showed contrition only decades later, and in the case of Japan only partially so? Did Germany's willingness to confront the dark corners of its history promote better relations with its European neighbors? Why did Austria, despite being deeply implicated in the crimes of the Third Reich, tackle the question of its moral culpability only much later? Why has Japan only reluctantly apologized for its Imperial past in Asia? Has Japan's relatively impenitent stance poisoned its relations with its neighbors, as is commonly assumed, or was the impact of its lack of contrition relatively marginal or outweighed by other geopolitical or geoeconomic factors?

These are perennial questions in the study of postwar Europe and Asia and have been the subject of considerable debate for decades. Since the end of the Cold War, however, they have become more pressing than ever. Despite Germany's continued contrition for the crimes of the past, new German concerns with commemorating not only the victims of Nazism, but also the millions of Germans who became the victims of aerial bombardment and ethnic cleansing, have raised troubling questions about whether the memory of the Holocaust is in the process of being relativized, possibly heralding the reemergence of a more self-centered and assertive Federal Republic. Concerns on this score have been particularly pointed in the context of the Federal Republic's relations with Poland and the Czech Republic, but have also been evident in

---

[1] The main focus for analysis will be the Federal Republic of Germany (West Germany).

I

some of the misgivings regarding the German response to the recent economic crisis in the Eurozone. In Austria, the rapid ascent of Jörg Haider's Freedom Party in the 1990s – culminating in its becoming part of the ruling coalition in 2000 – raised similar concerns and sparked a major diplomatic crisis within the European Union. Meanwhile, in Asia, Japan's relations with its neighbors – in particular with the People's Republic of China and South Korea – have been repeatedly paralyzed by tensions over historical issues. Incidents such as Prime Minister Koizumi Junichirō's repeated visits to the Yasukuni Shrine in Tokyo between 2002 and 2006 or the Ministry of Education's approval of revisionist textbooks for use in Japanese schools have stoked a nationalist backlash in neighboring countries, undermining efforts at building stronger regional institutions and spilling over dangerously into other areas, such as territorial disputes. Instead of fading with time, in many ways at the start of the twenty first century, the memory of World War II is more contentious – and more potent – than ever.

Over the years, many explanations have been advanced to explain the differences between Europe and Asia, beginning with Ruth Benedict's famous reflections on the impact of Asian "shame" versus European "guilt" cultures and Maruyama Masao's discussion of what he called Japan's "system of irresponsibility." These explanations often were based on an overly restrictive exploration of the politics of memory in a single country, or on a limited German-Japanese comparison. Moreover, the existing models of historical memory typically reflected the disciplinary concerns of the scholars who produced them: historians tended to focus on how our understanding of the past has distorted the way in which societies remember, sociologists on the implications of historical memory for social order, and so forth. Although many such models offered useful insights, they often rested on fairly simple understanding of how politics works and tended not to address some of the central concerns of policy makers, such as the ways in which government policies can shape the broader historical memory of a given society and how the official narrative of the state may influence international relations.

To address such concerns, a more comprehensive, practically oriented approach is needed, one that analyzes the politics of historical memory from the perspective of what might be called "Historical Realism." The term "Realism" is used here in two senses. On the one hand, it suggests that we need to be realistic about the place that history and historical memory occupies in political affairs. The ways in which most people remember the past is powerfully conditioned by the narratives generated by the state, which are, in turn, driven primarily by practical considerations of security and economic gain. States are not only capable of overriding the powerful feelings of anger, guilt, and resentment generated by memories that its people may have of the injustices that have been inflicted on them, but to a surprising – and perhaps saddening – degree they are able to ignore, defuse, and even redirect them. As we shall see, post-1945 Austrians, Japanese, and even Germans were for long stretches of time strikingly impenitent about the terrible atrocities they had committed in the past. This was true both of their governments and to a remarkable extent of their broader societies as well. Perhaps more surprisingly, some of the nations that had been the targets of their aggression – such as the People's Republic of China – were able to suppress the memories of the horrors their people had endured in order to pursue national economic and political objectives. At virtually every juncture of the evolution of the government policies that defined the official narrative, considerations of interest played a crucial, even decisive role.

At the same time, however, we also must be realistic about the limits of political power to reshape historical memory. This holds true not only for democratic societies, but for authoritarian ones as well, albeit it to a lesser degree. Although states can suppress the memories social groups and individuals may have, insurgent historical narratives can spring up that challenge the existing official narratives. These insurgent narratives evolve in response to forces that are only partly related to considerations of the material interests of the state or of the groups that promote them. They are rooted in the actual experiences of people, and they evolve according to a dynamic that cannot be explained by material considerations alone. Even though narratives can be ignored or suppressed by the state, over time they have real political effects that political leaders can ignore only at their own peril. Time and again, groups representing the victims of historical injustice, as well as groups who for their own reasons promote a historical narrative different from the existing official one, have been able to place their own concerns on the political agenda in ways that greatly complicate the efforts of political leaders to promote what they see as national interest.

The impact of such groups is particularly large in democratic countries. Yet they also can have a significant impact in authoritarian political systems where sharp divisions exist between political leaders and where history can become another arena for elite power struggles. Moreover, leaders themselves often become captive to the historical narratives that they or their predecessors had created, regardless of whether they do so in order to court the political support of the groups that promote them or because they actually come to believe in them. In this sense, historical memory as it is embedded in the political culture of a nation both conditions and becomes a constitutive element in the concrete interests of states and of political leaders and can have far-reaching consequences for the possibilities of conflict and cooperation, war and peace, in the international system.[2]

The Historical Realist perspective insists that to understand why countries choose to promote the kind of historical narratives that they do, scholars and analysts have to be sensitive to the interplay between material interest

---

[2] In this sense, the position outlined here is consistent with what is sometimes referred to as "thin" or "conventional" constructivism. See Ted Hopf, "The Promise of Constructivism in International Relations Theory," *International Security* 23:1 (Summer 1998), pp, 171–200, and John G. Ruggie, "What Makes the World Hang Together? Neo-Utilitarianism and the Social Constructivist Challenge," *International Organization* 52:4 (Fall 1998), esp. pp. 880–882.

and societal memory as it exists at a specific moment in time. To cope with the consequences of the past, political leaders and policy makers have to grasp both the ways in which historical memory shapes the present and gauge the extent to which government policy can assuage and reshape the emotional impact of the past. At times it may make sense to pursue reconciliation with other nations over historical issues; at other times it may be impossible or too costly to do so. It is the larger objective of this book to help develop the intellectual resources to help decide when it is appropriate – or productive – to do so.

## Acknowledgments

Appropriately for a work that has historical memory as a central focus, this book has a long history of its own. I have had a long-standing interest in the subject. In my earlier work on German and Japanese foreign and national security policies, I argued that the memory of World War II and the particular lessons both societies drew from the war had given rise to peculiar cultures of antimilitarism that discouraged them from assuming political-military capabilities commensurate with their formidable economic and technological resources.[3] While giving talks on the subject, I was confronted time and again with the question: If the lessons of the past had given rise to a comparable reluctance to use force in both societies, why was Japan so much more unwilling than Germany to acknowledge the terrible atrocities it had committed in the pre-1945 period? My standard answer to the question was that whereas Germany focused on the crimes it had committed against others, the primary concern in Japan was with the crimes that had been committed against the Japanese people *by their own military*. The Japanese people and many of the elite sectors in Japanese society, including even many of the conservative politicians who dominated postwar politics, blamed the Imperial army for having dragged the nation into a hopeless struggle against an overwhelmingly superior coalition of forces and subsequently carried on the fight even after all hope for an acceptable solution had vanished. As a result, Japan developed a historical narrative that placed responsibility for the war and the enormous cost in human life on the military. Consequently, the Japanese were as averse to relying on the military as a means for pursuing the national interest as were the Germans, albeit for entirely different reasons.

I was willing to offer some speculations as to why the Germans saw themselves as victimizers and the Japanese preferred to see themselves as victims, but in the end, it did not matter for my central argument. Demonstrating that these narratives existed and had a significant, even decisive impact on German and Japanese defense and national security policies was enough for my purposes.

[3] See Thomas U. Berger, "From Sword to Chrysanthemum: Japan's Culture of Anti-militarism," *International Security* 17:4 (Spring 1993), pp. 119–150, and Berger, *Cultures of Antimilitarism: National Security in Germany and Japan* (Baltimore: Johns Hopkins University Press, 1998).

In this sense, in my earlier work I was interested in historical memory as an independent variable – as the primary cause for the thing that I was seeking to explain, namely German and Japanese national security policy. I stubbornly resisted, however, being drawn into a systematic analysis of historical memory as a dependent variable – that is analyzing why the two countries developed these rather different narratives.

My resistance to examining the origins of German and Japanese historical narratives began to break down in 1998 after watching Japan's ambassador to the United States, Kunihiko Saito, debate Iris Chang, the celebrated author of the New York Times best seller, *The Rape of Nanjing: The Forgotten Holocaust of World War II* on American public TV. The ambassador – although a highly capable man – seemed totally out of his depth in his efforts to respond to Chang's emotionally charged accusations that Japan had not properly addressed the issue of its responsibility for wartime atrocities. His protestations that Japan in fact had apologized seemed unconvincing; his insistence that all claims for compensation had already been settled by treaty seemed both callous and legalistic. Even though his arguments may have been perfectly logical from the narrow perspective of international law, I was convinced that they would fall flat in the court of American and world public opinion and ultimately harm rather than further Japan's national interests. When soon thereafter John Ikenberry and Takashi Inoguchi invited me to explore the issue of historical memory for an edited volume they were putting together, I was ready and eager to accept their invitation.

The project took far longer than I had anticipated. I soon discovered that other disciplines – history, sociology, and social psychology in particular – have tackled the topic for many years, and that vast bodies of literature had grown up regarding the nature of historical memory and the forces that shape it. Political science, I learned, is a relative latecomer to the subject, and there has been a strong tendency on the part of political scientists to avoid dealing with the topic at all. The general view in the discipline is that historical memory is an issue for cultural historians and literary theorists; serious political scientists should focus on the ostensibly more substantive forces that really drive politics and international affairs, such as the balance of military power or the quest to maximize economic interests.

Yet, although at times the topic seemed overwhelming, in the course of my research, I also became convinced that there was an urgent need for political scientists to tackle the subject. As I worked, new political crises in both Europe and East Asia emerged that revolved around disputes over the past and underlined the saliency of the issue. Friends of mine who had gone into policy making in Washington – especially Mike Green and David Asher – frequently complained to me of the absence of practically oriented analyses of the impact of historical memory on international relations and further encouraged me to continue with the topic.

In the course of my research, I have accumulated many debts. I owe special thanks to the Japan Foundation and the Center for Global Partnership, which at a crucial juncture provided me with the funds to take time off from my research and concentrate on my writing. I am also grateful to Professor Jitsuo Tsuchiyama of Aoyama University in Tokyo for inviting me as a visiting lecturer and arranging a number of interviews and conversations with knowledgeable people. Innumerable people helped me at different stages in my research. I owe a particularly deep debt to Togo Kazuhiko, formerly Japan's ambassador to Holland and currently professor at Kyoto Sangyo University; Dr. Karl Kaiser, formerly head of the Deutsche Gesellschaft für Aussenpolitik and now lecturer at the Kennedy School at Harvard; and Dr. Thomas Novotny of the Austrian embassy in Washington, DC. Their perspectives as both scholars and practitioners were invaluable. Togo Kazuhiko in particular has been extraordinarily generous in providing support and guidance during my work on this topic. I am also indebted to some of my earlier interlocutors on German and Japanese foreign policy, especially Okazaki Hisahiko, Hata Ikuhiko, and Michael Stuermer.

During this period I was also invited to a number of workshops and conferences where I had the opportunity to present my ideas to knowledgeable audiences of scholars, journalists, and former policy makers. I owe special thanks in this regard to Jitsuo Tsuchiyama of Aoyama University, Martina Timmerman at the UN University in Tokyo, Eric Langenbacher and Yossi Schain at Georgetown University, Tsuyoshi Hasegawa of Santa Barbara University, Rogers Peterson of MIT, Lillian Gardner-Feldman of the American Institute for Contemporary German Studies, Ito Kenichi of the Japan Forum on International Relations, Jim Hollifield, director of the Tower Center at Southern Methodist University, and Gi-Wook Shin and Dan Sneider at the Shorenstein Center at Stanford. To both the organizers and to the many participants of these events, I wish to express my thanks for their thoughts and suggestions, as well as for an opportunity to publish some of my early work on this topic. I also thank Amy Catalinac and Shin Fujihira at the U.S.-Japan program at Harvard for arranging a smaller but very useful study group at Harvard University. Particular thanks are owed to Ide Hiroko for helping proofread the drafts of the chapters on Asia and catching mistakes in my transliteration of Japanese words.

Many colleagues in and around the Boston area have been the source of constant inspiration to me. Alexis Dudden, Yinan He, Jennifer Lind, Francisca Seraphim, and Catherine Yeh in particular were extraordinarily helpful and comradely in helping me think through the many complex issues involved in the study of historical memory. Ezra Vogel and Richard Samuels both generously agreed to read complete drafts of the book manuscript and offered plenty of both encouragement and constructive criticism. I cannot express the depth of my gratitude to these two extraordinarily accomplished and generous scholars. They truly are what one calls in Japanese my *Onshi* (teachers to whom one owes lifelong obligation).

Special thanks are also in order to Lew Bateman at Cambridge University Press, who was extraordinarily supportive of this project and who both wisely and patiently helped guide it to its conclusion. I also wish to thank the two anonymous reviewers for their careful reading of the manuscript and for their many thoughtful and often very useful comments.

Finally I want to thank the members of my family, my wife Sucharita and my children, Alex and Diya, who lived through their own history during the long and laborious completion of this project. I also want to thank my parents, Peter and Brigitte Berger, who shared with me their own historical memories and in a very real way are the origins of my fascination with the past. It is to them I wish to dedicate this book.

I

# Politics and Memory in an Age of Apology

We live in an age of apology and recrimination. Over the past two decades, the world has witnessed an unprecedented outpouring of expressions of contrition by political leaders for past injustices their countries are held responsible for. At the same time, there has been an upsurge in demands for apologies, restitution, and a variety of forms of compensation on the behalf of groups and nations that feel they have been victimized. The Federal Republic of Germany may well be the paradigmatic example of this trend. More than sixty years after the end of World War II, it continues to wrestle with the legacies of the Third Reich, offering long-overdue compensation to the hundreds of thousands of former slave laborers while arguing with the governments of Poland and the Czech Republic over how to commemorate the millions of ethnic Germans who were driven out of Eastern Europe in the aftermath of the war.[1] Germany might seem a special case in this regard, burdened as it is by an especially terrible history. Yet other examples abound: the bitter disputes between Russia and its neighbors over how to view the Soviet Union,[2] the disagreement between Israelis and Palestinians over whether the Arab population in Israel had fled or were driven from their homes in 1947,[3] or repeated accusations in Asia that Japan

---

[1] For a more complete discussion and list of references, see Chapter 2.

[2] For a general discussion of the formation of Russian accounts of World War II, see James Wertsch, *Voices of Collective Memory* (New York and Cambridge: Cambridge University Press, 2002). A recent example of the way in which these disputes are affecting Russia's relations to its former satellites is provided by Lithuania and Estonia's decision to boycott the celebration of the sixtieth anniversary of Russia's victory over Nazi Germany. See Roger Cohen, "1945's Legacy: A Terror Defeated, Another Arrives," *New York Times*, May 15, 2005, available at http://www.genocidewatch.org/opinion1945slegacy15mayo5.htm. On the European reaction to the trial in Turkey of Orhan Pamuk for his comments on the massacres, see the comments of the Council of the European Union, available at http://ue.eu.int/ueDocs/cms_Data/docs/pressData/en/cfsp/88108.pdf, as well as the editorial comment on the trial from *New York Times*, January 31, 2006, available at http://www.ahiworld.com/pdfs/020306_editorial.pdf.

[3] On the importance of lost territory to Palestinian national identity Susan Slyomovics, *The Object of Memory: Arab and Jew Narrate the Palestinian Village* (Philadelphia: University of

has failed to apologize adequately for its history of atrocity and aggression before 1945,[4] and the list could well be extended almost ad infinitum.

That the past and how it is represented is of political importance is nothing new. Rulers have long realized George Orwell's dictum, "Who controls the past controls the future; who controls the present controls the past."[5] What is novel about the current situation, however, is the degree to which history and memory have become contested, both domestically and internationally. In the past, states, by and large, have been able to promote laudatory depictions of their history by suppressing or driving under ground dissident, critical narratives, at least in the realm of public discourse. Under the modern Westphalian system of juridically independent, sovereign states, governments were given the right to do so without interference from outside actors. Yet in many liberal democracies, the dark and negative aspects of their national history have today become accepted, even required, parts of how the past is depicted. For instance, it has become de rigueur now not only for German school teachers and politicians to discuss the Holocaust and the crimes of the Third Reich but for their counterparts in France, the United States, or Australia to discuss – respectively – the atrocities committed by the Vichy government, the horrors of American slavery and racism, and the systematic abuse of indigenous Australian peoples. Whereas in the past history was written by the victors, today – as Elazar Barkan has pointed out – the victims have a say as well.[6]

Scholars have devised a number of explanations for the worldwide emergence of this phenomenon. Undoubtedly, a major factor has been the increased pluralization and democratization of modern political systems that allows for the expression of a broader range of different views regarding the past and has created a preference for a legalized settlement of historical wrongs.[7] Likewise, the spread of human rights norms throughout the international system has encouraged groups and individuals to pursue issues of historical justice. The victims of past injustices are supported by a growing network of international institutions and nongovernmental groups, such as the International Criminal Court and Amnesty International, who wish to help them recover from their trauma and to deter the reoccurrence of similar abuses in the future.[8] Other

---

Pennsylvania Press, 1998) and Robert Bower, *Palestinian Refugees: Mythology, Identity and the Search for Peace* (Boulder, CO: Lynne Rienner Press, 2003).

[4] See Chapter 5 of this volume for a more detailed discussion.

[5] George Orwell, *1984*, (New York: Harcourt, Brace and Company, 1949), p. 32.

[6] Elazar Barkan, *The Guilt of Nations: Restitution and Negotiating Historical Injustices* (Baltimore: Johns Hopkins University Press, 2001), pp. XVII–XVIII.

[7] On the impact of diversity, see Melissa Nobles, *The Politics of Apology* (New York: Cambridge University Press, 2008). On the democratic penchant to pursue historical justice issues through legal means, see David Bass, *To Stay the Hand of Vengeance: International War Crimes Tribunals* (Princeton: Princeton University Press, 2008).

[8] On the impact of human rights norms and the increased trend to ascribe rights not only to individuals, but to groups, see Barkan, *The Guilt of Nations*, ibid. On the importance of pursuing historical justice issues for the sake of helping their victims, see Martha Minow, *Between*

factors that could be pointed to include the transformation of how society remembers the past thanks to changes in the technology of data collection and dissemination,[9] the functional need to create identities on the basis of universal principles in an increasingly pluralistic, multicultural world,[10] and the singular impact of the Holocaust on contemporary politics and culture.[11]

Regardless of the underlying reasons for its emergence, it is clear that we are witnessing the emergence of an international trend toward apology and contrition. What is less clear, however, is why the phenomenon is so unevenly spread. Although guilt has become officially institutionalized on a global basis, it has not done so everywhere, in the same way at the same time, with the same results. Whereas the leaders of some countries express contrition for the past, others continue to deny that they have anything to apologize for. Whereas some countries offer generous compensation to former victims, others restrict themselves to offering only token apologies. Although, in some cases, apologies and efforts at reconciliations seem to lead to more stable interstate relations, in other cases any progress that has been made remains tentative and short lived. In short, the past has been politicized as never before, and the question of what kind of historical narrative (what will be referred to here as the "official historical narrative") a state chooses to promote has become a salient feature of both domestic and international politics.

Uncertainty reigns as well over the question of what the practical implications of this phenomenon may be. With some notable exceptions,[12] mainstream international relations and political science has tended to be dismissive, regarding questions of history and culture as essentially symbolic sideshows. Instead, most scholars – and many policy makers as well – have preferred to focus on the more concrete forces believed to really drive politics, such as the balance of power and considerations of material interests. The overheated passions that are stoked by fights over history tend to be viewed as either ephemeral – with little lasting impact on political affairs – or

*Vengeance and Forgiveness: Facing History after Genocide and Mass Violence* (Boston, MA: Beacon Press, 1998).

[9] Frances A. Yates, *The Art of Memory* (London: Pimlico, 1994).

[10] Jeffrey K. Olick and Brenda Coughlin, "The Politics of Regret: Analytical Frames," in John Torpey, ed., *Politics and the Past: On Repairing Historical Injustices* (Oxford: Rowman & Littlefield, 2003), pp.38–57.

[11] Geoffrey H. Hartman, ed., *Holocaust Remembrances: The Shapes of Memory* (Oxford: Blackwell, 1994).

[12] See for instance David Art, *The Politics of the Nazi Past in Germany and Austria* (New York: Cambridge University Press, 2006); Eric Langenbacher and Yossi Schain, eds., *Power and the Past: Collective Memory and International Relations* (Washington, DC: Georgetown University Press, 2010); Yinan He, *The Search for Reconciliation: Sino-Japanese and German-Polish Relations Since World War II* (Cambridge and New York: Cambridge University Press, 2009); Jennifer Lind, *Sorry States: Apologies in International Politics* (Ithaca, NY: Cornell University Press, 2008); Jan Werner Müller, ed., *Memory and Power in Post-War Europe: Studies in the Presence of the Past* (New York: Cambridge University Press, 2002); and Melissa Nobles, *The Politics of Apology*, op. cit.

epiphenomenal – the byproducts of disputes over other, more important issues. When the deep structures (the balance of power, economic interest, and so forth) that drive international and domestic politics favor conflict, historical narratives are generated that support conflict. When they do not, those narratives disappear, to be replaced by new narratives that support more cooperative and peaceful relations. To put it simply, it is money and bayonets that make the world go around, not whatever peculiar notions people may have about ancient grievances and past glories.

A significant and influential minority of observers, however, sees historical memory as having a decisive, even overwhelming, impact on politics. They maintain that the animosities generated by the past profoundly influence perceptions of whether a given nation or group of people is seen as reliable or not. Unless past grievances are addressed, they argue that it will be impossible to construct stable relations between the perpetrators of atrocity and their former victims. Not only will the victims of abuse be unable to heal from the traumas of the past but the groups to which they belong will distrust and even despise the unrepentant perpetrators. Left unattended, these feelings and perceptions can generate new tensions and confrontations. Only through a long and painstaking process of mutual acknowledgment of historical injustices can the process of reconciliation begin and a stable, more cooperative pattern of relations be established. This point of view is particularly popular among scholars who study the pursuit of justice in societies that have undergone a transition from authoritarianism to more democratic forms of government. It is also well represented among a wide range of nongovernmental activists, human rights organizations, political leaders, and a broad range of the general public in much of the democratic world. If one were to boil down their argument to a bumper sticker, it would read "no justice, no peace" – or at least not a stable and lasting one.[13]

In sum, although it is clear that we live in an era characterized by an increase in state apologies and expressions of contrition for the past, there remain two critical issues that need to be addressed. First, why do states adopt the kind of official historical narratives that they do? When do they choose to be apologetic for past wrong doings, and when do they not? Second, what are the consequences of their choosing to adopt penitent or impenitent narratives?

---

[13] For a good overview, see Ruti G. Teitel, *Transitional Justice* (New York and London: Oxford University Press, 2000). Others are interested in how history contributes to the perpetuation of domestic political conflict. See Consuelo Cruz, "Identity and Persuasion: How Nations Remember their Past and Make their Futures," *World Politics* 52:3 (April 2000), pp. 275–312; Roger D. Petersen, *Understanding Ethnic Violence: Fear, Hatred and Resentment in Twentieth-Century Eastern Europe* (New York: Cambridge University Press, 2002). For a study focusing primarily on Germany's relations with its European neighbors, see Andrei S. Markovits and Simon Reich, *The German Predicament: Memory and Power in the New Europe* (Ithaca, NY: Cornell University Press, 1997), as well as Lily Gardner-Feldman, "The Principle and Practice of 'Reconciliation' in German Foreign Policy: Relations with France, Israel, Poland and the Czech Republic," *International Affairs* 75:2 (April 1999), pp. 333–356.

## The Sources of Official Memory and the Impact of Controversy over Memory

Broadly speaking, there are three groups of explanations to these questions: those that stress the role of events themselves (Historical Determinist accounts[14]); those that focus on actors who manipulate the broader memory of a given society to serve their concrete material interests (Instrumentalist accounts); and, finally, explanations that emphasize the way in which existing cultural understandings, or discourses, define the boundaries of the kinds of official narratives that can be adopted (Culturalist accounts). Within each of these categories numerous refinements are possible, and it is possible to combine them, although if one does so one moves away from her core assumptions. In this sense, they are akin to what the German sociologist Max Weber called "ideal typical" forms of explanation, ones that for heuristic purposes express – perhaps in exaggerated form – certain central elements of a phenomenon, but that rarely exist in the real world in their pure form.[15]

Each of these three approaches identifies a different set of variables as the key to understanding the politics revolving around historical issues. To use the language of social science methodology, each specifies a different independent variable. They share, however, two common dependent variables: a common concern with explaining both why states adopt the kind of official narratives that they do and why those official narratives may become the source of political contention. Before going on to look at each of these three schools in more detail, it may be useful to more carefully delineate what these common dependent variables are and how they can be measured.

The official narrative is comprised of government policies across five domains: rhetoric (i.e., how political leaders talk about the past), commemoration (museums, monuments, holidays, etc.), education (especially school textbooks), compensation (policies aiming to help victims of past injustices), and punishment (both of perpetrators of injustice as well as policies that restrict freedom of speech and organization). Policies that reflect a sense of contrition for the past can be described as penitent; policies that do not reflect a sense of contrition and/or that actively deny any wrongdoing can be described as impenitent. Obviously, there may be tensions between and within these domains – political rhetoric may be penitent, whereas education and commemorative

---

[14] The term "experientialist" might be more appropriate for sophisticated versions of this approach, which understands that it is not directly the events themselves that drive policies but rather people's experiences of those events, however distorted and subjective those experiences may be. However, in the broader public debate there is often an assumption that the historical facts speak for themselves. The term "Historical Determinist" in this sense is the broader category and captures both the naïve and sophisticated versions of the argument.

[15] Max Weber, "Objectivity in the Social Sciences and Social Policy" in *The Methodology of the Social Sciences* ed. and trans. E. A. Shils and H. A. Finch (New York: Free Press, 1949), German original 1904.

policies may be more impenitent.[16] By looking at the overall range of policies – as opposed to a single policy – it may be possible to gauge more accurately the degree of contrition or impenitence of the official narrative.[17]

In this context, it is important to distinguish between the official narrative of the state and the array of memories that exist in the broader population (often referred to as the "collective memory" of the society).[18] Although the two are undoubtedly closely connected, they are by no means identical. Although the official narrative may be shaped by collective memory, or alternatively collective memory may ultimately be the byproduct of official memory, this is a matter for empirical investigation. We cannot assume the a priori dominance of one over the other. The collective memory of a society is reflected in various forms, including cultural artifacts, such as novels, plays, and films; personal stories that people may tell each other about the past; as well as various forms of public opinion data. The official narrative of states involves looking at the evolution of the different policy dimensions above. Tracing changes in the broader collective memory of a given society is a more challenging task and requires looking at this broader range of data. This volume does not try to explain the evolution of the overall collective memory of the society

[16] It would be tempting to try to devise a more elaborate schema reflecting different degrees of contrition or lack thereof in each dimension, however in practice, doing so creates a false impression of precision.

[17] The failure to compare different dimensions of a country's official narrative leads often to very different assessments of how contrite it is being about the past. For instance, Jane Yamazaki and Jennifer Lind, who emphasize the official statements of Japanese leaders, come to the conclusion that Japan has been quite penitent about its past misdeeds. See Jane Yamazaki, *Japan Apologizes for World War II* (London: Routledge, 2005) and Jennifer Lind, *Sorry States*, op. cit. George Hicks, on the other hand, who heavily emphasizes compensation for former comfort women and other victims, sees Japan as being relatively impenitent. See George Hicks, *Japan's War Memories: Amnesia or Concealment?* (Aldershot: Ashgate, 1997). Both sides effectively talk past one another by looking at the official narrative primarily along only a single dimension. Similarly, David Art, in his very detailed and careful study of the evolution of Austria's official historical narrative, argues that the Austrian government in the 1960s avoided coming to terms with its troubled past. David Art, *The Politics of the Nazi Past in Germany and Austria* (New York: Cambridge University Press, 2006). Although his broader point that Austria did not face up to its past in the way Germany did at the same time is undoubtedly correct, what he misses is the very significant shift in how the Austrians commemorated the victims of Fascism in the 1960s, marking the beginning of a trend away from blithely ignoring the dark sides of Austrian history.

[18] On the concept of collective memory see James V. Wertsch, *Voices of Collective Memory* (Cambridge: Cambridge University Press, 2002); Pierre Nora, *Rethinking France: Les Lieux de Memoire, Volume I: The State*, trans. Mary Seidman Troille (New York: Columbia University Press, 1997); and Paul Connerton, *How Societies Remember* (Cambridge: Cambridge University Press, 1989). The *locus classicus* is Maurice Halbwachs, *The Collective Memory*, trans. Francis J. Ditter and Vida Yazdi Ditter, (New York; Arno Press, 1975), French original, 1925. As was pointed out earlier, the term collective memory is a problematic one because it implies that there is (or should be) a certain homogeneity of views regarding the past. In fact, as numerous studies including this one confirm, the past is usually contested terrain, with a multiplicity of different views contending with one another for dominance. Nonetheless, the term is a useful one and will be used as a convenient shorthand.

per se, however because collective memory is an important variable for both the Historical Determinist and Culturalist approaches (albeit they have very different understandings of the phenomenon), it does try to track its evolution in the case studies through public opinion data and assessments offered by scholars who work on the topic.

The second dependent variable that is explored here is political conflict over history. Political conflict can take on a variety of different forms and can reach different levels of intensity, running a spectrum from minor to severe levels of contention. Domestically, low-level conflict may mean as little as low-level street demonstrations and heated debates over historical issues in the legislature. Internationally, diplomatic statements of protest or expressions of concern, as well as orderly societally based demonstrations and signature campaigns would constitute a comparable minor level of conflict. More severe (but still moderate) levels of contention might involve stoppages of the legislative process, inter- and intra-factional infighting, and less orderly political protests on the domestic level, suspensions in diplomatic talks, and economic boycotts internationally. Finally, severe levels of conflict would entail senior political leaders being forced to resign, domestic violence (riots, assassinations, etc.) or changes in government on the national level. Prolonged ruptures in diplomatic relations, a general breakdown in trust and cooperation (as reflected in failures in achieve previously agreed-on projects and sharp and sustained increases in elite and public expressions of distrust for another country), as well as violent militarized conflicts over historically laden issues represent severe international tensions.

Having delineated what it is that is being explained, it is time to turn our attention to the different ways of how to do so. Each of the three approaches – Historical Determinist, Instrumentalist, and Culturalist – is described in terms of what they see as being the determinants of the official historical narrative, the conditions under which conflict over historical issues is likely to emerge, as well as some of the policy prescriptions their adherents tend to draw from their analyses.

## Historical Determinism: History Creates Historical Memory

The approach of Historical Determinism is close to what is usually held to be a commonsense view of memory. Facts are facts and, sooner or later, they will impose themselves on the way people think about the past. Thus, the historical memory of a society is shaped by the facts – by what "actually happened."[19] Of course, the state or other powerful institutions may concoct official narratives

---

[19] In this sense, the Historical Determinist position is naturally link to the so-called positivist approach to history, which argues that the role of the historian is to uncover as objectively as possible the past as it actually was – famously associated with Leopold Ranke's famous injunction that the historian should embrace history as it actually was (*wie es eigentlich gewesen ist*).

that distort the past in order to serve this or that practical interest; however, such manipulations will come up against the sheer facts of real history anchored in the collective and individual memories of people – most powerfully in the generation that actually lived through these events but also in later generations to whom the past has been communicated through various cultural artifacts, including folklore, literature, oral histories told among families and friends, and so forth. If the official narrative differs greatly from the collective memory of the society, the costs of maintaining such a discordant official narrative is likely to rise and may become prohibitive, especially in democratic societies where groups who feel they have been neglected or mistreated are able to strongly register their views. In this sense, the facts set the parameters for the kind of official narrative that can be created and sustained over time.

Sophisticated versions of Historical Determinism recognize that the link between historical events and the official narrative of the state is far from straightforward. Various factors can distort or reshape societal memory. The most obvious of these are politically motivated interventions by the state or politically influential groups that try to manipulate individual and societal memory through their control over the media, arts, and education – either to make them reflect better their own memories of the past or in order to gain some type of commercial or political advantage. Although such blatant manipulations can be effective to some extent, they lack authenticity and lead people to produce insurgent historical narratives that can continue to exist on a subterranean level even in authoritarian societies where the expression of nonofficial views is forbidden. This is particularly true if the suppressed memories are important to the individuals who carry them, involving personal loss and trauma, or are connected to core beliefs such as ethnic or religious identity. When the vagaries of political fortunes shift, these insurgent narratives can erupt even after decades of suppression.[20]

In addition to political manipulation, psychologists and social psychologists who study memory formation on the level of the individual have uncovered a host of factors that may distort or alter the way in which people remember the past. The memory of individuals (or autobiographical memory, in psychological parlance) is episodic and fleeting – a set of sensory impressions that have to be contextualized and interpreted before they can be assigned meaning or become the basis of action.[21] Memories of emotionally traumatic events have been shown to be particularly susceptible to distortion, frequently leading to efforts to evade or repress them.[22] The complexity of memory formation is further increased by the interplay between individual and collective memory.

[20] See for instance the discussion in David E. Lorey and William H. Beezley, "Introduction," in Lorey and Beezley, eds., *Genocide, Collective Violence and Popular Memory* (Wilmington, DE: Scholarly Resources, 2002).

[21] For a more detailed discussion, see Endel Tulving and Wayne Donaldson, eds., *Organization of Memory* (New York: Academic Press, 1972).

[22] The original idea of suppressed memories and its association with various types of pathologies is closely associated with the work of Sigmund Freud and has in recent years been popularized

Although individuals may shape the collective memory by creating narratives on the basis of personal experiences, their own personal memory of events can be reshaped by the influence of the social environment in which they find themselves.[23]

The problems of distortion are magnified when moving from the individual to the collective level. When individuals relate their experiences to others, they do so by creating narratives. Every narrative is necessarily selective, including some elements of what was experienced while leaving others out.[24] Certain experiences cannot be conveyed to those who have not had comparable experiences. The terrors of war, hunger, pain, and suffering are simultaneously diminished and magnified for those who have never experienced such events. Conversely, the joys of, say, having been at Woodstock in 1968 can be similarly exaggerated or understated.[25] As a result, over time the content of collective memory tends to diverge increasingly from the original experiences. This process of mnemonic drift is compounded by generational change; as each new generation interprets received historical narratives against a background of experiences that are increasingly likely to differ starkly from that of earlier generations. Although this may lead to a gradual diminution in the emotional impact of memory in some cases,[26] memory is often given new strength through

again, to tremendous controversy, in the context of child abuse and posttraumatic stress disorder. It is one of the most controversial areas in the field of psychology. See Paul S. Applebaum, Lisa Uyehara, and Mark Elin, *Trauma and Memory: Clinical and Legal Controversies* (New York and Oxford: Oxford University Press, 1997).

[23] A particularly dramatic example of this process is illustrated in the work of Francesca Capelletto in her research of how communities in Italy recalled war time massacres by German forces. Those migrants who had left their villages to live in other parts of Italy had substantively different memories of the events from those who remained in the villages. At the same time, migrants to the villages, even though they had not experienced the massacres, would relate the events of the time in the same way, using the same visual imagery and emotional tropes, as did the actual survivors living in those villages. Francesca Capelletto, "Public Memories and Personal Stories: Recalling the Nazi-Fascist Massacres in Central Italy," in Capelletto, ed., *Memory and World War II: An Ethnographic Approach* (New York: Berg Publishers, 2005).

[24] For a discussion of these issues, see above all Hayden White, "The Question of Narrative in Contemporary Historical Theory," *History and Theory* 23:1 (February 1984), pp. 1–33, and White, *The Content of the Form: Narrative Discourse and Historical Representation* (Baltimore: The Johns Hopkins University Press, 1987).

[25] Perhaps the most powerful illustration of limitations of language is offered by the poems of Paul Celan. A Rumanian Jew from Czernowitz, Celan survived the concentration camps and the extermination of his family. After his liberation, Celan became a poet who dedicated his work to trying to convey his experiences to the rest of the world. Despite the undeniable power and artistry of his writing, there is reason to believe that in the end, Celan felt he failed in that task, leading to his suicide in 1970. For an overview of Celan's life and work, see Paul Felstiner, *Paul Celan* (New Haven: Yale University Press, 2001).

[26] Jon Elster, for instance, has argued that the memory of past injustices have a sort of mnemonic half life, causing them to fade over time. Jon Elster, *Closing the Books: Transitional Justice in Historical Perspective* (New York and Cambridge: Cambridge University Press, 2004), chapter 8, esp. p. 219, 222–227. This is a view that is commonly expressed in the media when discussing the history issue and has informed the thinking of, among others, many in the Japanese

their connection to new experiences. For instance, the memory of the suffering of black American slaves was given new meaning in the context of the American Civil Rights movement in the 1950s and 1960s.[27] In this way, collective memory becomes layered and more complex, as the same event is remembered in different ways – with different nuances and connections – at different points of time.

Given the range of forces that cause distortions in how people and societies remember the past, it is not surprising that there are often large and significant differences in how different groups remember the past. When sharply conflicting historical narratives are brought into confrontation with one another, they are likely to generate sharp reactions and political conflict. Faced with a historical narrative of an event that differs sharply from one's own, the initial reaction is likely to be one of incredulity and rejection. In the case of individuals whose personal experiences of suffering are left unacknowledged, such official narratives are likely to add to their pain and increase their anger. Likewise, an emotional response is likely on a collective level if the events that are being distorted are considered central to that group's identity, laying the foundations for bitter intergroup discord and conflict.[28]

A Historical Determinist description of the development of the official narrative might see it as going through a three or more stage process. In the first stage, the official historical narrative that a state adopts reflects in the first instance the actual historical experiences of policy makers and their supporters. In the second stage, the official narrative may then be modified by various domestic and international political considerations. Historical realities that are not reflected in the official narrative may serve as the basis of insurgent memories that continue to survive on the societal level. In more pluralist

government, who expect tensions over history to disappear when the last survivors of the war time and colonial period pass away.

[27] A less benign example can be seen in the former Yugoslavia of the 1990s, when Serb military and political leaders such as Radko Mladic and Slobodan Milosevic interpreted their struggles with the Muslim Bosniacs and Kosovars against the background of historical struggles against the Turks reaching as far back as the fourteenth century! For a discussion of the politics of history and the Yugoslav crisis, see Ilana R. Bet-el, "Unimagined Communities: The Power of Memory and the Conflict in the Former Yugoslavia," in Jan-Werner Müller, ed., *Memory and Power in Post-war Europe*, op. cit.

[28] Yinan He, *The Search for Reconciliation*, op. cit., pp. 30–31. On the importance of pursuing historical truth and searching for justice to reconciliation, see John Paul Lederach, *Building Peace: Sustainable Conflict Resolution in Divided Societies* (Washington DC: United States Institute of Peace, 1997), especially pp. 27–31. Many authors have recognized that there are risks involved in pursuing the truth and pushing for reconciliation, as well as the tensions between the goals of justice and truth telling. In general, however, they tend to nonetheless see the project as a necessary one for both ethical and long-term practical reasons. See Guillermo O'Donnell and Philippe Schmitter, "Transitions from Authoritarian Rule: Tentative Conclusions about Uncertain Democracies," in Neil J. Kritz, ed., *Transitional Justice Volume I: General Considerations* (Washington DC: United States Institute of Peace, 1995), p. 59 ff., and especially Priscilla Hayner, *Unspeakable Truths: Confronting State Terror and Atrocity* (New York: Routledge, 2002).

political systems, they are likely to serve as the basis of lobbying groups, such as veterans' organizations or victims' groups, who work to keep the insurgent memories alive and seek their inclusion in the official historical narrative. In the third and subsequent stages, changes in domestic and international political circumstances may strengthen the supporters of an insurgent narrative, who then force a renegotiation of the official narrative to better reflect the range of experiences of the historical event.

The Historical Determinist understanding of the politics of history has concrete policy as well as analytical implications. From a Historical Determinist's perspective, the best way to avoid conflict stemming from clashing historical narratives is to try to reconcile the contending view points and to create new narratives based on the historical facts by drawing on the experiences of both sides. This is the underlying premise of the movement to promote reconciliation in post-conflict societies through the establishment of truth commissions, criminal tribunals, as well as other forms of what is known as "transitional justice." These institutions – it is ardently hoped and believed – will uncover a body of evidence that will go into the historical record and will present both sides to a historical dispute with a body of incontrovertible facts that can then be used as the basis for a new historical narrative that both sides can agree on and will serve to forge a new relationship with one another.[29] The perpetrators of the Rwandan genocide, it can be argued, cannot pretend that they did not know what had happened or that the Tutsis had begun the genocide because of the existence of a large body of documents and testimonials that have been uncovered by the UN International Criminal Tribunal for Rwanda. Similar ideas are at the root of various efforts to promote cross-national research on textbooks, beginning with the first efforts promoted by the League of Nations after World War I.[30]

Of course, some facts are harder and more incontrovertible than others. That the Japanese Imperial Army captured Nanjing in December 1937 is a hard, incontrovertible fact. That a very large number of people died after the city was captured is likewise supported by a mass of historical documents and eye witness testimony. The exact number of people killed and the circumstances under which they died (whether they were killed in the cross fire, fell prey to

---

[29] For an excellent, if somewhat dense, overview, see Ruti G. Teitel, *Transitional Justice* (New York and London: Oxford University Press, 2000). On truth commissions, see Priscilla B. Hayner, *Unspeakable Truths: Confronting State Terror and Atrocities* (New York: Routledge, 2002). For an influential discussion of the relative virtues of trials versus truth commissions, see Martha Minow, *Between Vengeance and Forgiveness*, op. cit. For an important three-volume study of transitional justice pursued in different countries, see Neil Kritz, ed., *Transitional Justice*, op. cit. This idea is also at the root of various movements to promote the adoption of textbooks by international teams of scholars. See, for instance, Liu Jie, Mitani Hiroshi and Yang Daqing, *Kokyo o koeru Rekshininshiki: Nichū taiwa no Kokoromi* (Tokyo: Tōkyōdakgaku Shuppankai, 2006), and Yinan He, *The Search for Reconciliation*, op. cit.

[30] The leading European institution that has been born of these efforts is the Georg Eckert Institut in Braunschweig, Germany. See http://www.gei.de/.

rampaging groups of soldiers, or were deliberately massacred on order of the Imperial High Command) is considerably harder to establish.

The motives for Japanese actions and the complex combination of emotions and background factors that led to those actions – while undoubtedly real and important – are subject to a wide range of interpretations. By confronting these ambiguities, and by developing a better understanding of the historical complexities involved, Historical Determinists tend to believe that societies can develop a better understanding of their former adversaries and even though their perspectives on history are likely to remain different, by empathizing with them they can begin to reconcile. In short, good history ("history" here meaning the study of the past) can lay the foundations for good politics.

The official narrative of the state can thus promote reconciliation efforts between groups by exposing their members to the basic facts as well as the viewpoint of the other side. Conversely, the failure of the official historical narrative to recognize the perspective of a group or nation will hinder the recovery of traumatized individuals, breed resentment and discord between groups, and sow the seeds for future conflict

## Instrumentalism: Politics Creates Historical Memory

A sharply different perspective on the sources of collective memory is offered by Instrumentalist accounts, which focus on the ways in which individuals and groups manipulate the collective memory in order to advance their interests. Central to the Instrumentalist approach is the proposition that our knowledge of the past has little or nothing to do with the past; rather it is about the present and the future.[31] To put it differently, the formation of collective memory, and with it the development of the official narrative of the state, is all about what a number of scholars have called the search for a "usable past."[32] If Historical Determinism owes a great deal to the field of psychology and the pioneering work of Freud, Instrumentalism finds its inspiration in the study of politics and the spirit of Machiavelli.

Instrumentalism – in sharp contrast to the Historical Determinist position – is based on the proposition that collective memory is highly malleable. Individuals may have some independent knowledge of the world around them based on their own, immediate experiences. However, ordinary people's knowledge of the larger world, and their ability to interpret and evaluate that world, depend upon elites who control the flow of information and who can claim expertise

[31] A prime example of this type of analysis is Eric Hobsbawm and Terrence Ranger, *The Invention of Tradition* (Cambridge: Cambridge University Press, 1983).

[32] The term "usable past" was originally coined by the literary critic and historian Van Wyck Brooks in 1916, and the idea can be traced back even earlier to Friedrich Nietzche, who analyzed history in distinctly utilitarian terms. See Brooks, "On Creating a Usable Past," *The Dial* 64:7 (April 11, 1918), pp. 337–341: Friedrich Nietzsche, "Uses and Disadvantages of History for Life," in Nietzsche, *Untimely Meditations*, trans. R. J. Hollingdale (Cambridge: Cambridge University Press, 1983), orig. 1873.

that allows them to issue authoritative assessments. As a result, ordinary people are in a situation similar to Leonard Shelby, the hapless protagonist of the film *Memento*, who has lost the ability to form his own memories and who vainly tries to maintain his sense of purpose and direction based on the fragmentary evidence available to him in the form of notes, recordings, photos, and even messages tattooed upon his body. Like Shelby, society is vulnerable to exploitation and manipulation at the hands of those who discover this weakness and are in a position to alter or reinterpret the historical record to suit their own purposes. Elites, in contrast, are portrayed as cynical rational actors who are motivated by concrete interests, such as gaining or retaining control of political office, enhancing their power and material welfare. Sometimes, they may even be motivated by a concern for the national interest or for the collectivity as a whole.[33]

This does not mean, of course, that Instrumentalists deny that there are facts and that some events "actually happened" (although some postmodernist theorists concerned with power come perilously close to such a position when they contend that it is impossible to know what actually happened) any more than Historical Determinists will deny that the facts of the past can be manipulated or distorted to suit political purposes. The difference between the two approaches is the degree to which they see facts as being malleable. For the Instrumentalist, the official narrative can reshape the collective memory. For the Historical Determinist, the collective memory sets sharp limits to the official narrative.

The critical question in Instrumentalist analyses then becomes, which set of interests are in control of the process through which the official narrative is formed. The simplest and most obvious explanation is the state. By using its tremendous coercive and cultural resources, the state is able to create a single "master narrative" that is accepted as common sense by society and is only challenged at the margins.[34] Few states, however, enjoy such a high level of

---

[33] There is a considerable debate over the extent to which elites are motivated by their own narrow self-interests or the larger interest of the community of which they are a part. Realists tend to emphasize that, in the end, elites have to be mindful of the interests of the whole because their own fortunes are dependent on the well-being of the national community in which they are embedded. See Stephen R. Krasner, *Defending the National Interest: Raw Materials, Investments and U.S. Foreign Policy* (Princeton, NJ: Princeton University Press, 1978) and Barry R. Posen, *The Sources of Military Doctrine: France, Germany and Britain Between the World Wars* (Ithaca: Cornell University Press, 1984). Others, especially but not only left-wing critics of American foreign policy, argue that class or bureaucratic interests frequently predominate. See for instance Seymour Melman, *Pentagon Capitalism: The Political Economy of War* (New York: McGraw Hill, 1970) and Chalmers Johnson, *The Sorrows of Empire: Militarism, Secretism and the End of the Republic* (New York: Metropolitan Books, 2004). For the purposes of the present discussion, both positions can be classified as Instrumentalist.

[34] The most famous expression of this point of view is Antonio Gramsci's notion of "cultural hegemony," which has been a main stay of left-wing critical analysis of culture and politics ever since. See Antonio Gramsci, *The Prison Notebooks*, with an introduction by Joeseph Buttigieg, ed. and trans. J. Buttigieg and Antonio Callari (New York: Columbia University Press, 1992);

control over the public discourse (North Korea and other modern totalitarian societies come to mind as possible examples). In more pluralist political systems, a variety of different actors offer often sharply diverging historical visions, each associated with different policy programs. In such political systems, history becomes a battle ground, an arena in which different societal interests clash.

In such pluralized political environments, a broad variety of different kinds of interests may influence the construction of historical memory. Some of these may be purely political, of the sort described in the forgoing example. Others may be commercial. Publishers, editors, and authors have their own set of incentives to create historical narratives that appeal to the public.[35] In yet other cases, individuals may seek compensation for past wrongs[36] or to build and strengthen their own sense of identity as a group.[37] International considerations as well may intrude. States at war are likely to promote narratives that mobilize society for martial purposes. States at peace may choose instead to favor images that allow for reconciliation with former antagonists, promote peaceful coexistence with neighbors, and pave the way for deeper social, economic, and political integration on the regional level.[38]

Noam Chomsky, *Media Control: The Spectacular Success of Propaganda* (Westfield, NJ: Open Magazine, 1991) and Ernesto Lacalau and Chantal Mouffe, *Hegemony and Socialist Strategy* (London and New York: Verso, 1985).

[35] See, for instance, the discussion of the development of a market for Americana in the 1970s and 1980s in Michael Kammen, *The Mystic Chords of Memory: The Transformation of Tradition in American Culture* (New York: Vintage Books, 1993), pp. 669–678.

[36] For an excellent analysis based on direct experience of the efforts of victims of the Holocaust to collect compensation and of various actors – governments, firms, and attorneys – who sought to either profit from such claims or to insulate themselves from them, see Stuart E. Eizenstat, *Imperfect Justice: Looted Assets, Slave Labor and the Unfinished Business of World War II* (New York: Public Affairs, 2003). For a more polemical and far-reaching take on the same topic, see Norman G. Finkelstein, *The Holocaust Industry: Reflections on the Exploitation of Jewish Suffering* (New York and London: Verso Books, 2000). For an examination of how various groups in Japan vied for victim status, see Orr, *The Victim as Hero*, op. cit.

[37] For an interesting, if controversial argument along these lines, see Peter Novick, *The Holocaust in American Life* (New York: Mariner Books, 2000).

[38] For an example of how history can be reinterpreted for the purposes of fostering national reconciliation, see David W. Blight, *Race and Reunion: The Civil War in American Memory* (Cambridge, MA: Belknap Press, 2002). A comparable trend may be detected by a growing tendency in Europe to define the first and second as a "European Civil War." See, for instance, the comments "The Spiritual and Cultural Dimension of Europe," final report of a high level advisory group initiated by the President of the European Commission (Vienna Brussels, 2004), pp. 6–7, available at http://europa.eu.int/comm/research/social-sciences/pdf/michalski_281004_final_report_en.pdf. John Dower's *War without Mercy: Race and Power in the Pacific War* (New York: Pantheon, 1984) provides a particularly powerful example of how quickly narratives can change to suit national interests. During the Pacific War, both the Japanese and United States promoted images that portrayed the other side as savages. In Japanese propaganda, Americans were depicted as malicious demons; in the United States, the Japanese were presented as brutal, subhuman apes. These images encouraged brutal behavior on the battlefield and contributed greatly to the savagery of the conflict. Yet, once the war ended, these images were rather quickly discarded.

Which set of interests win out in the battle to shape the official narrative of the state as well as that of the collective memory of a society varies from case to case. Generally speaking, two variables are of critical importance in determining which historical narratives are ultimately favored by state policy: (1) to what degree key political actors are committed to the promotion of particular historical narratives; and (2) the relative power that different groups possess in the policy-making process. Although collective memory may be malleable, changing historical narratives may be costly for politicians if some of their constituents believe in them or are vested in them for other reasons. Similarly, whereas most political systems are to some degree pluralistic, pluralism does not translate into a level playing ground for all interests.[39] The representations of historical reality promoted by the states are as much the outcome of political bargaining as are other more mundane issues, such as taxes, farm subsidies, or community pest control. What actually happened, and whatever fragmentary images individuals may have of the past, is of little importance. Even the historical experiences or views of the elites are of secondary importance: The elites do not care about the past – they are concerned with concrete questions of interest.

From an Instrumentalist point of view then, the official historical narrative is an important reflection of the relations of power and interest both domestically and internationally. In the modern context in which political legitimacy depends upon the ability of the state and the political elite to create a sense of nation and in which nationalism is a powerful instrument for mobilizing societal resources, it is perfectly natural that history is disputed as never before.[40] To paraphrase Clausewitz's famous dictum about war, history has become the extension of politics by other means. A state's official narrative is also an important instrument of policy and a source of power. Consequently, a state's official narrative is watched closely by other states, particularly ones who might be threatened by it. Analysts who wish to understand the development of the official narrative are thus best served by understanding the constellation of power relationships that give rise to it, both in terms of the domestic political factors that give rise to a particular official narrative and the way in which these narratives than feed into relations between nations. The original historical events and the societal experiences based on them are of little consequence and can be safely ignored.

From a practical standpoint, the Instrumentalist perspective suggests that conflicts over history and official historical narratives are thus best and most efficiently dealt with by resolving the underlying conflicts in interest that give rise to them. If the clashes of interests behind historical disputes are intractable

---

[39] This is one of the central insights emerging out of the historical institutionalist literature of the 1980s. See Suzanne Berger, *Organizing Interests in Western Europe: Pluralism, Corporatism and the Transformation of Politics* (New York: Cambridge University Press, 1981).

[40] On the military uses of nationalism, see for instance Barry R. Posen, "Nationalism, the Mass Army and Military Power," *International Security* 18:2 (1994), pp. 80–124.

then so too are the conflicts over the official historical narrative. Conversely, if interests converge then so should the official narratives. Only to the extent that official narratives do not converge, or are difficult to harmonize despite common interests, does history become an important complicating factor in the management of political relations both domestically and internationally.

## Culturalist Explanations: Culture Creates Collective Memory

The third and final perspective on the sources of the official historical narrative is the Culturalist approach. The central insight of Culturalist accounts is that all individuals are embedded in a broader structure of ideas, beliefs, values, and social practices that together constitute a culture[41] and shape people's perception of the world and the way in which they relate to that world. Although cultures have no independent existence outside of the individual, individuals are culture-creating creatures who, to a large measure, are dependent on culture for guidance on how to think and behave.[42] Historical narratives – both on the official level and as embedded in the broader society – are an integral part of the overall cultural system that conditions the kind of official narrative that can be adopted by the state. This emphasis on culture as opposed to events and material interests places Culturalism at odds with both Historical Determinism and Instrumentalism.

Against Historical Determinism, Culturalists argue that people's experience of history is necessarily mediated by the preexisting set of cognitive lenses that are supplied by the culture in which they are embedded. A wink, as the noted cultural anthropologist Clifford Geertz once noted, can be more than a rapid contraction of an eyelid; it can signify a wide range of different things depending on the context and the kinds of meaning that people of a given culture may ascribe to that action.[43] Different people with different cultural backgrounds

---

[41] There exists a multitude of definitions of culture. Already in the 1950s a prominent survey identified well over fifty definitions. See A. L. Kroeber and Clyde Kluckhohn, *Culture: A Critical Review of Concepts and Definitions* (New York: Vintage Press, 1952).

[42] The cultural perspective is one of the great, meta-theoretical approaches in the social sciences, along with rationalism, that emerged out of the philosophical debates of the early nineteenth century, especially the works of the German philosophers, Hegel, Herder, and Fichte, who invented the concept of the *Kulturnation* as part of their critique of the universalistic and rationalistic nationalism of the French Revolution. Since that time, the idea of culture has been taken up in literally hundreds of different ways by scholars and researchers working across a wide spectrum of disciplines in the social sciences and the humanities. For a good overview of the some of the essential features of a culturalist perspective, see Harry Eckstein, "A Culturalist Theory of Political Change," in *Regarding Politics: Essays on Political Theory, Stability and Change* (Berkeley and Los Angeles: University of California Press, 1992). For a broader overview of the concept of culture as used in various social scientific disciplines, see Victoria E. Bonnell and Lynn Hunt, eds., *Beyond the Cultural Turn* (Berkeley and Los Angeles: University of California Press, 1999).

[43] Clifford Geertz, "Thick Description: Towards an Interpretative Theory of Culture," in *The Interpretation of Cultures* (New York: Basic Books, 1972), pp. 3–30.

will interpret the same set of events very differently. Whereas Culturalists would agree with Historical Determinists that the collective memory is very important and sets sharp boundaries to the kind of historical narrative that can be adopted and sustained over time, they would argue that both collective and individual memories are socially constructed and cannot be inferred from the events themselves.

Against Instrumentalism, Culturalists argue that the interests of individuals and groups – including those of elites – cannot be understood independent of the way in which the group and the individuals are culturally defined.[44] To put it another way, both historical experiences and interests are socially constructed categories. How an individual or group responds to a given situation depends very much on both how they define the situation and what they believe is appropriate for people like themselves to do in that particular situation.[45] Although interests may play an important role in the creation of the official narrative, those interests cannot simply be extrapolated from the material interests of the state and its elites. When political leaders adopt an official narrative that suits their interests but is dissonant with the collective memory of the society or of important groups in the society, they are bound to provoke resistance. Although such tensions may be manageable for a while, over time either the official narrative changes to reflect the collective memory – much in the way that Historical Determinists predict – or alternatively the societal discourse on the past, and with it the collective memory, changes – something which Historical Determinists would not predict.

Applied to the question where the official narrative and collective memory comes from, a Culturalist approach suggests that we must begin by focusing how new events are interpreted against the background of the existing memory of the past collectively held by a society and embedded in its culture. For instance, from a U.S. perspective, Saddam Hussein's invasion of Kuwait may have been seen as a reckless act of aggression by a brutal dictator, and the historical analogy that tended to be drawn by Americans was Adolph Hitler's invasions of Czechoslovakia and Poland half a century earlier. For many in the Arab world, however, the invasion was understood against the background of a history of Western dominance of the Middle East and the arbitrary drawing of boundaries by the imperial powers in the wake of the Ottoman collapse after World War I. By extension, the driving out of Saddam's forces by the U.S.-led coalition forces came to be seen by many, not as the ignominious defeat of

---

[44] See Friederich Kratochwil, "On the Notion of 'Interest' in International Relations," *International Organization* 36:1 (1982), pp. 1–30; Martha Finnemore, *National Interest and International Society* (Ithaca, NY: Cornell University Press, 1996).

[45] See the classic formulation in Berger and Luckman, *The Social Construction of Reality*, op. cit. This notion has been picked up very much by the recent Constructivist school in international relations. See in particular Alexander Wendt, *Social Theory and International Relations* (Cambridge and New York: Cambridge University Press, 1999). For an interesting, philosophically grounded take on these issues, see John Searles, *The Construction of Social Reality* (New York: The Free Press, 1995).

a brutal dictator, but yet another act of defiance of an Arab leader against the forces of the West. Thus, contrary to the hopes and expectations of many American analysts at the conclusion of the 1991 Gulf War, instead of being delegitimated by his defeat in Kuwait, Saddam Hussein was able to restore his authority, at least among his core constituency – the Sunni Arab population of Iraq.[46]

Assessing the cultural background of any given society is no easy matter. An earlier generation of researchers tended to simplify the task by assuming that culture is basically monolithic, static, and defined by its contents.[47] In recent years, however, all three of these assumptions have been subject to considerable challenge. Although some versions of cultural theory posit the existence of an all-powerful master discourse, increasingly culture has been shown to be made up of often quite disparate, even antagonistic, subcultures.[48] For instance, many analysts of French culture argue that it is constituted by two rival cultural currents: a Jacobin Republican tradition with its strong egalitarian, rationalist, and anticlerical traits, and a more traditionalistic, deeply Catholic current associated with French conservatism.[49] Each of these two currents has a radically different understanding of French history and, by extension, of the national interest. The competition between these two discourses is itself one of the central, defining features of French political culture and the discourse on national identity.

Similarly, in the past many scholars tended to see culture as permanent and unchanging, shaping the thought and behavior of societies for generations, if not millennia.[50] This static view of culture has come under sharp criticism from many quarters and today is frequently charged with serving as a way of justifying the scholar's own biases regarding a given society.[51] Instead, contemporary cultural theory tends to see cultures as fluid and protean, driven both by their own internal dynamics and by changes in the broader environment in which

[46] The author would like to express his thanks for Professor Nazli Choucri of MIT for her insightful comments on this issue.

[47] Yosef Lapid, "Culture's Ship: Returns and Departures in International Relations Theory," in Yosef Lapid and Friedrich Kratochwil, eds., *The Return of Culture and Identity in IR Theory* (Boulder: Lynne Rienner, 1996), especially pp. 6–9.

[48] Michel Foucault, *The Archaeology of Knowledge*. See also the debate between Aaron Wildavsky and David Laitin, "Controversies: Political Culture and Political Preferences," *American Political Science Review* 82:2 (June 1988), pp. 589–596.

[49] These two currents are referred to as the "red" and the "black" in Stendahl's novel of the same name. Although it is sometimes argued that these currents have largely disappeared in today's France, other analysts suggest that they live on in modified but recognizable form today, having crystallized around and revalorized by new issues such as immigration. See Pierre Birnbaum, *The Idea of France*, trans. M. B. DeBevoise (New York: Hill and Wang, 2001), French original, 1998.

[50] See, for instance, Louis Dumont, *Homo Hierarchicus*; Lucian Pye, *Asian Power and Politics: The Cultural Dimensions of Authority* (Cambridge, MA: Harvard University Press, 1985).

[51] For a particularly trenchant and influential example of this type of critique, see Edward W. Said, *Orientalism* (New York: Pantheon Books, 1978).

they operate. Sometimes change is slow and gradual. At other times, cultural change can be more rapid and profound, particularly in the wake of traumatic events that may compel members of a society to question their fundamental beliefs and values.[52] Even in such dramatic situations, however, previously held cultural beliefs and values will have some impact on what comes later. The slate is never fully cleaned, even if what comes next is defined as a total rejection of the beliefs and values of the old culture. This is often characterized as the "discursive" nature of cultural systems or practices.[53]

Finally, in the past cultures were viewed as having clear boundaries and as being defined by quite distinct sets of ideas and practices – beginning with early child rearing practices – that fit together in a holistic fashion, each part reinforcing the others.[54] In more recent years, however, there has been a growing appreciation of the amorphous boundaries of culture and the importance of markers as opposed to content in defining them. For instance, the cultural differences between urban Serbs, Croats, and Bosnians may have been quite marginal prior to 1990 – they spoke the same language, went to the same schools, had comparable levels of education, and even frequently intermarried. Once, however, religion was made into a salient marker, one that could make the difference between literally life and death under certain circumstances, they became sharply divided groups with, among other things, very different collective memories and definitions of identity.

In practice, this means that a Culturalist investigation of the official narrative of a state is an exercise in intellectual history. The new official narrative must be examined in relationship to the broader societal discourse on the past, which in turn is based on a pattern of interaction between various subcultures, each

---

[52] As argued cogently by Michael Thompson, Richard Ellis and Aaron Wildavsky, *Cultural Theory* (Boulder, CO: Westview Press, 1990), chapter 4. Jeff Legro has made the very important point in this connection that trauma is based not simply on the level of material damage sustained by a society but just whether events call into question the fundamental assumptions on which a culture is based. See Jeffrey Legro, "Whence American Internationalism," *International Organization* 54:2 (2000), pp. 253–289. Thus, although China underwent many waves of invasion in its history that were often far more devastating in terms of the number of people killed and territory lost than were the predations of the European Imperial powers from the mid-nineteenth century on, the European invasions were far more traumatic in cultural terms because they cast doubt on the fundamental assumptions of Chinese culture. See Joseph Levenson, *Confucianism and its Modern Fate* (Berkeley: University of California Press, 1968).

[53] See, for instance, Jeffrey Olick's very interesting discussion of discourse and dialogue in *The Politics of Regret: On Collective Memory and Historical Responsibility* (London and New York: Routledge, 2007), especially pp. 9–11, 55–60.

[54] Harry Eckstein referred to this fitting together of different cultural practices as "congruence." "Thin" constructivists believe that human behavior is shaped by an interaction between material forces and the cultural systems in which people are embedded. In contrast, "thick" constructivists believe that culture is so powerful that it trumps material concerns. Indeed, thick constructivists argue that people's perceptions – including social scientists who purport to study cultural systems – are so strongly conditioned by cultural lenses that it is impossible for them to even apprehend the true nature of the material world. See Eckstein, *Essays* op. cit., chapter 5.

promoting an account of the past that – although it is likely to overlap with that of other subcultures – differs on certain key points of interpretation and detail and from which it draws very different lessons. Tracing the ways in which those sub-narratives and their pattern of interaction changes becomes the central analytical task for researchers.

From a Culturalist perspective, the official narrative is likely to become the object of political contention when very different perspectives of the past are confronted with one another. When different subgroups in a given society have a very different perspective on the past, or when two states promote very different official narratives on the international level, tensions are likely to emerge. In such situations, political leaders and cultural elites come under pressure to change the official narrative in order to stabilize domestic and international relations. The new narrative will be successful only if it is accepted and internalized on a societal level. As in Instrumentalist accounts, people's understandings of the historical facts can be changed but only after a process of successful resocialization has occurred. Change in the official narrative is thus likely to be slower and more difficult than Instrumentalism suggests and will be accompanied by considerable political and emotional turmoil going beyond what the simple pursuit of material interests would dictate.[55]

Three additional prominent arguments have been made about the impact of culture on the ways in which societies view the past. The first refers to the ways in which societies evaluate the moral implications of the past on the basis of deeply rooted, essentially static cultural predispositions. This is most famously associated with the argument that Japanese see morally reprehensible actions in terms of "shame," whereas Westerners think instead in terms of "guilt." The second is the proposition that a global culture of contrition is coming fitfully into existence. Third, and finally, there is the idea that historical myths can become embedded in the official historical narrative that becomes difficult to control because of what some analysts describe as ideational "blowback." Each of these – the shame vs. guilt, global culture of guilt, and blowback hypothesis – deserves a few words of elaboration.

One of the oldest arguments regarding the impact of culture on history is the claim that different cultural backgrounds can lead different societies to have very different moral evaluations of the past. Ruth Benedict's famous distinction between shame and guilt cultures is a highly influential example of

---

[55] The argument here is similar to the thin constructivist argument that has been made by a number of international relations scholars regarding the role of ideational forces in foreign and national security policy. On "thin" versus "thick" constructivism. For a discussion of different versions of Constructivism, see Chris Reus-Smit, "Constructivism," in Scott Burchill et al., eds., *Theories of International Relations* 3rd edition (Basingstoke: Palgrave, 2005) and John Kurt Jacobsen, "Duelling Constructivisms: A Post-Mortem on the Ideas Debate in Mainstream IR/IPE," *Review of International Studies* 29:1 (January 2003), pp. 39–60. For an example of this type of analysis, see Thomas U. Berger, *Cultures of Antimilitarism*, op. cit.

this type of argument, and one that is particularly relevant to the concerns of this volume.[56] The main thrust of Benedict's argument is that there exists in the West a notion of a higher, transcendent set of principles against which actions in this world have to be judged. In Japan and other Asian cultures, however, the transcendent is seen as being imminent in this world and thus inseparable from the community in which the individual operates. These essentially religious ideas are deeply rooted in Japanese culture and have changed little over the course of the centuries. As a result, whereas Westerners, with their Judeo-Christian understanding of morality, may feel guilt over actions they judge to have violated God's will, Asians tend to see morality as defined by the situation in which they find themselves (so-called situational ethics). Therefore, Asians may feel ashamed when faced with public disapproval, but they are unlikely to feel guilt in the same way that Westerners do. This difference between Asian/Japanese and Western ways of evaluating the past, it is argued, leads to frequent misunderstanding and clashes because Westerners expect Japanese to evince feelings of guilt that are in fact alien to their culture.

A second, very different, but also very influential Culturalist argument emphasizes the role of globalizing human rights norms in defining the kinds of historical narratives that are deemed to be acceptable in modern societies.[57] State discourses on collective memory, from this perspective, are no longer operating within their own self-enclosed universe. Instead, they are increasingly subject to a broader set of discursive processes that reach across state boundaries and are transforming the ways in which societies, especially liberal democratic societies that are embedded in a complex network of interaction with other societies, think about the past. This emerging global culture of human rights insists on recognizing and condemning past human rights abuses, both in order to win justice for their victims and to delegitimate abuses in the present. Although leaders of individual countries may for their own reasons choose to ignore past abuses, such actions increasingly draw the condemnation of the international community.

A third and final argument about the impact of culture on the official historical narrative regards the way in which myths about the past originally created to serve the interests of elites pass into the general culture of a society and take on dynamics of their own. Thus, certain ideas about history may have been instrumental in origin, yet they become cultural in effect. The elites who

---

[56] Ruth Benedict, *The Chrysanthemum and the Sword Patterns of Japanese Culture* (Boston: Houghton Mifflin, 1946) and J. Victor Koschmann, ed., *Authority and the Individual in Japan: Citizen Protest in Historical Perspective* (Tokyo: University of Tokyo Press, 1978). Similar arguments have been made with respects to other religious traditions – for example, Judaism and the concept of forgiveness, or the relative receptiveness of Protestantism versus Catholicism.

[57] Elazar Barkan, *The Guilt of Nations*. See also Geoffrey Robertson, *Crimes Against Humanity: The Struggle for Global Justice* (New York: The New Press, 2002). On the development of the international human rights regime, see Thomas Risse, Stephen Roppe and Kathryn Sikkink, eds., *The Power of Human Rights International Norms and Domestic Change* (Cambridge and New York: Cambridge University Press, 1999), chapter 1.

created these myths frequently come to believe them themselves, especially over time and with the passing of generations. Even if elites do not believe in the myths they have created, they may still find their room for maneuver to be constrained once those myths become embedded in the broader society. As a result, conflicts that are deeply embedded in historical myths may become more intractable because – unlike in instrumental accounts – tensions will persist even if conflict is no longer in the interest of the state or of elite groups in society.[58]

Given the potential variability among cultural systems, it is difficult to generalize about the practical consequences of a Culturalist point of view. In general, Culturalists would argue that it is difficult to establish an official historical narrative that runs counter to the culturally embedded propensities of a given society. For example, it is difficult to impose a Western notion of guilt on a society where the culturally defined conception of guilt does not exist. Conversely, it is difficult to maintain an official historical narrative of impenitence if a broader, globalized discourse on human rights and historical justice are making inroads into society. Such trends can only be counteracted if it is possible to alter the dominant cultural currents that have given rise to them – something which governments and elites typically have great difficulty doing even on a local level: Very few countries can hope to shape culture on a global level. Finally, governments have to be very sensitive to the potentially pernicious effects of the historical narratives they create and take active measures to reverse them once they take hold. Although this may be difficult to do, states can use the official narrative to slowly reshape societal beliefs about the past in ways that serve the overall national interest.

## Summary

As was pointed out earlier, these three types of theoretical explanations regarding the sources of memory are far from mutually exclusive. Rather, they might better be thought of as Weberian "ideal types" – useful heuristic devices that identify some of the factors that drive the formation of the official historical narrative.[59] In the real world, a complete account of any given case necessarily would involve a combination of forces.[60]

---

[58] Yinan He, *The Search for Reconciliation* op. cit. pp. 25–34. A similar argument regarding patterns of expansionism and belligerence is made by Jack Snyder, *Myths of Empire: Domestic Politics and International Ambition* (Ithaca: Cornell University Press, 1991) and Stephen van Evera, *The Causes of War* (Ithaca: Cornell University Press, 2001).

[59] On the ideal type methodology, see Max Weber, "Objectivity in Social Science and Social Policy" in *The Methodology of the Social Sciences*, ed. and trans. E. A. Shils and H. A. Finch. (New York: Free Press, 1949) German original, 1904.

[60] See Rudra Sil, "The Foundations of Eclecticism: The Epistemological Status of Agency, Culture and Structure in Social Theory," *Journal of Theoretical Politics* 12:3 (2000), pp. 353–387; and Peter J. Katzenstein and Nobuo Okawara, "Japan, Asian-Pacific Security, and the Case for Analytical Eclecticism," *International Security* 26:3 (Winter 2003), pp. 153–185.

Nonetheless, there exist very real tensions between the different schools, and stressing one set of factors over another has important analytical as well as practical consequences.

Which type of factors are in fact the main variables that can help explain a particular outcome – for instance, whether a particular country chooses to apologize or not to apologize for past actions, what types of measures are taken to redress wrongs, and whether an effort is made to examine the darker sides of a nation's history, or to glorify it instead – needs to be determined on a case by case basis. There are no a priori theoretical reasons to favor one type of explanation over another in any empirical investigation. The core propositions of the different perspectives are summarized in Table 1.1.

The Historical Determinist school of thought would lead us to expect the original experiences of society to play a determining role in shaping its collective memory and, thus, setting the parameters for the official narrative states can sustain over time. States can promote official narratives that contradict the experiences imbedded in the collective memory, but there is a strong tendency for societally rooted challenges to emerge, particularly in times of political change. Social groups that keep historical memory alive play a key role in Historical Determinist accounts of the politics of the past. With the passing of generations, the Historical Determinist approach allows for change in the collective memory of societies and a diminishment in the intensity of emotions that can be aroused. Such shift is likely to be slow, however, and old memories can be given new vigor by their association with memories of more recent events. Historical Determinist accounts are weakened[61] to the extent that it can be shown that the collective memory can be changed over time and/or that it is in fact possible for states to sustain an official historical narrative that is sharply at odds with collective memory.

The Instrumentalist approach, on the other hand, is likely to stress the decisive role played by the objective interests of the state and its elites in shaping the historical narrative at any given point in time. Considerations of power and material gain are the key determinants here; states and politically influential groups, the main actors. Change in the official narrative can come relatively quickly and easily and is contingent upon changes in the relationships of power and interest. When material interests are in conflict, antagonistic official narratives are likely to emerge domestically as well as internationally. Instrumentalist accounts are weakened to the extent it can be shown that the collective memory makes it difficult to change the official narrative despite the objective material interests of the states or of their political leaders. Alternatively, Instrumentalism becomes less persuasive if it can be demonstrated that the way in which states

---

[61] In the language of social scientific methodology, uncovering of disconfirming or contradictory evidence is referred to as "falsification." Although it is important that scholars and analysts look for disconfirming evidence, this does not mean that one need subscribe to the rigid falsificationist view – associated with Karl Popper – that any disconfirmation means that a theory has been invalidated.

TABLE 1.1. *Summary of Different Approaches to Explaining the Determinants of Official Historical Narratives*

| Approach | Core Propositions |
| --- | --- |
| 1) Historical Determinism (History creates memory) | • The experiences of events is the basis for the collective memory of society, which in turn sets the parameters of the official narrative<br>• Memories can be encoded as cultural artifacts (books, films, monuments, etc.), which allow them to be shared<br>• Cultural artifacts that have a basis in the memories of the audience are more authentic in being anchored in the experiences of the creator of the artifact and are more persuasive than those that are not<br>• Collective memory is relatively not malleable<br>• Traumatic or politically inconvenient memories can be suppressed, but at a cost<br>• Exposure to cultural artifacts carrying different memories and that are based in historical facts can lead to a shift in the collective memory over time<br>• Generational and political changes allow for the emergence of previously suppressed memories and for the reinterpretation of existing memories |
| 2) Instrumentalism (Politics creates memory) | • The political interests of the state and/or elite groups in society determine the official narrative<br>• The collective memory of society is relatively malleable<br>• In pluralistic political systems, the official narrative is the product of the relative strength of elite groups and their commitment to a particular historical narrative<br>• The official narrative is likely to shift as a result of shifts in the domestic and/or international balance of power and interests |
| 3) Cultural (Cultural context and discourse creates memory) | • Both experience and interest are conditioned by culturally determined dispositions of society<br>• Culture is a more or less autonomous sphere, insulated from non-cultural forces<br>• Collective memory is the product of a culturally driven societal discourse on the past<br>• The collective memory sets the parameters for the official narrative<br>• Moral evaluations of the past are based on cultural – especially religious – traditions (the shame versus guilt hypothesis)<br>• Global and regional cultural discourses can reshape or put pressure on the official narrative of states (the global culture hypothesis)<br>• Myths about history created for instrumental purposes can become part of the culture of a society and take on a dynamic of their own (the blowback hypothesis) |

or leaders define their material interests is determined or strongly influenced by the collective memory.

The Culturalist approach, in contrast, emphasizes the role of culturally embedded predispositions in shaping the views of the past held both by elites and society in general. These views set the general parameters for the official historical narrative. If underlying cultural predispositions do not change (for example, religiously based notions of guilt versus shame), then it will be difficult to effect genuine, lasting changes in the official historical narrative. If they do, then change is likely to result. The Culturalist position can be weakened if it can be shown that non-cultural forces – such as material interests and historical experiences – shape the collective memory in rather predictable ways, or alternatively, if the official narrative is largely oblivious of the cultural discourse on history.

In addition to the main Culturalist argument, there are three other sub-hypotheses that are worth investigating – the shame vs. guilt, global culture of contrition and blowback hypotheses. Shame versus guilt would lead us to expect fundamentally different reactions to past historical injustices in the European versus Japanese contexts. If it can be shown that they behave in essentially similar ways, this argument loses credibility. The development of global cultural norms regarding historical justice suggests that, around the world, states are coming under increased pressure to face up to the dark sides of their history. For this hypothesis, variations in the level of pressure that states face is an anomaly that needs to be explained. Finally, the blowback hypothesis leads us to expect that historical narratives that were instituted at one point in time – perhaps to serve the interests of political elites – can become a hindrance for political elites at a later point. Like other variants of Culturalism, the blowback hypothesis is weakened if it turns out that such historical myths are easily discarded and have little impact on the evolution of the official narrative.

## Plan of the Book

To investigate empirically the dynamics and implications of contemporary controversies over history, this book will proceed to analyze the development of the politics of history and the memory of World War II in three concrete cases: post-1945 Germany, Austria, and Japan.[62] The year 1945 represents a convenient point of departure because World War II was a seminal experience as well as an apparent rupture[63] in the development of each country's national identity and political system. In addition, by dealing with an event that occurred

---

[62] In the case of Japan, the time frame that is relevant is somewhat larger than the other three, since the events of World War II are inextricably bound up with the larger issue of the development of the Japanese empire beginning in 1895.

[63] The extent to which 1945 really represented a rupture is, of course, itself a matter of considerable dispute.

at one common point in time, it will be possible to control for the impact of generational change as well as developments in the larger international system (the cold war, the development of the human rights regime, etc.).

By necessity, each case can be dealt with here only in broad brush strokes. The purpose is not to draw a comprehensive and precise picture of each case; fortunately, large and well-developed literatures are readily available on each one. Rather, a general overview of the development of debates over history will be provided with the aim of developing first-order answers to the larger questions posed in this study. In each of the three empirical cases, a three-stage research strategy will be employed.

First, it is necessary to get some gauge of what each country's populations experienced during the war years, in particular the numbers of people that were killed or injured as a result of state policy and the circumstances under which those killings occurred. Beyond the raw facts (to the extent that they are in fact observable) what is of particular concern here is the extent to which the population at the time was aware of what transpired, whether they felt they had any control over the course of events, and how they frame these experiences relative to other developments. This provides the baseline needed for investigating the historical determinist hypothesis.

Second, it is necessary to focus on the way in which these issues were defined in the immediate post-war period. Of particular importance here is the way in which the history issue was taken up by different political actors, both domestic and international, and the kinds of policies adopted that promoted particular historical narratives. Although the total range of such policies is potentially vast, the focus will be on the five dimensions of the official historical narrative: the rhetoric of political leaders, the establishment of commemorative sites and practices, educational policy, lustration policies – war crimes and amnesties, purges, limitations on the freedom of speech and various forms of compensation or restitution for groups and individuals defined as victims. Special attention will be paid to tracing the connections between the official narrative and broader political issues as democratization, partisan political interests, the development of regional institutions, and alliances.[64] The interaction of historical experience and political interest is central: The degree to which personal experience bows to practical expediency is of critical importance to gauging the relative importance of instrumental versus historical determinist factors.

Third, the evolution of each country's official narrative will be explored over time and compared to changes in its broader domestic and international political contexts. This will allow for the testing of some of the hypothetical relationships between broader politics and the official narrative. Such a diachronic analysis allows us to see whether insurgent historical narratives grounded in

---

[64] The aim here is to illuminate the casual connections between the different variables through careful tracing of the processes through which outcomes emerged. On the technique of process tracing, see Alexander George and Andrew Bennett, *Case Studies and Theory Development in the Social Sciences* (Cambridge: Belfer Center for Science and International Affairs, 2004).

personal experiences reemerge when a window of opportunity presents itself, as the Historical Determinist position might lead one to expect. It allows for the testing of the Instrumentalist proposition that changes in the distribution of power in the international system and in domestic politics translates into changes in the official historical narrative without evidence of significant levels of cognitive dissonance and political resistance. Finally, it allows us to test some of the central claims of the Culturalist position, to whit, whether the emergence of an international justice regime creates pressure toward a greater acknowledgment of past wrongs, or whether historical narratives once established become very difficult to change despite powerful normative (cultural) and pragmatic (instrumentalist) pressures to do so.

Finally, through comparison of the trajectory of the official narrative and the politics of the past in our three cases, it will be possible to achieve a certain degree of control of the variables and strengthen the testing of the hypotheses.[65] The proposition that the magnitude of the event impacts on memory and the propensity for disputes can be tested because the scale of the killings and the circumstances that they occurred under varied considerably between the three cases under review here. Similarly, the impact of deeply held cultural norms regarding guilt and responsibility can be explored because there are profound differences between Austria, Germany, and especially Japan on this score. Finally, the importance of regional variations can be controlled for in good measure by looking at cases situated in Asia and Europe.

---

[65] On the comparative case study method, Alexander George and Andrew Bennett, *Case Studies and Theory Development* (Cambridge, MA: MIT Press, 2005); and Adam Przeworski and Henry Teune, *The Logic of Comparative Social Inquiry* (New York: Wiley, 1970).

# 2

# Germany

## *The Model Penitent*

The burdens of history lie heavily upon the Federal Republic of Germany. Arguably, no nation in the world has committed greater crimes in the course of the twentieth century than Germany. In the popular mind, the atrocities of the Third Reich have come to define the outer limits of state-sponsored brutality and human cruelty. As a result, it might seem natural that no other country should do more to express remorse for its actions and to atone for its crimes. Since 1945, the leaders of the Federal Republic have made great efforts to apologize for the terrible suffering Germany had inflicted on the world. At times they have literally fallen to their knees and begged for forgiveness – as Chancellor Willi Brandt did during his famous visit to the Warsaw ghetto in 1970. The German State has paid well more than $100 billion in compensation to the victims of the Third Reich, and the crimes and horrors of the nation's past are commemorated with a thoroughness unparalleled in any other country. In 1985, President of the Federal Republic Carl Richard von Weizsäcker even went so far as to suggest that Germany's willingness to face up to its past is in fact the most distinctive and praiseworthy feature of the German nation. To put it another way, Weizsäcker was arguing that not only should Germans today feel guilty for the crimes of the past, but that this guilt should itself be a source of national pride (an attitude referred to as *Sühnestolz* in German).[1]

At the same time, arguably no other nation in the world has been as richly rewarded for expressing its guilt. Since 1945, the Federal Republic has been successfully reintegrated into the community of nations. Germany's democratic virtues are widely and generally celebrated. Its economic achievements are

[1] See Richard von Weizsäcker, "der 8.Mai 1945: 40 Jahre danach," in Weizsäcker, *Von Deutschland aus: Reden des Bundespräsidenten* (Munich: Deutscher Taschenbuch Verlag, 1987); English translation in Hartman, *Bitburg*, pp. 262–273.

Earlier versions of this chapter were presented at the International Studies Association Convention in San Diego in March 2006 and in Chicago 2007. The author would like to express his thanks to the commentators and panel members for their help and suggestions, especially Beverley Crawford, Gunther Hellman, and Ole Weaver.

formidable. The Federal Republic has been one of the driving forces behind European integration and generally is accepted as an important player in world affairs. So successful has the project of German rehabilitation been that in recent years Germans have been able to rediscover a sense of pride in their nation without provoking alarm and enmity among their neighbors.[2]

Not all of the Federal Republic's successes can be attributed to its penitent stance on history. Nonetheless, Germany is often held up to the rest of the world as an example of what a proper attitude of remorse and contrition can achieve. Advocates of the "historical justice regime" – that international network of scholars, lawyers, and activists who promote the rights of victims of state abuse and call on governments to face up to their past wrong doing – frequently point to Germany as the model other nations should emulate. There is an almost quasi-religious quality to their message: repent and you too can find redemption; speak the truth and it will set you free. Put simply, Germany has set the global gold standard for guilt – it is the model penitent for the world.

There is much to this narrative of Germany as former sinner who has been cleansed through acts of penance and contrition. Nonetheless, this narrative is in many respects a deceptive one. To begin with, there are a number of factual problems. For instance, German expressions of remorse have often been qualified by a powerful sense of German victimization, or by the fact that German expressions of remorse and efforts to paying compensation have been highly selective and were at least partly motivated by calculations of material interest. Arguably, it was not until 1985 that the Federal Republic fully adopted the penitent stance usually attributed to it, and it was not until the late 1990s that efforts were made to recognize and compensate the majority of those who had been victimized by the Third Reich. Despite repeated efforts to bring a closure to debates about the past, to this day history continues to be a sensitive and controversial political issue, both inside of Germany and in its relations with the outside world. Then there is the problem that this narrative of Germany as a model penitent overlooks the fact that Germany is highly unusual in its willingness to express remorse for the past. Many other countries have been responsible for terrible atrocities, yet typically they have been far more resistant to adopting a penitent official narrative.

---

[2] Perhaps the clearest recent example of this greater international tolerance of expressions of German nationalism came during the 2006 World Cup tournament held in Germany. For the first time in decades, it became acceptable for German fans to express their jubilation over the exploits of their nation's soccer team by waving the German flag and singing the national anthem – acts which in the past had generated considerable controversy in the German as well as international press and media. See, for instance, Richard Bernstein, "In World Cup Surprise, Flags Fly with German Pride," *New York Times*, June 17, 2006, available at http://www.nytimes.com/2006/06/18/world/europe/18germany.html?ex=1308283200&en=c077835a3e53b9ad&ei=5088& partner=rssnyt&emc=rss (accessed July 25, 2007). For a German commentary, see Alexander Marguier, "Deutschland und die WM," *Frankfurter Allgemeine Zeitung*, June 17, 2006, p. 1.

In short, Germany has not been as penitent as is often believed, nor may it easily serve as a model for the rest of the world. Rather than to expound on its virtues as a model penitent, it may be more fruitful for the student of international relations to ask, why is it that Germany has come to willingly adopt an official historical narrative that is so relentlessly negative about the past? Is the German readiness to be penitent the result of a genuine sense of guilt and moral repugnance regarding the crimes committed by Germans during the Third Reich? Such an interpretation would be consistent with some versions of the Historical Determinist position discussed in the Chapter 1. Alternatively, is it more plausible to argue that the Federal Republic's highly public display of remorse is a carefully calculated ploy designed to serve German national interests – as a cynical proponent of the Instrumentalist position would be likely to argue? Such an interpretation would be consistent with the Historical Determinist proposition that the magnitude of the atrocities committed by a country in the past should translate into powerful pressures for their acknowledgment.[3] Or, as the Historical Realist position maintains, is it a combination of these factors unfolding over time that determines both the official narrative and its impact on politics in general? To get a grip on this question, it is necessary to explore in greater detail the circumstances of the economic, social, and political realities with which Germany was confronted in the aftermath of its defeat in 1945.

## German Catastrophes

The destruction Germany wreaked upon Europe in the first half of the twentieth century was truly extraordinary. First, there was Germany's role in bringing about the disaster of World War I.[4] Before the fighting ended in 1918, over ten million lives had been lost on the field of battle, and much of central Europe lay in ruins. The processes that would lead to the dissolution of three great Empires – the Austro-Hungarian monarchy, the Ottoman Empire, and Imperial Russia – had been set in motion. In the aftermath of the slaughter in the trenches and the introduction of new, industrialized forms of warfare including aerial bombardment, the use of poison gas, and unrestricted submarine warfare,

---

[3] See Karl Wilds, "Identity Creation and the *Culture of Contrition*: Recasting 'Nor- mality' in the Berlin Republic," *German Politics*, 9:1 (2000), pp. 83–102.

[4] It is tempting to treat the disasters of the World Wars I and II separately, if only to simplify the analysis; however, the two wars are closely linked in any evaluation of German responsibility for the events of 1939–1945. A historical narrative that sees Nazism as the reaction to an unjust peace made in 1918 reduces German responsibility for the horrors after 1933. Conversely, a historical narrative that sees aggressive tendencies built into German society as a factor behind World War I heightens German culpability. For an overview of the German debate, see Klaus Große Kracht, *Die Zankende Zunft: Historische Kontroversen in Deutschland nach 1945* (Göttingen: Vandenhoek & Ruprecht, 2005), chapter 2. As we shall see, in Japan as well, the issue of pre–World War II history had a significant impact on how Japan evaluated its behavior during the war.

Western civilization as a whole had been shaken to its core.[5] Although many countries and leaders can be said to share responsibility for the outbreak of the war and its consequences, it would be difficult to absolve the Kaiser and his advisors of a major share of the blame.[6]

The horrors of World War I, however, were only the prelude to the even greater horrors of the World War II, which claimed between 40 million and 50 million lives in the European theater. The Soviet Union alone lost as many as 28 million – 10 million soldiers and 18 million civilians. Poland lost more than 3 million, or approximately 20 percent of its population. In the aftermath of the struggle, the economies of continental Europe had been shattered, and tens of millions of people had lost their homes and their livelihoods.

The destructiveness of the war was magnified by the savagery with which it had been waged. Massive aerial bombings aimed at instilling terror in the civilian populations had been conducted by both sides. Desperate resistance by partisan groups, particularly in Eastern Europe, had been met with savage counter insurgency operations marked by torture, the taking of hostages, and the punitive slaughter of entire communities. Millions of civilians in the territories occupied by the Wehrmacht were forcibly conscripted as laborers. By 1945, the Allies liberated over 8 million such slave laborers. Millions more had perished while being forced to work under inhuman conditions. Whereas Western prisoners of war were generally treated reasonably well by the Germans, the same could not be said of the Russian and other Eastern European soldiers who fell into German hands. Alone, between 1941 and 1942, over 3 million Russian prisoners of war were starved to death by their German captors. All of these horrors were in clear violation of the existing body of international law governing the conduct of war, the treatment of civilian populations in occupied territories, and the handling of prisoners of war.

Beyond these war crimes, the Third Reich was responsible for the systematic displacement and slaughter of millions of human beings on the basis of the Nazi racial ideology. The single largest group of victims was the Jews, approximately 6 million of whom were killed by the regime. In addition, millions of Poles, Gypsies (Roma and Sinti), homosexuals, handicapped people, and other groups designated as undesirable were liquidated by the Reich. All told, as many as 12 million people were exterminated by the Nazi regime.[7]

---

[5] On the impact of the War on Western thought and civilization, see Jay Winter, *Sites of Memory, Sites of Mourning: The Great War in European Cultural History* (Cambridge and New York: Cambridge University Press, 1995). On the ways in which World War I created a "culture of annihilation" in Europe, see Alan Kramer, *Dynamics of Destruction: Culture and Mass Killing in the First World War* (New York: Oxford University Press, 2007).

[6] For a recent reassessment that comes to this conclusion, David Fromkin, *Europe's Last Summer: Who Started the Great War in 1914* (New York: Alfred E. Knopf, 2004).

[7] Rudolph Rummel, in a meta-analysis of the estimates of the numbers killed, arrives at a staggering total of more than 12 million killed by the Third Reich, including Jews, gypsies, homosexuals, prisoners of war who starved to death while in captivity, reprisal killings of civilians in occupied

In light of this terrible past, it may seem obvious that the Germans should feel guilty after the war. Certainly the horrors of the war created a tremendous reservoir of anger, rage, and pain both inside and outside of Germany. There was a natural, human reflex to punish whoever might be held responsible. In many parts of Europe, this led to spontaneous, locally organized acts of violence, often followed by more sustained programs of persecution aimed at rooting out collaborators and others associated with the Nazi regime.[8] They also helped legitimate the subsequent efforts by the Allied governments to pursue the issue of war crimes and crimes against humanity.

However, the task of convincing Germans of their guilt – of impressing a sense of remorse into the collective consciousness of the German nation – was far from being the simple matter that it is sometimes assumed to have been today. There were at least four complicating factors: the degree to which ordinary Germans felt they had any knowledge of the crimes of the Nazi regime; a general sense that they had little ability to control the regime's actions; a sense of victimization on the part of the German population itself; and finally, the fact that German memories of the Nazi era were far from monochromatic and included positive as well as negative aspects. Each of these requires some further elaboration.

First, many, if not most, Germans claimed that although they were aware that something unpleasant (*etwas Unheimliches*) was going on during the Nazi years, few were aware of the full magnitude of what was taking place. Certainly, the Third Reich had made no secret of the fact that it viewed certain categories of people – Communists, homosexuals, Slavs, and especially Jews – as its enemies. Many Germans – especially in the armed forces – were well aware of the brutality with which the war was being waged and had direct knowledge of the fact that large numbers of people were being killed in anti-partisan operations and in programs aimed at rooting out racially undesirable elements. Likewise, the miserable condition of the large number of slave laborers was readily visible to the millions of Germans who came in contact with them. Nonetheless, it is also true that the Nazi regime went out of its way to conceal the true scope of its campaign of extermination. German propaganda films provided relatively benign images of conditions in the concentration camps and ghettos. Germans involved in the liquidation of the Jews and other targeted groups were forbidden to speak publicly about their actions. Certainly the Nazi-controlled media did not report on the homicidal nature of the regime's policies. Consequently, the murderous dimensions of what was taking place

---

territories, and massacres conducted by forces aligned with but not necessarily directed by the Third Reich. Rudolph J. Rummel, *Democide: Nazi Genocide and Mass Murder* (New Brunswick, NJ: Transaction Press, 1992) and *Statistics of Democide: Genocide and Mass Murder Since 1900* (New Brunswick: Transaction Press, 1997). Eleven million is the more common estimate.

[8] For an overview, see István Deák, Jan T. Gross, and Tony Judt, eds., *The Politics of Retribution in Europe: World War II and its Aftermath* (Princeton: Princeton University Press, 2000).

inside the territory of the Third Reich became apparent to most Germans only after 1945.[9]

Second, most Germans did not feel that they were responsible for or had any control over the actions of their government at the time. This diminished sense of responsibility had its roots already in the way in which Hitler came to power. Although Hitler had been elected in a free and open election in 1933, he had won only with a plurality of the vote, 33 percent of the total.[10] Once in power, Hitler then found a pretext for declaring an emergency – the burning of the Reichstag by a deranged arsonist – and then used the special powers granted to him to clamp down on domestic political opponents with startling speed and efficiency. By 1934, at the latest, National Socialist control over German politics was complete, and a highly effective program of ideological indoctrination and police control was put in place that stamped out all organized forms of resistance to the regime. On the ground, individuals and small groups at times were able to defy the orders of the state, and there was some organized opposition to the Hitler regime. On the whole, however, their actions were largely ineffective. As a result, after the war there was a general tendency to attribute responsibility for the crimes of the regime to a relatively small coterie of senior leaders, above all Adolf Hitler. Everyone below the top leadership was, as the famous line went, "just following orders." This sentiment was reflected in the common trope – popularized by the first German postwar chancellor, Konrad Adenauer, that terrible crimes had been committed "in Germany's name."[11] By implication, the German nation itself, and by extension, ordinary Germans were entirely blameless.

Third, especially in the early years after World War II, any German sense of guilt as perpetrators of atrocities was overshadowed by the powerful memories of the immense suffering of the Germans themselves. Whereas Germany had inflicted a catastrophic war on Europe, the war had been a catastrophe

---

[9] On the involvement of German soldiers in atrocities and broader social awareness of the crimes of the Third Reich, see Omer Bartov, *Hitler's Army* (Oxford University Press, 1991); Bartov, *Murder in our Midst: The Holocaust, Industrial Killing and Representation* (Oxford University Press, 1996); Christopher R. Browning, *Ordinary Men: Reserve Police Battalion 101 and the Final Solution in Poland* (New York: Harper, 1993). See also the discussion in Saul Friedlander, "The Wehrmacht, German Society and the Knowledge of the Mass Extermination of the Jews," in Omer Bartov, et al., eds. *Crimes of War: Guilt and Denial in the Twentieth Century* (New York: The New Press, 2002) as well as in Ian Kershaw, *Hitler, the Germans and the Final Solution* (New Haven: Yale University Press, 2008), chapters 5–9 and especially 6. Kershaw argues persuasively and on the basis of prodigious documentary sources that the Germans were neither ignorant – as many claimed – nor willing executioners – as famously argued by Daniel Goldhagen. Rather, their attitude was – with few exceptions – characterized by a "lethal indifference" to the fate of the Jews, cf. pp. 119–120.

[10] On mass electoral support, see Richard F. Hamilton, *Who Voted for Hitler* (Princeton, NJ: Princeton University Press, 1982). On the debate over Hitler's political support base, see Ian Kershaw, *The Nazi Dictatorship: Problems and Perspective of Interpretation*, Fourth edition (New York: Oxford University Press, 2000), chapter 3.

[11] Quoted in Jeffrey Herf, *Divided Memory: The Nazi Past in the Two Germanys* (Cambridge, MA: Harvard University Press, 1997), p. 282.

for Germany as well. Over 6.5 million Germans had been killed in the war – approximately half of them civilians. Millions more had been wounded or were left homeless.[12] The annexation of 22 percent of Germany's pre-1938 territory by Czechoslovakia, Poland, and Russia was followed by a wave of violence and ethnic cleansing that generated approximately 14 million refugees. Perhaps 500,000 more died in the violence or as a result of the resulting material deprivation.[13] Huge numbers of German women had been raped, especially in the East where the Soviet army was let loose on the civilian population of the liberated areas.[14] The Allied powers had taken more than 6 million German prisoners of war. Those who found themselves in Soviet hands were transported to Siberia where they were forced to labor under inhuman conditions, in many cases for more than a decade. Virtually every major German city lay in ruins, order had largely collapsed, and the economy in general had ceased to function. Caloric intake even in the relatively well-off American zone of occupation had fallen to 1,200 calories a day for ordinary workers, less for others.[15] By the winter of 1945, most of the German population felt brutalized, was cold and hungry, and faced a bleak future.

Taken together, these extreme conditions had two important consequences for the formation of German historical memory. First, although the deprivations undergone by the German population created a very real sense of anger at the regime for having inflicted this catastrophic war on the nation, most Germans in the immediate postwar years felt that they had other, more pressing concerns than pursuing questions of guilt or innocence. The first order of business was merely surviving; justice was a luxury that would have to be pursued later.

Second, German suffering also served to relativize feelings of guilt. Germans felt – with some justification – that the Allies as well had been guilty of atrocities. This was particularly true of the Soviet Union, whose reputation for brutality against the German as well as its own civilian population was matched only by that of the Third Reich; however, the Western Allies as well had not been above resorting to terror tactics in the pursuit of victory. Over 600,000 German civilians were killed by the bombing of German cities. Whereas in many instances, German civilian casualties were a byproduct of attacks on military and other

[12] On Germany's material losses, see Dennis L. Bark and David Gress, *A History of West Germany: From Shadow to Substance* (Cambridge, MA: Blackwell, 1982), p. 42.

[13] The division of Germany and its human costs has been the focus of a great deal of recent writing. For relatively early works, see Herman Graml, *Die Alliierten und die Teilung Deutschland's Konflikte und Entscheidungen 1941–1948* (Frankfurt am Main: Fischer, 1985); and Alfred M. de Zayas, *Nemesis at Potsdam: The Anglo-Americans and the Expulsion of the Germans* (London: Routledge and Kegan, 1979). For more recent works, see Wolfgang Benz, ed., *Die Vertreibung der Deutschen aus dem Osten: Ursachen, Ereignisse, Folgen* (Frankfurt am Main: Fischer Verlag, 1995); and Erik K. Franzen, *Die Vertriebenen – Hitler's letzte Opfer* (Berlin: Propyläen Verlag, 2001).

[14] Antony Beevor, *Berlin: The Downfall* (New York and London: Viking, 2002).

[15] Bark and Gress, *From Shadow to Substance*, op. cit. pp. 130–131.

strategic targets, in other cases – notably the fire bombings of Dresden and Hamburg – the quite deliberate goal had been to break the morale of the German population.[16] In the eastern parts of Germany, the Red Army had engaged in a wild orgy of destruction as it advanced into German territory, partly out of a desire to exact retribution on the Germans for the damage that they had inflicted on Russia, partly because the Soviet leadership had little interest in restraining them. Even after the first shock of conquest, Germans in the East continued to suffer under Soviet occupation. Entire factories were carted off to the Soviet Union as reparations. Large numbers of people, in particular from the East German land-owning class, were imprisoned or deported, and a harsh Communist dictatorship was imposed replete with prison camps, secret police, and the ultimate threat of Soviet military intervention.

Consequently, there developed a strong sense of victimization on the part of the German people after 1945, a feeling that they too had been victims of the war and were deserving of help and pity. Germans in general felt that in many respects they had been doubly victimized, first by their own government, and second by the Allied powers.[17] So powerful was this sense of victimization that in the rhetoric of the time, the suffering of the German people was often equated with that of the Jews.[18] Many leading political and cultural figures, including many who had been victims of Nazi persecution, expressed such views.[19]

Further complicating the effort to pursue the issue of German guilt in the immediate postwar period was the fact that whatever knowledge Germans may have had of the dark sides of the regime was tempered by more mundane, even benign memories of the time between 1933 and 1945. During this period, millions of people went to school or work, went on picnics, got married and otherwise led perfectly normal lives. The regime was able to command the loyalty of the population because it seemed to have made some significant achievements. The often violent struggle between the Far Right and the Far Left that had characterized the Weimar period had been put to an end. Hitler's economic policies appeared to bring Germany out of the malaise of the Great Depression considerably earlier than was true of other great powers, including the United States. National Socialist welfare policies were generally popular

---

[16] Jörg Friedrich, *Der Brand- Deutschland im Bombenkrieg 1940–1945* (Munich: Propyläen Verlag, 2002).

[17] Frank Biess, "Men of Reconstruction – the Reconstruction of Men: Returning POWs in East and West Germany," in Karen Hagemann and Stefanie Schüler-Springorum, *Home/Front: The Military, War and Gender in Twentieth-Century Germany* (Oxford: Xoford University Press, 2002).

[18] Jeffrey K. Olick, *In the House of the Hangman: The Agonies of German Defeat, 1943–1949* (Chicago and London: University of Chicago Press, 2005), pp. 175–177; and Robert Moeller, "The Politics of the Past in the 1950s," in Niven, ed., *Germans as Victims*, pp. 36–37.

[19] See for instance the comments of Reichstag deputy Paul Löbe before the Bundestag in 1949, quoted in Peter Reichel, *Vergangenheitsbewältigung in Deutschland: Die Auseinandersetzung mit der NS-Diktatur von 1945 bis heute* (Munich: Verlag C.H. Beck 2001), p. 68.

and appeared to be promoting greater social equality while improving the lot of the ordinary German.[20] Finally, Hitler could claim that he had reestablished Germany's standing as a great power and to have rectified some of the injustices of the Treaty of Versailles.

With the annexation of Austria in 1938, he even achieved the great nationalist dream of uniting virtually all the German speaking peoples of Europe into a single state. As a result, until well into the 1950s, public opinion data suggested that significant numbers of West Germans believed that Nazism had "been a good idea that had gone wrong."[21]

In sum, from a Historical Determinist perspective, the notion that Germans should automatically feel guilty for the crimes of the Nazi regime is far from self-evident. The combination of limited knowledge, the feeling that they had little control, and a powerful sense of victimization, all served to mitigate any sense of remorse that ordinary Germans may have felt in the early postwar years, both individually and as a nation. In a grim way, the German stance after 1945 is reminiscent of the old joke about the man who is charged with poisoning his parents and defends himself by claiming that first, he had not known that it was poison that he had put into their soup, second, that the bottle had fallen inadvertently out of his hand, third, that his parents had drunk the soup before he could stop them, fourth, in any case many people poison their parents, and finally, by begging for mercy from the court on the grounds that he is an orphan.

Of course, such exculpatory arguments could be countered, and eventually the Germans themselves came to reject them. Nonetheless, the fact remains that there were a great many experiences that Germans in the postwar years could draw on to construct a historical narrative, some of which were a source of guilt and shame, and others that fed a sense of aggrievement and victimization. To understand why the Federal Republic in the end adopted the kind of official historical narrative that it did, we need to go beyond the historical experiences themselves and examine the political climate in which the official narrative was formed in the early postwar years.

## Imperfect Reckoning: The Allied Pursuit of German War Guilt, 1945–1952

The first effort to establish an official narrative of guilt was undertaken by the victorious Allied powers. Already before the war had ended, fierce debates had raged among the leaders of the Allied forces over how to deal with a defeated Germany. That some sort of reckoning was necessary never was in question. Public opinion in the Allied countries overwhelmingly favored severe punishment for the hated Axis powers. The chief question was what form that

---

[20] David Schoenbaum, *Hitler's Social Revolution* (Garden City, NY: Doubleday, 1966).

[21] According to an October 1948 survey, 57 percent of all Germans above the age of 18 years agreed with this statement.

reckoning should take. Some favored immediate and direct punitive action, designed to punish Germany for its crimes and to cripple the German economy so as to make it physically impossible for Germany to become a military power ever again. Others, however, felt that it might be possible to reeducate the German population through a program of reeducation. In the end, the more lenient approach won the day, in part because there was a growing appreciation that the rehabilitation of Germany would be needed for both the economic recovery of Europe and to create a bastion against the further spread of Communism.[22]

In many respects, the Allies appeared to be in an ideal position to pursue questions of historical justice in Germany. In the aftermath of the war, Germany lay broken and prostrate at their feet. Unlike many other occupations – notably that of Afghanistan or Iraq – there was virtually no organized opposition to the occupying forces.[23] The German government had largely disintegrated, as had the economy. The maintenance of social and political order lay almost wholly in the hands of the occupation authorities, and the German populace was in desperate need of Allied economic assistance to meet their basic needs. Thanks to meticulous German record keeping, the Allies had ready access to the information that they needed to pursue historical justice issues.[24] Most importantly, there was a considerable willingness on the part of German elites and the population as a whole to investigate crimes of the Nazi regime. Large numbers of Germans had been victims of the regime's policies, and the postwar political leadership was dominated by men who had been persecuted by the Nazis.[25] Public opinion data from early in the occupation showed that over half of Germans surveyed supported the purges, and a similar percentage felt at the outset that the Nuremberg trials against the top Nazi leadership were fair and just.[26]

Despite these initial advantages, during the seven-year occupation period, Western efforts to pursue the issue of German responsibility for the war was

---

[22] For an excellent summary of Allied debates about the occupation of Germany, see Jeffrey Olick, *In the House of the Hangman: The Agonies of German Defeat, 1943–1949* (Chicago: University of Chicago Press, 2005), Part I.

[23] For a comparison of the German and Japanese occupations with the problems facing the United States in Afghanistan and Iraq, see Thomas Berger, "Political Order in Occupied Societies: Realist Lessons from the Germany and Japan," *Asian Security* 1:1 (2005), pp. 3–24.

[24] In Japan, in contrast, much of the documentary evidence was lost or destroyed before they could fall into Allied hands.

[25] To cite just a few examples, Konrad Adenauer, who became head of the Christian Democratic party, had lost his position as Mayor of Cologne as a result of Nazi pressure and had been briefly arrested and interrogated by the Gestapo. The head of the Social Democratic Party, Kurt Schumacher, had been interned in a concentration camp and severely tortured. Thomas Dehler, one of the chief figures in the Free Democratic Party, had suffered persecution because he refused to divorce his Jewish wife.

[26] See Reichel, *Vergangenheitsbewältigung in Deutschland*, op. cit., p. 34, 69–71; Anna Merritt and Richard L. Merritt, eds., *Public Opinion in Occupied Germany* (Urbana: University of Illinois Press, 1970), pp. 307–308. Observers at the time cautioned, however, that there appeared to be a gap between what the survey data seemed to show and public opinion as reflected in published sources at the time. Reichel, *Vergangenheitsbewältigung in Deutschland*, p. 47.

flawed at best, and by the end of the occupation era they were deemed by many, including some of the officials who had been put in charge of the process, to have been a failure. Many years later, when asked to comment on the war crimes tribunals, the military governor in charge of the American zone of occupation, General Lucius Clay, was reported to have begged off, saying only, "Don't remind me of the biggest mistake."[27] The West's efforts to pursue the issue of Nazi guilt may have had some benefits in terms of meting out justice to some of the worst evil doers and in helping cleanse the German political system of possibly dangerous elements. However, the larger project of convincing the Germans that they bore a special burden of guilt as a nation was by and large unsuccessful.

Three factors contributed to this failure. First, there were the deficiencies of the main instruments – trials and the purges – the Allies used to pursue German guilt. Second, there was the concomitant German dissatisfaction with what they perceived as being a one-sided and disruptive Allied campaign to punish Germany for its misdeeds. Third and finally, there was the growing pressure of the cold war, which forced a dramatic reordering of Western policy goals in favor of the speedy reconstruction of Germany and the rehabilitation of German military men at the expense of a rigorous persecution of those responsible for the crimes of the Nazi era.

From the start, the Allied War crimes tribunals – especially the politically important showcase trial of the top Nazi leadership at Nuremberg – were beset with problems. The most fundamental issue was that many of the crimes with which the Nazi leadership was charged – crimes against peace and crimes against humanity – were not crimes at the time they were committed. There was, thus, a post hoc quality to the proceedings that opened them up to the charge of victor's justice, more concerned with satisfying the Allies' thirst for revenge than in defending fundamental principles of justice. The prosecutors at Nuremberg were well aware of this problem and, therefore, focused on those crimes that had a clearer basis in international law, such as the mistreatment of prisoners in violation of the Geneva Convention or the waging of aggressive war in violation of the Kellog-Briand Pact of 1928. Remarkably, from a contemporary perspective, the more heinous crimes of the Holocaust and the mass extermination of people on the basis of racial criteria received comparatively little attention. Although the proceedings did document in great detail the horrors of the concentration camps and the slaughter of the Jews, there was a certain ambiguity about how these crimes should be punished, even though the revelations provoked universal shock and revulsion.[28]

Equally problematic was the theory of collective guilt that was used to justify the prosecution of the top German leadership for the actions of literally

---

[27] Quoted in Lutz Niethammer, *Die Mitläuferfabrik Entnazifisierung am Beispiel Bayerns* (Berlin: Dietz Verlag, 1982), pp. 15–16. The author is also indebted for his insights on this issue to Professor Bill Griffith of MIT, who had been involved in the denazification program in Bavaria during the occupation period.

[28] Olick, *In the House of the Hangman*, op. cit., pp. 105–110.

hundreds of thousands of people working together in large organization. In total, twenty-eight members of the German military and political elite were put on trial as class A war criminals who bore political responsibility for the crimes committed by four organizations that were suspected of having carried out criminal acts: the Nazi party, the High Command of the Wehrmacht, the SS, and the administration in charge of conquered territories. The idea that individual leaders could be held responsible for the actions of their underlings was a novel one at the time and had originated in American antiracketeering case law developed to fight organized crime. Perversely, the decision to put the top leadership on trial had the effect of exculpating those who were not put on trial, including the German people as a whole.

The arbitrary nature of the proceedings was underlined by the fact that although German crimes were pursued, the issue of possible Allied war crimes was never seriously raised. The United States and Great Britain had conducted a brutal campaign of aerial bombardment of German population centers during the war, and Allied forces had often been guilty of depredations against civilians. Particularly problematic, from the point of view of the German population, was the presence of a Russian judge at the proceedings, even though the Soviet Union had clearly been guilty of many of the same crimes the German defendants were accused of.

Similar problems afflicted the lower-level war crime trials conducted by the Allied powers. These were broken into two groups: individual trials of class B and C war criminals and collective trials for the leaders of organizations accused of criminal acts – the German military command, the personnel who ran the concentration camp system, doctors who had been involved in medical experiments on prisoners and the euthanizing of the disabled, as well as the judiciary charged enforcing the edicts of the Hitler regime.[29] In total, in the Western occupied zones (the parts of Germany under control of the Americans, British, and French), 5,025 persons were found guilty of war crimes or crimes against humanity, of whom 806 were sentenced to death.[30] Another 13,000 were convicted in the Soviet-controlled zone, plus several thousand more who were tried and punished outside of Germany – mostly in Eastern Europe.[31]

Although these were substantial numbers of people (well over 20,000), they paled in comparison with the number of victims of Nazi crimes. Moreover, there were many instances in which men who arguably deserved to be punished were allowed to go free, and other cases in which those who were punished bore less guilt than those who were not or were punished at a later date. The

---

[29] Reichel, *Vergangenheitsbewältigung in Deutschland*, op. cit., pp. 59–66. A recent, thorough investigation shows slightly lower number of 4,410 guilty sentences in the West zone. See Norbert Frei, "Einführung und Bilanz," in Norbert Frei, ed., *Transnationale Vergangenheitspolitik: Der Umgang mit deutschen Kriegsverbrechern in europa nach dem Zweiten Weltkrieg* (Göttingen: Wallstein, 2006), esp. Table 1, pp. 31–32.

[30] Jeffrey Herf, *Divided Memory*, op. cit., p. 206.

[31] Reichel, *Vergangenheitsbewältigung in Deutschland*, op. cit., p. 72. Frei comes up with a total of nearly 96,798 in all of Europe. Frei, *Transnationale Vergangenheitspolitik*, op. cit., p. 32.

arbitrary and incomplete nature of the proceedings was underlined by these gross asymmetries of justice.

Even more problematic than the trials were the purges of individuals and organizations that had supported the Nazi regime. The logic of the reeducation project demanded that German society be rid of baneful influence of those contaminated by Nazism if a new start was to be made and democracy to flourish. The chief problem was the sheer numbers of people involved. Given the totalitarian nature of the regime, virtually every single person with any degree of authority had been drawn into the Nazi party, and virtually every single organization, from nursing associations to chess clubs, had been incorporated into the political system in one way or another. The Nazi party alone had more than 8 million members by the end of the war, disproportionately drawn from the most capable and well-educated sectors of society – the doctors, lawyers, business leaders, and others whose skills and talents were needed if Germany was to be rebuilt. In addition, many of the organizations that were deemed suspect and whose operations were suspended were responsible for providing vital social services, such as caring for the more than 2 million severely wounded and disabled former soldiers left behind by the war.[32]

As a result of these obstacles, the purges were beset with difficulties from the beginning, and throughout the early stages of the occupation, the Western powers struggled to find some sort of mechanism that would allow them to balance the objective of getting rid of dangerous, tainted elements in German society with the practical needs of running the country. Initially, the Allies leaned toward thoroughness, and entire categories of people deemed to be dangerous were subject to "automatic arrest" and placed in internment camps based on their membership in certain designated organization. Half of these were released by the end of 1946, although members of the Nazi party leadership, the SS, and the Gestapo remained imprisoned longer.[33] In the spring of 1946, the Western allies then set up instead special courts (*Spruchkammern*) that were charged with screening people who might be purged. Run by Germans with no legal training but from an untainted political background (often former exiles returning from abroad or ex-Communists), the *Spruchkammern* were supposed to examine virtually the entire adult German population and sort them out into five different categories according to their level of involvement with the previous regime.

To aid with the screening process, a survey was passed out in the American zone of occupation asking questions regarding the respondents' pasts. Every German over the age of 18 was required to fill out the survey. Over 13 million such surveys were filled out. Approximately 3.4 million cases came to the attention of the *Spruchkammern*, and over a third of these actually resulted in trial, with the accused having to prove their innocence. In every case,

---

[32] Kurt P. Tauber, *Beyond the Eagle and the Swastika: German Nationalism Since 1945* (Middleton, CT: Weslyan University Press, 1967).

[33] Reichel, *Vergangenheitsbewältigung in Deutschland*, pp. 30–31.

documents had to be collected, witnesses interviewed, a defense appointed, and a judicial process initiated before a verdict could be handed down. Even then, there was an opportunity to appeal. In short, the purge set into motion a vast bureaucratic-judicial exercise that caught up millions of people in its operations and far outstripped the limited resources of a military government struggling to deal with such urgent problems as rebuilding shattered cities, resettling millions of refugees and displaced persons, maintaining law and order, and feeding a desperate, hungry population.

Inevitably given the mismatch between goals and resources, this process quickly broke down. In practice, informal networks quickly sprang up whereby alibis were manufactured (the so-called *Persilschein*, or certificate of innocence, named after the ticket used for bleached items at laundry stores) and various ways were found to circumvent or expedite the judicial process. Typically, those with the best connections or other resources were the most adept at evading the purge machinery. As a result, the impression was created that the cards were stacked against the ordinary citizen – or as the saying at the time put it, "they hang the little ones and let the bigger ones go free" (*"Die Kleinen hängt man, und die Großen lässt man laufen"*).[34] The *Spruchkammern* were forced to let the vast majority of those who they examined go free, the majority without even coming to trial. Only 23,600 were judged to have been primarily responsible or responsible, and many of these were later recategorized as less guilty. As one German commentator sarcastically put it, the purges created a *Mitläuferfabrik*, a judicial factory that pumped out millions of fellow travelers, not guilty enough to deserve being purged, but not entirely innocent either.[35]

As a result of the manifest deficiencies of the trials and the purges, whatever public support there may have been for pursuing the issue of Nazi crimes evaporated. Already in March 1946, Konrad Adenauer, the emerging leader of the conservative Christian Democratic Union (CDU), in a speech at the University of Cologne, said that the Nuremberg trials had gone on long enough, that those members of the Nazi party who had been guilty of crimes should be punished, but those who were not "should finally be left in peace and quiet to get on with their work."[36] A few months later, in a speech in Munich-Gladsbach, he went further, stating that the Allies were doing more to encourage nationalism and militarism through their misguided policies than the Nazis had ever been able to.[37]

The CDU's stance on the issue was at least partly motivated by electoral calculations. Former Nazis and ex-soldiers numbered in the millions, and if one included their families, there was scarcely a household in Germany that was not in some way affected by the trials and the purges. This was a

---

[34] Reichel, *Vergangenheitsbewältigung in Deutschland*, op. cit., pp. 32–24.
[35] Niethammar, *Mitläuferfabrik*, op. cit.
[36] Quoted in Jeffrey Herf, *Divided Memory*, pp. 222–223.
[37] Quoted in Herf, *Divided Memory*, op. cit., pp. 223–224.

potential voting block that no politician could ignore. The Free Democrats, who appealed strongly to veterans of the Wehrmacht, were similarly highly critical of the purges and the trials.[38] Adenauer's Social Democratic opponents were generally more supportive of punishing former supporters of the Nazi regime, especially those responsible for the prosecution of the Jews; however, for electoral reasons, they too were reluctant to pursue the issue too aggressively, pushing for restitution for the victims of Nazism instead.[39]

Influential interest groups, for example the German Protestant and Catholic Churches, also spoke out in favor of ending the trials and the purges.[40] Even former victims of the Nazi regime who had returned to prominent positions in German intellectual life criticized the Allied policies. For instance, Eugen Kogon – who had survived Buchenwald and became an influential Catholic commentator and publisher after the war – wrote of "the right to make political mistakes." Similarly, Martin Niemöller, a prominent Protestant clergyman who had been imprisoned in the Sachsenhausen concentration camp for his opposition to the regime's policies, called for a boycott of the trials and the purges.[41]

During the 1949 Federal elections, the first since the war, the question of historical justice emerged as a central campaign issue. Despite some reservations, the Social Democratic Party (SPD) under Schumacher generally favored continued confrontation with the past and bringing those guilty of war crimes to trial. Adenauer and the CDU, on the other hand, emphasized leniency and the reintegration of former regime supporters instead. Both sides linked their positions on the trials and the purges to their broader political world views and policy agendas. Although party interest played a central role in shaping their preferred policies – at a minimum, the ideological worldviews associated with the subcultures of the major political actors, like CDU and SPD, gave those interests a particular form and linked them together in ways that were perfectly understandable – they were not necessarily based on interest alone.

For the CDU, Nazism and Communism both were part and parcel of the same phenomenon, a broader deformation of Western civilization that denied all human and ethical values in favor of the quest for absolute political power – what political writers such as Hannah Arendt and Carl Friedrich (both German exiles who had settled in the United States) called the "totalitarian project." The overriding challenge of the day, from this perspective, was to rebuild Germany as a free, market-oriented, democratic state and to anchor it in the nascent Western military alliance, the North Atlantic Treaty Organization (NATO), to protect it from the threat of resurgent nationalism as well as of the godless Bolshevik menace from the East. Anti-Communism could thus be equated with

---

[38] Even Thomas Dehler, who had been imprisoned by the regime and whose wife was Jewish, was highly critical of the purges on the grounds of their faulty legal basis.

[39] Herf, *Divided Memory*, op. cit., pp. 223–224.

[40] Reichel, *Vergangenheitsbewältigung in Deutschland*, op. cit., p. 70.

[41] Reichel, *Vergangenheitsbewältigung in Deutschland*, op. cit., pp. 35–36.

anti-Nazism, and it became possible to sharply condemn Adolf Hitler and the Nazi regime while supporting the rehabilitation of large numbers of former Nazis in the name of building a strong and stable democracy.

Intellectuals on the Left, in contrast, tended to emphasize Nazism's roots in German bourgeois society and the peculiar path of German socioeconomic and political development – the so-called German *Sonderweg* – that had given birth to militarism and Fascism. They argued that unlike other Western societies, Germany had undergone industrialization and modernization without experiencing a bourgeois revolution of the sort the United States had undergone in 1776 and France in 1792. As a result, the German bourgeoisie had developed a mentality of extreme dependence on the bureaucratic state and were hostile to democratic processes in ways that made them susceptible to the authoritarianism of the Nazi regime. These views had practical, political consequences. Domestically, the Social Democrats were inclined to believe that Germany had to aggressively root out those elements that had supported the Nazi regime – through the continuance of trials, reeducation, and purges, but also through the nationalization of key industrial sectors and the redistribution of economic resources – if it was not to succumb to similar impulses in the future. In the realm of foreign policy, the SPD opposed German rearmament and joining the Western alliance. They feared the possible political impact of a revived military and believed doing so would make German reunification impossible for the foreseeable future. Instead, the SPD supported the adoption of a stance of strict neutrality between East and West and the maintenance of a minimal, defense-oriented military establishment.[42]

Both parties' stances on the issues reflected the views and preferences of their constituencies. The SPD's economic policies reflected the positions of its supporters in the powerful German trade union movement and were rooted in its traditional Marxist ideological world view. There was an element of political calculus as well, for its foreign policy stance held out the hope of speedy reunification with the East, where many of the SPD's pre-1933 bastions of electoral strength were located. For its part, the CDU received strong support from the German business community and historically drew much of its electoral support from the heavily Catholic Southern and Western regions of the country. Speedy reunification threatened to tip the electoral balance in favor of the Social Democrats and was viewed with suspicion by the traditionally anti-Protestant sentiments of many Christian Democrats. Adenauer in particular was widely rumored to have had a strong aversion to the Prussian East, which he associated with militarism and political intolerance. Although no German leader at the time could afford not to support the cause of reunification, it was relatively easier for the CDU to contemplate a longer division as part of a capitalist West than was true of the Social Democrats.

---

[42] On German foreign policy and its linkage to domestic politics at the time, see Thomas Berger, *The Cultures of Antimilitarism: National Security in Germany and Japan* (Baltimore: Johns Hopkins University Press, 1998), chapters 2 and 3.

In the end, the CDU won a narrow victory over the SPD in the 1949 elections, gaining 139 seats in the Bundestag to the SPD's 131. With the support of the Free Democratic Party's (FDP) 51 seats, the CDU was able to put together a solid parliamentary majority, and Adenauer was elected the first chancellor of the Federal Republic. Although a number of factors played a role in the outcome, the CDU's relatively lenient approach to historical justice issues certainly did not hurt it. As a result, the official historical narrative of the newborn German Federal Republic moved decisively in a relatively impenitent direction.

In his inaugural speech that September, Adenauer announced that the time had come to end the denazification process and consider granting an amnesty for the large majority of those who had been purged. Germany, he declared, should not be divided into two classes of people, those who were politically unburdened by the past and those who were not (*politisch einwandfrei* and *nichteinwandfrei*).[43] The legal basis for such a shift in policy already had been laid with the passing of the new German constitution, the Basic Law (or Grundgesetz), in May 1949. Article 103 of the Basic Law forbade post hoc justice, and actions that had been legal at the time they had been committed were not prosecutable.[44] Exceptions were made for certain types of crimes, especially those involving war crimes or crimes against humanity. Nonetheless, over the course of the next four years, the conservative-dominated German Bundestag passed a series of laws that exempted growing numbers of people from prosecution for a wide range of acts – including murder and aiding or abetting murder – that they may have committed during the Nazi period, so long as those actions could be considered to have been legal at the time, that is, permissible under German and international law.[45]

As a result of this change in policy, large numbers of former Nazis and supporters of the Nazi regime were able to return to positions of authority in many walks of life, including the business world, the bureaucracy, and academia (although a Nazi past remained an insurmountable electoral liability). Perhaps the most glaring example of this was Konrad Adenauer's own chief of staff, Hans Globke, a prominent and highly capable jurist who also happened to have written the commentaries to the 1934 Nuremberg laws, which defined citizenship on racial grounds and laid the legal basis for the prosecution of German Jews.

At first, the Western Allies remained implacable in the face of the rising tide of criticism. In November 1946, for instance, the American military governor, General Lucius Clay, firmly warned that there would be no return to German self-government without denazification.[46] Gradually, however, the

---

43 Jeffrey Herf, *Divided Memory*, op. cit., p. 271.

44 Peter Reichel, *Vergangenheitsbewälitigung in Deutschland*, p. 25.

45 For a thorough study of the politics surrounding these laws, see Norbert Frei, *Adenauer's Germany and the Nazi Past: the Politics of Amnesty and Integration*, trans. Joel Golb (New York: Columbia University Press, 2002), original *Vergangenheitspolitik* (Munich: C. H. Beck, 1997).

46 Peter Reichel, *Vergangenheitsbewälitigung in Deutschland*, op. cit. p. 35.

U.S. position softened as the failures of the purges and the trials became manifest and the need to rebuild Germany as a cold war bastion against Communism increased. Two issues loomed particularly large in American calculations at the time. First, there was the need to prevent Germany from falling under Soviet control. The industrial and military resources of a united Germany could tip the global balance of power in favor of the Soviet Union and its allies. Even a neutralized Germany in the center of Europe would greatly reduce the strength and cohesion of the Western alliance.[47] In this context, the United States was eager to create a pro-Western political constituency inside of Germany and had no desire to clash with Adenauer over the issue of historical justice, even if it meant that some reprehensible characters might return to positions of power.

Secondly, the United States soon realized that it would need many of those who it had once been inclined to view as criminals if Germany was to be an effective member of the Western military alliance. In this regard, the rehabilitation of the German officer corps was of particular importance. As momentum for rearmament began to gather, many former German officers threatened to refuse to serve if their honor was not restored. As a result, the United States began to actively support the curtailment of some of the war crimes trials that it had aggressively pursued in the early stages of the occupation. A particularly dramatic illustration of the shift in U.S. position is offered by the Malmédy trials of seventy-four former members of the Waffen SS men who had been convicted of massacring American prisoners of war during the Battle of the Bulge. All of the defendants were found guilty, and forty-three were sentenced to death by an American military tribunal in July 1946. Soon thereafter, however, doubts about trial procedure were raised, and there was growing political pressure from both the German Federal Government and the U.S. Senate to reconsider the verdicts. Although the legal proceedings would drag on for a while, by 1951, all of the sentences were commuted, and the prisoners were let go.[48]

In sum, by the early 1950s, the initial American-led effort to pursue German war crimes by and large had ended in failure. The trials were sharply curtailed, and the purges had been reversed. Whereas substantial numbers of particularly odious individuals may have been punished, on the whole, the judicial results might well seem paltry in light of the enormity of the crimes that had been committed. More importantly for the purposes of the present discussion, the societal perspective on the past that emerged in the Federal Republic during

---

[47] Marc Trachtenberg, *A Constructed Peace: The Making of the European Settlement, 1945–1963* (Princeton, NJ: Princeton University Press, 1999), pp. 104–108; John Lewis Gaddis, *The United States and the Origins of the Cold War* (New York: Columbia University Press, 1972), chapter 4.

[48] For an overview of the trials, see James Weingartner, *A Peculiar Crusade: Willis M. Everett and the Malmedy Massacre Trial* (New York: New York University Press, 2000).

this time period was a strikingly impenitent one. The popular sense that Germany had been guilty of uniquely evil crimes was distinctly weak, whereas the feeling that Germans had been victims of particularly savage atrocities – based above all on societal memories of Soviet depredations – was strong. The CDU government capitalized on these sentiments – in part for instrumental political reasons – to create an official historical narrative that, to a considerable extent, was exculpatory in tone, placing all responsibility for whatever crimes had occurred on a small group of Nazi leaders while absolving the vast majority of Germans. Pragmatic interest triumphed over outrage; German memories of being victimized won out over whatever sympathy Germans may have had for their victims.

Despite the failures of these initial efforts to achieve a thorough reckoning with the past, the Federal Republic did not adopt an entirely impenitent stance. Domestic and international pressures, in fact, did force Germany to pursue some kind of penance, albeit a highly imperfect one.

### Imperfect Penance

Although by the late 1940s the German public and much of the German political elite had turned against the trials and the purges, the leaders of the Federal Republic could not afford to ignore the issue of historical justice altogether. Too many people, many of them in countries with considerable influence over the Federal Republic, had been victimized by the Nazis and demanded both compensation for the injuries they had suffered and reassurance that Germany would not become a threat to the world once again. Too many Germans as well clamored for compensation for their injuries, and the fear that democracy could collapse again if the bacillus of Nazism was not contained was widespread among German elites on both the Left and the Right.

In response to these fears and demands, the newly founded Federal Republic instituted two sets of policies that would have long-term consequences for the development of the German official narrative. First, it launched a series of initiatives that, albeit on a highly selective basis, paid out large sums of money in restitution to people who could be defined as victims of Nazism. Second, the Federal Republic put into place a variety of institutional mechanisms that allowed the government to clamp down and suppress organizations and groups that were viewed as threats to German democracy, including any organization that espoused a revisionist view of German history or sought to revive the ideas and symbols of the Third Reich.

Already in 1944, before the Hitler regime had been defeated, the leaders of the Allied powers at their summit meeting in Yalta had agreed that Germany would be forced to pay $20 billion in reparations. In 1946 a reparations agreement was reached in which the victor powers were awarded percentages of German property in lieu of cash payment. At this stage the primary concern was with compensating Allied governments, although special provisions also were made early in the occupation to compensate Jewish victims of the Nazism.[49]

Disagreements between the Western Allies and the Soviets soon led to a break down in the implementation of the reparations accord. For their part, the Americans increasingly became concerned that an overly draconian reparations regime would further complicate the already immensely difficult task of rebuilding the German economy and thereby create the conditions under which extremist movements, both on the Left and the Right, could flourish. The post-World War I settlement was widely credited with having ruined the economy of the fledgling Weimar economy and for paving the way for Hitler's ascent to power. In 1952, at the behest of the United States, the Western powers (albeit reluctantly on the part of France) agreed to scale back the size of the reparations demanded from Germany. Although the Soviets were strongly critical of the new American policy, they were unable to extract reparations from the Western part of Germany without U.S. support and were forced to content themselves with what they could extract from the East.[50]

Despite the technical closure of the reparations issue at the intergovernmental level, there remained the question of how to meet the demands of the vast numbers of individuals who had suffered because of the war and Nazi persecution. Here the German Federal Government committed itself to a far-reaching program of paying compensation to the victims of Nazism, in part to meet the pressures from their own citizens, but also critically to win political acceptance from the Western powers. Four sets of measures were taken to meet their demands. First, there was the Burden Sharing Law (*Lastenausgleichgesetz*) aimed at compensating all German citizens who had suffered property losses during the war – including the 14 million or so refugees who settled in the territory of the Federal Republic. Over the next five decades, this mammoth program would pay out close to $100 billion in compensation.[51] Second, there was the 1953 Supplementary Law for the Compensation for the Victims of National Socialist Persecution – BEG (*Bundesentschädigungsgesetz* – revised in 1956) whose stated goal was to "compensate those persecuted for political, racial, religious or ideological reasons," as well as surviving family members. This law, however, applied only to residents of the Federal Republic (although an exception was made for those residing in Israel). Repeated efforts by residents of other countries to apply for compensation under its provisions were

---

[49] Elazar Barkan, *The Guilt of Nations: Restitution and Negotiating Historical Injustices* (New York: Norton, 2000), pp. 6–7.

[50] David Forster, *Wiedergutmachung in Österreich und der BRD im Vergleich* (Innsbruck, Vienan, Munich: Studien Verlag, 2001), pp. 64–65.

[51] "Vertriebene-Organization will gegen Polen klagen," *Frankfurter* Allgemeine, August 3, 2004, at http://www.faz.net/s/Rub28FC768942F34C5B8297CC6E16FFC8B4/Doc~E67755 E46B2974FA295853C69DC7AEC4D~ATpl~Ecommon~Scontent.html (accessed August 17, 2004).

repeatedly turned down by the German courts.[52] Third, there were a series of bilateral treaties signed between the Federal Republic and twelve Western states – all of them either military allies through NATO or important trading partners[53] – under whose provisions the German government paid compensation to individual claimants living in those countries. Between 1959 and 1964, the Federal Republic of Germany (FRG) paid almost one billion marks to victims of Nazi persecution in neighboring countries.[54]

Finally, and most controversially, there was the Luxembourg Agreement of 1952 in which Germany sought to make amends to the world Jewish community as represented by the State of Israel. Jewish groups had been pressing hard for some form of special compensation as early as 1943.[55] In 1947, Kurt Schumacher and the SPD had adopted the issue and urged that such restitution be offered. The CDU, in contrast, was at first reluctant. Although opinion polls showed considerable support for helping Jewish victims of Nazism (68 percent of those surveyed said they were in favor), there was even greater popular support for aiding the German victims of the war – in particular veterans and refugees from the East.[56]

In the 1951 Bundestag debates on the Luxembourg Agreement, considerable reservations were expressed by conservative law makers regarding the legality of Jewish claims as well as the Federal Republic's ability to meet them without damaging its still fragile economy. In the end, Adenauer was able to win Bundestag approval to negotiate an agreement by citing not only Germany's moral obligations but its national interests as well. Without reconciliation with the world Jewish community, Adenauer claimed, Germany would not be able to restore its image in the world. Moreover, he argued that given the influence of Jews in world financial circles, an accord would be in Germany's economic interests as well.[57] Although he did not mention it in his speech, he and his

---

[52] For a detailed discussion of German reparations, see Constantine Goschler, *Schuld und Schulden: die Politik der Wiedergutmachung für NS-verfolgte seit 1945* (Göttingen, Wallstein: 2005).

[53] Austria, Belgium, Britain, Denmark, France, Italy, Luxembourg, Greece, the Netherlands, Norway, Sweden, and Switzerland.

[54] See Susanna Schrafstetter, "The Diplomacy of Wiedergutmachung: Memory, the Cold War and West European Victims of Nazism, 1956–1964," *Holocaust and Genocide Studies* 17:3 (Winter 2003), pp. 459–479; and Schrafstetter, "Die einfachen Leute werden für die Gerechtigkeit sorgen! Die deutsch-britischen Verhandlungen über ein Abkommen zur Entschädigung von Opfern nationalsozialistischer Verfolgung, 1956–1965." *Zeitenblicke* 3:2 (2004), online at http://zeitenblicke.historicum.net/2004/02/schrafstetter/index.html

[55] A substantial literature has grown regarding Jewish claims during this period. For early works written from a firsthand perspective, see Siegfried Moses, *Die Judischen Nachkriegsforderungen* (Tel Aviv: Bitaon, 1946); Kurt R. Grossman and Earl G. Harrison, *Germany's Moral Debate: The German-Israel Agreement* (Whitefish, MT: Literary Licensing, 2011); and Rolf Vogel, ed., *Deutschland's Weg nach Israel: Eine Dokumentation mit Geleitwort von Konrad Adenauer* (Stuttgart: Seewald, 1967).

[56] Information Services Division of the American Army (December 5, 1951) cited in Kurt R. Grossman, *Germany's Moral Debate: The German-Israel Agreement*, op. cit. p. 18.

[57] Herf, *Divided Memory*, op. cit., p. 286.

advisors were particularly concerned that a failure to reach an agreement could be prejudicial to German interests at the upcoming London Conference aimed at resolving questions revolving around German debt and financial obligations vis-à-vis the outside world. [58]

In the end, in the final formulation of the agreement in 1952, Germany agreed to pay an initial settlement worth $1 billion, with an understanding that further payments could be made.[59] The Bundestag approved, but only after sharp debate: 239 voted for the treaty (including the Social Democratic opposition), 35 voted against, and 86 abstained. Most of those abstaining were from Adenauer's own party, the CDU.[60]

The Federal Republic's decision to pay compensation to the victims of Nazism was a crucially important step, one that committed the fledgling nation to maintaining an at least partially penitent official historical narrative. At the same time, it also played an exculpatory role. Even the German term for restitution – *Wiedergutmachung*, to make good again – was reflective of its morally restorative implications, and it was part of an array of policies paying compensation to the victims of the war, including German victims, that underlined the victimization of the German nation as well as that of others. Moreover, the German policy of paying compensation was highly selective, reflecting its instrumental as well as moral side. Compensation was paid to those who could influence German interests – first and foremost the German people themselves, then the citizens of Germany's Western allies and trading partners, and then the Jewish people as represented by the state of Israel. The vast majority of the victims of Nazism, however, lived on the other side of the Iron curtain and was therefore excluded. Clearly, German morality was strongly tempered by calculations of German national interest.

A second aspect of the Federal Republic's attempt to come to terms with the legacy of Nazism was its determination to prevent a renewed breakdown of democracy. Traumatized by the memory of how the liberal institutions of the Weimar Republic had allowed extremist movements to flourish and ultimately erect a totalitarian regime, Germany's leaders were determined to create new institutional structures that would check the growth of extremism. The underlying philosophy of this new approach was labeled "militant democracy" (*Streitbare* or *Wehrhafte Demokratie*). The Federal Republic, unlike its Weimar predecessor, would defend itself from its enemies. To this end, extensive legal instruments were placed at the disposal of the state to help it clamp down on extremist movements. Political organizations and groups who were judged to be "enemies of the Constitutional order" (*Verfassungsfeindlich*) could be banned, their assets seized, and their members placed under arrest. This ban was first exercised in 1952 when the German Constitutional Court approved banning the neo-Nazi *Sozialistische Reichs Partei* (SRP), which had been making some

---

[58] Konrad Adenauer, *Erinnerungen 1953–1955* (Stuttgart: DVA, 1965).

[59] Adenauer, *Erinnerungen 1953–1955*, op. cit., pp. 140–142.

[60] Carlo Schmid, *Erinnerungen* (Stuttgart: Hoser, 1979), p. 512.

inroads in local elections. In 1956, the German Communist Party (KPD) was outlawed as well, thus extending the ban from the right end of the political spectrum to the left – a move that was consistent with the antitotalitarian ideology espoused by German conservatives at the time. Organizations deemed extremist could also be banned, including sports groups or clubs that espoused a Nazi or neo-Nazi ideology. Limits were placed on the freedom of speech as well. In particular, the dissemination of Nazi propaganda – including the sale of Hitler's *Mein Kampf* – was outlawed. The use of certain symbols – such as the Swastika or the Nazi salute – was forbidden, and the government began to run background checks to prevent people with an extremist background from gaining employment in the public sector.[61]

There is an obvious paradox, and obvious dangers, in trying to defend democracy through undemocratic means, that is, by curtailing such civil liberties such as the freedom of speech and the freedom of association. In its decision to allow the ban of the Communist party, the German Constitutional Court set a high standard that would have to be met before a political party could be outlawed. In the following decades, despite several attempts, no other political party would be so outlawed. The ban on prohibiting radicals was only partially implemented. Although it was possible to fine or even arrest people for selling *Mein Kampf*, other ways were found to disseminate neo-Nazi ideas or to employ symbols associated with the Hitler regime.

Nonetheless, the German traditions of militant democracy had a chilling effect on the development of extremist movements, especially on the Right. Numerous Far Right organizations (often posing as shooting or sports clubs) were banned, and the very fact that a group or party was being investigated as a possible extremist organization tended to have a stigmatizing effect on its political fortunes. There were several periods during the cold war when Far Right parties seemed poised to make a break through from successes at the local level – in the late 1950s, the late 1960s, and again the early 1990s.[62] However, in contrast with almost every other Western European country – including, as will be shown later, Austria – at no point did a Far Right party manage to establish itself on the national scene.[63] Just as importantly, German militant democracy very effectively served to delegitimize Nazism and the nationalist

---

[61] For an overviews of the various aspects of militant democracy, see Markus Thiel, ed., *Wehrhafte Demokratie: Beiträge über die Regelung zum Schutze des freiheitlichen demoktatischen Grundordnung* (Tübingen: Mohr Siebeck, 2003). For a critical evaluation of the effectiveness of these methods, see Hans-Gerd Jaschke, "Sehnsuch nach dem starken Staat – was bewirkt Repression gegen rechts?" *Aus Politik und Zeitgeschichte* 39 (2000), online at http://www.bpb.de/publikationen/B7J06R,0,0,Sehnsucht_nach_dem_starken_Staat.html. Accessed January 8, 2011.

[62] For a useful overview of the electoral fortunes of the Far Right in the Federal Republic between 1945 and 1991, see Eckhard Zimmerman and Thomas Saalfeld. "The Three Waves of West German Right-Wing Extremism," in Peter H. Merkl and Leonard Weinberg, eds, *Encounters with the Contemporary Radical Right* (Boulder: Westview, 1993), pp. 50–74.

[63] This is the main argument of David Art, *The Politics of the Nazi Past.* op. cit., see especially chapter 5.

traditions associated with it, and it firmly anchored an official historical narrative that at least was highly critical of the recent German past, if only partially penitent.

Both main political parties, the SPD and the CDU, supported these policies because they reflected their unhappy experiences from the 1930s and 1940s, and because they also served to help stabilize the party political landscape in their favor. With the Far Right and Far Left ends of the political spectrum closed off to competitors, the two parties were able to consolidate their political hold on power, with the Free Democrats acting as the holder of the balance of power between them for over forty years.

In sum, by the mid-1950s the Adenauer government had managed to devise a set of policies that helped the Federal Republic meet the complex and potentially disruptive pressures it faced regarding the Nazi past. In retrospect, given the broad popular resistance to these purges and the war crimes trials, the passage of some sort of amnesty appears to have been almost inevitable. This closure, however, came at a price. There was an economic price in terms of material compensation to the victims of Nazism and a political price in the form of a militant vigilance against its reappearance. By 1952, however, a balance had been found between domestic political interests and a collective historical memory that favored a relatively impenitent stance toward history on the one hand, and the international political pressures that forced the leaders of the Federal Republic to accept historical responsibility for the crimes of Nazism on the other. There followed a general silence – whether comfortable or uncomfortable – inside German society regarding the Nazi past. Most Germans actively avoided discussing the past – although its mementos were all around them. Individuals who sought to bring up the past often were treated with indifference, if not open hostility.[64] Later many would criticize this period as an era of active suppression of the past (*Vergangenheitsverdrängung*),[65] yet at the time many Germans would have agreed with the then German Federal President Hermann Lübbe when he argued that in the 1950s the Federal Republic was in need of "a certain stillness" (*eine gewisse Stille*).[66]

---

[64] An excellent cinematic portrayal of this period is Paul Verhoeven's 1990 film *Das Schreckliche Mädchen* (released in the US in 1991 under the title *The Nasty Girl*), which depicts the persecution faced by a Bavarian school girl who begins to delving into her home town's Nazi past

[65] See, for instance, Alexander and Margarete Mitscherlich, *Die Unfähigkeit zu Trauern* (Munich: Piper, 1967); and Ralph Giordano, *Die Zweite Schuld oder Von der Last Deutscher zu Seien* (Hamburg: Rausch und Röhring, 1987).

[66] Lübbe, "Der Nationalsozilaismus im politischen Bewusstsein der Gegenwart," in Martin Broszat, ed., *Deutshclands Weg in die Diktatur: Internationale Konferenz zur nationalisozialistischen Machtübernahme im Reichstagsgebäude zu Berlin* (Berlin 1983), pp. 334–335. There is some debate on how still this stillness in fact was. See Hartmut Berghoff, "Zwischen Verdrängung und Aufarbeitung," *Geschichte in Wissenschat und Unterricht* 49 (1998), pp. 96–114.

## The Return of Memory and the Wars over History – 1965–1982

Germany's silence on the past was never complete. Time and again internal or external events would seize hold of public attention. In 1958 Germans were horrified when a senior police official was put on trial in a court in Ulm for his participation in the infamous special missions groups (*Einsatzgruppen*) responsible for the liquidation of Jews and other undesirables in the field.[67] In 1959, neo-Nazi attacks on a newly opened Jewish synagogue in Cologne, coming on the heels of the success of a Far Right party in local elections in Schleswig Holstein rekindled German fears of a nationalist revival.[68] The 1961 trial in Jerusalem of Adolf Eichmann, who had been in charge of transporting prisoners to Auschwitz, received enormous media coverage and sparked a vehement domestic debate over the complicity of ordinary Germans and their mentality of orderliness and obedience in the atrocities of the Third Reich.[69] Likewise, the trial of concentration camp personnel from Auschwitz that began in 1963 attracted tremendous media attention and served to preserve and strengthen public interest in the crimes of the Nazi era.[70]

In many cases, it was the mechanisms of militant democracy that triggered bouts of German wrestling with their past, in particular the trials of war criminals and the continued vigilance against extremist organizations. In other instances, external events acted as a catalyst for debate. The trial of Adolf Eichmann received intense coverage in the German press, as did the publication in East Germany of the "Black Book," which listed prominent West Germans with a tainted past. Developments in the cultural field could also have had an impact. For instance, the 1957 staging of the *Diary of Anne Frank* as a play in several major German cities spurred an outpouring of anguished memories over the systematic annihilation of Europe's Jewish population.[71]

---

[67] Ute Frevert and Aleida Assmann argue that 1958 and the Ulm trials in fact mark the beginning of a new era in German thinking. See Assmann und Frevert, *Geschichtsvergessenheit, Geschichtsversessenheit: Vom Umgang mit deutschen Vergangenheiten nach 1945* (Stuttgart: Deutsche Verlags-Anstalt, 1999), p. 144. After the Ulm trials, a special center to coordinate efforts for pursuing war crimes was set up in Stuttgart (*Zentrale Stelle der Landesjustizverwaltung zur Aufklärung von NS-Verbrechen*). This was, however, more aimed at deflecting criticism, and the genuine breakthrough in terms of the politics of official history came later. See Mary Fullbrook, *German National Identity after the Holocaust* (Oxford and Malden, MA: Polity Press, 1999), pp. 68–69.

[68] See Ekkart Zimmerman and Thomas Saalfeld, "The Three Waves of West German Right-Wing Extremism," in Peter H. Merkl and Leonard Weinberg, eds., *Encounters with the Contemporary Radical Right* (Boulder, CO: Westview Press, 1993), pp. 50–74.

[69] For a firsthand collection of documents from the time, see Hans Lamm, *Der Eichmann-Prozess in der deutschen öffentlichen Meinung: Eine Dokumntationsammlung* (Frankfurt am Main: Ner-Tamid Verlag, 1961).

[70] See Jennifer Wittman, *Beyond Justice: The Auschwitz Trial* (Cambridge, MA: Harvard University Press, 2005), especially chapter 7.

[71] See Andreas Huyssen, "The Politics of Identification: 'Holocaust' and West German Drama," *New German Critique* (1980), pp. 117–136.

Despite these and other incidents, the overall parameters of the political discussion of the past, and of the German official historical narrative, remained
relatively unchanged.

By 1965, however, the confluence of a number of structural factors raised
the debate over the German past to a fever pitch and set into motion developments that would turn it into the "model penitent" it typically is depicted as
being today. Three factors in particular deserve to be singled out: generational
change and the emergence of the student movement, the development of détente
and the subsequent restructuring of the Federal Republic's relations with Eastern Europe, and the emergence of the SPD as a governing party as of the
mid-1960s.

Generational change during the 1960s had an enormous impact on the politics and societies of countries around the world. From New York to Frankfurt,
from Paris to Tokyo, from Mexico City to Beijing, young people – generally
from the better educated and privileged strata of their respective societies –
challenged the existing cultural and political order. In each country the youth
movement took on quite different forms. In Austria and Japan, as we shall
see, the student protestors and young radicals did not actively take up the
question of their nation's responsibility for wartime atrocities. In Germany, on
the other hand, they did. Young radical leaders like Daniel Ben-Condit and
Rudi Dutschke – who collectively came to be referred to as the "68ers" in the
German media – pilloried the older generation for its complicity in the crimes
of the Nazi era. They argued that the German political system was permeated
with old and new Nazis who sought to use the oppressive apparatus of the state
to reimpose an authoritarian, fascist dictatorship. To counter this threat, they
called on the students and Germany's youth to take over the campuses and
challenge the reactionary police forces in the streets.[72] Professors, journalists,
and politicians with a tainted past were exposed by left-wing students and the
media. The habits and virtues of the older generation, the "bourgeois camp"
(*das Bürgerliche Lager*) were dismissed as being the same qualities needed
to run a concentration camp. Everywhere, history became a weapon in the
arsenal of the young as they launched their assault on the bastions of "the
establishment." Left-wing intellectuals and the liberal press adopted many of
the students' themes and brought them to the attention of a larger audience,[73]
causing conservative leaders such as CDU Chancellor Ludwig Erhard to deplore

---

[72] The manifesto of the new movement was Uwe Bergmann, Wolfgang Lefevre, and Bernd Rabehl,
*Die Rebellion der Studenten oder die neue Opposition* (Hamburg: Rohwolt, 1968).

[73] Of special importance was the idea of a German Sonderweg, a deformed pattern of German
industrialization that led to a particularly murderous form of dictatorship, which was popularized by many authors in the 1960s. See, for example, Ralf Dahrendorf, *Society and Democracy
in Germany* (Garden City, NY: Doubleday, 1967); and Georg Iggers, *The German Conception of History: The National Tradition of Historical Thought from Herder to the Present*
(Middletown, CT: Weslyan University Press, 1968).

what they characterized as a cynical instrumentalization of the past and the undermining of a healthy sense of patriotism.[74]

From a Historical Determinist perspective, these generational changes opened a window for changing the historical narrative. Young people, unburdened by direct experiences of the Nazi past, were free to accept or reject the official narrative and the broader societal ways of remembering the past. A significant segment of the generation that grew up in West Germany after 1945 chose to reject the relatively impenitent narrative of their parents and to even take a certain relish in doing so.

The second major development of the 1960s was the development of détente and the pressures it placed on the foreign policies of the Adenauer period. During the first half of the cold war, the Federal Republic had been one of the most resolute supporters of the policy of confrontation and containment of the Soviet Union. A major driver of German policy was the continued reality of German national division. The policy of the Adenauer government was to limit German cooperation with the governments of the Communist bloc as long as Germany remained divided. The Federal Republic even refused to grant diplomatic recognition to countries that had normal diplomatic relations with the German Democratic Republic (GDR) in the East. Adenauer's basic strategy – sometimes referred to as the "magnet theory" – was that if Germany and the Western allies remained resolute and united in their opposition to the Soviet Union, eventually Moscow would be forced to negotiate for German reunification on favorable terms.[75] One important consequence of this policy was that it helped justify, on pragmatic grounds, the Federal Republic's refusal to pursue the issue of historical justice with Eastern Europe.

As the cold war dragged on, however, this policy proved increasingly difficult to sustain. The Soviet Union's hold on Eastern Europe proved stronger and more durable than Adenauer and his advisors had hoped. As Soviet military and diplomatic strength continued to grow, Western capitals increasingly sought to reach some sort of accommodation with the Soviet Union, culminating in Henry Kissinger's policy of détente and the establishment of separate U.S. and Soviet spheres of interest. As German foreign policy increasingly appeared out of step with that of its allies, broad segments of German public and elite opinion came to support seeking some sort of new *modus vivendi* with the East. Inevitably, any diplomatic *rapprochement* with the East would involve the issue of reparations and with it the question of German responsibility for Nazi atrocities.[76]

---

[74] Aleida Assmann und Ute Frevert, *Geschichtsvergessenheit, Geschichtsversessenheit: Vom Ungang mit deutschen Vergangenheiten nach 1945* (Stuttgart: Deutsche Verlags-Anstalt, 1999), especially p. 59 ff.

[75] See William G. Gray, *Germany's Cold War: The Global Campaign to Isolate East Germany, 1949–1969* (Chapel Hill, NC: University of North Carolina Press, 2007).

[76] One of the best studies of the development of Ostpolitik remains William E. Griffith's *The Ostpolitik of the Federal Republic of Germany* (Cambridge, MA: MIT Press, 1978). For a more

The third and final element was the continuing evolution of the Social Democratic Party. After the historic party congress in Bad Godesberg in 1959, in which the SPD accepted Germany's entry into NATO and abandoned much of its overtly Marxist ideology, the party had moved toward the center of the German political spectrum. Under the direction of a new generation of technocratic party leaders such as Helmut Schmidt and Hans Apel, the party established itself as a responsible, left-of-center modernizing force in German politics and society. In 1964, it entered government as part of a coalition with the Christian Democrats. In 1969, it became the dominant member of a coalition government with the FDP with the charismatic former mayor of Berlin, Willi Brandt, as chancellor.

The party's forward-looking stance on questions of dealing with the Nazi past was central to its efforts to promote its image as a rejuvenating force in Germany and became an important instrument in its efforts to attract support of the younger generation and the student movement. The key issue with which the party sought to develop its profile on this issue was the debate over the extension of the statue of limitations (*die Verjährungsdebatte*). Under German law, even the most severe crimes – including murder – were no longer prosecutable after twenty years. This meant that even those involved in the most horrendous atrocities of the Third Reich could no longer be prosecuted after 1965. Already in 1960, the SPD had sought to extend the statue of limitations, but was stymied by fierce resistance from the Christian Democrats. In 1965, however, against the backdrop of the Auschwitz trials and the burgeoning student movement, the political tide turned.

External pressures as well played an important role. At the time, there were continued suspicions regarding the German propensity for nationalism and anti-Semitism, leading many prominent voices in the United States and Great Britain to express reservations over plans to include Germany in a planned joint European nuclear multilateral force. Allaying such fears was a matter of considerable concern to German policy makers at the time.[77] After fierce and impassioned debates, the SPD, with some support from within the CDU and the FDP, finally pushed an extension of the statute of limitations through the Bundestag, albeit initially only a four-year one. In subsequent years, however, the Bundestag would extend the statue of limitations for crimes against humanity twice more before lifting it permanently in 1979.[78]

Once the SPD became the dominant party in power, the push to revise the official narrative became all the stronger. In his inaugural speech, Willi Brandt

recent study using recently available archival material from Russia and the former GDR, see Mary Sarotte, *Dealing with the Devil: Détente and Ostpolitik 1969–1973* (Durham: University of North Carolina Press, 2001).

[77] See Susanna Scharfstetter, "The Long Shadow of the Past: History, Memory and the Debate over West Germany and Nuclear Weapons, 1954–1969," *History & Memory* 161 (2004), pp. 118–145, especially pp. 126–131.

[78] Reichel, *Vergangenheitsbewältigung in Deutschland*, op. cit., chapter 9.

called on the country to "risk more democracy" (*mehr Demokratie wagen*) – by which he meant far-reaching reforms not only in economic, social, and educational policy but also in the launching of an ambitious new program of diplomatic rapprochement with the East. In the eyes of many Germans, *Ostpolitk* was not merely a question of coming to terms with the diplomatic realities of détente but also one of dealing with its history. The two issues were, in fact, inseparable. Karl Jaspers, the leading philosopher of the time, and one of the Federal Republic's most influential public intellectuals, argued that only by acknowledging its guilt and apologizing for its crimes would Germany be in a position to enter into negotiations with Eastern Europe.[79]

Brandt succeeded brilliantly in making the theme of facing up to the past a central element of his diplomatic campaign to normalize relations with the Eastern European nations. Most dramatically, on December 7, 1970, while visiting Poland, Brandt fell to his knees before the memorial commemorating the victims of the 1943 Warsaw ghetto uprising. The image of the somber-looking chancellor kneeling at the site of one of the most brutal massacres of the war was captured by the international media and disseminated across the world and would go on to become the most powerful and enduring symbol of German penance.[80] It played no small role in Brandt later being awarded the Nobel Peace Prize.

The new German official narrative now firmly emphasized the need to apologize to all the victims of German atrocities and crimes. Questions regarding the victimization of Germans, such as compensation and apologies for the expulsion of millions of ethnic Germans, were deliberately placed on the sidelines. As a result of Brandt's efforts, the official historical narrative of the Federal Republic took a decisive step in the direction of contrition.

Although Germany's new official stance was much celebrated outside of Germany, inside the Federal Republic, it remained controversial. Public opinion was deeply divided, and the conservative Christian Democrats were critical of Brandt's stance on history as well as his policies in general. A public opinion poll taken by the prominent left-liberal magazine, *Der Spiegel*, right after Brandt's dramatic visit to Warsaw showed that 48 percent of those surveyed felt that Brandt's gesture had been "exaggerated," whereas only 41 percent thought that it was "appropriate."[81] Brandt's one-sided interpretation of history was one of the main points attacked by the opponents of Ostpolitik in the Bundestag debates on the ratification of the treaties that had been negotiated with the governments of Eastern Europe. In the end, the treaties were approved by the narrowest of margins – two votes. After the Cold War, it was revealed that

---

[79] Karl Jaspers, *Wohin treibt die Bundesrepublik?* (Munich: Piper, 1966).

[80] For a recent, critical retrospective on the event, see Michael Wolffsohn and Thomas Brechenmacher, *Denkmalsturz? Brandt's Kniefall* (Munich: Olzog, 2005).

[81] Data cited in "Willi Brandt: Person of the Year," *Time*, January 4, 1971, available at http://www.time.com/time/subscriber/personoftheyear/archive/stories/1970.html (accessed July 11, 2007).

they had only passed thanks to the bribing of two deputies by the East German secret service.

Although by the early 1970s a substantial segment of the German population clearly was ready to accept a more penitent narrative based on their own views regarding the nation's history, there was no societal consensus on the issue. Resistance stemmed in part from the conservative political interests; in addition, it resonated with the personal memories of a substantial portion of the German population. Instrumentalist calculations of national and party political interest had tipped the balance in the official narrative, but it had been close. Instrumentalist factors determined the direction of change, but Historical Determinist variables helped dictate the rate at which change could be achieved.

Despite the important shift in emphasis in the German official historical narrative, it is also important to note that there were limits to how far the Federal Republic was ready to go. In the area of compensation for past atrocities, for instance, the German courts in 1973 again rejected claims from former slave laborers residing in Eastern Europe on the grounds that these issues could not be pursued by individuals.[82] That same year, in negotiations with the Communist government in Prague, the federal government also agreed that the 1938 annexation agreement, which representatives of the Czech government of the time had been forced to sign, was null and void but insisted that ethnic Germans who had been driven out in 1945 and 1946 were at the time German citizens and, therefore, according to the federal Government, had the right to be compensated.[83] Feelings of victimization and societal pressures from the expellee organizations clearly continued to play a role in West German policy.

Nonetheless, the changes in the official narrative made under Brandt had far-reaching consequences. Aided by both the increased global awareness of the Holocaust, as well as by the efforts of the SPD-led government to stake out a penitent stance on history, over the next decade the view of Germans as victimizers became more broadly accepted in German society as a whole. The turning point in terms of public opinion came in 1979, in the context of the fourth German debate on the extension of the statute of limitations. The critical catalyst for change was not so much a political event as a cultural one. That year, an American-made miniseries, *Holocaust*, portraying the travails of a German-Jewish family during the Nazi era and starring Meryl Streep, was shown on German television. The series was viewed by a huge audience, and its impact on German public opinion and on the debate over the statute of limitations was enormous.[84] Before the broadcast, 64 percent of those surveyed

---

[82] Marie Cornelia Raue, "Doppelpunkt der Geschichte: Die Prager Deutschlandpolitik 1990–1997." Unpublished disertation, Humboldt University, Berlin, September 2000, pp. 60–61.

[83] Raue, *Doppelpunkt der Geschichte*, ibid., p. 60.

[84] On the show's impact, see Susanne Brandt, "Wenig Anschauung? Die Ausstrahlung des Films 'Holocaust' im westdeutschen Fernsehen (1978/79)," in Christoph Cronelißen, Lutz Klinkhammer, and Wolfgang Schwenker, eds., *Erinerungskulturen: Deutschland, Italien und Japan seit 1945* 2nd edition (Frankfurt am Main: Fischer Taschenbuch Verlag, 2004), pp. 257–268.

agreed one should draw a line through the Nazi past (*einen Schlußstrich ziehen*) and opposed the extension of the statute; only 34 percent believed Nazi crimes should be pursued further. After the airing, there was a startling shift: 50 percent wanted to pursue the issue further, and only 46 percent wanted to leave the issue behind.[85]

The shift in public opinion had a decisive impact on parliamentary proceedings. Despite continued resistance from conservative ranks, the statute of limitations was extended by a vote of 255 to 222. Although the Bundestag had twice before agreed to extend the statute, this was the first time that an indefinite extension was agreed to for crimes against humanity. A deputy from the FDP, Werner Maihofer, poignantly expressed the new mood, "Above the (grave) of every murder, the grass eventually grows again; as a rule it does so after a generation. But grass will never grow above Auschwitz, not even after a hundred generations have passed."[86] A tipping point had been reached where the broader collective memory of the society had shifted in favor of greater contrition, allowing the German government to consolidate and strengthen a penitent official historical narrative that had originally been adopted thanks to largely instrumental calculations. The strength of that new consensus would soon be tested.

### The Birth of a Culture of Contrition: 1982–1989

During the 1960s and 1970s, the period of liberal ascendancy in German politics and culture, the move toward a more contrite posture regarding the past seemed slow, but inexorable. In the early 1980s, however, the tenor of the times changed once more. The failure of the Keynsian-inspired economic management to deal with the economic slow down and growing unemployment of the 1970s led to a return of a more market-based approach across the industrialized world, beginning with the triumph of Thatcherism in Great Britain. The perceived excesses of the counterculture provoked the reassertion of middle-class values. Perhaps most importantly, the collapse of détente in the face of the continued Soviet military buildup and the expansion of Soviet influence in the developing world (Afghanistan, Nicaragua, and Vietnam) led to a re-intensification of Cold War tensions and a renewed commitment by Western governments to redouble their efforts in the area of defense. These changes were matched by a general reassertion of national pride and optimism

---

The fact that the protagonists were German speakers from an educated, middle-class background may have helped many Germans to identify with them.

[85] Data cited in Joyce Mushaben, *From Post-War to Post-Wall Generations: Changing Attitudes the National Question and NATO in the Federal Republic of Germany* (Boulder, CO: Westview Press, 1998), p. 58.

[86] Peter Reichel *Vergangenheitsbewältigung*, op. cit., chapter 9. The original German is as follows: "Über der Mord wächst irgendwann eimal Gras, und zwar im Regelfall schon nach einer generation. Über Auschwitz aber wächst kein Grass, noch nicht einmal in 100 Generationen" (translation by the author).

in many countries of the world and a general shift in an ideologically more conservative direction.

In the Federal Republic, the change in the spirit of the times was marked by the collapse of the coalition between the Social Democrats and the FDP, and its replacement with a new FDP-CDU government led by Chancellor Helmut Kohl. From the beginning, Kohl made the development of a "healthy sense of patriotism" an integral part of his administration. In May 1983, in his first speech as chancellor, after winning reelection in a momentous campaign fought largely over the issue of the stationing of a new generation of medium-range missiles in Western Europe, Kohl announced plans to open a museum of West German history in Berlin to celebrate the achievements of the Federal Republic. In the speech, he argued for a more balanced view of history: "We Germans must stand by our history with its greatness and its misery, not taking anything away, but also not adding anything." He went on to emphasize that German history must provide the youth of Germany with a spiritual home and highlight its positive sides.[87]

Kohl's statements came against the backdrop of deep divisions in German society over national security policy. The preceding Social Democrat-led government of Helmut Schmidt had been paralyzed by infighting over the proposed deployment of a new generation of middle-ranged nuclear missiles (the Pershing II), and by the early 1980s, the German peace movement – which had been quiescent since the late 1950s – had roared back to life. The newly formed Green party and the left wing of the SPD were outspoken in their criticism of the proposed missile deployments. All through the first half of the decade, German cities were rocked by massive demonstrations often numbering in the hundreds of thousands. Although the Christian Democrats' coalition with the FDP was contingent on continued support for Ostpolitik and diplomatic relations with the East (a policy that caused a great deal of consternation in Washington at the time), there also was solid support in both parties for standing up to the Soviet Union at the same time.

The question of how to deal with Germany's history provided a central battleground in the ideologically polarized battles of the time and was closely linked to debates on defense and national security. For the Left, the Kohl administration was pushing Germany back in the direction of militarism and self-destructive belligerence, this time under the banner of NATO instead of the Swastika. The end result of this mindless bellicosity would be, to use one of the more provocative slogans of the time, a "Nuclear Holocaust."[88] A central

---

[87] For the text of the speech, see Helmut Kohl, *Der Kurs der CDU: Reden und Beiträge des Bundesvorsitzenden 1973–1993*, Peter Hintze and Gerd Languth, eds. (Stuttgart: Deutsche Verlags-Anstalt, 1993).

[88] For an excellent overview of the battle over German security policy of the time, see Thomas Risse-Kappen, *Krise in der Sicherheitspolitik:Neuorientierungen und Entscheidungsprozesse im politischen Systems der Bundesrepublik Deutschland, 1977–1984* (Mainz: Grünwald, 1988), as well as Jeffrey Herf, *War by Other Means: Soviet Power, West German Resistance and the Battle over the Euromissiles* (New York: Free Press, 1991). The author has written on this

element of the Left's worldview was a militant antimilitarism, combined with a fervent anti-nationalism, which saw all soldiers as murderers and all calls for national unity as opening the way for Fascism.[89]

Joining the fray on the side of the Kohl government was a network of conservative intellectuals and journalists who sought to counter the Left's influence by promoting a more positive view of German history and what they termed "a healthy sense of patriotism." Drawing on ideas and arguments that dated back to the 1950s, conservative historians such as Andreas Hillgruber, Ernst Nolte, and Michael Stürmer placed the emergence of Nazism and Fascism in the broader context of the emergence of totalitarianism. They stressed the baneful impact of the Soviet Union and the Communist International on political developments inside of Germany in the 1920s and 1930s, and they sought to humanize German soldiers on the Eastern Front by depicting them as men caught in the contradictory currents of the time, fighting bravely on behalf of a criminal regime against a vicious and implacable enemy.[90] By implication, efforts by Germans in the contemporary period to bolster the defense of the free world in the face of a renewed menace from the East should not be condemned but welcomed as building on the positive aspects of the German tradition. In essence, they argued that at least sometimes German soldiers should be seen as heroes, not murderers, and that calls for national unity and sacrifice were acts of patriotism rather than the tools of dictatorship and deception.[91]

The response from the Left, spearheaded by the prominent philosopher and public intellectual Jürgen Habermas, was devastating. The Right, they charged, was obscuring the issue. Although there had been other atrocities committed by other nations, the Holocaust was a uniquely evil event, and Germany had to face moral responsibility for it. For much of the 1980s the German press and intellectual world was roiled by a fierce, often polemical debate between the two sides in the so-called war of the historians, or *Historikerstreit* in German.[92]

---

period as well, with a special emphasis on the impact of historical memory on national security policy, in *Cultures of Antimilitarism: National Security in Germany and Japan* (Baltimore: Johns Hopkins University Press, 1998), chapter 5.

[89] The phrase "soldiers are murderers" was one of the slogans of the peace movement, and in the late 1980s led to a series of legal cases pitting accusations of defamation against the freedom of speech. See Michael Hepp and Viktor Otto, eds., *Soldaten sind Mörder. Dokumentation einer Debatte* (Berlin Ch. Links Verlag, 1996).

[90] This was the view first advanced by Ernst Nolte, writing in the conservative *Frankfurter Allgemeine Zeitung*, in 1980. See Nolte, "Between Historical Legend and Revisionism," reprinted in James Knowlton and Truett Cates, eds., *Forever in the Shadow of Hitler? Original Documents on the Historikerstreit concerning the Singularity of the Holocaust* (Atlantic Highlands, NJ: Humanities Press, 1993).

[91] The author would like to express his special thanks to Wolfgang Bergsdorf, Joachim Fest, Josef Joffe, Christian Hacke, and Michael Stürmer for explaining the background of the debate from their perspective.

[92] The *Historikerstreit* has been the subject of immense interest and has generated a considerable literature. For useful overviews, see Richard J. Evans, *In Hitler's Shadow: West German Historians and the Attempt to Escape from the Nazi Past* (New York: Pantheon, 1989); Charles Maier, *The Unmasterable Past: History, Holocaust and German National Identity* (Cambridge, MA:

The high point of the political controversy came in 1985, the year that marked the fortieth anniversary of Germany's defeat in World War II and that continued to be colored by the ongoing confrontation between the United States and the Soviet Union. Chancellor Kohl, eager to garner international support for his efforts to foster a healthy sense of patriotism, invited President Ronald Reagan to visit the German military cemetery in the small town of Bitburg. A year earlier, the Federal Republic had not been invited to participate in the festivities celebrating the fortieth anniversary of the Allied landings at Normandy, despite expressions of interest on the part of the German government. Kohl's advisors were concerned that some gesture of Allied solidarity was desperately needed, especially because the deployment of the middle range missiles arguably placed Germany – a divided nation on the front lines of the East-West conflict – more at risk than any other NATO power.[93] A few months earlier, French President Francois Mitterand had given Kohl what he needed, when the two men made a joint visit to the military cemetery at Verdun, standing (improbably) hand in hand before the tomb of the Unknown Soldier. Now Kohl felt he needed a similarly powerful gesture from the United States.[94]

News of the proposed U.S. visit triggered a massive controversy, both inside and outside of Germany. Unlike Verdun, Bitburg touched on the ultrasensitive subject of Nazism and Germany's responsibility for the horrors of World War II. The controversy was further heightened by the discovery that at least forty-three of the soldiers buried there had been members of the elite Waffen SS. Prominent German opponents of the visit, such as the Nobel Prize winning author Günter Grass, were joined by a chorus of international critics – including fifty-three U.S. senators – in condemning the planned visit. German conservatives such as the CDU Bundestag Deputy Alfred Dregger fired back, stressing the symbolic importance of the trip to their constituents and pointedly asking whether the United States was an ally or not. Chancellor Kohl begged the U.S. president not to cancel the trip, warning that the CDU-led government could fall if he did. In the end, Reagan was persuaded to follow through, but important symbolic touches were added to make the trip more palatable to international mainstream opinion. After a brief ceremony in which the two leaders silently laid a wreath at the military cemetery, they traveled to

Harvard University Press, 1988); and Wolfgang J. Mommsen, *Nation und Geschichte: Über die Deutschen und die deutsche Frage* (Munich: Piper, 1990).

[93] A joke making the rounds at the time went, What is the NATO definition of a tactical nuclear weapon? Any nuclear weapon that goes off on German soil.

[94] For an interesting analysis of the 1984 event, see Ulrich Krotz, "Social Content of the International Sphere: Symbols and Meaning in the Franco-German Relationship," Program for the Study of Europe and Germany Working Paper No.02.2 (Cambridge, MA: Mina de Gunzberg Center for European Studies, Harvard University), pp. 31–34, available at http://www.ces.fas.harvard.edu/publications/docs/pdfs/Krotz2.pdf (accessed November 13, 2007). For a photo of the famous event, see http://www.dhm.de/lemo/objekte/pict/NeueHerausforderungen_photoKohlUndMitterrand/.

the nearby site of the concentration camp Bergen Belsen to lay a wreath there as well.[95]

Symbolically, the trip appeared to mark a significant step in a more conservative direction in the German official historical narrative. At the same time, it demonstrated the limits of what could be achieved, even by a powerful German chancellor with a commanding domestic political position and strong international support. At the time, the CDU and its coalition partners, the FDP, had a commanding parliamentary majority of 278 out of 498 seats in the German Bundestag, and opinion polls showed that 64 percent of Germans approved of the Bitburg visit. Ronald Reagan as well appeared to accept the core elements of the historical narrative Kohl was seeking to promote.[96] In an interview with journalists, the American president remarked that there was nothing wrong with commemorating the fallen soldiers at Bitburg, the majority of whom were between the ages of 17 and 19 when they were killed: "They were victims just as surely as victims of the concentration camps." From an Instrumentalist perspective, if there ever was a time when conditions were ripe for German conservatives to reverse the course set out under Brandt and move the official historical narrative in a more impenitent direction, it was the first half of the 1980s.

Despite all these political advantages and despite the fact that the conservative elites around Kohl believed that doing so would be in their own and the national interest, the German political culture had evolved in such a way that a wholesale revision to the less penitent narrative of the time before Brandt was impossible. The power of the newly embedded cultural discourse of Germany as a victimizer could hardly have been more palpable.

A few weeks later, the limits of the conservative drive to reshape the historical narrative received further confirmation in a remarkable speech made by the president of the Federal Republic, Richard von Weizsäcker. Speaking before the Bundestag on the fortieth anniversary of the German capitulation to the Allied powers on May 8, 1940, Weizsäcker, although a member of the CDU, broke with conservative ranks and argued that the Third Reich's defeat was a day of liberation for Germany as well as the rest of Europe and should be celebrated as such. Weizsäcker explicitly rejected the argument that contrition conflicted with the possibility for a healthy national identity. On the contrary, he argued, the ability to show remorse for the past was the duty of every German citizen and should itself be a source of pride for the German nation.[97]

---

[95] For a thorough recounting of the events surrounding the Bitburg visit and a collection of many of the key contributions of the debate it sparked can be found in Ilya Levkov, ed., *Bitburg and Beyond: Encounters in American, German and Jewish History* (New York: Shapolsky Publishers, 1987). For a recent assessment written by the former mayor of Bitburg, see Theo Hallet, *Umstrittene Versöhnung: Reagan und Kohl in Bitburg, 1985* (Erfurt: Sutton, 2005).

[96] "Struggling with a Dark Past," *Newsweek*, May 13, 1985, p. 34.

[97] Richard von Weizsäcker, "der 8.Mai 1945: 40 Jahre danach," in Weizsäcker, *Von Deustchland aus: Reden des Bundespräsidenten* (Munich: Deutscher Taschenbuch Verlag, 1987), English translation in Hartman, *Bitburg*, pp. 262–273.

With this argument, Weizsäcker had brilliantly fused the Left's preferred historical narrative of Germany as a victimizer with the conservatives' efforts to promote a positive sense of nation.

The speech was wildly successful. Weizsäcker received over 60,000 letters about the speech, the vast majority supportive. Newspaper editorialists and intellectuals both on the left and right ends of the political spectrum praised the speech as a watershed in post-1945 German national identity. The noted author Heinrich Böll even called for distributing the speech to all German high school students, a suggestion that was subsequently acted upon both by the traditionally conservative German State of Bavaria as well as the liberal state of Hesse.[98]

After Weizsäcker's speech, the battle over history dragged on for several more years. In retrospect, however, it is difficult to avoid the impression that the subsequent attacks and counterattacks in the media were little more than after-shocks of the massive seismic shift that had occurred in German political culture in 1985. By 1988 virtually all of the major protagonists on the Right, with the exception of Ernst Nolte, had ceased writing actively on the topic. German politicians and opinion leaders – including Weizsäcker, Kohl, and the conservative *Frankfurter Allgemeine Zeitung* – had accepted much of the Left's historical narrative, emphasizing the uniqueness of the Holocaust and the necessity for Germans to continue to face up to the moral consequences of their past.[99] With both sides of the ideological spectrum in agreement on this central point, Germany's culture of contrition was finally consolidated. For the first time, the Federal Republic truly became the model penitent that it is often held up to be. Rather than marking the end of the history of the battle over history, however, new events soon conspired to move the debate in new and unexpected directions.

## Travails of the Model Penitent – Preaching the Gospel of Guilt

The fall of the Berlin wall in November 1989 and the subsequent collapse of the Soviet Union shifted fundamentally the domestic and international political parameters within which the German official historical narrative operated. With German reunification came the gargantuan task of creating a new national identity and a new official historical narrative that would help integrate 17 million former East German citizens into the West German social and political systems. The disappearance of the East-West divide also reopened the question of how to structure Germany's relations with its Eastern neighbors and once again raised the issue of how to deal with the thorny legacies of World War II. Of particular urgency was the question of how to meet the demands for compensation from the many surviving victims of Nazism residing in the former Communist states as well as by the groups representing the millions of

---

[98] David Art, *The Politics of the Nazi Past*, op. cit., pp. 73–74.
[99] David Art, *The Politics of the Nazi Past*, op. cit., pp. 76–77.

Germans who had been expelled from Eastern Europe. At the same time, the Federal Republic's new international environment generated powerful pressures for Germany to assume an expanded international security role and send its armed forces on missions beyond territorial defense. How to legitimate such missions in a country that for over forty years had eschewed such a role on the grounds of its history would pose a monumental challenge to both conservative and Social Democratic governments. These changes did not lead to a complete reworking of the official German historical narrative nor to an end to the culture of contrition; on the contrary, in many respects they led to a reinforcement of the Germany's stance as a model penitent. To the disappointment of those who predicted a revival of German nationalism, and with it a return to great power politics,[100] the Federal Republic continued down the path of relative restraint in the expression of nationalist sentiments as well as in its use of military power – even though from a purely Instrumentalist perspective, the possibility for a very different definition of the national interest and with it the official historical narrative had not only become possible, but even probable.[101]

In the longer run, however, significant, yet subtle changes began to take place, shifts that led to a peculiar re-contextualization of both German foreign policy and its official historical narrative. Although the Federal Republic continued to practice the art of penance for its past sins, increasingly it began to preach the gospel of guilt worldwide, calling on other countries to acknowledge historical injustices they had committed, including against Germans. Not surprisingly, these calls led to frictions so that by the early twenty-first century, the problem of German history, instead of disappearing, returned with a vengeance, albeit in new forms.

At first, the end of the cold war led to a further strengthening of German official penance. The collapse of Communist regimes in Eastern Europe and their replacement with democratic governments, especially in Poland and the Czech Republic, opened the way for a new round of reconciliation efforts. For both sides, considerable interests were at stake. From the point of view of Prague and Warsaw, the path to rejoining Europe ran though the Federal Republic, and German support was critical if their plans to gain membership in NATO and the European Union (EU) were to succeed. For Germany, the stakes were equally high. The newly united German state had over 800 miles of

---

[100] Jacob Heilbrun, "Germany's New Right," *Foreign Affairs* 75:6 (November/December, 1996), pp. 80–98; John Mearsheimer, "Back to the Future," *International Security* 5:56 (Summer 1990), pp. 5–56.

[101] As has been argued by Andrei S. Markovits and Simon Reich, *The German Predicament* (Ithaca, NY: Cornell University Press, 1997); Thomas Banchoff, *The German Problem Transformed* (Ann Arbor: Michigan University Press, 1999); and Peter J. Katzenstein, ed., *Tamed Power: Germany in Europe* (Ithaca: Cornell University Press, 1997), as well as Thomas Berger, *Cultures of Antimilitarism*, op. cit.; Berger, "A Perfectly Normal Abnormality: German Foreign Policy after Kosovo and Afghanistan," *Japanese Journal of Political Science* 3:2 (Winter, 2002), pp. 173–193; and Berger, "The Past in the Present: Historical Memory and German National Security Policy," *German Politics* 6:1 (April 1997), pp. 39–59.

border with its Eastern neighbors, and it needed their cooperation to deal with a broad range of issues, including migration, pollution, and organized crime. In addition, Czechoslovakia and Poland represented considerable potential markets for German goods and investment.

The newly elected Polish Prime Minister Tadeusz Mazowiecki called for reconciliation between the German and Polish peoples along the lines of what had been accomplished between Germany and France. In the Czech Republic, Vaclav Havel, the former dissident turned prime minister, similarly took bold steps in condemning the expulsion of ethnic Germans after the war. In June 1991, a German Polish Treaty on Good Neighborliness and Friendly Cooperation was negotiated in which the two sides pledged to work together to improve societal level understanding of one another through youth and cultural exchanges. In February of the following year, a similar treaty was negotiated between Germany and Czechoslovakia. Although many critical issues could not be settled – including the questions of restitution for German expellees and compensation for the surviving Czech and Polish victims of National Socialism – the treaties represented a considerable step forward. The readiness of the Czech and Polish governments to deal with these issues, and their capacity as democratically elected governments to speak on the behalf of their peoples in a way that their Communist predecessors during the era of Ostpolitk never could, created considerable hope that Germany's penitent stance would achieve reconciliation with Eastern Europe as it had with the West.[102] As the decade proceeded, these hopes appeared to be in the process of being realized.[103]

In addition, progress was made on the issue of compensating the victims of Nazism, beginning in 1993 with the revision of the German law on compensation, BEG, to include the residents of Eastern Europe. Separate compensation funds were then established for Belorussia, Poland, the Russian Federation, and the Ukraine. Similarly, various groups that had suffered vicious persecution under the Nazis but who, for decades, had been relatively neglected, such as the Roma and Sinti (gypsies) and homosexuals, were given new recognition and included in German apologies, commemorations, and efforts at compensation.[104] In December 2000, after long and difficult negotiations led by the

---

[102] On the background of the German-Czech treaty, see Raue, *Dopplepunkt der Geschicthe*, op. cit., chapter 5. On the German-Polish relationship, see Dieter Bingen, "die deutsch-polnischen Beziehung und die polnische Binnenpolitik 15 Jahre nach der Unterzeichnung des Partnerschaftsvertrag," 2006, pp. 2–4, available at http://student.org.uni-hamburg.de/fsr-Osteuro pastudien/download/ring_bingen.pdf (accessed July 6, 2007). For a general overview of German-Central European relations, see Peter J. Katzenstein, ed., *Mitteleuropa: Between Europe and Germany* (Providence, RI: Berghahn Books, 1997).

[103] For instance, in 1997 the Germany and the Czech Republic signed a declaration on Mutual Relations and their Future Development in Prague in which the two sides agreed that "injustices inflicted in the past belong in the past," and a special German fund was set up to compensate the victims of Nazism residing in the Czech Republic. The text of the agreement is available at htttp://www.mzv.cz/servis/soubor.asp?id=8627.

[104] In the case of the Roma Sinti, German courts had ruled that they were eligible for compensation already in the 1960s, but full eligibility as victims of racial persecution was finally granted only

former head of the FDP Otto Graf von Lambsdorf, an agreement was reached in Berlin to compensate the remaining slave laborers in Eastern Europe through the establishment of a special fund, entitled Compensation Fund Recollection, Responsibility and Future Foundation, set up with 10 billion marks ($6.3 billion) – half from the German government and half from German industry.[105]

There were numerous signs of a continued deepening of the culture of contrition inside of Germany as well. The 1990s, for instance, saw an explosion in commemorative sites and memorials dedicated to the victims of Nazism, capped by the creation of a massive monument commemorating the Holocaust in the heart of the new capital, Berlin.[106] Likewise, an enormously controversial and influential exhibition of photographs taken by ordinary German soldiers fighting on the Eastern Front was organized that included disturbing images of atrocities committed in the Soviet Union and elsewhere. These photos challenged one of the most cherished popular myths regarding World War II, namely that the ordinary German infantryman had been largely uninvolved in, and ignorant of, the crimes of the Third Reich, and it raised once again the question of to what degree the German nation as a whole had to acknowledge direct responsibility.[107]

The general tendency to portray Germany as a victimizer continued to be challenged by conservatives, and there were signs that the commemoration of the Holocaust and other crimes of the Third Reich had taken on an increasingly ritualistic character.[108] Nonetheless, on the whole, the Federal Republic's official stance as a penitent nation remained unshaken and, if anything, was

---

in 1979, and even then they received considerably less attention than did Jews in terms of apologies, commemoration, or apology. Homosexuals were even more neglected. Weizsäcker had recognized homosexuals as victims of Nazism in 1985, the first major German political figure to do so. The first commemoration service for homosexuals was held only in 1999 at the Sachsenhausen concentration campsite. The first formal apology from the German government came only in December 2000, and belatedly homosexuals were encouraged to apply for compensation.

[105] For an overview of the development of the slave labor issue see Matthias Arning, *Späte Abrechnung* (Frankfurt am Main: Fischer, 2001). For a detailed account of the negotiations by an insider, see Stuart E. Eizenstat, *Imperfect Justice: Looted Assets, Slave Labor and the Unfinished Business of World War II* (New York: Public Affairs, 2003), chapters 10–13.

[106] This topic has received a great deal of attention in recent years. See James E. Young, *The Texture of Memory: Holocaust Memorials and Meaning* (New Haven: Yale University Press, 1993); Rudy Koshar, *Germany's Transient Pasts: Preservation and National Memory in the Twentieth Century* (Chapel Hill: University of North Carolina Press, 1998); and Peter Reichel, *Politik mit der Erinnerung – Gedächtnisorte im Streit um die nationalsozialistische Vergangenheit* (Munich: Carl Hanser Verlag, 1995). For a critical look at the politics surrounding the Holocaust memorial, see Claus Leggewie and Erik Meyer, *'Ein Ort an den man gerne geht': Das Holocaust-Mahnmal und die deutshche Geschichtspolitik nach 1989* (Munich: Hanser 2005).

[107] Bill Niven, *Facing the Nazi Past: United Germany and the Legacy of the Third Reich* (London: Routledge, 2002), pp. 143–174.

[108] For instance, in 1998 the German intellectual scene was rocked by a fierce debate between the author and critic Martin Walzer and the head of the Jewish community in Germany

strengthened and deepened by developments on the societal level. Political leaders who challenged that consensus quickly found themselves in deep trouble.[109]

At the same time, however, there emerged a new tendency to generalize from the German experience and, in effect, to preach a gospel of guilt beyond the parameters of the confrontation with the Nazi past. The first manifestation of this tendency came as the newly united Germany began to wrestle with the legacy of Communism on German territory. In the aftermath of unification, the question of how to deal with the crimes of the East German Sozialistische Einheitspartei Deutschland (SED) regime emerged. The conservative Kohl government felt it natural that the crimes of the East German communists should be punished with the same vigor the crimes of the Nazis had been. Former communists were purged from the bureaucracy and the academy, members of the old regime – most notably Markus Wolff, the head of the old East German intelligence agency – were placed on trial, and a systematic effort was made to reeducate East Germans in West German ways of thinking.

These attempts ultimately failed.[110] The crimes of the East German regime, bad as they were, were simply of a different order of magnitude than the crimes of the Nazi regime, and support from the international system for defining them in a way that equated them was critically absent. In addition, as in West Germany after the collapse of the Third Reich, the problems of integrating the elites of the old regime necessitated compromises in punishing the guilty. The vast majority of the most dynamic and capable individuals in the former East Germany had been to some degree or another compromised by the old regime and its hated secret service, the Stasi. Efforts to purge the German system of all who were tainted threatened to lead to a virtual cleansing of all East Germans from positions of authority, reinforced the image of a de facto colonization of the East by the West, and helped kindle a deep-rooted resentment in the East German population. The emergence of the PDS (*Partei des Deutschen*

Ignatz Bubbis over the instrumentalization of the Holocaust. See Frank Schirrmacher, ed., *Die Walzer-Bubbis-Debatte: Eine Dokumentation* (Frankfurt am Main: Suhrkamp, 1999); Bill Niven, *Facing the Nazi Past: United Germany and the Legacy of the Third Reich* (London: Routledge, 2002), pp. 175–193. On the increasingly ritualistic character of Holocaust remembrance in Germany, see Jeffrey Olick, "What Does it Mean to Normalize the Past? The Path of Official Memory in German Politics Since 1989," *Social Science History*, 22:4 (Winter 1998), pp. 547–571.

[109] For instance, in October 2003 the CDU deputy Martin Hohman, in a talk in his constituency, said that the Jews as well were victimizers (*ein Tätervolk*), citing the role played by Jews in the Russian revolution and the Soviet secret police. He was criticized not only by the Left, but also by many leading conservative politicians. Eventually he was forced out of the Christian Democratic caucus in the Bundestag and then out of the party with a vote of 78 percent in favor of expulsion. Domnik Cziesche, et al. "Der ganz rechte Weg," *Der Spiegel* 45 (November 3, 2003), pp. 40–42.

[110] For an overview of the problems of transitional justice in the East German context, see Markovits, *Imperfect Justice: An East-West German Diary* (Oxford and New York: Oxford University Press, 1995); Anna Sa'adah, *Germany's Second Chance: Truth, Justice and Democratization* (Cambridge, MA: Harvard University Press, 1998); and Timothy Garton Ash, *The File: A Personal History* (New York: Basic Books, 1997).

*Sozialismus*), which drew heavily on the votes of former supporters of the East German regime and whose strong showing in the East was viewed with alarm by the traditional West German parties, was one reflection of these trends.

There is a certain irony that West German conservatives, who in the past had rejected "vengeful" efforts to actively punish the perpetrators of historical injustices, should encounter the same frustrations in dealing with the legacy of Communism as the Allies and the West German Left had encountered in their efforts to come to terms with the legacy of Fascism. However, despite their ultimate failure in trying to prosecute and punish the former communists, the debate over the misdeeds of the Communist regime led to a certain relativizing of the crimes of the Nazi era. This trend received reinforcement from official German commemorative practices such as the erection of monuments dedicated to the victims of the communist era, notably the *Neue Wache* in Berlin. Under the communists, this highly visible and centrally located memorial had been dedicated to the victims of Fascism, but in 1993 it was rededicated to commemorate victims of "war and the rule of violence," including the fallen soldiers of two world wars, the innocent citizens who lost their lives in the fighting, those who had suffered in captivity or had been driven out of their homeland (a code word for referring to the ethnic German expellees), as well as the Jews, Sinti, and Roma, and homosexuals.[111]

The trend toward relativizing German guilt was further reinforced by changes in German foreign policy. During the cold war, German defense and national security policy had been overwhelmingly focused on the problem of territorial defense. The Soviet Union, with over 300,000 soldiers stationed in the territory of the GDR, represented a clear and present danger that had commanded the attention of German defense policy makers for over four decades. Germany's wretched history of past aggression had made the presence of German soldiers in the rest of the world undesirable for both domestic and international political reasons. Thus, there was little need, and little interest, in having the Federal Republic become directly involved in international security questions beyond the scope of NATO.

With the end of the East-West conflict, however, this state of affairs changed dramatically. First with the Gulf War in 1991, and then with the series of security crises resulting from the disintegration of the former Yugoslavia, pressures for a German military contribution to international security beyond its borders escalated dramatically. The Federal Republic's willingness to make such a contribution, however, was sharply constricted by a political culture that linked a passive stance on military security to the moral consequences of its Nazi past. At the same time, German foreign policy elites were convinced that Germany had no choice but to meet the expectations of its allies if it did not want to risk undermining the security structures, especially NATO, on which it

---

[111] Bill Niven, "Introduction: German Victimhood at the Turn of the Millenium," *Germans as Victims*, op. cit., p. 6. See also Young, *The Texture of Memory*, op. cit., and Koshar, *Germany's Transient Past*, op. cit.

had come to rely.[112] Consequently, German governments, beginning with the Kohl administration, began to lay the legal, political, as well as psychological groundwork for a new approach, beginning with a historic ruling by the German Constitutional Court (BVG) in 1994 that permitted German participation in military operations outside of the territory of NATO (so-called out-of-area missions) providing that they are undertaken in a multilateral framework and that they are approved by the Bundestag. The ability of first the CDU-FDP and subsequently the SPD-Green coalition to hold together in support of a more activist security policy was the important political corollary.

The critical breakthrough in terms of public attitudes, and with it the ways in which the German state and political elites drew lessons from the past, came only four years later – in 1999 – during the war over Kosovo. Once again, pressures mounted for German participation in the U.S.-led campaign to stop Serbia from ethnically cleansing Kosovo. Despite strong internal opposition, the new SDP-Green coalition led by Chancellor Gerhard Schroeder and his foreign minister Joschka Fischer determined early on that it was in the national interest of the Federal Republic to offer direct military support to its alliance partners. To legitimate German participation and win over opponents in his own party, Fischer drew on Germany's past to argue that Germany was morally obligated to respond to the massive violation of human rights perpetrated by the Serbian government of Slobodan Milosevic in Kosovo. Once again, in the heart of Europe, Fischer and Schroeder argued, a brutal regime was persecuting people on the basis of their ethnicity, massacring them, driving them from their homes, and placing them in concentration camps. Precisely because Germany had been guilty of similar crimes in the past, it could not remain indifferent to their repetition in the present. Fischer's rhetorical strategy was successful, winning him enough support within his party – despite its pacifist roots – and the broader public to legitimate direct German participation in at least aerial combat missions.[113] The decision to do so, however, was by no means easy. Opposition to the war, especially on the Left, was intense. Much as the Culturalist model would suggest, there was a wrenching sense of psychological dissonance even among supporters of the war.[114]

Kosovo represented an important turning point not only in German foreign policy, but also in the ways in which Germany dealt with its history. Fischer, a man of the Left, had implicitly accepted many of the key arguments traditionally made by the Right. The evils of Nazism, although unique in terms of scale and

[112] The author would like to express his thanks to former German Minister of Defense, Volker Rühe, as well as managing editor of *Die Zeit* and long-time analyst of German defense policy, Josef Joffe, for their insights on this topic.

[113] For a more detailed discussion of Kosovo and the evolution of German foreign policy up to that point, see Thomas Berger, "A Perfectly Normal Abnormality: German Foreign Policy after Kosovo and Afghanistan," *Japanese Journal of Political Sciencel* 3:2 (Winter, 2002), pp. 173–193.

[114] See for instance, the interview with German author Durs Grünbein in *Der Spiegel* no.15 March 12, 1999, p. 262.

viciousness, were not uniquely German. Other countries as well committed similar crimes, and countries that try to draw moral consequences from their past need to respond to those crimes with the same resolution that they face up to the crimes of Nazism. It almost seemed as if Fischer was channeling the spirits of Hannah Arendt and Carl Friedrich, who had helped invent the theory of totalitarianism so much favored by the German conservatives in the 1950s. Only this time, the source of moral legitimacy for German military efforts was not the liberal West, as it had been for Adenauer, but a broader, more diffuse international community propagating the norms of universal human rights.

After Kosovo, the floodgates of history seemed to open. German left-wing historians and intellectuals began to reexamine the issue of German civilian suffering during World War II through new lenses. The Nobel Prize winning author Günter Grass led the way with his celebrated novel, *Krebsgang*, which focused on the 1945 sinking of a ship packed with German refugees from the East and how the memory of that event continued to haunt the memory of contemporary Germany. Literary critic and novelist W. G. Sebald attracted enormous attention with his essay *Luftkrieg und Literatur* on the fire bombing of German cities and their impact, or to be more precise their apparent lack of impact, on German collective memory. *Der Spiegel*, arguably the flagship of the left-wing media in Germany, ran a long series on the expulsion of Germans from the East as well as the firebombing of German cities. Although these themes had long been a staple of the right-wing discourse on history, suddenly it became acceptable, even fashionable, for the Left as well to broach the subject of German victimization.[115]

In a strange way, much as Weizsäcker's acceptance of elements of the liberal historical narrative had consolidated on the Right Germany's culture of contrition in the 1980s, Fischer's linking of Auschwitz to ethnic cleansing can be said to have consolidated on the Left a German consensus in favor of reminding others of their historical sins.

The most important manifestation of this trend was the reemergence of a powerful movement in German politics for commemorating the suffering of the ethnic Germans expelled from Eastern Europe and placing diplomatic pressures on the Czech and Polish governments to express some degree of remorse and possibly to offer compensation for the expulsion of ethnic Germans in 1945–1946. Predictably, these moves sparked a strongly negative response from Germany's Eastern neighbors. Despite the steps taken toward reconciliation on these issues earlier in the decade, the new emphasis on German civilian suffering filled many Czechs and Poles with alarm.

The opening shot of this new battle over history came in May 1999 – only two months after the start of the war in Kosovo – when the Bundestag passed a resolution calling for a resolution of "still open history questions," that is. the expulsion of ethnic Germans after the war. In response, the Polish legislature

---

[115] For an excellent overview of these developments, see Bill Niven, ed., *Germans as Victims* (New York: Palgrave Macmillan, 2006), chapter 1.

passed a resolution condemning the Bundestag motion. Echoing concerns in the popular press that Polish accession to the EU would open the way for a return of the German ethnic minority to the areas from which they had been expelled over half a century earlier, the Polish legislature warned that Poland would not accept any challenge to Polish territory and property and accused the German Bundestag of "dangerous tendencies" that threatened the stability of Europe. Similar concerns were expressed in the context of German-Czech relations, and leading Czech politicians angrily rejected German calls for rescinding the decrees (the Benes decrees) that had authorized the expulsions after 1945.[116]

Over the next decade Germany's relations to its Eastern neighbors were repeatedly roiled by emotional disputes over history. For example, in 2002, the Czech foreign minister Milos Zeman, in an interview with the Austrian news magazine *Profil*, justified the expulsions saying that the German ethnic minority had served as Hitler's fifth column. In response German conservatives, led by the chief minister of Bavaria Edmund Stoiber demanded that the Czech Republic be barred from joining the EU until it repudiated its position on the expulsions.[117] In 2005, the mayor of Warsaw Lech Kaczynski called for further German compensation for the damage inflicted on Poland, asserting that 40 billion euros would not be enough for Warsaw alone. Public opinion data at the time showed that 64 percent of Poles supported making further demands for compensation.[118] That same year, Kaczynski's party, the nationalist Law and Order Party, took power. For the next few years, German-Polish relations seemed to enter a new ice age. Disputes over historical issues became the central point of contention between the two governments.

Perhaps the low point came in the summer of 2007, during the EU summit in Brussels. On the agenda was the vital issue of a new constitutional order for Europe, which the new German Chancellor Angela Merkel had made her top diplomatic priority. From the start, Poland was determined to block what

---

[116] On the development of German-Polish tensions at this time, see Henning Tewes and Roland Freudenstein, "Germany and Poland Hit a Sour Patch," *Internationale Politik* (Summer 2000), available at http://en.internationalepolitik.de/archiv/200/summer2000/germany-and-poland-hit-a-sour-patch.html (accessed July 6, 2007) and *The Sejm International Chronicle*, 37:341 (July 22–28, 1998), available at http://kronika.sejm.gov.pl/kronika.97.3/text/en/ic-37.htm (accessed July 6, 2007). On German-Czech relations, see Vladimir Handl, "German-Czech Relations: The New "Normality" and Lack of Empathy," in Marco Overhaus, Hanns Maul and Sebastain Harnisch, eds., *Germany, Poland and the Czech Republic – A New Era on the Eve of EU Enlargement?* German Foreign Policy in Dialogue, Newsletter – Volume 3, Issue 8, September 30, 2002, pp. 26–27, available at http://www.deutsche-aussenpolitik.de/newsletter/issue8.pdf (accessed February 17, 2005).

[117] For a blow by blow description of the events between January and March 2002, see "Schwerpunktthema: Die Diskussion um die 'Benes-dekrete'" *Collegium Carolinum Vierteljahresbercht* (January-March 2002), available at http://www.collegium-carolinum.de/publ/vjb/2002/2002-1-Text-CR.pdf (accessed July 20, 2007).

[118] "Polen erwarten von Deutschland Reparationszahlungen," *Der Spiegel* 39 (September 22, 2004), available at http://www.speiegel.de/politik/ausland/0,1518,319231,00.html (accessed September 22, 2004).

it saw as a German bid to expand the FRG's influence in Europe. The Polish government insisted that Poland be awarded votes in EU councils on the basis of what its population *would have been* if Germany had not killed so many Poles during World War II (66 million as opposed to 38 million). In the end, Merkel, with strong support from other Western European nations, was able to overcome Polish objections and see through a compromise, but only after the negotiations had broken down several times and the entire conference seemed on the verge of collapse.[119]

Despite these tensions, a fundamental rupture in relations between the Federal Republic and its Eastern neighbors was avoided. Tourism, trade, and investment continued to flourish, and the three governments continued to cooperate on a wide range of important issues, including at times clamping down on tensions stemming from their dissonant views on the past. Moreover, public opinion surveys suggested that, with the exception of the history issue, Germans, Czechs, and Poles on the whole had fairly positive views of one another – much better than they had been in the immediate aftermath of the cold war.[120] Twenty years of promoting reconciliation between Germany and its Eastern neighbors had borne fruit, despite the acrimonious disputes over history.

For the first time in its history, however, the way in which the Federal Republic officially defined its past was creating significant and overt tensions in its relations with neighboring countries. Ironically, as the consensus on history between the Left and Right inside of Germany grew stronger, the gap between Germany and at least some of its neighbors deepened. The model penitent may have been ready to preach the gospel of guilt, but not everyone, and certainly not the nationalist politicians in Prague and Warsaw, was ready to convert.

## Conclusions Based on the German Case

A comprehensive analysis of the development of the German official narrative over time highlights the utility of the Historical Realist approach and allows us to arrive at a more nuanced answer to the question that was asked at the outset of this chapter: Why has the Federal Republic been such a model penitent? Although each of the other three perspectives on the origins and the impact of the official historical narrative – the Historical Determinist, Instrumentalist, and Culturalist – help illuminate and explain many aspects of the German case, the German case also shows up the limitations of any one of these paradigms

---

[119] "Schwierige Verhandlungen in Brüssel," *Frankfurter Allgemeine Zeitung* (June 23, 2007), pp. 1–2; "Europa sucht neue Wurzeln," *Frankfurter Allgemeine* (June 24, 2007), p. 1.

[120] See the very useful survey material collected by the Warsaw-based Institute on Public Affairs, especially Mateusz Falkowski and Agnieszka Popko, *The Germans about Poland and the Poles 2000–2006*; Mateusz Falkowski, *Meinungen der Polen über die deutsch-polnischen Beziehungen nach dem Regierungswechsel in beidern Länder* (November 2005), especially p. 3, 7, and 8; and Jaroslaw Cwiek-Karpowicz, *Public Opinion on Fears and Hopes Related to Russia and Germany*, available at http://www.isp.org.pl/?v=page&id=285&ln=eng (accessed July 19, 2007).

used in isolation from the others. Tracing the interplay of these different forces over time underlines the virtues of an eclectic approach while delineating more precisely their relative importance in specific instances.

In the initial period after the war, German leaders were confronted with the dilemma of reconciling the practical need to satisfy Allied demands for justice with the equally practical necessity of rehabilitating the large number of Germans who had been implicated in the crimes of the Nazi era but were needed to rebuild Germany. Compounding their difficulties was the reality that the personal experiences of most Germans did not fit the historical narrative of the Allies, which one-sidedly emphasized German guilt without acknowledging the immense suffering that had been inflicted on the German people. Already before the Cold War, German leaders had rejected a narrative based on the notion that the Germans bore some sort of collective responsibility for the crimes of the Nazi period. Once the Americans became convinced of the necessity for rebuilding Germany as an anti-Communist bastion, it became possible for Adenauer to introduce an only partially penitent official narrative. On the one hand, on a rhetorical level the German Federal Government acknowledged that terrible crimes had been committed during the Nazi period and offered substantial compensation to its victims, at least those in the West. At the same time, the purges and trials were to a large extent reversed or discontinued, and concomitantly penitent commemorative and educational policies were not put in place. This partially penitent official narrative was awkwardly paired with a largely impenitent societal collective memory.

By the second half of the 1960s, increased German prosperity reduced the practical (Instrumentalist) obstacles to greater penance, while the rise of a new generation reduced the psychological (Historical Determinist) barriers. This combination of factors, however, only created a window of opportunity. Instrumental variables, in the shape of the political calculations of the Brandt government, encouraged the German government to take advantage of that opportunity. Brandt and others on the political Left thought that a more penitent stance would simultaneously appeal to a new generation of young Germans who were inclined to be sharply critical of their elders while also helping open the way for a bold new foreign policy of rapprochement with the East. Although this posture enabled Brandt to implement a more penitent rhetorical stance on history, his efforts provoked sharp resistance from his political opponents on the Right that was bolstered by significant portions of German society whose memory of the pre-1945 period was sharply at odds with the new official narrative. The practical interests of the German state alone could not have explained the strength of the opposition that Brandt faced to his policies. Even though the Christian Democrats had a powerful incentive to do whatever they could to block the Social Democrats, the emotional depth of the resistance on which the conservatives were able to capitalize was rooted in the collective memories of German victimization that existed on the societal level.

In the early 1980s, the vagaries of domestic and international politics shifted again, bringing the Christian Democrats back into power. In the meantime, however, a culture of contrition had taken hold both in Germany and abroad. Whereas the government of Helmut Kohl sought to push the official narrative in a more impenitent direction, the German population had become more receptive to confronting the crimes of the Nazi era, as reflected by the remarkably positive response to the TV mini-series *Holocaust* and the subsequent shift in the German debate over the extension of the statute of limitations for crimes committed during the Nazi period. At the same time, international opinion as well had become increasingly sensitive to the issue of Nazism, as could be seen not only in the allergic global reaction to Kohl's visit to Bitburg but also in the fierce French debates over the role of the Vichy government in the prosecution of the Jews[121] and in the increasingly sharp criticism of Austria for its unwillingness to face up to its role in the Holocaust. These shifts in German and international political culture increased the cost of impenitence for the Federal Republic and caused even conservative leaders like Richard von Weizsäcker to part company with his government. As a result, the domestic battle over history led to a consolidation of support for a penitent policy. For the first time, German policy and German collective memory became more or less congruent.

In the late 1990s, Instrumental variables again led to an important shift in the official narrative. The need to legitimate German participation in the military intervention into Kosovo led Chancellor Gerhard Schroeder and his foreign minister Joschka Fischer to place the ethnic cleansing taking place in the former Yugoslavia in the same category as the atrocities of the Third Reich. In so doing, they implicitly relativized Nazi misdeeds even as they continued to insist that Auschwitz occupied a unique moral space and that Germans continued to need to atone for the past. This had the entirely unexpected consequence of opening the door for social groups such as the *Vertriebenen* organizations led by Erika Steinbach to push for the integration of their version of history in the larger official narrative of the Federal Republic. Neither Schroeder nor Fischer intended this to happen – in fact, Schroeder at the time was actively trying to prevent the reemergence of expellee demands for compensation.[122] However, the shift in political rhetoric taken for tactical reasons had in effect triggered a cultural shift that empowered social groups to redefine in important ways the terms of the political debate over the past.

The actions of the expellee organizations can be partially understood in terms of their material interests. Undoubtedly, the hope for some form of material compensation loomed large in the minds of many; however, it also clearly fits the increased official Historical Determinist hypothesis that social groups are liable to preserve and promote their memories of a traumatic past in

---

[121] See Henri Rousseau, *The Vichy Syndrome: History and Memory in France Since 1944*, trans. Arthur Goldhammer (Cambridge, MA: Harvard University Press, 1991); Rousseau and Eric Conan, *Vichy: An Ever Present Past* (Hanover: University Press of New England, 1998); and Joan B. Wolf, *Harnessing the Holocaust: The Politics of Memory in France* (Stanford, CA: Stanford University Press, 2004).

[122] In "Heftige Kontroverse um Schröeders Rede," *Der Spiegel*, August 2, 2004, available at http://www.spiegel.de/politik/deutschland/0,1518,311324,00.html (accessed August 17, 2004).

the form an insurgent narrative even in the face of decades of official opposition. Moreover, the powerful and emotional response in Poland and the Czech Republic that increased recognition of the expellee narrative provoked cannot be understood in terms of national interests alone. Although political actors such as the Kaczynski brothers certainly benefited from the nationalist sentiments that were aroused, the prolonged war of political recrimination and diplomatic tensions was neither in German nor Polish or Czech national interests, and any gains made by political parties in those countries were short lived at best. The eventual diffusion of these tensions testifies to the ability of pragmatic leaders to prevent such sentiments from getting out of hand, at least in the context of a well-ordered and highly structured international environment such as that of the European Union. Their emergence, on the other hand, speaks to the continued power of emotional currents of nationalist sentiment and historical memories to have a disruptive effect on interstate relations even after the passing of many decades.

In sum, the German case sheds a great deal of light on the general dynamics behind the formation and impact of a country's official historical narrative. The interplay of historical experience and practical necessity shapes a historical narrative that subsequently becomes embedded in society in the shape of a set of slowly evolving collective memories. These collective memories, and the larger domestic as well as international political culture in which they are embedded, anchor the historical narrative over time and give it a certain degree of permanence (or perhaps inertia) that outlives the original constellation of historical and instrumental factors that had given rise to it in the first place. At the same time, however, it is important to keep in mind that shifts in the domestic and international system can give rise to new dynamics that have the potential to cause leaders to try to alter or shift the official narrative, giving rise to new conflicts and tensions that may manifest themselves in unexpected ways, as we can see on hand of the German experience in the 1990s.

In many ways the German case may seem *sui generis*. The sheer magnitude of the crimes of the Nazi era arguably inclined Germany toward penance in the long run. Likewise, the German official historical narrative unfolded in a uniquely difficult international environment and against the backdrop of unique German cultural traditions. Would a country that was not divided and on the frontlines of the Cold War have been willing to adopt a penitent stance on history? Would a country that did not have Germany's particular cultural traditions, for instance its strong sense of Lutheran ethics and deep rooted appreciation of the importance of guilt, have acted in the same way? Comparison with other cases is necessary to get a firmer grasp on the weight of the different variables at play.

# 3

# Austria

## The Prodigal Penitent

It has been said that Austria's greatest accomplishment in the twentieth century was to convince the world that Beethoven was Austrian and Hitler was German, when in fact, the reverse is true. Behind this joke is a cruel criticism of Austria's ability to forget: to forget the fact that like the Federal Republic, the Republic of Austria was a successor state to the Third Reich; to forget the role many individual Austrians played in the worst crimes of the Nazi era; to forget the wild scenes of jubilation that greeted Hitler during his triumphal tour of Austria following the *Anschluß*; and to forget the shameful way in which many Austrians participated in, and often profited from, the destruction of Austria's Jewish community.

For decades, Austria was able to hide from both itself and from the world this darker side of its history thanks to the convenient myth, first propagated by the Allied Powers in 1943, that Austria had been the "first victim of Nazism." The myth of Austrian victimhood became the basis of a resolutely impenitent official historical narrative, one that denied any Austrian responsibility for the crimes of the Third Reich, neglected the legal pursuit of the perpetrators of atrocities, and paid relatively paltry sums of compensation to the victims of Nazism and their families.

Since the early 1990s, however, Austria has adopted an appreciably more penitent stance regarding its history. Austrian political leaders have admitted that Austria shares a considerable measure of responsibility for the crimes of the Third Reich. The Austrian state has paid substantial amounts of compensation and restitution to the surviving members of the Austrian Jewish community living both in Austria and abroad, as well as to former slave laborers who had been forced to toil on its territory. Prodded on by the Austrian government, a culture of commemorating the horrors of the 1938–1945 period has sprung up that is comparable to that of Germany's in its depth and intensity. Austria, which once more than Germany or even Japan could be said to have suffered from historical amnesia, has joined the community of those professing their guilt. If Germany is the model penitent, Austria is the prodigal penitent.

Why was the trajectory by which Austria came to penance so different from that of Germany's? Why was Austria initially so much more impenitent? What were the factors that led it to greater contrition? In the following, the path to penance taken by Austria will be traced in some detail to ferret out the respective impact that factors of historical experience, political expediency, and cultural-normative values exercised on this winding path. The appropriate starting point for our investigatory journey is the original historical experiences that Austria and Austrians had under the Third Reich.

### Austria and the Third Reich

In many ways, Austria was an integral part of the murderous apparatus of racial genocide created by the Nazis. Although Austria comprised only 8 percent of the Reich's population, 13 percent of the SS, 40 percent of the staff of the concentration camps, and over 70 percent of the camp commanders were Austrians. Many of the figures involved in planning and executing the final solution had been Austrian, including Ernst Kaltenbrunner, the second in command of the SS, and Adolf Eichman. One of the most notorious concentration camps, Mauthausen, where an estimated 195,000 people were killed, was located outside of Linz.[1] One of the six major euthanasia centers, Castle Hartheim, where over 20,000 people were gassed, was also located in Austria. In addition, at least 800,000 people were compelled to toil as slave laborers on Austrian territory during the war. Many of these were "murdered" in the closing days of the war.

Popular support for Nazism was strong in Austria. After Germans troops crossed the border in 1938, Hitler was greeted as a conquering hero in his hometown of Braunau as well as in other major Austrian urban centers, including Linz and Vienna. Many ordinary Austrians joined with gusto in the widespread and systematic persecution of the Jews that commenced immediately after the German takeover.[2] Of the over 180,000 Jews living in Austria at the time of the *Anschluß*, approximately 65,000 were killed, and most of the remaining 120,000 were forced to flee.[3] If involvement in atrocities were a factor in shaping a society's collective memory and thus setting the parameters of its official historical narrative, Austrians should have felt as guilty as the Germans did.

At the same time, many of the factors that helped mitigate feelings of guilt in Germany were also obtained for Austria. As in Germany, the degree to which ordinary Austrians were aware of the full scale of the atrocities of the Nazi period, or were in a position to prevent them, was limited. In certain respects, the Austrian sense of responsibility was even more attenuated than that of Germany's because Austria had been an independent state prior to

[1] See David Art, *The Politics of the Nazi Past*.
[2] David Art, *The Politics of the Nazi Past*, ibid.
[3] David Art, *The Politics of the Nazi Past*, ibid.

the German takeover in 1938. While support for the *Anschluß* was particularly strong in some sectors of the population, there was also considerable
resistance, especially among conservative Catholics who had been the main
source of support for the conservative Schuschnigg regime that was toppled
by the German takeover, as well as among the Socialists who together with
the pro-German nationalists and the Catholics reflected the major currents in
pre-1938 Austrian politics. If a fair plebiscite on unification with Germany
had been held, as the Schuschnigg government proposed just days before the
German armed forces crossed the border, it is far from clear that the pro-
unity forces would have won.[4] Despite desperate entreaties from the Austrian
government, the international community – which in 1934 had helped block
earlier German efforts to take over Austria – remained impassive in the face
of German aggression. As the *Wehrmacht* gathered on the border, Chancellor Schuschnigg resigned after instructing the Austrian military not to resist.
Once German forces had crossed into the country and established control, the
secret police moved quickly and efficiently to suppress all possible sources of
resistance. Within days over 70,000 Austrians were arrested. Deals soon were
worked out with both the Catholic Church led by Cardinal Innitzer and the
moderate Socialists led by Karl Renner in which concessions were made in
return for their acquiescence to the takeover. Only once the Third Reich had
established political control and it was clear that resistance was useless was
a plebiscite held; 99.73 percent voted in favor of joining the Third Reich.[5]
Austria was renamed the *Ostmark* and was reduced to the status of a German
province. Although there existed powerful popular support for the Nazis in
Austrian society and politics, it is also clear that there were even more powerful sectors that were opposed, or at least acquiesced only under duress, to the
German takeover.

As in Germany, the new Nazi regime was able to claim some important
accomplishments. Most importantly, union with Germany helped address the
deep sense of malaise that had gripped Austria since the collapse of the old
Hapsburg Monarchy after World War I. Now Austrians, who had wrestled
with their sharply diminished status as a central European state of less than
7 million, could take pride in their membership in the much larger and more
powerful Third Reich: a pride magnified by the fact that one of their own,
Adolf Hitler, was the head of state and government. The deep rooted and often
violent divisions between pro-German nationalists, Socialists, and Christian
Socialists that had dominated Austrian social and political life after 1918 had

---

[4] It should be recognized, however, that the plebiscite, if it had been conducted as planned by
the Schuschnigg government, would have been far from fair. There was only one "yes" or "no"
question, Are you "for a free and German, independent and Social, for a Christian and United
Austria, for peace and work, and the equality of all those who declare themselves for Nation
and Fatherland?" Only "yes" ballots were distributed. Those wishing to vote "no" were to have
to provide their own (possibly invalid) ballots.

[5] Barbara Jalevich, *Modern Austria* (New York: Cambridge University Press, 1994), pp. 216–224.

been resolved decisively in favor of the nationalists.[6] Germany's subsequent conquest of Czechoslovakia and Poland reunited millions of ethnic Germans – many of them former citizens of the Austro-Hungarian monarchy – with their kinsmen, thus redressing what many perceived as one of the great wrongs of World War I. For millions of Austrians who initially may have felt ambivalent about, or even opposed the *Anschluß*, the Nazi regime offered a powerful, new identity.[7] As a result, there was no wholesale desertion of Austrian troops from the *Wehrmacht*, nor the emergence of a significant Austrian resistance to the Nazi regime, unlike in Vichy France or Fascist Italy.[8]

As in Germany, any feelings of guilt that Austrians may have harbored were overshadowed by even stronger feelings of victimization resulting from the hardships undergone by Austrians during and immediately after the war. Although Austrian material losses were proportionately lighter than those suffered by Germans dwelling in the territory of the Third Reich prior to 1938, they were still significant. Out of the 1,286,000 Austrians who served in the German armed forces, 240,000 died between 1939 and 1945 – 19 percent of the total.[9] Hundreds of thousands more were taken prisoner. Industrial centers in Austria were heavily bombed, including Vienna Neustadt, which was 88 percent destroyed, and over 9,000 civilians died in air raids. As a result of combat operations on Austrian soil, 20 to 30 thousand more civilians were killed. At the end of the war, 430,000 persons sought refuge in Austria, the large majority ethnic Germans from the territory of Czechoslovakia. In addition, as the Red Army rolled into Austria, its forces committed countless acts of brutality, including rape, murder, and looting. After the war, the country was gripped by hunger and despair. Average daily caloric intake dropped at

[6] Jalevich, *Modern Austria*, chapter 4, provides a ready and accessible review of the politics of this period.

[7] Kurt Waldheim, the future Secretary General of the UN and controversial president of the Austrian Second Republic, might be taken as a paradigmatic example. According to his own description, he came from a conservative Catholic family who had been opposed to the takeover. In 1988, Waldheim would recall in an interview the tears that ran down his mother's face as they listened to Schuschnigg's speech asking his country to accept the *Anschluß*. Yet, this did not prevent young Waldheim from enlisting in the *Wehrmacht* and serving first on the Eastern front and then as an intelligence officer in the Balkans. Nothing in his military record – which would be reviewed with excruciating care in the 1980s and 1990s – indicated that he was anything less than a loyal soldier of the Reich.

[8] To be sure, there was an Austrian resistance, and in the post-war period a concerted effort was made to document and underline its size and significance. According to official figures, 2,400 Austrians were executed by the Third Reich for their opposition to the regime. Another 16,000 perished while in prison or in concentration camps; Jelavich, *Modern Austria* p. 241. These are significant figures, however, it should be pointed out that there was also an equally significant, or insignificant, German resistance to Hitler.

[9] Rüdiger Overmans, "German and Austrian Losses in World War II," in Gunter Bischof and Anton Pelinka, eds., *Austrian Historical Memory and National Identity* (New Brunswick, NJ: Transaction Publishers, 1997), pp. 293–301. In the German case, the percentage was much higher: 29 percent of total forces, or over 4 million soldiers, were killed.

one point to 800, and food rationing would continue until September 1948.[10] In short, like Germany, Austria had suffered greatly during the war, and in the immediate aftermath, the memories of that suffering weighed heavily on the minds of the Austrian people.

A final factor that may have played a role in the Austrian case is the historical strength of Austrian anti-Semitism. Anti-Semitism has long and deep roots throughout Western Europe reaching back to the Middle Ages, and anti-Semitism as a political factor was a particularly potent force in the Old Hapsburg monarchy. The large, well-educated Jewish middle class in major urban centers such as Vienna, Budapest, and Prague was the object of widespread resentment in non-Jewish sectors of society, especially in the middle and lower-middle classes. These sentiments were seized upon by unscrupulous politicians, including the German nationalist Georg von Schönerer as well as Karl Lueger, the populist mayor of Vienna between 1896 and 1910. Both men had a considerable impact on Adolf Hitler and figured prominently in his manifesto, *Mein Kampf*. In many instances, Austrian political anti-Semitism was divorced from personal anti-Semitism. Karl Lueger, for instance, when asked about his many Jewish friends, responded brusquely, "Wer ein Jud ist, bestimm ich" (I determine who's a Jew). Nonetheless, the anti-Semitic sentiments stirred by Lueger and others had a profound impact on Austrian society and laid the foundations for the eager participation of many Austrians in the Holocaust.[11] These sentiments (as will be shown later in this chapter) would surface again at various points in Austria's post-1945 history, and it can be argued that this deeply rooted anti-Semitism helped desensitize Austrians to Jewish suffering during the war. Even after 1945, substantial numbers of Austrians felt that the Jews were at least partially responsible for their own persecution.[12]

None of these mitigating factors, however, were necessarily greater in Austria than in Germany. Neither the fact that the *Anschluß* was the result of coercion nor that popular support for the Nazi takeover was less total than is often believed relieves Austrians of moral responsibility for their role in the crimes of the Third Reich. After all, in the January 1933 elections in which Hitler took power in Germany, the National Socialists received only 32 percent of the vote. The suppression of opposition inside Germany after the

---

[10] Jelavich, *Modern Austria*, pp. 254–255.

[11] On the history of anti-Semitism in Austria, see Peter Pulzer, *The Rise of Political Anti-Semitism in Germany and Austria*, revised edition, (Cambridge, MA: Harvard University Press, 1988) and Bruce F. Pauley, *From Prejudice to Persecution: The Rise of Austrian Antisemitism* (Chapel Hill: University of North Carolina Press, 1996).

[12] In 1947, in response to the question, "Under the Nazis the Jews got what they deserved," 38 percent of all respondents said they agreed partially with the statement (only 1 percent agreed fully, and 54 percent disagreed). In 1966, in response to the statement, "It is no accident that Jews have been persecuted throughout history; they are in part responsible for it," 27 percent agreed fully and 45 percent partially. See Heinz Wasserman, *Naziland Österreich!? Studien zu Antisemitismus, Nation und Nationalsozialismus im öffentlichen Meinungsbild* (Innsbruck, Vienna, Munich and Bozen: Studien Verlag 2002), pp. 68–69.

*Machtergreifung* in 1933 was similarly brutal and effective. Many of the benefits that the Third Reich brought to Austria it also brought to Germany. Anti-Semitism was deeply rooted in Germany as well as Austria, even if it was perhaps not as strong a political factor before 1933.[13] Finally, the suffering endured by Austrians, although terrible, was also significantly less than that suffered by Germans.[14]

In sum, although the experiences of the war had significant and lasting implications for the politics of the past in Austria, as in Germany, on balance, it should have been neither more or less difficult for Germans to create an exculpatory narrative. The Germans too could claim to have been Hitler's victim to the same degree that the Austrians could be considered his accomplices. The reasons behind why the two countries developed very different initial official narratives of history and historical responsibility lie not in the differences between their historical experiences with Nazism – significant though those differences might have been. Rather, the source of Austrian impenitence can be found in the very different ways in which after 1945 the Allied powers and the international system encouraged German and Austrian post-War elites to deal with the past.

## "The First Victim of Nazism" – The Allied Powers and the Emergence of Impenitent Austria, 1943–1948

Like the Federal Republic, at the end of World War II, Austria was a broken nation: defeated militarily, ruined economically, and occupied by the Allied powers. Austria, however, differed in three crucial respects from the Federal Republic. First, the Allies defined Austria as the "first victim of Nazism." This definition in turn led the Allies to give the Austrian government a significant measure of control over their own affairs, including over the construction of their official historical narrative. Second, although there were fierce German battles over the kind of nation the new Germany should be – whether it should be a western bulwark against communism as opposed to a central European bridge between the East and the West – there never was any question over whether there was a Germany to begin with. In contrast, post-1945 Austria's sense of self was far more fragile, and Austrian elites at the time were deeply concerned with the question of how they could create a national identity that could reintegrate their small and fragmented nation. Third, and directly related

---

[13] As was argued most forcefully, and controversially by Daniel Goldhagen in his book, *Hitler's Willing Executioners* (New York: Knopf, 1996). For a nuanced and critical take on the Goldhagen thesis, see Dieter Pohl, "Die Holocaust Forschung und Goldhagens Thesen," *Vierteljahresschrift für Zeitgeschichte*, 45 (1997), pp. 1–48.

[14] Of Austrians serving in the armed forces, 19 percent were killed as opposed to 29 percent of Germans. Under 4 percent of the total population was killed, as opposed to nearly 10 percent of the German population. And only approximately 1 in 15 Austrians were refugees, compared to nearly 1 in 6 Germans. Also Germany was partitioned and lost 33 percent of its pre-1938 territory, whereas Austria was to reemerge after 1945 more or less intact.

to the previous point, after an initial period of quite vigorously pursuing denaz-ification, the Austrian government became after 1947 increasingly preoccupied with reintegrating former supporters of the Nazi regime into Austrian society. The competition between the main Austrian political parties to win the support of this potentially large electoral bloc played a key role in leading the govern-ment to de-emphasize not only Austrian complicity in Nazi atrocities but the fact that such atrocities had occurred on Austrian soil at all. The interaction of these three factors would lead to the establishment of a resolutely impenitent Austrian official historical narrative that would endure for decades. Each of these factors is worth examining in some greater detail.

Allied policy toward Austria and the subsequent development of an Austrian national identity was profoundly shaped by the Allies' decision to define Austria as the first victim of Nazism. In October 1943, a month after Benito Mussolini had been deposed by an internal coup in Italy, the foreign ministers of the Soviet Union, the United Kingdom, and the United States met in Moscow and issued a declaration that defined Austria as the "first free nation to fall victim to Hitlerite aggression" and announced their commitment to the creation of a free and independent Austria. The chief aim of the declaration was to encourage elements inside Austria to challenge the Nazi regime, as they had done in Italy. The promise to establish an independent Austria was intended as an incentive for Austrian soldiers and political elites to defect from the Axis. At the same time, the Allied leaders also warned darkly that Austrians bore a responsibility for participating in the war on the side of Nazi Germany and that in the final settlement of the war, as the Moscow declaration put it, "account would be taken of her own contribution to her liberation." In this way, the stick of Allied postwar retribution was tied to the carrot of Austrian independence.[15]

Allied hopes for an Austrian uprising were disappointing. Whereas some small groups of Austrian soldiers tried to cooperate with the advancing Allied forces, the vast majority of Austrian soldiers fought loyally in the defense of the Reich right to the end. Vienna was taken by the Red Army after five days of fierce fighting, on April 13, 1945, and German forces – including many Austrians – continued to fight on Austrian soil until May 7, more than a week after Hitler had taken his own life in Berlin and only a day before Germany accepted unconditional surrender on May 8.

Like Germany, Austria was divided into four zones of occupation: one under the control of the British, one under the French, one under the Russians, and one under the United States. Vienna was divided into four zones, which were

---

[15] A copy of the text of the Moscow declaration is available at http://www.ibiblio.org/pha/policy/1943/431000a.html (accessed April 16, 2006). For a detailed discussion of the diplomacy surrounding the Moscow declaration, see above all Robert H. Keyserling, *Austria in World War II: An Anglo-American Dilemma* (Kingston-Montreal: McGill-Queen's University Press, 1983). See also Hella Pick, *Guilty Victims: Austria from the Holocaust to Haidar* (London: I.B. Tauris, 2000), pp. 17–23, and Gerald Strouzh, *Um Einheit und Freiheit: Staatsvertrag, Neutralität und das Ende der Ost-West-Besetzung Österreichs 1945–1955* (Vienna: Böhlau Verlag, 1998), pp. 11–28.

jointly managed by the four Allied powers. Nonetheless, the Allies continued to define Austria as a liberated nation. As the commander of U.S. forces in Austria General Mark Clark put it: "Austria was drawn into the war after the Nazi invasion. Our task is to create a democratic and independent government capable of running the country on its own. It must be separated from Germany and free of Nazi influence. Austria must be treated better than Germany." Clark's Russian and British counterparts made similar statements.[16]

The political definition of the situation had immediate consequences on the ground. Although there was widespread looting and rape of the civilian population by Soviet forces, the level of abuse was reportedly less severe than on German territory. More importantly, at least in the long run, the governing of Austria was largely left to the Austrians themselves, albeit under Allied supervision. Representatives of the three designated democratic parties of Austria – the Austrian Peoples Party (*Österreichische Volkspartei*, or ÖVP), the Social Democratic Party of Austria (*SozialdemokratischePartei Österreichs*, or SPÖ), and the Communist Party (*Kommunistische Partei Österreichs*, or KPÖ) – were invited to form a provisional government, under the leadership of the venerable Socialist party politician, Karl Renner, who despite his endorsement of the *Anschluß* still enjoyed a substantial political following. On April 27, as fighting still raged in parts of Austria, the leaders of the three parties met in Vienna and issued a Declaration of Independence. In it, the new Austrian government declared that the annexation was null and void and, adroitly using the language of the Moscow declaration, portrayed Austria as an innocent victim of Nazism. The 1938 annexation, they insisted, had been imposed by means of an external military threat assisted by a treacherous Nazi-fascist minority. As a result, the country had been led into a catastrophic war that "no Austrian had ever wished for" against peoples toward whom "no true Austrian ever felt any animosity or hatred."[17]

Austria's leaders, thus, eagerly bought into the line that Austria was a liberated, not defeated, country. At the same time, they recognized that they had not been able to significantly contribute to their own liberation, as specified in the Moscow declaration. They were therefore eager to demonstrate their commitment to the Allied cause by vigorously pursuing the purge of former Nazi members from the government, a policy that many doubtless relished because a very large percentage of Austria's post-1945 leadership either had been imprisoned or fled into exile after the *Anschluß*.[18] Throughout the period between 1945 and 1947, Austria's leaders were repeatedly reminded that their

---

[16] Quoted in Hella Pick, *Guilty Victims*, op. cit., p. 38.

[17] "Proklamation über die Selbstständigkeit Österreichs vom 27, April 1945," available online at http://www.verfassungen.de/at/unabhaengigkeit45.htm (accessed December 4, 2007). The excerpted passages are from the second page.

[18] According to Dr. Thomas Nowotny, close to 70 percent of the first Austrian parliament had either returned form exile or from prison. Many of the leading Austrian political leaders of the time had been persecuted by the Nazis, including future chancellors Julius Raab, Leopold Figl, and Bruno Kreisky. Interview with Dr. Novotny, Spring 2008, in Washington DC.

efforts at denazification were scrutinized by the occupying powers and would be used as a criterion for determining when the occupation would end.[19]

As a result, at least initially, the Austrian government went about the task of denazification with considerable vigor. On May 8 and June 26 laws were passed, the *Kriegsverbotsgesetz* and the *Kriegsverbrechergesetz*, establishing special Peoples Courts (*Volksgerichte*) to try Austrians for crimes against humanity, torture, and other offenses that in contemporary parlance would be termed human rights abuses, as well as for aiding and abetting the Nazi takeover of Austria. Nearly 137,000 individuals were investigated by the *Volksgerichte* of whom 28,000 were brought to trial and 13,607 were convicted.[20] Forty of those convicted were sentenced to death. Many others suffered substantial financial penalties or received lengthy prison sentences. In addition 135,000 Austrian civil servants were purged because of their connection with the old regime.[21] An even larger group of Austrians who had joined the Nazi party – over 500,000 – suffered a suspension of their civil liberties, including the right to vote.[22] These Austrian efforts at self-cleansing were in addition to the trial of Austrian war criminals and purges conducted by the Allied powers, and at least in quantitative terms, they compared favorably with the efforts undertaken by the Allied powers in occupied Germany, including Soviet occupied East Germany.[23]

Commemorative practices in this period as well reflected the narrative of Austria as a victim of Nazism. The old Austrian Imperial Eagle was revived as the state symbol with the addition of burst strings of chain adorning its breast to symbolize Austria's newly liberated status. The government sponsored a special anti-Fascist exhibition Never Forget (*Niemals Vergessen*) in which exhibits detailing the criminal character of the Nazi regime were

---

[19] For instance, during the 1946 Paris conference dealing with the issue of signing peace treaties with Germany's minor allies – Bulgaria, Finland, Hungary, and Rumania – Soviet Foreign Minister Molotov raised the denazification issue as one of the reasons for excluding Austria from the negotiations. See Hella Pick, *Guilty Victims*, p. 22. A constant fear during this period was that if the occupation did not end, it could solidify and result in a de facto partition of their country, as happened in Germany.

[20] Annette Weinke, "Bundesrepublik, DDR und Österreich," in Norbert Frei, ed., *Transnationale Vergangenheitspolitik: Der Umgang mit deutschen Kriegsverbrechern in Europa nach dem Zweiten Weltkrieg* (Göttingen: Wallstein 2006), pp. 65–71.

[21] Fred Parkinson, ed., *Conquering the Past: Austrian Nazism Yesterday and Today* (Detroit: Wayne State University Press, 1989), p. 323.

[22] What the French refer to as the *morte civile* – or civil death. For an overview of Austrian denazification efforts, see Dieter Stiefel, *Entnazifisierung in Österreich* (Vienna: Europa Verlag, 1981).

[23] In West Germany between 1956 and 1955 there were 31,563 similar investigations resulting in 5,969 convictions. In East Germany, there were over 38,371 investigations and 12,776 convictions. Thus, despite the fact that Germany had over ten times the population, there were more investigations in Austria and over two-thirds as many convictions. See the data supplied by Weinke, "Bundesrepublik, DDR und Österreich," p. 31. However, a certain degree of caution is in order, as it is not entirely clear to what extent the trials in Austria overlapped with what was dealt with under the purges in Germany.

displayed.[24] An annotated collection of documents concerning the Austrian resistance, the *Rot-Weiß-Rot-Buch* (red-white-red being the Austrian national colors) was issued by the Austrian government and widely distributed.[25] In many parts of Austria, monuments were raised commemorating the suffering of concentration camp victims and Austrian resistance fighters. Thus, when references were made to Nazi atrocities, they consistently were depicted as having been planned and orchestrated by the Third Reich with the help of a small minority of Austrians.[26] The dirty little secret that many Austrians had participated in – and benefited from – the crimes of the Third Reich was conveniently swept under the carpet.

The emphasis on Austrian victimization was important not only for foreign policy purposes but also for the new government's domestic political priorities. The inability of the First Republic to create a strong sense of identity after 1918 was seen as one of the chief factors behind the collapse of the First Republic, and Austria's post-1945 leaders feared that Austria's weak sense of nationhood could once again become a source of instability. The results of the first survey of Austrian national identity taken in 1956 suggested that these fears were well grounded. When asked the question, "Are you personally of the opinion that we are a subgroup of the German people, or are we an Austrian people of our own?" 49 percent of those surveyed indicated that they thought Austrians represented a separate people, whereas 46 percent still saw themselves as part of the German people.[27] By portraying Austria as a victim of German aggression and stressing the resulting suffering of the Austrian people, the Austrian government hoped to create a popular sense of estrangement from Germany and to lay the foundations for a separate, Austrian sense of identity.

Further distance was created by portraying Nazi atrocities as something alien to the Austrian nation. The crimes of the Third Reich were described as being uniquely German in character, the product of a Northern, Prussian culture of hierarchy, militarism, and obedience that was the polar opposite of the Austrian national character, depicted in school books that began to be issued in the fall of 1945 as "modest, cosmopolitan, conciliatory, humorous and good-hearted," and an "integral part of the region around the Donau river since time immemorial."[28] Although this Austrian strategy of nation building

[24] Wolfgang Kos, "Die Schau mit dem Hammer. Zur Planung, Ideologie und Gestaltung der Antifaschistischen Ausstellung 'Niemals Vergessen!'" in Wolfgang Kos, *Eigenheim Österreich. Zu Politik, Kultur und Alltag nach 1945* (Vienna: Sonderzahl, 1994), pp. 7–58.

[25] Günter Bischof, *Austria in the First Cold War, 1945–1955: Leverage of the Weak* (Basingstoke: Macmillan, 1998), pp. 64–65.

[26] Uhl, "From Victim Myth to Co-Responsibility Thesis," op. cit., pp. 42–43.

[27] Cited in Uhl, "From Victim Myth to Co-Responsibility Thesis," p. 43.

[28] Heinz P. Wasserman, *Verfälschte Geschichte im Unterricht. Nationalsozialismus und Österreich nach 1945* (Innsbruck, Vienna, Munich and Bozen: Studien Verlag, 2004), pp. 21–22. See also Peter Utgaard, *Remembering and Forgetting Nazism: Education, National Identity and the Victim Myth in Post-war Austria* (New York: Berghahn Books, 2003).

through victimization was successful in the long run,[29] it came at the price of neglecting Austrian responsibility for the war and the Holocaust. Austria's leaders evidently feared that the notion that Austrians could be both victims and perpetrators would create a level of ambiguity that the Austrian people were not ready to accept.

Austria's unwillingness to accept any responsibility for Nazi atrocities was further reinforced by the problem of how to eventually reintegrate the very large number of Austrians who had been purged. As in Germany, it soon became apparent even to the Allied authorities who oversaw the Austrian denazification process that the effects of the program were arbitrary, costly, and dangerously unpopular. As Lord Schuster, director of the legal division of the British occupation authority, noted in April 1946:

What we are doing by this present measure is to create a large body of unemployed and unemployable persons, who will have no means of livelihood, and who will form themselves centers of dissatisfaction or will readily turn to whatever disaffected or more dangerous elements there may be lurking in the country. . . . this policy is discrediting the Austrian government in the eyes of its people . . . [denazification] if pursued to the extent now contemplated, will destroy any hope of sound government in Austria.[30]

By 1947, the growing cold war competition between the United States and the Soviet Union began to overshadow the Allies' original focus on denazification, and the Austrian government was allowed, even earlier than in Germany, to reverse many of the measures they had previously taken. In 1947 and in 1948, the legislature passed two laws granting amnesty to over 500,000 of those who had been purged for relatively minor offenses. Although the *Nationalrat* also passed a law forbidding the propagation of Nazi ideas or the formation of a new Nazi organizations (the *Verbotgesetz*), the law was relatively weakly enforced and by the late 1950s was largely moribund. Militant democracy never took hold in Austria the way it did in the Federal Republic. Certainly, there was nothing comparable to the juridical apparatus created in West Germany allowing the banning of anti-system organizations and parties.[31] By 1957, virtually all of those who had been affected by the purges were rehabilitated. In 1949, many of the former purgees formed their own political party – the Federation of Independents (*Verband der Unabhängigen – VdU*). They were joined by veterans groups (*Kameradschaften*), especially those representing former members of the *Waffen* SS and represented a considerable electoral bloc, winning 12 percent of the vote in the lower house (*Nationalrat*) elections of 1949. Potentially at least, they held the balance of power between the two major parties,

[29] By the 1960s, a clear majority of those surveyed identified themselves as Austrian, and by the 1990s over 90 percent did so. See the compilation of data in Heinz P. Wasserman, *Naziland Österreich*, op. cit., chapter 3, and especially p. 110.

[30] Original document partially reproduced in Siegfried Beer, "Hunting the Discriminators: Denazification in Austria, 1945–1957," in *Discrimination, Imperialism and Fascism*, p. 191.

[31] For the background and development of the *Verbotgesetz*, see Felix Müller, *Das Verbotgesetz im Spannungsverhältnis zur Meinungsfreiheit* (Vienna: Österreich Verlag, 2005).

the Peoples Party (ÖVP) and the Socialists (SPÖ)[32] and both sides began to actively court their support.[33]

The drive to reintegrate former Nazis led to a sharp change in Austrian attitudes toward their recent past. As Heidemarie Uhl has shown in her pioneering study of commemorative culture in Austria, by 1948 references to the horrors of the concentration camps, the extermination of the Jews, and the execution of Austrian resistance fighters virtually vanished. Instead, new monuments commemorating the hundreds of thousands of Austrians who had served in the German military were erected throughout the country, and new emphasis was placed on the suffering of all Austrians, both those who had served the Nazi regime and those who had suffered at its hands.[34] Former concentration camp prisoners were urged to no longer speak of the horrors of the camps because "people just didn't want to hear about it anymore."[35] In the process, the focus of Austrian victimization subtly shifted. Not just the Nazis, but the Allies as well (especially the Soviets), were identified as Austria's tormentors. So complete was this transformation, that when the occupation of Austria finally ended in 1955, the Austrian Foreign Minister at the time, Leopold Figl, proudly announced that 17 years of occupation – that is, the period from 1938 to 1955 – had finally come to an end.[36]

All political parties in Austria were complicit in sustaining this new narrative. The conservative ÖVP avoided talking about Karl Renner and the trade unions' support for the *Anschluß*. In return, the SPÖ eschewed attacking the deals the Catholic Church had made to preserve its independence under the Nazis. The returning soldiers were absolved of guilt for participating in a brutal war of annihilation that killed millions of civilians across Europe, and the former Nazi bureaucrats who had helped administer the murderous apparatus of the Reich were allowed to resume normal existences. All were united in what Peter Utgaard has referred to as a "community of suffering."[37] This rush to integrate all elements in Austrian society and to create a united front made

---

[32] The Communists, who had been weak in the prewar period, were weaker still after 1945, in part because of their association with the Soviet Union. In the first elections held in November 1945, they were barely able to muster 5 percent of the popular vote and, by the end of the decade, had faded away into insignificance.

[33] David Art, *The Politics of the Nazi Past*, op. cit., pp. 109–111.

[34] Uhl, "From Victim Myth to Co-Responsibility Thesis," pp. 44–53. On the soldiers as a symbol of Austrian victimization, see E. Hornung, "Trümmermänner: Zum Schweigen östereichischer Soldaten der Wehrmacht," W. Kos and G. Rigle, eds., *Inventur 45/55, Osterreich im ersten Jahrzehnt der Zweiten Republik* (Vienna, Sonderzahl, 1996).

[35] According to former resistance fighter, concentration camp survivor and postwar socialist trade union leader Josef Hindel, speaking about how he was pressured to stop talking about his experiences in the early postwar period, quoted in Heidemarie Uhl, "Das 'erste Opfer' Der Österreichische Opfermythos und seine Transformationin in der Zweiten Republik," *Österreichische Zeitschrift für Politikwissenschaft* 30 (2001), pp. 19–34, cited on p. 22.

[36] Quoted in Uhl, "From Victim Myth to Co-Responsibility Thesis," op. cit., p. 46.

[37] Peter Utgaard, *Remembering and Forgetting Nazism*, p. 15. Other authors, such as Heidemarie Uhl and Günter Bischoff devise similar terms to describe the same phenomenon.

perfect political sense, both in light of recent Austrian history and in view of Austria's precarious position as a small, occupied nation on the front lines of the cold war and still uncertain of its relationship with its much larger German neighbor. Yet, submerged in the rush to unity were the interests of those who had been the special targets of Nazi persecution – the resistance fighters, homosexuals, handicapped patients, slave laborers, Roma-Sinti, and, above all, Jews. In many ways, they were the first victims of the "first victims" twice over: first after 1938, when they became the targets of brutal persecution under the Nazis, and then again after 1945, when their quest for restitution, justice, and even acknowledgement of their suffering at Austrian hands was denied.[38] Although there were similar tendencies in West Germany during this same period, based on similar psychological (Historical Determinist) and practical (Instrumentalist) factors, in Austria the convenient myth of first victimhood allowed for the emergence of a very different pattern of politics and policies.

## Impenitent Austria – 1948–1962

The impenitent Austrian official narrative that had emerged by the late 1940s had effects beyond the spheres of rhetoric and symbolism. It had a concrete impact on several dimensions of Austrian state policy – specifically on issues pertaining to the compensation of the victims of Nazism and the pursuit of those guilty of atrocities and war crimes. Together with statements made by leaders, commemorative practices and educational policies as well as the criminal prosecution of those guilty of war crimes and other atrocities were the main constitutive elements of the Austrian official historical narrative.

One of the starkest points of contrast between Austria and the Federal Republic during this period is offered by the different ways they handled the question of restitution and compensation for the victims of Nazism. Between 1946 and 1949, the Austrian government passed no fewer than seven acts concerning the restoration of property that had been seized by the Nazi regime. By and large, however, these measures benefited only Austrian citizens living on the territory of the Second Republic. Citizens of other countries, or former Austrian citizens residing in other countries, were by and large excluded – that is, the vast majority of the close to one million people who had been forced into slave labor on the territory of the Second Republic as well as the approximately 110,000 Austrian Jews who had managed to escape abroad.

Austrian unwillingness to make special provisions for the victims of Nazism did not escape the world's attention. The Allied powers – in particular the United States – repeatedly enjoined the Austrian government to address the restitution issue. From early on, U.S. occupation authorities insisted that special provisions be made for concentration camps survivors and other so-called

---

[38] The phrase "first victims of the first victims" was coined by Thomas Albrich. See Albrich, "Holocaust und Schuldabwehr. Vom Judenmord zum Kollektiven Opferstatus," in Rolf Steininger and Michael Gehler, eds., *Österreich im 20 Jahrhundert*, Vol. 2 (Vienna, 1997), p. 85.

displaced persons (DP) who were gathered in special camps on Austrian soil. On several occasions the United States threatened to cut or suspend aid if the Austrian government was not more forthcoming in providing restitution.[39] Pressure also came from the Jewish community overseas, especially in the United States. In 1953, shortly after the successful conclusion of the Luxembourg Agreement with the Federal Republic of Germany, the World Jewish Congress formed an Austrian Claims Committee to begin negotiations with the Austrian government.[40]

The Austrian government, however, was far less responsive to these pressures than its German counterpart under Adenauer. The Austrian official narrative that Austria had been the first victim of Nazism and that individual Austrians had by and large been Hitler's unwilling accomplices led to a blanket denial of responsibility for the crimes of Nazism. The essential position of the Austrian government was that because the Austrian state had ceased to exist after the *Anschluß*, it could not be held responsible for the actions of the government that was in control at the time: the government of Hitler's Third Reich.

In this, they were backed by Austrian popular as well as elite sentiment, which was strongly opposed to making special provisions for any group outside of Austria. Often, the debate took on strongly anti-Semitic overtones. Already in 1945, in closed cabinet meetings, the socialist Chancellor Karl Renner bitterly complained that it was unreasonable on the part of the Allies to demand Austria help Jewish victims of Nazism and asked rhetorically, How could the government help any particular group when an entire class – the working class – and an entire movement – the Socialist movement – had been dispossessed?[41] When trains packed with Jewish refugees from Poland pulled into the main station in Vienna in 1945, they were greeted by crowds of protestors. One of the speakers at the station, Leopold Kunschak – who a few weeks earlier had signed the Declaration of Independence as the ÖVP's chief representative – declared that the refugees were not Austria's responsibility and added, "I am an anti-Semite and have always been an anti-Semite." The crowd reportedly clapped and cheered in response.[42] In 1947, demonstrations broke out in front of the main DP camp outside Vienna. The protestors blamed shortages in bread and milk on the purported special treatment that was being given to the Jews.[43]

---

[39] Robert Knight, *Ich bin dafür, die Sache in die Länge zu Ziehen: die Wortprotokolle der österreichschen Bundesregierung von 1945 bis 1952 über die Entschädigung der Juden* (Frankfurt am Main.: Athenäum, 1988), p. 217.

[40] Christian Thonke, *Hitlers Langer Schatten*, op. cit., pp. 54–55.

[41] Robert Knight, *Ich bin dafür, die Sache in die Länge zu Ziehen*, op. cit.

[42] Cited in Olivier Rathkolb, "Zur Kontinuität antisemitischer und rassistischer Vorurteile in Österreich 1945/1950," *Zeitgeschichte*, 16 (1988/89), p. 169.

[43] Hella, Pick, *Guilty Victims*, pp. 205–206. Note that Heinz Wasserman's analysis of survey data shows a discernible up tick in anti-Semitism at the time, although it should be noted that the data is fragmentary and clearly anti-Semitic opinions remained in the minority. See Heinz Wasserman, *Naziland Österreich*, op. cit., pp. 63–64.

Beyond simple bigotry,[44] considerable material interests were at stake. The value of the property that had been confiscated under the Nazi Aryanization policies was immense. Whereas Austrian restitution laws had provided for compensation for the 4,300 or so large-scale enterprises that were taken over under the Nazis, no provisions were made for the 30,000 small businesses that had been stripped away from their owners. In addition, hundreds of millions of dollars had been extorted from the Jewish community in the form of special property taxes and "flight taxes" (i.e., the cost of permits allowing Jews to flee the country).[45] Then, there was the thorny issue of unredeemed life insurance policies, valued at 2 billion Reichsmarks ($1 billion).[46] These sums would be considered substantial even decades later, when serious efforts at restitution were finally made. For Austria in the 1940s and 1950s, they represented a potentially crushing economic burden. Even more sensitive politically were questions of what to do about the houses and apartments that had been confiscated and auctioned off – often at bargain basement prices – to non-Jewish families. An estimated 60 to 70,000 such apartments existed in Vienna alone.[47] Potentially hundreds of thousands of Austrians had some reason to fear that under a strict restitution regime, they would be forced to give up their homes and/or businesses. The situation in the Federal Republic at the time confirmed these fears. As a result of strong pressure from the Western occupation authorities, Aryanized Jewish properties in West Germany were restituted to their former owners, and compensation was paid for property damages.[48] Alone in

---

[44] It is difficult to determine the level of anti-Semitism in Austria, although there is ample anecdotal evidence that it survived the war and was more clearly manifest in Austria than in Germany. Survey data, including the few early surveys taken in the 1940s after the war, suggest that overtly anti-Semitic sentiments were in a minority. When asked, "Does it bother you to work or live with a Jew?" or "Do you think it wrong that a non-Jewish girl marry a Jew?" large majorities of those surveyed answered in the negative. These expressed views jibe with the insistence in the Austrian media of the time that anti-Semitism was largely a thing of the past. However, anti-Semitic attitudes could be discerned with reference to particular issues or events, such as whether Austria owes a special moral responsibility to the Jews or whether the Jews are responsible or partially responsible for the persecution that they have suffered in the past. These more indirect expressions of anti-Semitic sentiments or feelings of ambivalence regarding Jews tended to increase sharply in the wake of controversies over Austria's past. For instance, in response to the question, "The Jews got what they deserved under the Nazis" in 1947, 1 percent of respondents said yes, 38 percent said partially correct, 54 percent said no. In 1948, as the debate over restitution heated up, 4 percent said yes, 56 percent said partially so, and only 34 percent disagreed. See Wasserman, *Naziland Österreich*, op. cit., p. 11–13 and 68. A similar upswing in anti-Semitic attitudes could be seen following the Waldheim affair beginning in 1986 (see below). One, thus, had the paradoxical situation in Austria after 1945 of a kind of anti-Semitism without any Anti-Semites (at least over ones) and without hardly any Jews! See Wasserman, ibid., p. 11.

[45] Stuart Eizenstat, *Imperfect Justice*, op. cit., p. 302.

[46] Stuart Eizenstat, *Imperfect Justice*, op. cit., p. 311.

[47] David Foster, *Wiedergutmachung in Österreich und der BRD im Vergleich* (Innsbruck, Vienan, Munich: Studien Verlag, 2001), p. 128.

[48] David Foster, *Wiedergutmachung in Österreich und der BRD im Vergleich*, ibid., pp. 47–55, 57–65.

the U.S. zone of occupation, the value of restituted property was estimated at over 1 billion marks.[49] Given the proportionately larger size of the Austrian Jewish community, the economic burden of a comparable restitution program would have been several times greater.[50]

These material interests translated into powerful political currents that had a major impact on Austrian politics. In late 1948 an Association of the Victims of Restitution" (*Verband der Rückstellungsbetroffenen*) was founded to block and, if possible, reverse government restitution policies. With their own newspaper and strong representation in the political parties, the opponents of restitution represented a formidable political lobby.[51] The League of Independents (*Verein der Unabhänigigen*, or VdU) was a similarly potent electoral bloc, representing the interests of the 500,000 or so people who had been purged from the political system in 1945–1946 but were rehabilitated in 1948. In contrast, the Jewish population in Austria after 1945 numbered only 5,000. Although the VdU was incapable of taking power from the SPÖ and the ÖVP, they potentially held the balance of power between them, and both parties catered to Far Right voters. In the 1954 election, for instance, ÖVP candidates complained of greedy *émigrés* (the code word of the time for Jews who had fled the country) who lived on fat incomes abroad and now were demanding their property back. That same year, the SPÖ-ÖVP coalition government sought to pass measures that would reverse some of the earlier restitution laws that focused on the victims of Nazism and compensate instead former Nazis and war criminals for the property that had been confiscated from them – property that, in many cases, had originally been plundered from Jewish families.[52]

In West Germany as well, there had been strong initial resistance to restitution.[53] Unlike Austria, however, as the government of a defeated nation, the Germans had virtually no choice but to accede to foreign pressures. In addition, as was shown in the Chapter 2, the desire of the Adenauer government to join the West through NATO and the embryonic institutions of the European Union (beginning with the European Coal and Steel Community founded in 1951) ensured that even after Germany regained some measure of sovereignty in 1952, it would remain sensitive to Allied pressures on issues of historical justice. Austria, in contrast, was in a relatively insulated position.

In a pivotal cabinet meeting in November 1948, the Austrian government debated how to respond to Western pressures regarding the issue of Jewish

---

[49] David Foster, *Wiedergutmachung in Österreich und der BRD im Vergleich*, ibid., p. 49.

[50] The Jewish population of Germany prior to the Nazi takeover was estimated at 500,000, out of a total population of over 70 million, or about seven-tenths of 1 percent. In Austria, it was 180,000 out of 6 million, or close to 3 percent, over four times the size in relative terms.

[51] David Foster, *Wiedergutmachung in Österreich und der BRD*, p. 138.

[52] Christian Thonke, *Hitlers Langer Schatten*, p. 59. These measures were blocked by the American occupation authorities. The Allied veto sparked outrage in the Austrian press at the time, which denounced the United States as a bastion of world Jewry ("*eine Hochburg des internationalen Judentums*").

[53] David Foster, *Wiedergutmachung in Österreich und der BRD im Vergleich*, op. cit., p. 47.

reparations. Some, like Peter Krauland of the ÖVP, espoused an Adenauerian line, arguing Austria had to be responsive because of Jewish influence in the world. Others, however, such as Oskar Helmer of the SPÖ, argued that Jewish power was overrated and probably declining and advocated a strategy of prevarication instead. The chancellor Leopold Figl agreed with Helmer, noting that the contrast between a generous treatment of Jews and a harsh treatment of the former supporters of the Nazi regime could be damaging politically.[54]

Although the Austrian government met numerous times with representatives of the World Jewish Congress (WJC) and the Jewish Claims Conference, the Austrian government insisted that, during the Third Reich, Austria had been in no position to protect the rights of its Jewish citizens and, therefore, was under neither legal nor moral obligation to provide compensation or restitution. So steadfast was the Austrian government in its protestations of innocence that the head of the World Jewish Council, Nahum Goldman, joked bitterly during a 1953 meeting with Austrian Chancellor Julius Raab, "Yes, Herr Chancellor. That is why I have come to ask you how much money the Jews owe the Austrians."[55]

Despite such recriminations, the international political situation favored Austria. Following Stalin's death in 1953, both the West and the Soviet Union were prepared to end the occupation. In 1955, during the final negotiations over the State Treaty that the Austrian foreign minister (formerly Chancellor) Leopold Figl was able to convince the great powers to reaffirm the 1943 Moscow declaration's definition of Austria as the first Victim of Nazism. At the same time, he managed to remove from the final version of the treaty the language in the original Moscow declaration that had insisted that Austria should be reminded of its responsibility for participating in the war on Hitler's side. Although some limits were placed on Austrian sovereignty (including a ban on advanced weapons systems, a guarantee that Austria would not rejoin Germany, and a commitment to dissolve Nazi successor organizations), the

---

54 Robert Knight, *Ich bin dafür, die Sache in die Länge zu Ziehen: die Wortprotokolle der österreichschen Bundesregierung von 1945 bis 1952 über die Entschädigung der Juden* (Frankfurt am Main: Athenäum, 1988), pp. 195–199. Ironically, that same evening Figl attended a rally commemorating the persecution of the Jews at which he made a passionate speech saying that such events must never be allowed to happen again.

55 Art, *The Politics of the Nazi Past*, op. cit., pp. 108–109. Goldman cited on p. 108. It has to be noted, however, that the Jewish position was considerably weakened by the fact that in 1944 the WJC had accepted the Moscow declaration's position that Austria was the first victim of Nazism. In addition, before the negotiations with Germany, the WJC delegation had sought to convince the FRG to accept financial responsibility for the compensation of Austrian Jews, a position that the West Germans rejected on the grounds that the most violent anti-Nazis had been frequently Austrian. See Thonke, *Hitlers Langer Schatten*, op. cit., pp. 77–78. This led to considerable tensions between Bonn and Vienna. When pushed by his Austrian counterpart to accept responsibility for the claims of Austrian Jewish victims, the chief German negotiator famously snapped back, "We'll gladly take back responsibility for the Austrian victims of Nazism, if you will take back responsibility for Hitler!" The author would like to thank Dr. Thomas Nowotny for relating this anecdote.

Allied powers also agreed not to pursue claims for compensation on Austria arising from the state of war in Europe after September 1, 1939. Article 26 of the treaty committed Austria to return sequestered property or to pay their former owners compensation within 18 months of its signing. Austria, however, was able to largely dodge this requirement by instituting procedures for the payment of restitution and compensation that made it virtually impossible to apply for people living in wealthy countries abroad.[56] As a result, on May 15, 1955, Austria was permitted to reemerge as an independent, sovereign nation largely free of any legal burden pertaining to its Nazi past.[57]

Although not a specific part of the treaty, it was also understood at the time of the signing that Austria would become a neutral country. On October 26, 1955, the Austrian government instituted the policy of permanent neutrality under whose terms Austria vowed not to join any military alliances nor allow the stationing of foreign troops on its soil.[58] In 1959, Austria was granted special access to European markets as a founding member of the European Free Trade Association (EFTA). Unencumbered by formal membership in either NATO or the European Community, while still enjoying the benefits of free trade and peace in Europe, Austria was thus relatively insulated from pressures from the United States or neighboring European countries regarding historical justice issues. Like the von Trapp family in the popular 1965 film, *The Sound of Music*, who had escaped the clutches of the Nazi past by crossing the mountains, Austria was absolved from its complicity in the crimes of the era to find sanctuary in pristine, Swiss-style neutrality.

The establishment of this official narrative of Austria as a victim had very real practical consequences. Although in the early 1960s small amounts of compensation were eventually paid to the Jewish Claims Committee and the World Jewish Congress, the amounts involved were relatively small, principally a $22 million settlement arrived at in 1962. At the same time, with the threat of an Allied veto removed, the Austrian government passed a succession of measures that compensated former Nazi officials and other "victims" of the occupation.[59] In contrast, the Federal Republic began its quest for reconciliation by paying $1 billion to the State of Israel as part of the Luxembourg agreement of 1952. Even given the very different sizes of the two countries, the imbalance was striking.

---

[56] Thonke, *Hitlers Langer Schatten*, op. cit., pp. 64–65.

[57] The most thorough review of the negotiation of the treaty is offered by Gerald Stourz, *Um Einheit und Freiheit: Staatsvertrag, Neutralität und das Ende der Ost-West-Besetzung Österreichs, 1945–1955* (Vienna: Böhlau Verlag, 1998). See also Hella Pick, *Guilty Victims*, op. cit., chapter 2, and Bischof, *Austria and the First Cold War*, pp. 517–522.

[58] Paul Luif, "Austria's Permanent Neutrality – its Origins, Development and Demise," In Günter Bischof, et al., eds., *Neutrality in Austria: Contemporary Austrian Studies Volume 9* (New Brunswick, NJ: Transaction Books, 2001).

[59] Thonke, *Hitlers Langer Schatten*, pp. 64–68; David Forster, *Wiedergutmachung in Österreich und der BRD*, pp. 154–159; Bruce Pauley, "Austria" in David S. Wyman, ed., *The World Reacts to the Holocaust*. (Baltimore, MD: Johns Hopkins University Press, 1996), pp. 496–497.

A similar pattern emerged in the area of the pursuit of Nazi war criminals. In both Austria and the FRG, after 1947 the judicial machinery charged with prosecuting those guilty of crimes during the Nazi period slackened its pace considerably. In the Austrian case, however, the process ground to a virtual halt after 1955. In December of that year, the *Volksgerichte* were finally and formally closed. Although some jury trials of war criminals were held thereafter, the numbers were tiny. Only 46 cases were heard between 1956 and 1975, and guilty verdicts were handed down only in 18 cases. In contrast, during the same period nearly 12,000 cases were processed in the Federal Republic.[60] Austrian public opinion overwhelmingly favored ending the trials – according to a 1976 survey, 83 percent favored ending the trials, whereas only 16 percent favored continuing them.[61] However imperfect the West German pursuit of justice may have been, a serious effort was made and continued after West Germany had become an independent state. In Austria, the cause of historical justice for the victims of Nazism was basically abandoned.

In the years following the signing of the State Treaty, Austria would cultivate its image as a peace-loving, neutral state between the superpowers by championing idealistic causes such as human rights, overseas development, the North-South dialog, and international disarmament. At times, this idealism took quite concrete, even costly, forms. For instance, after the 1956 Hungarian uprising, Austria took in 180,000 refugees, 10,000 of whom would settle permanently in Austria.[62] After the Prague uprising in 1968, Austria again took in over 90,000 refugees. In addition, in the 1970s, Austria became the major conduit through which hundreds of thousands of Soviet Jews were allowed to emigrate to the West. Even as Austria vigorously pursued moral causes in the present, however, it turned a blind eye to the moral failings of its past.

Like the Federal Republic, by the mid-1950s Austria had found an equilibrium that satisfied the contradictory internal and external pressures it faced in dealing with its Nazi past. However, whereas Germany under Adenauer had settled on an official historical narrative that can be described as one of imperfect penance, Austria under the leadership of Julius Raab of the ÖVP and Leopold Figl of the SPÖ had seized upon one of resolute impenitence. That Austria should have done so was perfectly sensible in light of the conditions at the time and easily explicable from an Instrumentalist perspective. If it had been afforded the opportunity by the outside world, one might well wonder whether Germany might have adopted a similarly impenitent stance. In both countries, the resistance to paying compensation and pursuing war criminals was great, while the economic and political costs of doing so were significant.

However, although internal and external conditions may have set the parameters for action, they did not dictate policy. Arguably, Adenauer had done the

[60] Annette Weinke, "Bundesrepublik, DDR und Österreich," in Norbert Frei, *Transnationale Vergangenheitspolitik*, pp. 71–74.

[61] Wasserman, *Naziland Österreich?!*, op. cit., p. 161.

[62] Pick, *Guilty Victims*, op. cit., pp. 58–61.

maximum that was possible for a German leader at that time to pursue reconciliation with the victims of Nazism[63]; demonstrably, Raab and Figl had done
the minimum. Although it may have been impossible, given scarce resources
and enormous needs, for the Austrian government to have commenced a full-
scale restitution of Aryanized property or the payment of large sums of compensation, it is difficult to imagine that the politically stable and increasingly
prosperous Austria of the early 1960s could not have managed to cough up a
bit more than $22 million.

That Austria chose not to do so was the result of a number of factors, including such cultural elements as the lingering power of anti-Semitism in Austrian
society, as well as the influence of a peculiar sort of socialist idealism that denied
special status to the demands of ethnic groups.[64] Just as importantly, Austria's
decision to opt for impenitence was a result of the utility of the narrative of
Austrian victimization as a way of uniting a country that historically had been
deeply divided and for reintegrating the large numbers of people who had been
implicated in the Nazi regime. This identity had taken root and formed a kind
of culture of impenitence that differed sharply from the Federal Republic's then
nascent culture of contrition. In this sense, cultural variables (national identity
and discourses on class and ethnicity) conditioned the instrumental calculations
of political actors. A more farsighted calculation of Austrian interests, one that
took into account the damage that the decision to ignore these demands would
inflict on Austria's image, might have led to a more sensitive response to Jewish demands for compensation. Nonetheless, the official historical narrative
of impenitence that had emerged in the 1940s and 1950s remained viable,
even attractive in a narrow political sense into the 1960s and 1970s. With the
passage of time, however, it would prove increasingly costly to maintain.

### The Costs of Impenitence – 1962–1991

Austria steadfastly maintained its impenitent stance on the past for several decades, despite recurring bouts of domestic political controversy and

---

[63] It is interesting to speculate what might have occurred had the Social Democrats gained power in
Germany. Certainly, the Social Democratic party, as a whole, was receptive to a more vigorous
pursuit of historical justice issues, including the prosecution of war criminals. However, the
Social Democrats – like their Austrian counterparts – were worried about the potential loss of
votes such policies would have resulted in and, hence, were ready to support the CDU's amnesty
programs. See Norbert Frei, *Adenauer's Germany and the Nazi Past*, op. cit., pp. 307–312.

[64] The insistence that the operative moral and political categories are class and not identity based
is a central feature of much Marxist-inspired thinking and was not, as such, unique to Austria.
Although outside the purview of the current study, the Socialist government of Eastern Germany
denied all responsibility for Nazi atrocities on similar grounds and chose to reinterpret the
Holocaust in class-based terms, thus obscuring the racial ideology that was at the core of
Nazism. Nazism and Fascism were seen movements that mobilized the lower middle class to
protect the interests of the bourgeois-capitalist state. Its primary target was the working class.
Thus, the German Democratic Republic, as part of the international socialist movement that
under the leadership of the Soviet Union had defeated Nazism, bore no responsibility for the
crimes of the Third Reich. See Jeffrey Herf, *Divided Memory*, op. cit.

mounting international criticism. As we have seen, the official historical narrative had both strong societal and political roots. Like in the Federal Republic, there existed a powerful tendency on the societal level to suppress uncomfortable memories pertaining to the Nazi past into the 1960s. This tendency could often be observed in the popular culture at the time.[65] For instance, when the *Sound of Music* was filmed in Salzburg in the early 1960s, the local government tried to prevent the film crew from hanging up Nazi flags to illustrate the change in atmosphere that took place following the *Anschluß*. They argued that hanging such flags would be historically inaccurate because there had been no Nazis at the time in Salzburg. The municipal authorities relented only when the film's producers threatened to use news reels from the period instead, ones that showed not only Nazi flags but cheering crowds of Austrians as well. The film went on to be a box office hit worldwide, and the generally positive image that it projected was a major boon to the Austrian tourist industry. Inside Austria itself, however, the film was a flop, closing within days of its opening in Salzburg, Linz, and other major urban centers.[66]

Similar critical reactions attended the televised broadcast of the immensely popular cabaret *Der Herr Karl*. While widely regarded as a masterpiece of social satire, the cabaret was also fiercely criticized for its less than sympathetic portrayal of the average Austrian of the wartime generation as shameless opportunists who were – among other things – happy to go along with the Nazis and not above profiting from the regime's Aryanization policies.[67]

On the political level, the Austrian political system was characterized by a high degree of consensus and collusion between the major parties, a feature that it shared with other postwar consociational democracies such as Switzerland and the Netherlands. Unpleasant and controversial issues, such as questions concerning Austria's complicity in the crimes of the Third Reich, were swept under the carpet for the sake of national unity.[68]

At the same time, both the ÖVP and the SPÖ continued to compete fiercely with one another within the unwritten limitations of the corporatist system they had created. Both parties, therefore, were eager to win the backing of the former supporters of the Nazi regime, as represented first by the Union of Independents (UdV) and, after 1954, by the Freedom Party of Austria (FPÖ), which won between 6 and 12 percent of the popular vote in elections for the Austrian *Nationalrat* between 1953 and 1986.[69] The consociational character

---

[65] Unfortunately, public opinion surveys on Austrian attitudes regarding Nazism were quite scarce between the late 1940s and the late 1970s.

[66] Hella Pick, *Guilty Victims*, op. cit., pp. 172–173; and Robert von Dassanowsky, "An Unclaimed Country: The Austrian Image in American Film and the Social Politics of *The Sound of Music*," *Bright Lights Film Journal*, 41, (August 2003), available at http://www.brightlightsfilm.com/41/soundofmusic.htm (accessed August 21, 2009).

[67] Uhl, "From Victim Myth to Co-Responsibility Thesis," op. cit., pp. 56–57.

[68] See Anton Pelinka, *Austria: Out of the Shadow of the Past* (Boulder, CO: Westview Press, 1998), p. 15, 22–24.

[69] There is a certain degree of similarity between the FPÖ and the FDP in Germany, especially in the early days of the Federal Republic. The FDP as well included a large number of former

of the Austrian system helped encourage the integration of the former Nazis into the political system; the competitive nature of party politics encouraged the mainstream parties to court them. The resultant unwillingness of the Austrian mainstream parties to alienate the FPÖ firmly anchored Austria's impenitent official historical narrative and helped it withstand for decades a slowly growing tide of domestic and international criticism.

Perhaps the best example of this tendency came in the mid-1960s, when left-wing students and intellectuals – like their counterparts in Germany – raised the issue of the older generation's involvement in the crimes of the Third Reich. In 1965, a group of left-wing students called for the retirement of Taras Boro-dajkewycz, professor of economic history at the College of World Trade at Vienna, for his outspoken neo-Nazi and anti-Semitic views. A series of confrontations ensued between socialist students and Borodajkewycz's supporters, mainly young men from the youth wing of the FPÖ. At a demonstration on March 31, the two sides first taunted one another – the right-wingers reportedly held up signs saying "long-live Auschwitz" – and then began attacking one another physically. In the fracas, an elderly bystander – a former communist and concentration camp survivor – Ernst Kirchweger was killed by a student with a radical right-wing background. The incident provoked a storm of consternation in the press and resurrected fears that Austria could descend back into the type of internecine struggles that had led to the establishment of the Austro-fascist dictatorship in the 1930s. Both the SPÖ and the ÖVP – which were in coalition at the time – were united in condemning the violence. Virtually the entire government – with the exception of a few ÖVP politicians – joined the massive (by Austrian standards) 25,000-person funeral procession that was held for Kirchweger on Vienna's stately *Ringstrasse* in April.[70]

Although the incident was regarded as the most serious since the founding of the Second Republic twenty years earlier, the political fallout was relatively mild. Borodajkewycz was forced into early retirement, but with a full pension. Kirchweger's assailant, a fourth-year chemistry student, was given a relatively light sentence – ten months imprisonment – and was not even expelled from the university system. The mainstream political parties did go to some lengths to distance themselves from the Far Right wing views of Borodajkewycz and

soldiers, both among its constituents and in the ranks of its leadership, and it was the heir to a particular German nationalist tradition. The FDP, however, although quite nationalistic, never was as outspoken in its conservative views as the FPÖ was, in part because of the FRG's strong system of militant democracy. In addition, it had a greater diversity of views in its ranks, including a powerful pro-business wing and a social libertarian wing. In the 1960s, after it was pushed out of government to join the ranks of the opposition, it dropped much of its nationalist ideology and became resolutely pragmatic in its pursuit of power. See Dietrich Wagner, *Die FDP und Wiederbewaffnung* (Boppard am Rhein: Harald Boldt, 1978).

[70] See Gerard Kasemir, "Spätes Ende für 'wissenschaftlich' vorgetragenen Rassismus. Die Borodajkewycz Affäre von 1965," in Gehler and Hubert Sickinger, *Politische Affäre und Skandale in Österreich*, op. cit., pp. 486–501; David Art, *The Politics of the Nazi Past*, op. cit., pp. 111–115; Uhl, "From Victim Myth to Co-Responsibility Thesis," op. cit., pp. 55–56.

his supporters. On April 27, a new monument in memory of the Austrian resistance to the Nazis was dedicated at the Hofburg palace in Vienna. At the dedication ceremony, the president of the *Nationalrat* Alfred Maleta of the ÖVP emphasized that "We pardoned individuals, but we do not share their conception of the Nazi past."[71]

Beyond a new emphasis on remembering the Austrian resistance to Nazism – in many ways a return to the official historical narrative that had begun to take shape in the 1945 to 1947 period – no serious effort was made to delve further into Austria's Nazi past. Unlike in France and Germany during the same period, there did not emerge a class of engaged and enraged students and intellectuals committed to pursuing the question of the older generation's complicity in the crimes of the Third Reich. Indeed, the students were actively discouraged from doing so by the Austrian Socialist party, which was seeking the support of the FPÖ at the time. As a result, in the 1960s and 1970s the official historical narrative was never challenged in the Austrian context the way it was in the Federal Republic or in France. Austria continued to define itself as Nazism's first victim and to deny any responsibility for what had happened between 1938 and 1945.[72]

A pivotal role in shaping the SPÖ's political strategy in this era was played by one of the most brilliant and complex figures in post-1945 Austrian politics, Bruno Kreisky. Kreisky, who was Jewish and had lost several members of his family in the Holocaust, was also a dedicated Socialist who dreamed of shifting Austrian politics decisively to the left. Like his good friend Willy Brandt, Kreisky had spent the war years in exile in Sweden, where he watched with admiration how the Swedish socialists had managed to achieve a hegemonic position by splitting the bourgeois vote. Kreisky hoped to do the same in Austria, and to this end he began to cultivate ties with the FPÖ leadership, led at the time by Friedrich Peter, a former member of the *Waffen SS*. Although Kreisky and other Socialists did not subscribe to the nationalist views on a wide range of issues, they saw in them useful allies in what they perceived to be their major struggle, the age-old battle against the conservative Catholics. In addition, during the pre-*Anschluß* many of the Social Democratic and Nationalist leaders had been cell mates imprisoned by the Schuschnig regime.

As a result, Kreisky generally chose to avoid dealing with issues pertaining to historical justice, although as foreign minister in the early 1950s, he had been instrumental in engineering the 1962 $22 million settlement with the Jewish Claims Committee. Kreisky's cultivation of the Far Right eventually paid off. In 1970, the Social Democrats finally managed to take control of the Austrian government without entering into a coalition with the ÖVP, forming a minority government with the support of the FPÖ. Kreisky became the new chancellor.

---

[71] Cited in Uhl, "From Victim Myth to Co-Responsibility Thesis," op. cit., pp. 56–57.

[72] David Art, *The Politics of the Nazi Past*, op. cit., pp. 114–116. On the weakness of the Austrian student movement in general, see Paulus Ebber and Karl Vocelka, *Die Zahme Revolution: '68 und was davon bliebt* (Wien: Ueberreuter, 1998).

The Socialists' success came at a high price, however. In return for the FPÖ's support, five of the eleven members of the 1970 cabinet were former members of the Nazi party. Ironically, there were thus more Nazis in the first Kreisky cabinet than there had been in the Seyss-Inqhart cabinet that had taken over after the *Anschluß* in 1938. This proved a precarious arrangement. The renowned Nazi hunter Simon Wiesenthal was instrumental in revealing that at least one of the new cabinet members Hans Öllinger had been a member a Waffen SS unit notorious for perpetrating large-scale massacres on the Eastern front. The international reaction was scathing, and Öllinger was forced to resign, only to be replaced by another former Nazi from the FPÖ. In 1975, on the eve of national elections, tensions between Kreisky and Wiesenthal flared up again when Wiesenthal released new information revealing that FPÖ chief Friedrich Peters, like Öllinger, had been a member of an SS unit responsible for numerous massacres in Eastern Europe. Kreisky was furious, believing that Wiesenthal's campaign was part of an ÖVP-led plot to undermine the Socialist government. He savagely attacked Wiesenthal in the media, calling him a "Jewish fascist" and accusing him of using "mafia methods." In response, Wiesenthal sued Kreisky for libel, whereupon Kreisky then moved to initiate an investigation into the finances of Wiesenthal's nonprofit Documentation Center based in Vienna.[73] Throughout the controversy, Austrian public opinion and the press strongly supported Kreisky: 59 percent of those polled agreed that "Wiesenthal's goal is to see as many Nazis convicted as possible, regardless of whether they are guilty or not"; only 24% disagreed.[74] The SPÖ, however, became increasingly concerned that the scandal was ruining the chancellor's image. Eventually, a compromise was worked out whereby Wiesenthal agreed to drop his suit, and Kreisky called off the investigation of the Documentation Center.[75]

Matters did not end there, however. Although after the 1976 elections, the SPÖ was able to govern without FPÖ support, in1983 they lost the majority in the Austrian parliament and had to turn back to the FPÖ. Once again, the Socialists' dependence on the FPÖ created renewed controversy. In 1985 the minister of defense Friedhelm Frischenschlager of the FPÖ went to the airport in Graz to shake hands with Walter Reder, a former SS major and convicted war criminal[76] who had just been released on humanitarian grounds from prison in Italy. Once again, there was blistering international criticism,

---

[73] David Art, *The Politics of the Nazi Past*, op. cit., p. 114; Hella Pick, *Guilty Victims*, op. cit.

[74] Heinz Wasserman, *Zuviel Vergangenheit tut nicht gut!*, op. cit., p. 82.

[75] Hella Pick, *Guilty Victims*, op. cit., p. 108. For a more detailed discussion, see Ingrid Böhler, "Wenn die Juden ein Volk sind, so ist es ein Mieses Volk: Die Kreisky-Peter-Wiesenthal-Affäre 1975," in Michael Gehler and Hubert Sickinger, *Politische Affäre und Skandale in Österreich: Von Mayerling bis Waldheim* (Thaur: Kultur Verlag, 1995), pp. 502–531.

[76] Reder, a member of the Totenkopf SS, had been sentenced in 1951 for the destruction of the town of Marzabotto – where 1,830 civilians died – and for giving the command for the execution of an additional 2,700 civilians in reprisal for partisan attacks.

and this time, many inside the SPÖ were critical as well. The opposition ÖVP, naturally, exploited the situation to put pressure on the government.[77]

Despite repeated embarrassments, the Socialists, both under Kreisky and his successor Fred Sinowatz, continued to rely on the FPÖ for political support for over fifteen years. The SPÖ's calculated interest in staying in power clearly outweighed whatever ideological or moral compunctions some of its members may have felt. Over time, however, the costs of the alliance with the Far Right continued to rise. Whereas in the 1960s and 1970s there was hardly any broader public criticism of the government's stance on the history issue, by the early 1980s, there were signs that the mood of the country had begun to change. In 1983, when Friedrich Peter was being considered for the post of president of the *Nationalrat*, demonstrations and a mass media campaign criticizing Peter induced the government to pass him over.[78] Pro-socialist intellectuals and journalists were now critical of their party's attachment to the FPÖ in a way that had not been true in the 1960s and 1970s. And as in the Federal Republic, public opinion data showed a slow, steady trend in favor of confronting the Nazi past. Whereas in the 1970s fewer than half of all respondents favored continued remembrance, in the 1980s over 50 percent did. By the 1990s, that figure would rise to over 60 percent.[79] The coalitional logic of looking to the far right for support had not changed for the Socialists, but the broader, global cultural currents favoring confrontation with the Nazi past were slowly but surely having an effect in Austria as well.

As a result of these trends, when in 1986 the FPÖ shifted dramatically to the right by electing the charismatic but controversial Jörg Haider as its leader, the SPÖ alliance with the Far Right finally collapsed. Haider, the governor of the state of Carinthia, was well known for his archconservative views, including positive comments he had made regarding the Waffen SS and Nazi social policies. It was a sign of how much the times had changed that Socialists were unwilling to accept a defender of the Waffen SS in the 1980s but had been willing to accept working with a party led by actual Waffen SS members – some with blood on their hands – in the 1970s.[80]

Despite the rejection of the FPÖ, there was no immediate impetus to change Austria's impenitent official historical narrative. The Socialists new coalition partner, the ÖVP, showed little interest in the issue, and the SPÖ as well had

---

77 Heinz P. Wasserman, *Zuviel Vergangenheit tut nicht gut!*, op. cit., pp. 130–135.

78 Uhl, "From Victim Myth to Co-Responsibility Thesis," pp. 59–60; Anton Pelinka, *Die Kleine Koalition: SPÖ-FPÖ, 1983–1986* (Vienna: Böhlau 1993), pp. 30–33.

79 Heinz P. Wasserman, *Naziland Österreich!?*, op. cit., p. 160. As in Germany, many commentators stressed the impact on public opinion of the mass media and, in particular, the broadcast of the American-made for television miniseries *Holocaust*. See Gunter Bischof, "Victims? Perpetrators? 'Punching Bags' of European Historical Memory? The Austrians and their World War II Legacies," *German Studies Review* 27:1 (February 2004), p. 24; Uhl, "From Victim Myth to Co-Responsibility Thesis," op. cit., pp. 60–61; Wasserman, *Zuviel Vergangenheit tut nicht gut!*, op. cit., pp. 294–348.

80 Pelinka, *Die Kleine Koalition: SPÖ-FPÖ*, op. cit.

other priorities, although some changes in the area of education policy were visible already in 1985.[81] However, the issue of Austria's part in the Third Reich refused to die away, and almost immediately after the coalition formed, a new controversy broke out over Austria's Nazis past that overshadowed all previous incidents.

In 1985 former secretary general of the United Nations Kurt Waldheim had decided to run for the largely ceremonial post of the Austrian presidency. Waldheim was widely viewed as a shoo-in for the job and was jointly nominated by both major parties. In 1986, however, reports emerged in the media that Waldheim had lied about his wartime record. In the past, Waldheim had claimed that after being wounded on the Eastern front in 1941, he had spent the rest of the war as a law student in Vienna. In fact, journalists working for the German magazine *Stern* and the Austrian weekly *Profil*, revealed that Waldheim had been a member of Wehrmacht intelligence during the brutal counterinsurgency campaign in the Balkans. Although it was never proven that Waldheim personally had committed any crimes, his claim that he had been unaware of the large-scale atrocities taking place all around him were widely regarded as unpersuasive.[82]

Despite the fiercely critical international scrutiny that these revelations generated, Waldheim handily won the election for the presidency with 53.9 percent of the vote, the best showing ever for a nonincumbent. During the election, the conservative press made much of an international conspiracy to ruin Waldheim and besmirch Austria's reputation. This "rally around the flag" message found considerable resonance, especially among older voters.[83] Waldheim's election, however, was a major embarrassment for the government, especially for the Socialists. As a result, Fred Sinowatz was forced to resign as chancellor, to be replaced by Franz Vranitzky, also of the SPÖ.

---

[81] In early 1980s, some Austrian textbooks began refer to racial ideology, anti-Semitism, and organized killing of the Jews as part of Austrian history. They were, however, more the exception than the rule. Heinz P. Wasserman, *Verfälschte Geschichte im Unterricht. Nationalsozialismus und Österreich nach 1945* (Innsbruck, Vienna, Munich and Bozen: Studien Verlag, 2004), p. 41; Utgard, *Remembering and Forgetting*, op. cit., pp. 102–104.

[82] Waldheim had been on the staff of General Alexander Löhr, who was hung in 1947 in Yugoslavia for war crimes. Although Waldheim did not have command responsibility, in his position he could hardly have avoided knowing about the anti-partisan operations. Waldheim had also been stationed in Salonika when virtually the entire Jewish population of that city was deported for extermination. It would take an exceptionally obtuse intelligence officer not to notice the disappearance of 25 percent of the local population. See the conclusions of the International Commission of Historians Designated to Establish the Military Service of Lt. Kurt Waldheim *The Waldheim Report* submitted February 8, 1988, to Federal Chancellor Dr. Franz Vranitzky (Copenhagen, Denmark: Museum Tusculanum Press, University of Copenhagen, 1993).

[83] Heidemarie Uhl, "Generationen-Gedächtnis-Wissenschaft: Thesen zum 'Perspektivenwechsel' in der österreichischen Zeitgeschichte," in Martin Horvath, Anton Legerer, Judith Pfeiffer, and Stephan Roth, *Jenseits des Schlussstrichs: Gedenkdienst im Diskurs über Österreichs national-sozialistische Vergangenheit* (Vienna: Löcker, 2002).

International and domestic criticism of Waldheim and of Austria's stance on history continued to intensify after his election. In April 1987, the Reagan administration (possibly seeking to improve its image after the debacle of the Bitburg trip) placed Waldheim on the watch list of individuals forbidden from entering the United States. Other governments followed suit. With the exception of a single trip to the Vatican in May 1987, for the next six years the Austrian president was unable to make any state visits, arguably the most important function performed by his office. Inside Austria, the newly formed Green party and left-wing intellectuals, including many associated with the Socialist party,[84] staged numerous demonstrations accusing Waldheim of duplicity and calling for his resignation. In response, the Austrian Foreign Ministry set up a special international committee of historians to investigate the charges against Waldheim.[85]

Even before he had received the commission's report, however, Vranitzky and his advisors were coming to the conclusion that a major shift in Austria's official narrative was inevitable. In 1987, a memorandum prepared by one of Vranitzky's advisors, the veteran journalist Hugo Portisch, urged the chancellor to make a major policy speech at the earliest time admitting Austria's complicity in the crimes of the Third Reich. Portisch also advised the chancellor to take up the issue of restitution for the non-Austrian victims of Nazism, especially the Jews. Portisch argued that both national self-interest as well as moral considerations made it imperative that the Austrian government abandons its legalistic and ungenerous stance on the issue.[86] Others outside of the Socialist party were moving in the same direction. In 1987, Cardinal Franz König of Vienna – a highly influential figure in Austrian circles – made a speech in which he declared Austria shared some responsibility for the atrocities of the Nazi era. And in 1988, in an emotional televised speech marking the fiftieth anniversary of the *Anschluß*, Waldheim himself acknowledged Austrian shared responsibility (*Mitverantwortung*) with the Federal Republic for the horrors of the Nazi era.[87]

---

[84] Gerhard Botz and Gerald Sprengnagel, editors, *Kontroversen um Österreichs Zeitgeschichte. Verdrängte Vergangenheit, Österreich-Identität, Waldheim und die Historiker* (Frankfurt am Main/New York: Campus Verlag, 1994). See also Anton Pelinka and Erika Weinzierl, eds., *Das Grosse Tabu: Österreichs Umgang mit der Vergangenheit* (Vienna: Verlag der Österreischischen Stattsdrukerei, 1987).

[85] David Art, *The Politics of the Nazi Past*, op. cit., pp. 111–130. The Waldheim affair has generated quite a large literature. Particularly useful were Richard Mitten, "Bitburg, Waldheim and the Politics of Remembering and Forgetting," in David F. Good and Ruth Wodak, eds., *From World War to Waldheim: Culture and Politics in Austria and the United States* (New York: Berghahn, 1999), pp. 51–84; and Michael Gehler, "'... eine grotesk überzogene Dämonisierung eines Mannes...' Die Waldheim Affäre 1986–1992," in Michael Gehler and Hubert Sickinger, *Politische Affäre und Skandale in Österreich: Von Mayerling bis Waldheim* (Thaur: Kultur Verlag, 1995), pp. 614–665.

[86] Hella Pick, *Guilty Victims*, op. cit., pp. 197–199.

[87] The full text of the speech is available at http://zis.uibk.ac.at/quellen/gehler1.htm#dok3. For a discussion of the speeches impact, see Uhl, 2001, p. 8.

In the late 1980s, however, Vranitzky was still unable to take the sort of decisive action that he might have liked. Alois Mock, the leader of the ÖVP, maintained that the international campaign against Waldheim was an attack on Austria and insisted that the coalition government stand by its embattled president. The Austrian conservative press and a substantial portion of public opinion were on Waldheim's side as well.[88] Although Vranitzky repeatedly threatened to resign as chancellor if Waldheim remained, he never made good on the threat, perhaps because he feared that if he did, the ÖVP could turn the tables on the Socialists and go into coalition with the FPÖ instead.[89] As a result, Waldheim was allowed to serve out his term as federal president until it ended in 1992, symbolizing Austria's impenitent stance on the past. However, the controversy over Waldheim had a catalytic effect, and the forces favoring a transformation of Austria's official historical narrative had been set into motion already well before he left office.

The contrast between Austria and the Federal Republic of Germany is striking. The sustained influence of the Far Right on Austrian politics throughout the post-1945 period and the open espousal of neo-Nazi views by important political figures are difficult to imagine in the German context. Likewise, there is nothing in the German case that compares with Austria's prickly defense of figures like Friedrich Peter or Kurt Waldheim (to say nothing of Walter Reder) that in Germany would have been deemed totally indefensible. Whereas in France and the FRG the generational shift of the 1960s had created a window of opportunity to pursue issues of historical justice, in Austria the window was kept shut. Additionally, whereas in Germany the dynamics of party political competition created incentives for a charismatic left-wing politician like Willy Brandt to harness the winds of generational and international change to open a new political debate on the past, in Austria they worked in the opposite direction. They encouraged Brandt's Austrian counterpart – Bruno Kreisky – to resolutely, if vainly, try to keep Austria's Nazi past off the political agenda.

Despite these striking points of contrasts between Austria and the French and German cases, there are also a number of important similarities. First, despite Austria's foundational myth as the first victim of Nazism, Austrian public opinion slowly but surely began to change in the 1970s and 1980s, so that by the mid-1980s there was a general readiness to confront the past that had not existed earlier. It should not be forgotten in this connection that in Germany, Brandt's policies – such as his famous genuflection before the Warsaw Ghetto monument in 1970 – had been controversial in the Federal Republic and that like Austria, it was not until 1985 that the German public was ready to embrace President Weizäcker's designation of May 8 as a day of liberation. In both countries, a combination of generational change (a Historical Determinist variable) and broader, international cultural forces (a Culturalist one) seemed to be slowly reshaping societal attitudes toward greater acceptance of a more

[88] David Art, *The Politics of the Nazi Past*, op. cit., pp. 111–130.
[89] Hella Pick, *Guilty Victims*, op. cit., p. 190.

critical look at the recent past. Nonetheless, the gap between Austrian and German public opinion on many specific issues remained large. For instance, whereas a plurality of Germans favored an extension of the statute of limitations for the prosecution of war crimes by the late l970s, a clear majority of Austrians opposed further prosecutions. Nonetheless, the direction of change was similar in both countries.[90]

A second point of similarity between Austria and Germany is that in both cases international pressure to deal with the Nazi past began to grow already in the 1980s. In the 1970s, despite an international media outcry, there was little official response to the FPÖ's joining the Austrian government. By the 1980s, the United States had set up a watch list barring entry to the United States of people who could be shown to have been involved in the racially or ethnically motivated violation of human rights.[91] In 1987, U.S. Secretary of State George Schultz overruled his own advisors and insisted that Waldheim be placed on the watch list of those denied the right to enter the United States. To do otherwise, he reportedly said, would be a "travesty."[92] Other states, beginning with the nations of the European Community, had followed the U.S. lead. In this sense, whereas the Federal Republic had been ahead of the curve on historical justice issues, Austria had been behind the curve. By the 1990s, however, both countries' official narratives were evolving in similar directions, even though they had begun at very different starting points. Global cultural forces were reducing the internal, societal barriers toward changing the official historical narrative of Austrian innocence, while international political pressures were increasing the costs of trying to hold on. Austrian leaders were then induced, on instrumental grounds, to adjust the official narrative in response to the shifting domestic and international realities in which they found themselves.

### The Prodigal Penitent Returns

In the early 1990s, the Austrian official narrative underwent a fundamental transformation. Both on the level of symbolic politics and with respect to policies regarding historical justice issues – especially restitution and compensation – Austria moved decisively from its position of resolute impenitence toward the acceptance of shared responsibility for the Holocaust. The political forces favoring a shift toward contrition, however, were not entirely consolidated by the early 1990s, and there remained considerable resistance on the right end of a political spectrum. It would take a decade before a new equilibrium was established.

---

[90] In 1979, 75 percent of Austrians surveyed favored ending war crimes trials, whereas only 31 percent favored continuing them. In 1991, a clear majority remained opposed – 56 versus 38 percent Wasserman, *Naziland Österreich!?*, op. cit., pp. 161–162.

[91] The watch list had been created as a result of the 1978 amendment by Elizabeth Holtzman of Immigration and Naturalization Act. For details, see *Final Report*, pp. 34–35.

[92] Hella Pick, *Guilty Victims*, op. cit., p. 162.

On the level of political symbolism, the change was already visible in 1988, the fiftieth anniversary of the *Anschluß*. Officially designated Austria's year of remembrance and reconsideration (*Bedenkjahr*), 1988 saw a number of small gestures indicating growing official acceptance of the view that Austrians had been the perpetrators as well as victims of Nazi crimes. A major monument was erected (over objections from the ÖVP) in Vienna's Albertinaplatz commemorating the victims of war and Fascism. A central component of the monument was a stone statue of a bearded man on his hands and knees scrubbing the sidewalk – a reference to the public humiliation endured by many of Vienna's Jews following the *Anschluß*.[93] That same year, Chancellor Vranitzky made a speech in which he acknowledged that many individual Austrians had been guilty of atrocities during the Nazi period, and the Austrian government offered a small amount of compensation, about $400 per person – described as a token payment of a "debt of honor" – to former Austrian Jews living abroad.[94]

These initial, tentative steps gave way to bolder measures after the SPÖ strengthened its political position in the 1990 Nationalrat election. The Socialists held on to nearly 43 percent of the popular vote, while their conservative coalition partners slid nine points to 32 percent. Much of the ÖVP's decline in electoral strength could be attributed to the FPÖ, which increased its share of the vote to a post-war high of 16.6 percent. Although numerically the ÖVP and the FPÖ were in a position to form a government, the conservatives considered the FPÖ under Haider unacceptable as coalition partners. Instead, the conservatives and the Socialists chose to work together to contain the Far Right, successfully toppling Haider as the governor of the province of Carinthia in 1991.[95]

Emboldened by his improved position, Vranitzky began to decisively change Austria's official historical narrative. In July 1991, the chancellor made a speech before the parliament in which he again stressed that individual Austrians should be held responsible for their past actions.[96] A second, stronger statement followed in 1993, when Vranitzky, as the first Austrian chancellor to visit Israel, spoke at Hebrew University and publicly acknowledged that Austria as a nation – and not just individual Austrians – bore responsibility for the Holocaust.[97] In his 1992 inaugural speech, Thomas Klestil, Waldheim's successor in the office of the president, called on Austria to face the truth about

---

[93] See Eva Kuttenberg, "Austria's Topography of Memory: Heldenplatz, Albertinaplatz, Judenplatz and Beyond," *The German Quarterly*, 80:44 (October 2007), pp. 468–491.

[94] The amount was 2,500 schilling, the equivalent of $400 at the time.

[95] Similar patterns could be observed elsewhere in Europe in this period. For instance, French conservatives worked together with their Socialist rivals to contain the rise of the far right Front National under Jean Marie Le Penn.

[96] Gerhard Botz and Gerald Sprengnagel, eds., *Kontroversen um Österreichs Zeitgeschichte. Verdrängte Vergangenheit, Österreich-Identität, Waldheim und die Historiker* (Frankfurt am Main/New York: Campus, 1994), pp. 575–576. Journalist Hella Pick sees it as a bigger gesture, *Guilty Victims*, op. cit., pp. 199–120.

[97] Uhl, "From Victim Myth to Co-Responsibility Thesis," op. cit., p. 63.

its history, with its dark as well as light sides, and in 1994 he made a follow-up speech before the Knesset in which he repeated Vranitzky's message.[98] Austrian public opinion data showed strong support for the government's new stance on history: 81 percent of Austrians surveyed supported the chancellor's remarks, only 17 percent opposed.[99]

Changes in rhetoric were soon matched by changes in Austrian compensation and restitution policies. In 1994, Austria came under pressure from the European Union to address the issue.[100] The government was exceptionally sensitive to these pressures because Austria was negotiating to join the Union in 1995, and in a national referendum, two-thirds of Austrians already had voted in favor of accession. In 1994, the Nationalrat approved the creation of a new organization, the National Fund of the Republic of Austria for Victims of National Socialism (or *Nationalfond*), which was to provide compensation to former Austrian Jews living abroad. Beginning in 1995, the fund began making payments of up to 70,000 schillings ($4,500) to all survivors it could locate. Additional funds were set aside for supporting Jewish museums, synagogues, hospitals, and old-age homes.[101] During the same period, the Austrian government also undertook steps to deal with the complex issue of restoring art treasures that had been forcefully taken away from their Jewish owners during the Nazi era. In 1994, the government also transferred control over the repository of looted art at the Mauerbach Monastery to the Austrian Jewish community, which agreed to sell those items whose original owners or their heirs could not be identified and to use the proceeds for the benefit of Austrian Holocaust victims.

Although there were no new war crimes trials as a result of the change in the historical narrative, there was a significant shift in Austrian policy regarding the legal pursuit of Holocaust deniers. In 1992, the *Nationalrat* revised the long moribund *Verbotgesetz*, which forbade the propagation of Nazi propaganda, to make it illegal to deny, belittle, or justify the National Socialist genocide. Although initially few cases were brought to trial, by the end of the decade a substantial number of people were brought to trial and punished under the provisions of the revised law. Between 1999 and 2005, 191 guilty verdicts were handed down. The most controversial of these was the 2005 arrest of the British historian and prominent Holocaust denier, David Irving, while on a trip to

---

[98] Uhl, "From Victim Myth to Co-Responsibility Thesis," op. cit., p. 63.

[99] Heidemarie Uhl, "Das'erste Opfer'. Der Österreischische Opfermythos und seine Transformationin in der Zweiten Republik," *Österreichische Zeitschrift für Politikwissenschaft* 30 (2001), pp. 19–34, data cited on p. 27.

[100] During the accession negotiations, it had become apparent that Austria would need to take further measures to improve its image on the issue of historical justice. The establishment of the *Nationalfond* was in certain respects a tacit precondition for Austrian accession to the EU. Günter Bischoff, "Victims? Perpetrators? 'Punching Bags' of European Historical Memory? The Austrians and their World War II Legacies," *German Studies Review* 27:1 (February 2004), p. 26.

[101] David Foster, *Wiedergutmachung in Österreich und der BRD*, op. cit., pp. 171–175.

Vienna. In 2006, Irving was sentenced to three years in prison for his revisionist views.[102] As in France, which a few years earlier had passed laws making denial of the Holocaust a criminal offense, the strengthened *Verbotgesetz* was aimed at weakening the Far Right and the FPÖ.

Despite these measures, international pressures to pay further compensation to the victims of Nazism continued to grow. Of critical importance in this context were pressures emanating from the United States. In June 1998, the U.S. Congress passed the War Crimes Disclosure Act, which established a Nazi War Criminal Records Interagency Working Group inside the U.S. government to oversee the identification and disclosure of all documents pertaining to commission of war crimes between 1939 and 1945. A new wave of official documents was made available to Holocaust survivors and their lawyers that enabled them to more effectively pursue their claims. In December 1998, a lawsuit was filed against the Bank of Austria as well as other Austrian and German financial institutions on the behalf of Holocaust survivors seeking compensation and restitution for lost assets. Austria also faced growing pressure to address the issue of former slave laborers who had been put to work on the territory of the Austrian Republic during the Nazi period.

In response to these developments, the Austrian government set up a huge, 150-member historical commission to investigate the expropriation of property under Nazi rule and the way in which restitution issues had been handled during the Second Republic.[103] On the selection committee for the commission was Simon Wiesenthal and other long-time critics of the Austrian government's previously obstructionist policies regarding compensation and restitution.

In 2000, however, Austria once again became the focus of international criticism when the far-right FPÖ party under Jörg Haider went into coalition with the ÖVP to form a new government. Despite his efforts to burnish his democratic credentials, Haider had continued to promote revisionist views regarding history throughout the 1990s. In 1996, Haider had praised members of a *Waffen SS* veterans' group for their sense of loyalty and duty.[104] During the 2000 *Nationalrat* elections, Haider also suggested that if restitution were made to Jews, ethnic Germans who had been driven out of Poland and Czechoslovakia should also get their property back, and he accused the head of the Austrian Jewish community Ariel Muzicant of manufacturing anti-Semitic letters in the Austrian press to create the image that anti-Semitism was alive and well in

---

[102] *Der Spiegel*, 9 (February 25, 2006), p. 182. The decision has spurred quite a controversy over the freedom of speech, and Irving was released after serving only half of his sentence. For more on the *Verbotgesetz*, see Felix Müller, *Das Verbotgesetz im Spannungsverhältnis zur Meinungsfreiheit*. op. cit.

[103] Clemens Jabloner, et al., eds., *Schlussbericht der Historikerkommission der Republik Österreich: Vermögensentzug während der NS-Zeit sowie Rückstellungen und Entschädigungen seit 1945* (Vienna: Oldenbourg, 2003).

[104] Haider had made a series of such comments, dating back to 1985. See "Haider in his own Words: A Chronology of Comments," *Time Europe*, February 14, 2000.

Austria and thus rally support for Jewish claims.[105] Bolstered by popular concerns over immigration and capitalizing on voter dissatisfaction with the long-term domination of Austrian political life by the two major parties, Haider's party vaulted to its best electoral performance ever, winning 26.9 percent of the popular vote and 52 seats in the *Nationalrat*. The FPÖ was now tied with the SPÖ as Austria's second largest party. Although the leader of the ÖVP Wolfgang Schüssel had said before the election that his party would not enter into coalition with the FPÖ, he changed his mind after protracted negotiations with the SPÖ broke down. Apparently Schüssel calculated that Haider could be better contained within the framework of a coalition than outside of it and that the burden of governance would weaken rather than strengthen the rightists.[106]

Schüssels' decision sent shock waves throughout Europe and beyond. Unlike the 1970s, when the Kreisky government went into coalition with the FPÖ, international political sensitivity to the historical issue had increased greatly. In addition, since the end of the cold war, European Far Right parties, beginning with the Front National in France and the Lombard League in Italy, had been enjoying levels of electoral success not seen since the 1930s. It was feared in many European capitals that the FPÖ's success would have a contagion effect, signaling that Far Right parties were acceptable coalition partners and, thus, change political dynamics far beyond the borders of Austria. In response, the fourteen members of the European Union, spearheaded by France and Belgium, imposed unprecedented diplomatic sanctions on the Republic of Austria. All bilateral contacts between Austria and the other members of the EU were suspended, and Austrian candidates were not supported by the other members when EU offices were to be filled. From the start, it was clear that these measures were largely symbolic in nature. Austrian participation in EU committees, where most of the international decision making within the EU takes place, continued without interruption. Nonetheless, the Union's willingness to make such a costly signal created an immediate sense of crisis in the beleaguered Alpine Republic.[107] The United States as well joined in the international campaign to isolate the new government, recalling its ambassador for "urgent consultations" and instructing its U.S. diplomats to have no contact with Haider or other FPÖ members who joined the Austrian government.[108] Inside Austria, critics of the new government – spearheaded by the SPÖ

---

[105] Eizenstat, *Imperfect Justice*, op. cit., p. 284.

[106] According to an advisor to the ÖVP interviewed by the author.

[107] See Michael Merlingen, Cas Mudde, and Ulrich Sedelmeier, "The Right and the Righteous? European Norms, Domestic Politics and the Sanctions against Austria," *Journal of Common Market Studies*, 39:1 (March 2001), pp. 59–77; and Michael Gehler, "Kontraproduktive Intervention: Die 'EU 14' und der Fall Österreich oder vom Triumph des 'Primates der Innenpolitik' 2000–2003," in Michael Gehler, Anton Pelinka, and Günter Bischof, eds., *Österreich in der Europäischen Union: Bilanz einer Mitgliedschaft* (Vienna: Böhlau Verlag, 2003), pp. 121–181.

[108] "U.S. Acts over Austrian Far-Right," *BBC News*, February 4, 2000. Available at http://news.bbc.co.uk/1/hi/world/europe/631376.stm (accessed on May 8, 2006).

(now in the opposition) and a large network of activists – took to the streets, organizing large-scale demonstrations in Vienna, Linz, and Salzburg.[109]

Faced with a growing domestic and international political crisis, the new government redoubled Austria's efforts to address the issue of its responsibility for the horrors of Nazism. On February 3, 2000, at the request of President Thomas Klestil, Schüssel and Haider signed a historic declaration acknowledging Austria's shared responsibility for the crimes of the Third Reich and underlining the Second Republic's commitment to democracy, human rights, and ethnic tolerance. The key passage in the declaration read:

Austria accepts her responsibility for the tragic history of the 20th century and the revolting crimes of the national-socialist regime. Our country acknowledges the light and dark sides of its past and the deeds of all Austrians, good as well as bad, as its responsibility. Nationalism, dictatorship and intolerance brought war, xenophobia, bondage, racism and mass murder. The uniqueness and singularity of crimes of the Holocaust are an exhortation to permanent alertness against all forms of dictatorship and totalitarianism.[110]

The statement was more nuanced in its acknowledgement of guilt than Weizsäcker's 1985 speech on the fortieth anniversary of the German surrender, and the subsequent outline of the government's political program (*Regierungserklärung*) that was presented to the Austrian National Assembly was considerably less forthcoming in acknowledging Austrian guilt.[111] Nonetheless, in the Austrian context, the declaration had a watershed effect similar to that of the Weizsäcker speech in Germany, consolidating support for a contrite approach to the past on both the Right as well as the Left ends of the political spectrum.

Just as importantly, the new government quickly moved to carry out and expand the previous government's policies in the area of reparations and restitution. Aware that the European Union was looking closely at how the new government would deal with the slave labor reparations issue, within days of taking office in February 2000, Schüssel called on Maria Schaumayer, the widely respected former head of the Austrian National Bank, to negotiate an agreement that would offer compensation to those surviving slave laborers who had been put to work on Austrian territory.[112] A few months later, in May, Schüssel charged Ambassador Ernst Sucharipa, director of Austria's Diplomatic

---

[109] For a detailed overview, see Isolde Charim and Doron Rabinovici, eds., *Österreich. Berichte aus Quarantanien* (Frankfurt am Main: Suhrkamp, 2000).

[110] Official translation available at http://www.oe-journal.at/0300/06_030300_e.htm.

[111] See Regierungserklärung, February 9, 2000, especially p.16, which says only that Austria's Nazi past requires a vigorous discussion of the past and sensitivity to how the unjust Nazi system functioned. Available at http://www.bundeskanzleramt.at/2004/4/7/Regerkl%C3%A4r.pdf (accessed May 8, 2006).

[112] The pressure to address the slave labor issue had been building for several years before then, and already in 1998 the Austrian government had set up a historical commission to study the issue. The initial report was published in February 2000.

Academy, with improving how Austria dealt with providing restitution for those who lost their property as a result of Nazi Aryanization policies – a topic of particular concern to the United States. On July 7, the *Nationalrat* approved the creation of a reconciliation fund (*Versöhnungsfond*) that would pay out the equivalent of $550 million to the estimated 150,000 surviving former slave laborers. A few months later, on March 6, 2001, after protracted and difficult negotiations mediated by Stuart Eizenstat of the U.S. Treasury Department, the Austrian government agreed to amend the 1995 *Nationalfond* and pay out an additional $150 million in compensation to former Austrian Jews and their descendants[113] for material losses resulting from Nazi Aryanization policies. Approximately 21,000 people were expected to be affected by this law.[114] In a separate agreement, the Austrian government also agreed to supplement with $150 million legal claims that had been pressed against Austrian banks regarding frozen or unclaimed accounts left over from the Nazi period.[115]

Politically speaking, these actions had their desired effect. On September 12, the European Union lifted the diplomatic *cordon sanitaire* that had been imposed on Austria. Likewise, after the signing of the March 6 agreement amending the National Fund, the U.S. government helped end the legal challenges faced by the Austrian government and Austrian firms in the United States. At several points in the negotiation, Secretary of State Madeline Albright and other U.S. representatives had warned the Austrian government of the potential repercussions for Austrian economic interests if the Aryanization issue was not effectively addressed.[116] Now these threats were dispelled, and Austria's diplomatic isolation had been ended. For the space of nine months, however, the issue of historical justice and Austria's Nazi past had held the center stage in Austrian domestic and international politics.

In stark contrast to the 1960s and 1970s, when the SPÖ's political dependence on the FPÖ had stiffened Austrian unwillingness to face the Nazi past, the ÖVP's coalition with the FPÖ in 2000 had accelerated and consolidated Austria's conversion to contrition. Several factors lay behind these two very different outcomes. First, and most importantly, international pressure on the issue had greatly intensified. Both Western Europe and the United States

---

[113] The law covers all those persecuted by the National Socialist regime on grounds of politics, origin, religion, nationality, sexual origin, or of physical or mental handicap. The overwhelming majority of those covered by the law, however, were Jewish. The complete text of the Reconciliation (slave labor) and the National Fund laws, as well as ancillary speeches, texts, and comments, are available in both English and German at http://Vienna.usembassy.gov/en/policy/restitution.htm.

[114] See Eizenstat, *Imperfect Justice*, op. cit., chapters 14 and 15; Thonke, *Hitlers Langer Schatten*, op. cit.

[115] See Eizenstat, *Imperfect Justice*, op. cit., p. 306.

[116] Eizenstat, *Imperfect Justice*, op. cit., pp. 296, 309. The Clinton administration was especially sensitive to the potential impact of the issue on Jewish support for the Democratic Party and insisted on a close coordination of U.S. mediation efforts with representatives of the World Jewish Congress. The fact that 2000 was a closely fought election year heightened administration concerns. See ibid., pp. 296–300.

assigned the issue of historical justice a far higher level of diplomatic priority than they had during the days of the cold war. Just as importantly, in an
international environment characterized by what Robert Keohane and Joseph
Nye have called "complex interdependence,"[117] Austria was far more susceptible to international pressure than it had been at any time since the days of
the occupation. The Austrian government faced powerful diplomatic pressures
through the institutions of the European Union, and Austrian firms faced damaging legal challenges, and a potentially even more damaging threat to their
corporate image, in the United States.[118]

In addition to these changes in the international political environment, conditions inside Austria had shifted as well. The tone of the Austrian discourse
on history had been changing slowly but surely to the point where the popular
response to the debate over Haider in 2000 bore little resemblance to the Waldheim or Peter controversies of the 1970s and 1980s. Gone was the outraged
press commentary protesting the outside interference in Austrian sovereign
affairs, and there were few signs of popular opposition to the new, more penitent stance on history adopted by the Schüssel government. Even the FPÖ
remained relatively quiescent, apparently satisfied with its new role as coalition partner and with a few compensatory gestures made to its Far Right
constituency – primarily in the form of a new law offering increased compensation to former prisoners of war. Although Schüssel in November 2000 gave
a controversial interview with the *Jerusalem Post* in which he reiterated the old
line that Austria had been Nazism's first victim, nonetheless, he also underlined
that Austria bore a moral responsibility to address the injustices of the Nazi
era.[119]

In the years that have followed, Austria has settled into its new mode as
a penitent. In 2001, payments began to be disbursed to former slave laborers
and to those who had lost property as a result of Aryanization policies. In
certain respects, Austria became a pioneer in certain aspects of restitution
policy, especially with regard to the return of looted art treasures. Exhibitions
and commemorative events dedicated to the victims of the Holocaust fell into
the regular, ritualized mode that can be seen in Nazi Germany, with a new
high point reached in 2005 on the sixtieth anniversary of the end of World
War II.[120]

Although the ÖVP's coalition with the FPÖ continued until 2006, the Far
Right was beset by internal rivalries, leading to a major split in the party

---

[117] Robert O. Keohane and Joseph S. Nye, *Power and Interdependence: World Politics in Transition* (Boston: Little Brown, 1977).
[118] The Austrian government, like many others at the time, was struggling with privatizing formerly state owned or co-owned firms while at the same time reducing trade and investment
barriers, so it was especially concerned that its newly independent firms would be competitive
internationally.
[119] "Das erste Nazi-Opfer," *Die Presse*, November 10, 2000, p. 10.
[120] See Bischoff, "Victims? Perpetrators? 'Punching Bags' of European Historical Memory? The
Austrians and their World War II Legacies," *German Studies Review*, 2004, op. cit.

in 2005. In 2006, the ÖVP and the SPÖ went back into coalition, and the Far Right returned to the opposition, although the combined share of the Far Right parties approached fifteen. Increasingly, however, the Austrian Far Right parties focused on immigration and opposition to Turkey's proposed entry into the EU, rather than on historical issues. Austria's new penitent official narrative was no longer a central issue either inside or outside of Austria. After more than half a century, the prodigal penitent had returned to inherit the dark legacies left behind by its history.

## Conclusions Based on the Austrian Case

The Austrian case, like that of the Federal Republic, generally fits the Historical Realist model outlined earlier. As in the Federal Republic, an initial combination of personal experiences (a Historical Determinist variable) together with pragmatic considerations (Instrumentalist factors) inclined Austria toward an impenitent stance. In Austria's case, however, the international political environment – that is, the myth conveniently supplied by the Allied powers that Austria was Nazism's first victim together with Austria's relative insulation from the pressures of the cold war and its only very attenuated integration in the political structures of the European Union – allowed Austrian leaders to maintain a far more impenitent official historical narrative for far longer than the Federal Republic.

Also as was the case in Germany, the emergence of an international discourse focusing on the crimes of the Holocaust helped reshape the way in which Austrian society looked on its Nazi past, thus shifting the incentives that its political leaders had for dealing with the issue. Whereas in the 1960s Austrian Socialists found reasons to suppress critical discussion of the past, beginning in the 1980s, growing numbers of party members rejected turning a blind eye. Much as in Germany after the airing of the TV mini-series *Shoah*, the parameters of the political debate on history had changed, paving the way for a decisive shift in the official narrative. With the end of the cold war and mounting pressures for Austria to join the EU, these international cultural forces were joined by geoeconomic incentives, triggering a far-reaching reformulation of the official narrative.

Much as a Historical Realist position would suggest, however, when the consolidation of the Austrian official narrative in favor of greater penitence did come, it did not come easily. Although Instrumentalist factors as well as international cultural trends pointed in the direction of greater contrition by the middle of the 1980s, it took nearly fifteen years for a consensus supporting a complete shift to emerge. Whereas the Kohl government in the first half of the 1980s found its efforts to promote a healthy sense of nationalism stymied by a waxing German culture of contrition, successive Austrian governments beginning with that of Vranitzky in the late 1980s found its efforts to move the official narrative in the direction of greater penance blocked by the continuing influence of an Austrian culture of impenitence. Even Chancellor Schüssel, who in 2000 had tried to satisfy the international community that his government accepted Austrian co-responsibility for Nazism, lapsed into the language of Austrian victimization (in an interview with the *Jerusalem Post* no less!). The rallying of many Austrians to the defense of Peters and Waldheim could be understood in instrumental terms (i.e., as an effort to avoid having to pay compensation), however, the widespread persistence of the view – as reflected in the large body of survey data – that Austria was being unfairly singled out,[121] bespeaks of a more deeply rooted world view.

To be sure, there were many Austrians who benefited materially from holding such views – beginning with the members of the FPÖ.[122] Likewise, there were others, such as Bruno Kreisky, who benefited politically from espousing an impenitent stance. The number of individuals who benefited materially from impenitence, however, was far less than the large numbers of Austrians who were impenitent or were in some sense suspicious of a penitent stance. This trend is consistent with the culturalist proposition that the official historical narrative and the collective societal memory in which it is embedded are likely to evolve in a *discursive* manner – that is, that the way in which an issue is defined at point A in time conditions the way in which that issue is defined subsequently at point B. Change in views on history in Austria has been slow and incremental, arguably slower than the changes in its international environment, and has generated considerable cognitive as well as political dissonance.

At the same time, although the Austrian case fits the general pattern we have seen in the Federal Republic, it also differs in a number of important ways, allowing us to control for historical, political, and cultural variables and to arrive at a more fine-grained analysis of their relative impact. This is particularly true with regard to the influence of history and historical experience on the official narrative. The actual experiences that members of Austrian and German society had with war and persecution were quite similar. After 1938, Austria became an integral part of the Third Reich; its people received German citizenship; and both Germans and Austrians participated on more or less

---

[121] According to 1991 GALLUP poll, when asked "Do Jews use the Holocaust for their own purposes?" 32 percent agreed, 36 percent disagreed and 32 percent gave no answer. The same question, asked by GALLUP in 1995, showed 28 percent agreed, and 44 percent disagreed. Wasserman, *Naziland Österreich*, op. cit., pp. 164–165. The change with respect to was Austria a victim or a co-victimizer is even starker. In 1987, 48 percent saw Austria as a victim, and only 24 percent, a co-victimizer. By 1991, 34 percent saw Austria as a victim, and 39 percent, as a co-victimizer, ibid., p. 142. Note, however, the increase in the numbers who refused to answer the question – 33 percent in 1991.

[122] Jörg Haider might be viewed as a paradigmatic case. As the leader of the FPÖ he, of course, was beholden to interest groups such as the SS veterans' organizations who favored a revisionist world view. In addition, Haider's own personal fortune had been inherited from his uncle, who in turn had bought for a very low price a large 3,800-acre estate that had been Aryanized in 1938. The Jewish family who had originally owned the estate had settled in Israel and was still seeking compensation for it in the 1980s, a claim that Haider unsurprisingly dismissed as "absurd." Hella Pick, *Guilty Victims*, op. cit., pp. 186–187; Eizenstat, *Imperfect Justice*, op. cit., p. 285.

equal terms in the war as well as in the Holocaust and other Nazi crimes. One might, therefore, expect the two societies to have broadly similar reactions to these experiences. To a certain extent, they did. In both countries, on a societal level there was a marked reluctance to confront the question of their own responsibility for the crimes of the Third Reich. Instead, Austrians and Germans alike preferred to focus on their own suffering and to view themselves as the victims of war and tyranny, rather than as victimizers. Likewise, in both countries, this unwillingness to recognize moral responsibility for the horrors of the Nazi period only abated with the passage of time and the change of generations. The Historical Determinist hypothesis that a certain amount of distance must be achieved before a society is willing or able to acknowledge its guilt seems to be confirmed by the Austrian case.

This having been said, there remain some fundamental differences between the Austrian and German cases that raise serious doubts about the validity of a strict Historical Determinist position. First and foremost, regardless of the popular feeling of victimization on the societal level, the Federal Republic's official historical narrative during the 1950s through 1980s was considerably more penitent than that of Austria: in terms of rhetoric used by its leaders, in terms of commemorative policies, in terms of policies regarding restitution and compensation for the victims of Nazism, and in terms of the pursuit of the perpetrators of Nazi atrocities. Although societal memories may set the parameters for the official narrative, those parameters are quite wide, giving elites considerable latitude to shape the official narrative according to other factors, such as instrumental calculations of interest.

Second, although generational change may have created opportunities to reexamine the nation's responsibility for the crimes of the Third Reich, there was nothing automatic about the process. In Austria, the first postwar genera-tion – the young people who came of age in the 1960s – did not pursue the issue with anywhere near the vigor that their counterparts in the Federal Republic did. Although after the Taras Borodajkewycz affair in 1965 there was a revival of the memory of the Austrian resistance to Nazism and a certain distancing of the major parties from revisionist historical views, it was not until the 1980s and 1990s that the issue of Austria's moral responsibility became the focus of a serious protest movement.

This takes us to the final set of questions posed in the theoretical chapter: What kind of impact did the official narrative have on domestic and interna-tional politics? The Austrian case reinforces the Historical Realist view that his-tory can become a significant issue with ramifications that reached far beyond the symbolic realm. This is particularly true on the domestic political level, where the battle for the support of the FPÖ was a decisive factor in Austrian coalitional calculations throughout the postwar period. Not until 2000, when the FPÖ was willing to at least formally abandon its revisionist views did the politics of history cease to have a decisive impact on coalition building.

On the international level, whereas the issue of how Austria dealt with its past did not appear to significantly affect Austrian security interests nor did the occasional storm of controversy over Austrian impenitence greatly affect Austrian national economic performance, it did have a major impact on Austrian diplomacy. At least twice, during the Waldheim affair of 1988 to 1992, and then again in 2000, after Haider's FPÖ joined the government, Austria was faced with major, long-lasting diplomatic crises resulting from its impenitent official historical narrative.

Moreover, throughout the postwar period, Austrian leaders found themselves compelled to spend significant amounts of time on the issue – in 1955 (with the State Treaty), in 1965 (after the Borodjakwyzch affair), in 1992 (with Vranitzky's speech and the replacement of Waldheim with Klestil), and in 2000 (with the ÖVP-FPÖ joint declaration). Each time, eventually, Austria made adjustments to its official historical narrative around which a new equilibrium between domestic and international interests could be established. However, this was by no means an easy task. In the short run – until a new equilibrium could be established – the official historical narrative played an important independent role in shaping a number of political outcomes. In the longer run, the official narrative was a very important intervening variable.

The Austrian case, instructive as it is, still leaves many questions open. In many respects, Austria and Germany are too similar, resembling one another closely in terms of the original historical experiences that they had as constituent elements of the Third Reich; in terms of their common cultural background as Christian, German speaking nations; and in terms of their common geopolitical location as Western democratic nations in an increasingly integrated European regional system. As a result, it is still difficult to say to what extent the commonalities we have observed in the politics of history in Austria and the Federal Republic – the pattern of the suppression of guilt followed by eventual acceptance of responsibility, the impact of increased integration, and of international normative shifts – are the result of these similar preconditions or whether they are reflective of broader dynamics common to the politics of historical responsibility. A further expansion of cases is needed to arrive at a more robust and nuanced analysis.

# 4

# Japan

## *The Model Impenitent?*

Japan is often depicted as suffering from a particularly severe form of collective amnesia regarding its recent past. While the Japanese people remember in excruciating detail their own sufferings during the war, especially the atomic bombings of Hiroshima and Nagasaki, they are said to overlook the immense suffering their country inflicted on other peoples.[1] To be Japanese, as the noted Japan critic and commentator James Fallows put it, means never having to say you're sorry – at least to non-Japanese. For much of the period since 1945, Japan's status as a victim, rather than as a victimizer, has dominated not only the official historical narrative of the Japanese state but also the collective memory of the Japanese people.

This impenitent stance is widely believed to have had consequences. Just as Germany is widely seen to have benefited from its penitent stance on history, it is commonly argued that Japan's lack of contrition has placed it at odds with its Asian neighbors and, at times, even with its principal ally and protector, the United States. Tensions over history are said to have heightened suspicions regarding Japan's military intentions – increasing the risk of military conflict and a potentially destabilizing regional arms race[2] – inflamed nationalist feeling in its East Asian neighbors, and all but wrecked efforts to create a strong network of international institutions in East Asia.[3] If Germany is the model penitent in international affairs, than Japan is the model impenitent.

---

[1] See for instance Iris Chang, *The Rape of Nanjing: the Forgotten Holocaust of World War II* (London and New York: Penguin, 1997); George Hicks, *Japan's War Memories: Amnesia or Concealment?* (Aldershot: Ashgate, 1997); and Nicholas Kristof, "The Problem of Memory," *Foreign Affairs* 77:6 (November/December 1998), pp. 37–49.

[2] Thomas Christensen, "China, The U.S.-Japan Alliance and the Security Dilemma in East Asia," *International Security* 23:4 (Spring 1999), pp. 49–80; Paul Midford, "Japan's Leadership Role in East Asia: Security Multilateralism," *The Pacific Review* 13:3 (Fall 2000), pp. 367–397.

[3] Edward J. Lincoln, *East Asian Economic Regionalism* (Washington, DC: Brookings, 2004), pp. 37–38; Gilbert Rozman, *Northeast Asia's Stunted Regionalism: Bilateral Distrust in the Shadow of Globalization* (Cambridge: Cambridge University Press, 2004).

There is more than a grain of truth to this portrayal of Japan. For decades, the Japanese government assiduously avoided assuming any formal responsibility for the horrors of the war in Asia and the preceding colonial era. Even in the early twenty-first century, more than six decades after the war, attempts to adopt a more contrite official historical narrative are often undermined by the steady revisionist drumbeat emanating from the right end of the Japanese political spectrum. It is also true that recriminations over Japan's relatively impenitent stance on history have been a central feature in its relations with the outside world, especially in East Asia. In addition, it cannot be denied that disputes over Japan's official historical narrative have often dominated the regional diplomatic agenda and severely impaired its relations with China and South Korea as it did during the 2001–2007 period.

Nonetheless, this narrative of Japan as a model impenitent is misleading. Far more than is commonly realized, both the Japanese people and the government of Japan have acknowledged that Imperial forces were responsible for atrocities in the period before 1945 and have tried to make amends, especially in recent decades. On a societal level, a case can be made that Japan has never suffered from "historical amnesia." The case can even be made that there was greater public awareness of the atrocities committed by the Imperial forces at an earlier date than in Austria, France, or even Germany.[4] This awareness was fueled by fiery debates over the legitimacy of the war and who bore responsibility for it (frequently referred to as *Sensōsekininron* in Japanese) that has colored Japanese public life from 1945 on.[5] In this respect, Japan, with its supposedly collectivistic, consensus-oriented political culture, has been more prone to dissent than were the supposedly more individualistic and open societies of Austria, France, and Germany. Japan began offering apologies for its pre-1945 record (albeit quite tepid ones) as early as 1965 and since the 1980s, it has sought reconciliation with its Asian neighbors.

The net result of Japan's various efforts to pursue reconciliation, however, have failed to meet expectations. Despite a social and political readiness to adopt a more contrite historical narrative – and despite strong international pressures to do so – Japan's apologies have been limited in scope, challenged domestically, and singularly unsuccessful in improving Japan's relations with its Asian neighbors. Instead of resolving the history issue, tensions over Japan's official narrative have mounted over the years, resulting in a string of major diplomatic crises over historical and related territorial issues at the beginning of the twenty-first century. Although certain parallels can be made with the

---

[4] See Petra Buchholz, "Tales of War: Autobiographies and Private Memories in Japan and Germany," in Takashi Inoguhi and Lyn Jackson, eds., *Memories of War: The Second World War and Japanese Historical Memory in Comparative Perspective* (Tokyo: United Nations University, 1998), available at http://www.unu.edu/unupress/m-war.html#tales (accessed August 4, 2010).

[5] A number of recent studies have strongly challenged the myth of Japanese historical amnesia, demonstrating conclusively that war memory has been woven into the fabric of post-1945 Japanese politics. See especially Franziska Seraphim, *War Memory and Social Politics in Japan, 1945 to 2005* (Cambridge, MA: Harvard University Press, 2006), esp. pp. 4–5.

European cases, the international tempests over history in Asia were far more severe – and potentially dangerous – than the Austrian crises over Waldheim and Haider or the FRG's problems with Poland and the Czech Republic in the early 2000s.

These conspicuous differences between Japan and the two European cases examined earlier raise two sets of intriguing questions: First, why has Japan been unwilling or unable to adopt as penitent an official narrative as did Germany or (albeit after a considerable delay) Austria, despite a comparably bloody recent history and despite being subject to intense international pressures to do so? Second, why has the "history problem" been so much more intractable and disruptive in the Asian context than in the European?

This chapter is dedicated to pursing the first issue, focusing on the development of the Japanese official narrative during the cold war era. Chapter 5 continues the analysis into the postwar era and pays special attention to the second question.

## The Legacy of Empire – Historical Determinist Factors

Similar to Germany and Austria, Japan's problems with its past are in the first instance the product of a particularly brutal history. The scope of that history (or at least that part of its history that became controversial after 1945), however, is considerably longer and more complex than was true in Germany and Austria. Between 1895 and 1945, Japan carved out a vast empire in Asia, encompassing at its height Korea, Taiwan, Manchuria, virtually all of South East Asia, most of coastal China, and most of the islands of the Western Pacific. To build this empire, Japan fought five major wars: the Sino-Japanese War of 1894–1895, the Russo-Japanese War of 1904–1905, World War I (fighting on the side of the Western Allies), the second Sino-Japanese War beginning in 1937, and finally the War in the Pacific, which commenced with the attack on Pearl Harbor in 1941.[6] To maintain control over the various peoples it conquered, Japan employed not only a variety of tools, including persuasion and co-optation,[7] but also more brutal methods, such the savage persecution of dissidents, torture, and large-scale massacres.

---

[6] In addition to these wars, Japan conducted numerous lesser wars and undertook countless military expeditions, including the international campaign to suppress the Boxer rebellion in 1900, the Japanese expedition into Siberia from 1919 to 1925, and the military takeover of Manchuria in 1931.

[7] Far more often than is commonly recognized today, Japan had considerable success in co-opting its colonial peoples. This was particularly true of Taiwan, where the indigenous elite were unusually pliant and the local attachment to an alternative locus of identity – in this case China – was relatively tenuous. The situation was somewhat different in Korea and mainland China, both of which had a well-developed sense of identity and many of whose elites were actively opposed to incorporation in the Japanese Empire. Nonetheless, even in China and Korea hundreds of thousands were successfully incorporated into the colonial apparatus as soldiers, policemen, judges, and bureaucrats, and much of the local business elite (especially in Korea) benefited greatly from Japanese rule. See for instance, Carter Eckert, *Offspring of Empire: The*

The human cost of building and maintaining this empire was appalling. The number of people killed in Asia after 1937 is usually estimated at around 20 million. Hundreds of thousands perished before then as well.[8] The price paid in less tangible things, such as national pride and human freedom, is incalculable. Although it is impossible to review this history in any detail here, for the purpose of the present analysis, it is necessary to briefly list the key sets of issues that would become particularly salient in the post-1945 debates over Japanese history. *The first complex of issues revolves around Japanese colonial policy*, in particular the annexation of Korea and the political and cultural assimilation of Koreans. *The second set of issues concerns the forced conscription of millions of laborers* by the Japanese armed forces and Japanese firms, particularly after the outbreak of the Second Sino-Japanese War in 1937. Of particular notoriety in this connection was the recruitment, often through violence or duplicity, of approximately 100 to 200 thousand women (the so-called comfort women) to serve as prostitutes for the Japanese army.[9] Also closely connected to the story of forced labor was the horrendous treatment

*Koch'Ang Kim and the Colonial Origins of Korean Capitalism, 1876–1945* (Seattle: University of Washington Press, 1996).

[8] It is difficult to determine how many in fact died in the Asia-Pacific theater between 1937 (the start of the Japanese invasion of North China) and 1945, although the usual estimate is around 20 million, including 10 million Chinese, 4 million Indonesians, and around 3 million Japanese. American military and civilian losses in the Pacific theater were probably under 110,000. These statistics, however, do not include the approximately 1 million Vietnamese and the 3 or so million Indians who are estimated to have died as a result of the disruption in food supplies that caused the Japanese invasion of Burma. In addition, there is considerable uncertainty about the actual numbers of deaths in China. Rudolf Rummel, op. cit., for instance, estimates that the total number of those killed in China at 19,605,000. Of these, he estimates Chinese Communist and nationalist military deaths at 3.4 million; the number of Chinese killed while serving in the Japanese military at 432,000; the number of civilians killed as a result of combat operations, 3,250,000, plus an additional 56,000 people killed in internal clashes. To this already staggering total comes an estimated 3,949,000 deliberately killed by Japanese forces; another 5,907,000 killed by the Chinese nationalists; 250,000 by the Chinese Communists; and another 110,000 killed by Chinese warlords. In addition, Rummel puts the number of Chinese who died as a result of famine at 2,250,000. See Rudolf Rummel, *China's Bloody Century* (New Brunswick, NJ: Transaction Books, 1991), Table 5a. Official Chinese estimates go even higher, suggesting that as many as 30 million died during this period. All of these numbers, however, should be viewed as suspect given the poor state of record keeping, and efforts to attribute deaths to one side or another are even more problematic. There is no estimate that the author is familiar with that tries to estimate the total number of people killed by the Japanese Imperial forces from the start of the empire in 1895 to its demise in 1945.

[9] George Hicks, *The Comfort Women: Japan's Brutal Regime of enforced Prostitution in the Second World War* (New York: Norton, 1994); Yuki Tanaka, *Japan's Comfort Women: Sexual Slavery and Prostitution during World War II an the US Occupation* (London: Routledge, 2002); Yoshiaki Yoshimi, *Comfort Women: Sexual Slavery in the Japanese Military during World War II* (New York: Columbia University Press, 2000). For a critical take on the issue by a highly respected conservative Japanese historian, see Ikuhiko Hata, "The Flawed UN Report on Comfort Women," *Japan Echo* 23:3 (Autumn, 1996), pp. 66–73. His more detailed criticism pointing out the methodological problems involved in establishing the dimensions of the comfort woman issue appeared in Japanese as *Ianfu to Senjo no Sei* (Tokyo: Shinchosha, 1999).

of Allied prisoners of war, nearly a third of whom died while in captivity.[10] *The third complex of issues centers on Japan's history of aggression against China*, especially the numerous atrocities committed by Japanese forces against the civilian population in China after 1937. Of particular importance in this connection is the massacre and brutalization of Chinese prisoners and civilians after the fall of Nanjing in 1937 (although numerous other similarly horrific and often better documented atrocities took place throughout Asia, including Hong Kong, Manila, and Singapore) and the development and use of chemical and bacteriological weapons in China.[11] *A fourth and final set of issues involves Japan's decision to go to war with the United States in 1941*, a decision that turned the war with China into an even larger war waged across the entire Asia-Pacific region.

Each of these issues would become the subject of considerable controversy in the postwar period. Critics of Japan would point to them as particularly shameful episodes in Japanese history and argue that the Japanese government should seek to make amends for them through apologies and by offering compensation. In contrast, defenders of Japan insist that the gravity of these offenses were exaggerated and should be viewed from a broader perspective that takes into account both the positive aspects of what the Japanese Empire accomplished as well as the pressures that its leaders found themselves under as a result of the equally or even more atrocious behavior of the other powers.

There are five important differences between the atrocities attributed to Japan and the crimes of the Third Reich that have to be noted. If one subscribes to the Historical Determinist proposition that past events set the parameters for the kind of historical narratives that countries can adopt, it follows that such differences should have a sizeable impact on the way post-1945 Japan came to view its recent past:

(1) Regardless which estimates one comes to rely upon, the numbers of those killed in Europe were far greater than in Asia. Between 1939 and 1945 an estimated 50 million people were believed to have been killed in Europe. In contrast, all but the highest estimates place the numbers of those killed in Asia between 1937 and 1945 at around half that number. The number of those killed by deliberate Japanese policy – that is, beyond those killed

---

[10] Gavan Daws, *Prisoners of the Japanese: Prisoners of War in the Pacific* (New York: William and Morrow, 1994); Van Waterford, *Prisoners of the Japanese in World War II: Statistical Narratives and Memorials Concerning Camps and Hellships, Civilian Slave Laborers and Others Captured in the Pacific Theater* (Jefferson, NC: McFarland and Company, Inc., 1994); and Yuki Tanaka and Toshiyuki Tanaka, *Hidden Horrors: Japanese War Crimes During World War II* (Boulder, CO: Westview Press, 1998), chapters 1 and 2. For a powerful, personal testimonial, see Lester I. Tenney, *My Hitch in Hell: The Bataan Death March* (Washington, DC: Brassey's, 1995).

[11] Sheldon Harris, *Factories of Death: Japanese Biological Warfare, 1932–1945 and the American Cover-up*, 2nd edition (New York: Routledge, 2001); and Hal Gold, *Unit 731 Testimony* (Tokyo: Yen Books, 1996).

as a result of the war and the chaos that it created – is similarly figured to around half of the numbers killed by the Nazis.[12]

(2) The documentary evidence on Japanese atrocities is much poorer than is the case in the European theater. Unlike the Nazis, who were meticulous record keepers, the Japanese left few written documents behind (an unknown number of documents were destroyed between the time of surrender and when the Allied occupation authorities arrived). Moreover, the pattern of decision making in the Japanese military and bureaucracy tended to be more diffuse than was the case in Germany, making it more difficult to establish that any given atrocity was a result of deliberate Japanese policy. This is not to deny that very large numbers – in the millions – were killed as a result of Japanese actions. The volume of evidence of Japanese atrocities – in the form of eye witness accounts and physical evidence – is overwhelming. There can be no doubt, for instance, that the Japanese army went berserk in Nanjing, killing many tens of thousands captured Chinese soldiers as well as countless civilians and raping and brutalizing thousands more after the fall of the city. However, whether the total numbers killed were 40,000 (as conservative but serious Japanese historians such as Hata Ikuhiko estimate) or over 200,000 (as was maintained by the Allies in the postwar trials) or 300,000 (as adamantly insisted upon by the Chinese government) is impossible to decide definitively.[13]

(3) While the Japanese military undoubtedly killed huge numbers of people, no systematic effort was made to exterminate entire groups of people on the basis of their putative racial characteristics, as the Nazis did with the Jews. Although Japan established a racialized hierarchy in the territory under its control, the Japanese concept of race appears to have been more porous than that of the Nazis.[14] Likewise, although there were slave labor camps in which hundreds of thousands perished and special

---

[12] Rummel estimates that the total number of those killed as a matter of deliberate Japanese policy to be 5,964,000. See his Web site, http://www.hawaii.edu/powerkills/SOD.CHAP3.HTM (accessed May 16, 2006). However, in any given instance, there exists a great deal of uncertainty over the actual numbers killed. Over 12 million were killed by the Third Reich.

[13] . For a high estimate relying heavily on Chinese official sources plus recently uncovered historical documents, see Iris Chang, *The Rape of Nanjing: The Forgotten Holocaust of world War II* (New York: Basic Books, 1997). For a contrasting view, see Masahiro Yamamoto, *Nanking: The Anatomy of a Massacre* (Westport, CT: Praeger, 2000). For a highly balanced collection of essays examining the controversy from all sides, see Joshua Fogel, ed., *The Nanjing Massacre in History and Historiography* ((Berkeley: University of California Press, 2000), as well as David Askew, "The Nanjing Incident: Recent Research and Trends," *Electronic Journal of Japanese Studies*, April 4, 2002, available at http://www.japanesestudies.org.uk/articles/Askew.html (accessed on May 13, 2006).

[14] On the Japanese understanding of race and ethnicity, see Michael Weiner "The Invention of Identity: Race and Nation in Pre-war Japan," in Frank Dikötter, ed., *The Construction of Racial Identities in China and Japan* (Honolulu: University of Hawaii Press, 1997), pp. 96–117.

facilities such as the Unit 731 where Japanese forces conducted horrific medical experiments on thousands of prisoners, these monstrosities were dwarfed by the even more monstrous extermination camps set up by the Third Reich in Europe.[15]

(4) The official Japanese rationale for waging war and the circumstances under which it went to war were different from that of Germany's. Similar to the Nazis, Japan sought to construct a "new order" in Asia, centered on a "Greater East Asian Co-Prosperity Sphere"; however, Japan did not launch wars of aggression against independent, more-or-less democratic countries as Hitler did when he invaded first Austria, then Czechoslovakia, Poland, and finally the rest of Western Europe.[16] Instead, Japan fought first against a notoriously corrupt Yi Dynasty in Korea and the Qing and Chinese Nationalist Regime in China, as well as assorted Chinese warlords who were arguably as thuggish toward their own people as the Japanese. After 1940, Japan waged war against Western colonial powers who themselves had forcibly imposed their rule on the countries of the region and were facing increasing resistance from the local population. As a result, many Japanese, including Japanese leftists and intellectuals who were otherwise critical of the conservative elites who dominated Japanese politics before 1945,[17] thought of Japan's imperial expansion not as a war of aggression, but rather as one of liberation, aimed at freeing the rest of Asia from the shackles imposed by corrupt local power brokers and the white, racist, imperial powers.

Furthermore, it was widely believed in Japan that were it not for the creation of its empire, Japan itself might have become a target of

---

[15] Although it is worth noting that fairly large numbers of Jews, perhaps as many as 150,000, were Aryanized and served in the German armed forces during World War II. See Bryan Mark Rigg, *Hitler's Jewish Soldiers* (University Press of Kansas, 2002). In addition, Germany was able to mobilize large numbers of Russians, Poles, Lithuanians, and others to serve alongside the Wehrmacht. As many as a million Russian volunteers served in a support and logistic role during the war, and several SS divisions were recruited from the conquered territories, including the Charlegmagne and the Nordland Divisions, which were among the final forces holding out in Berlin during the Russian assault in April 1945. Race was not as clearly defined in the Nazi case as sometimes believed, and Nazi efforts to establish objective criteria for determining race were farcical at best. One popular joke during the Third Reich went as follows: What does a true Aryan look like? A true Aryan is tall like Goebbels (who was 5'4), thin like Goering (who weighed nearly 250 lbs.), and blond like Hitler!

[16] Poland had ceased to be democratic after the May 1926 coup d'etat, and in both Czechoslovakia and Poland, there were substantial minorities who felt that their interests were not respected by their respective governments. Nonetheless, even in Poland there continued to be elections after 1926, and the Pilsudski regime could be fairly described as far more representative of the majority of the population than was true of the majority of the governments of the countries invaded by Japan.

[17] On the participation of Japanese leftists in the creation of the Japanese Empire, see especially Louise Young, *Japan's Total Empire: Manchuria and the Culture of Wartime Imperialism* (Berkeley, CA: University of California Press, 1999).

Western imperialism, or at the very least, found itself cut off from the raw materials and markets it would need to survive and prosper. Imperial expansion therefore tended to be seen as having a defensive dimension as well as a liberating mission – in Korea, China, and elsewhere the choice was to either take control of these regions for Japan or to see them fall under the control of other, potentially hostile powers.[18]

Of course, other, less noble motives also were at play behind the creation of the Japanese Empire, including the quest to maximize Japanese power and to bolster the legitimacy of its ruling elites.[19] Nonetheless, there was a considerable difference between the circumstances under which war broke out in Asia as opposed to Europe, and a plausible case can be made – as Japanese conservatives often did after 1945 – that Japanese motives were more legitimate than those of the West even by the higher normative standards obtained after 1945. Thanks in part to the shattering blow the Japanese invasions dealt to the Western colonial structures, the dismantling of the European empires and their spheres of influence in East and South-East Asia was greatly accelerated. Moreover, the regimes that emerged out of the ruins of the Japanese empire were not, in the main, any more democratic than that of the Japanese colonial administrations (with the important exception of the Philippines), and a good case could be made that Japanese rule had contributed considerably to their economic and social development.[20]

(5) The fifth and final factor that made the attribution of responsibility for the war and its consequences to Japan was the fact that Japanese imperial expansion took place over a considerable period of time, under several different governments operating under changing international circumstances. There was no single leader like Adolph Hitler, nor a single political party, like the Nazis, who dominated decision making during Japan's gradual expansion into Asia. While Emperor Hirohito was the head of state from 1926 on, most historians agree that he wielded power only sporadically and cannot have been said to have been the mastermind behind Japan's decision to go to war with China and the West (although he was certainly more of an active participant in Japanese policy making than the mild-mannered marine biologist that Japanese governments made him out to be after 1945).[21] Moreover, Japanese decision making was extraordinarily complex and opaque, with competing power centers

---

[18] W.G. Beasley, *Japanese Imperialism, 1894–1895* (Oxford: Oxford University Press, 1987), pp. 46, 79–80.

[19] Michael Barnhart, *Japan Prepares for Total War: The Search for Economic Security* (Ithaca, NY: Cornell University Press, 1987).

[20] On Japanese contributions to the development of the region, see Atuhl Kohli, "Where do High-Growth Political Economies Come From? The Japanese Lineage of Korea's 'Developmental State,'" in Meredith Woo Cummings, ed., *The Developmental State* (Ithaca, NY: Cornell University Press, 1999), pp. 93–136.

[21] Herbert P. Blix, *Hirohito and the Making of Modern Japan* (New York: Harper Collins, 2000).

and deeply rooted institutional rivalries that prevented the formulation of anything akin to one coherent grand strategy.[22]

As a result, it is difficult to disentangle the history of Japan's involvement in World War II from the broader sweep of Japan's imperial history. Although the Third Reich was obviously the product of modern German history, the singular character of Auschwitz and the Nazi regime and the clear political shift that occurred in Germany as a result of Hitler's ascent to power in 1933 provided a convenient (some would say all too convenient) break point around which all subsequent discussions of German guilt are organized. In contrast, there is no comparably clear watershed in the history of Japanese expansion and the descent into militarist rule in the 1930s and 1940s. The events of 1941–1945 (the War in the Pacific) are closely linked to the events of 1937–1941 (the War against China), whose origins in turn can be traced back to the Manchurian incident in 1931, when Japan took over much of Northern China. Although many historians would argue that the Manchurian incident represented a significant departure from the more moderate diplomatic policies pursued by Shidehara Kijuro, it too was in many respects an extension of the Japanese policy toward China that began with the first Sino-Japanese War of 1894–1895.

Consequently, efforts to attribute responsibility for any particular set of atrocities to any particular leader or group of leaders would be very problematic, a fact that would greatly complicate the efforts of the Allies to prosecute Japan's wartime leadership for war crimes and crimes against humanity. Moreover, the complexity of the historical issues driving the evolution of the empire would strengthen Japanese resistance to accepting blame for any given atrocity. Whereas most Germans could readily agree that the invasion of Poland was the result of Hitler's megalomania, the invasion of China in 1937 tended to be viewed as the product of the broader sweep of modern Asian history going back all the way to Japan's forcible opening by the West by Commodore Perry's black ships in 1854.[23]

---

[22] Perhaps the most incisive commentary on Japanese prewar decision making remains Maruyama Masao, in *Thought and Behavior in Modern Japanese Politics*, trans. Ivan Morris, (London and New York: Oxford University Press, 1963). Maruyama argued that everything was done in the name of the emperor, but no single figure coordinated, much less controlled, the various actions that were taken. As a result, there was no one leader or group of leaders who could be said to control Japanese policy. Japanese policy making could be likened to a web without a spider. Maruyama called this the "structure of irresponsibility" (*musekinin no Kozo*).

[23] One of the chief ideologists of Japanese Imperial expansion and architect of the 1931 Manchurian incident, Ishiwara Kanji argued in his trial after the war that all of Japan's actions, up to 1941, needs to be understood as a long and protracted defensive reaction to the aggressive imperialism of the Western powers who had forced Japan out of its feudal seclusion under the Tokugawa Shogunate. See Mark Peattie, *Ishiwara Kanji and Japan's Confrontation with the West* (Princeton: Princeton University Press, 1975), and Gewn and Meirion Harries, *Sheathing the Sword: The Demilitarization of Postwar Japan* (New York: MacMillan, 1987).

In sum, from a Historical Determinist position, there are numerous reasons to believe that Japan should develop a very different historical narrative from that of postwar Germany, one with a far more attenuated sense of guilt or responsibility. The war and Japanese occupation of conquered countries had been less destructive; the evidence of Japanese atrocities was less solid; there had been no genocidal plan for the destruction of an entire people; Japan's motives for going to war were more complex and perhaps even more justifiable by contemporary standards than those of Germany; and finally, it is far more difficult to assign to individual leaders the responsibility for the decision to go to war.

Japanese feelings of responsibility were further attenuated by many of the same factors that played a mitigating role in the German and Austrian cases. The Japanese people as well had been at the receiving end of a tremendous amount of violence. Approximately 3 million Japanese had died during the war, including close to a million civilians who perished as a result of the fire bombings and the atomic bombings of Hiroshima and Nagasaki. Japanese civilian casualties during the invasion of Okinawa had been particularly high. As many as 200,000 – one-third of the island's population – perished during the campaign, including many thousands who were forced to commit suicide by the military rather than suffer the indignity of surrender. Most major Japanese cities had been reduced to rubble by intense bombings. Food intake had been reduced to around 1,000 calories a day for the majority of the population. By the end of the war, economic production had collapsed, and many Japanese civilians were starving to death. Only a massive injection of food aid by the American occupation averted a major famine in the winter of 1945–1946. Adding to the misery were the 3 million Japanese refugees generated by the collapse of the empire, many of whom had suffered greatly at the hands of Soviet forces who had plunged into Manchuria and Northern Korean in the final days of the war.[24] Even on the American occupied main islands occurred many incidents of violence, in particular those of a sexual nature. In 1945, there were 40 reported incidents of rape a day involving Allied forces.[25]

In addition, as in Europe, ordinary Japanese felt they had only limited control over the course of events. Even at the height of Taisho democracy in the 1920s, when universal manhood suffrage was introduced and there was considerable freedom of debate and expression, Japanese politics was dominated by a closely integrated – if fractious – set of economic, social, and political elites. Although there were elected officials, the ability of Japanese political parties to influence the actions of the state was decidedly limited, especially in the critical domains of defense and foreign policy. What freedoms there were slowly evaporated

---

[24] See John Dower, *Embracing Defeat: Japan in the Wake of World War II* (New York: W.W. Norton, 1999), pp. 45–52, 89–92; Lori Watt, *When Empire Comes Home: Repatriation and Reintegration in Postwar Japan* (Cambridge, MA: Harvard University Press, 2009).

[25] Dower, *Embracing Defeat*, op. cit., p. 579, footnote 16.

during the 1930s, as the military consolidated its power through a series of coups, assassinations, and foreign crises (many of which had been engineered by the Japanese armed forces).[26] Discipline inside the military was brutal, and wartime controls and censorship of the civilian population – although not as harsh as in the Third Reich – were nonetheless quite effective in squelching domestic opposition to Imperial policies.

Nonetheless, it is important to recognize the limitations of the simple Historical Determinist argument that, because the Japanese had done less awful things than the Germans, they were less inclined toward contrition. The destruction caused by the war and Japanese Imperial policy had been immense. The Allied powers presented clear and overwhelming evidence of large-scale brutality committed by Japanese forces, and there is considerable evidence that many Japanese were well aware that atrocities had taken place, even if they could not be sure of the scale of the crimes. One reflection of this was the relative willingness of postwar Japanese writers – as compared to their German and Austrian counterparts – to write openly about their experiences. Beginning quite early in the postwar period, there was an outpouring of literature in Japan dealing with the experience of war (*sensō taiken ki*). Although until the 1970s there existed a tendency to avoid the subject of Japanese atrocities, references were in fact made to them. For example, Yukio Mishima's 1955 short story "Botan" (peonies) centers on a character, the retired army Colonel Kawamata, who after the war plants a peony in his garden for every one of the 580 women he personally killed in China – not in penance, but as obscene trophies of his crimes. Although the official narrative adopted after the occupation would generally avoid any expression of guilt, on the unofficial level at least, there was a great deal more public awareness of the horrors of the war than is often assumed outside of Japan.[27]

Comparison with other cases underlines the limits of a simple Historical Determinist argument as well. Other countries responsible for smaller-scale crimes would come to show at least as much guilt as postwar Japan did. For example, in the 1970s France became virtually obsessed with the role the Vichy regime played in the Holocaust, even though the crimes committed by the French – atrocious as they were – involved vastly fewer victims and

---

[26] Gordon M. Berger, *Parties out of Power in Japan, 1931–1941* (Princeton: Princeton University Press, 1977).

[27] Petra Buchholz has gone so far as to suggest that there has been a greater willingness on the part of the Japanese to describe their wartime experiences, including atrocities, than was true in the German case, perhaps because in the German case there was a well-grounded fear of prosecution. See Buchholz, "Tales of War: Autobiographies and Private Memories in Japan and Germany," in Takashi Inoguchi and Lyn Jackson, *Memories of War: The Second World War in Japanese Historical Memory in Comparative Perspective* (Tokyo: United Nations University Press, 1995). For a more detailed, side-by-side comparison of postwar German and Japanese fiction, see Ernestine Schlant and J. Thomas Rimer, eds., *Legacies and Ambiguities: Postwar Fiction and Culture in West Germany and Japan* (Baltimore, MD: Johns Hopkins University Press, 1991).

occurred under even more extenuating circumstances.[28] On the other hand, other countries that were directly implicated in even worse atrocities than those of Imperial Japan have evinced even less a sense of responsibility, as was the case in Austria until the 1990s. In addition, although Japanese feelings of victimization and powerlessness in the early postwar period may have helped suppress feelings of guilt, as we have seen elsewhere, this does not explain why Japan failed to develop a more contrite historical narrative, as occurred in West Germany in the 1960s or in the Austria of the 1990s. In other words, although actual historical events undoubtedly had an important impact on the official historical narrative that Japan has constructed, as in the other cases discussed, we are compelled to look elsewhere for a more complete explanation of why Japan's official narrative was relatively impenitent.

### Shame Versus Guilt: Cultural Explanations

Could Japanese culture be the explanation for Japan's relative lack of remorse? This was not as much of an issue in the cases previously examined because, despite the significant differences between Austria and Germany, overall the two nations are culturally quite close. In the Japanese case, however, we have to examine the degree to which Japanese reactions may have been shaped by the very different religious and philosophical traditions of Asia. From early on in discussions of why Japan may have been unwilling to confront its moral responsibility for the horrors of the war, there have been those who argued that culture may have played an important role. The first and most prominent exponent of this argument was Ruth Benedict, whose extraordinarily influential *The Chrysanthemum and the Sword* helped shape the debate on this issue for over a generation.

Ruth Benedict and her intellectual successors argued that in Japanese society control over its members is exercised by means of the inculcation of a sense of shame. Failure to adhere to the norms of the group results in ostracism. This leads to a system of what Benedict calls "situational ethics." Individual behavior is judged by whether that behavior was approved by the social group at the time and the place where that behavior occurred. In contrast, she argued,

---

[28] On French debates over history, see above all Henry Rousso, *The Vichy Syndrome: History and Memory in France since 1944* (Cambridge: Harvard University Press, 1991); and Eric Conan, Henry Rousso, Nathan Bracher, trans., *Vichy: An Ever-Present Past* (Hannover, NH: Dartmouth Press, 1998). French collaboration in the Holocaust led to a great many deaths. At the same time, the scale of the crimes (perhaps 60,000 people deported) and the circumstances under which they occurred suggest that France, even more than Japan, should have a diluted sense of responsibility for the crimes of the 1940 to 1944 period. Instead, beginning already in the 1970s, there emerged a burning political debate over the willing participation of many Frenchmen in the extermination of the Jews and the establishment of authoritarianism in France. This led to the establishment of an official historical narrative that was at least as penitent of Japan during the same time period. Indeed, the official French narrative was in several respects more penitent than that of Japan – for instance, Holocaust denial was made a crime.

in the West social control relies on feelings of guilt. The individual is expected to obey a moral code that is to be found inside him or herself. It is therefore possible for the individual to feel guilt about actions even if those actions were deemed appropriate by the group at the time they occurred.[29]

Benedict's basic argument has been elaborated upon over a generation of scholars. For instance, the eminent historian J. Victor Koschmann built on Benedict's ideas by tracing the origins of situational ethics back to differences between how Christianity and Asian religions such as Buddhism and Shintoism conceive of the relationship between the mundane and the transcendent worlds. Unlike in the Western Judeo-Christian tradition, he argues, there is no clear distinction in Asian thinking between the sacred and the profane, the law of god and the law of man. In the Asian tradition the divine is immanent in the world as it is. Therefore, there is no higher moral standard that can serve as a guide for action other than the standards that are created in this world. The system of situational ethics as opposed to individual conscience (or shame versus guilt, to use Benedict's terminology) is thus rooted in radically different understandings of the sacred and the profane.[30] This particular view of the relationship between this world and the divine dovetails with the Japanese emphasis on the group as the primary source of ethical and moral standards. As a result of these profound differences in cultural understandings, many commentators have expressed doubt whether it is possible – or fair – to expect the Japanese to exhibit feelings of guilt in the Western sense.[31]

It is possible to question these arguments on numerous grounds. For one, it is open to debate whether Benedict's and Koschmann's portrayals of Japanese culture were accurate even at the time they were made. Their applicability to contemporary Japan is more questionable still.[32] More plausible are the arguments made by numerous commentators who, rather than singling out "unchanging"(that is, more or less permanent) cultural elements as the reason for Japan's attenuated sense of guilt, focus on specific features of Japanese culture and society during the time of the Japanese empire. Among the first to do so was Maruyama Masao, one of the most influential figures in postwar Japanese intellectual life, who argued that the structure of Japanese society in the early twentieth century created both a sense of helplessness on the part of individual Japanese and a propensity toward brutality on the part of Japanese society as a whole. Maruyama argued that the opaque system of decision making in Japan, where everything was done in the name of the Emperor, but the emperor himself played no active role, created a situation in which individual leaders did not feel responsible for their actions. As Maruyama famously put it in his comparison of the Tokyo War crimes trials with Nuremberg, whereas

---

[29] Benedict, *Chrysanthemum and the Sword*, op. cit., chapter 10.

[30] Victor Koschmann, "Introduction," op. cit.

[31] Gwenn and Merion Harries, *Sheathing the Sword*, op. cit., pp. 176–178.

[32] For a review of Benedict's reception in Japan, see Sonia Ryang, "Chrysanthemum's Strange Life: Ruth Benedict in Postwar Japan," *The China Review* 1:2 (Spring 2002), pp. 1–28.

Goering admitted his guilt and roared with nihilistic laughter, Tojo and the other defendants feebly protested that they had no choice but to act as they did. Maruyama referred to this phenomenon as Imperial Japan's "system of irresponsibility" (*musekinin no taisei*) and argued that as a result Japan lacked the strong sense of guilt that Germany developed. This system of decision making was rooted in and reinforced by the ideology of the Imperial state, where the emperor was the divine sovereign (*Kokutai*) and the people, his subjects. According to Maruyama, this system effectively obliterated any sense of individual morality, and made any action, no matter how atrocious, acceptable as long as it ostensibly was done for the good of the empire. Maruyama also argued that the hierarchical structure of Japanese society, with the Emperor at its apex and the conquered or colonized Asian peoples at the base, encouraged a pattern of brutality in which those at higher rungs of authority reflexively dominated and bullied those below them.[33] Ironically, although Maruyama himself favored confronting the question of Japan's moral responsibility for its actions, his analysis likewise shifted the blame from individuals to the ideological and social system in which they were embedded.[34]

Other commentators, such as Gwen and Merion Harries, similarly have argued that the military ethos that characterized Imperial Japan, together with the increasingly virulent anti-Western propaganda and a growing sense of Japanese racial superiority in the 1930s and 1940s, help explain the readiness of the Japanese to perpetrate atrocities. The Japanese army in particular, with its emphasis on tight military discipline, its ready recourse to extreme forms of punishment, and its use of a romanticized image of the samurai as a role model for it soldiers (what sometimes has been referred to as "neobushidosim"), made the Imperial forces particularly prone to violence. The Harries and other observers note that during earlier periods, Japanese forces were highly praised for their discipline and restraint in dealing with the local population. For instance, during the Boxer rebellion of 1900, the Japanese expeditionary forces were far less likely to prey upon the civilian population than were their French, German, and Russian counterparts. Likewise, during the Russo-Japanese War of 1904–1905, the Japanese treated captured prisoners of war fairly and in accordance with international law. The Russians, in contrast, brutalized captured Japanese soldiers, many of whom died while in captivity. The savagery, with which the Japanese army behaved during World War II[35]

---

[33] Maruyama Masao, *Thought and Behavior*, op. cit., p. 19.

[34] See Rikki Kersten, *Defeat and Democracy in Post-war Japan: Maruyama Masao and the Search for Autonomy* (London: Routledge), pp. 31–35.

[35] Harries, *Sheathing the Sword*, pp. 177–179, and Harries, *Soldiers of the Sun: The Rise and Fall of the Imperial Army* (New York: Random house, 1994). This line of reasoning is more consonant with more contemporary views of the nature of culture. Earlier generations of cultural research have tended to see culture as a fixed or at least enduring feature of a social system that is largely homogenous and with clearly demarcated boundaries. In recent decades, researchers

was thus a historically contingent phenomenon, the product of the political and ideological climate within the empire at the time of the war.

However, even if one grants that there were cultural, ideological, or sociological factors – be they of an enduring nature or reflective of more transitory historical conditions – that may have encouraged violence in Japanese society before 1945 and weakened any sense of individual responsibility the Japanese may have felt for their actions, this does not necessarily mean that the Japanese in the postwar era did – or do – not have a capacity to feel some basic sense of remorse for the past. There is evidence that after 1945 many Japanese did indeed exhibit very real and profound feelings of remorse. Even during the war, Imperial censors went to some lengths to prevent reports of Japanese brutality from reaching the Japanese public, suggesting that even at the time at least some Japanese viewed the widespread depredations against the local civilian population as unacceptable.[36] Later, when the occupation authorities first began to share with the Japanese public reports of wartime atrocities, there were considerable expressions of mortification on the part of at least some Japanese. The mother of one young soldier went so far as to say that if he were guilty of the sort of atrocities that were being reported, it would be better if he were executed than if he were to come home.[37] Other Japanese went further, trying to gather the bones of Chinese and Korean forced laborers who had died or been killed during their time in Japan and return them to their families in their home countries.[38]

Indeed, it is precisely because the knowledge of atrocities provokes feelings of remorse in ordinary Japanese that history has become such a contentious issue in Japanese politics. If the Japanese had no capacity to have such feelings, there would be little need for internal debate on the matter. However, the Left (especially in recent decades) has sought to emphasize Japanese wrongdoing to provoke feelings of remorse that would bolster their antimilitary agenda. In contrast, their opponents on the Right deplore such a "self-flagellating" view of history and try to deny or downplay Japanese atrocities to foster what they characterize as a healthy sense of national pride. Neither strategy would make

---

have tended to view culture as dynamic and evolving sets of beliefs and values that are unevenly spread across a social system that is often highly fractured and with ambiguous boundaries. For analyses of Japanese culture in these terms, see Stephen Vlastos, ed., *Mirror of Modernity: Invented Traditions of Japan* (Berkeley: University of California Press, 1998), and Tessa Morris-Suzuki, *Re-Inventing Japan: Time, Space, Nation* (Armonk, NY: M.E. Sharpe, 1998).

[36] See introduction to Tatsuzo Ishikawa, *Soldiers Alive*, trans. Zljko Cipris (Honolulu: University of Hawaii Press, 2003).

[37] See John Dower, *Embracing Defeat: Japan in the Wake of World War II* (New York: Norton, 1999), p. 506, and pp. 504–508.

[38] Some of the Japanese who the author has interviewed expressed considerable anguish over the treatment of Korean laborers that they had witnessed during the war years. Inoki Masamichi, a prominent defense intellectual, for instance recalled vividly watching the transport of such laborers in obviously miserable condition toward the end of the war.

much sense in a society where the concept of guilt and remorse – or something quite close to it – did not exist.[39]

Arguments that the relative lack of Japanese remorse is rooted in Japanese culture are further weakened when we consider the Japanese case from a comparative perspective. Whereas Christian Germany has shown a greater sense of guilt, as we have seen, equally Christian Austria has for considerable periods of time been even less remorseful than Japan. A particularly stubborn advocate of a "thick" culturalist explanation for guilt might choose to emphasize the role of Catholicism. As the Federal Republic after 1945 was approximately 50 percent Protestant, and Austria was almost totally Catholic, it might be reasoned that Catholicism, with its more forgiving stance on questions of guilt, might explain why Austria was less remorseful than West Germany. Does it, however, explain why the official narrative of Buddhist-Shintoist Japan was – as we shall see – relatively more remorseful than Austria until the 1990s? Although it might be possible to push the argument further, at a minimum the credibility of a simple Culturalist explanation is weakened considerably.

If neither historical circumstances nor deeply rooted cultural predispositions provide us with an adequate explanation for the development of Japan's official narrative, it is logical to examine next the possible influence of the ways in which the issue of Japanese responsibility for the horrors of the war in the Pacific was pursued in the postwar period. To what degree did Instrumentalist factors play the key role in creating a relatively impenitent official narrative in Japan? The logical point of departure for such an analysis is the U.S.-led occupation of Japan.

## Rice Bowl Penitents: America and Japanese Guilt 1945–1952

As in Germany, the Allied Powers were determined to hold Japan's wartime leadership responsible for the war and its immense horrors. Behind this determination were strong domestic political as well as practical foreign policy considerations. First, within the Allied nations public opinion strongly favored punishing Japan. From the standpoint of the American public, it was Japan that had started the war with its sneak attack on Pearl Harbor, and close to half of all U.S. casualties during the war had been suffered in the Pacific theater. Far from being a "forgotten Holocaust," in 1945, the crimes of the Japanese vied with those of the Germans as the epitome of evil in American eyes, a perception that was greatly reinforced by wartime propaganda that portrayed the Japanese as a vicious, subhuman enemy.[40] Once Japan had surrendered, the overwhelming public mood in the United States was that the time for a

---

[39] For an example of right wing portrayal of Japanese history, see for instance Fujioka Nobukatsu and Nishio Kanji, *Kokumin no Yudan: Rekishi Kyōkasho ga abunai* (Tokyo: PHP Kenkyūjo, 1996); and *Kyōkasho ga oshienai Rekishi* (Tokyo: Sankei Shuppan, 1996).

[40] For a brilliant comparison of American and Japanese wartime propaganda, see John Dower, *War without Mercy*, op. cit.

reckoning had arrived. According to public opinion polls after the war, fully 88 percent of the American public supported war crimes tribunals, and 67 percent favored the execution of Tojo Hideki, the Japanese prime minister at the time of Pearl Harbor, and the rest of the senior Japanese leadership. The American press was similarly eager for punishment, and State Department analyses of the American press and media indicated that the predominant view was that the occupation was too lenient with the Japanese.[41]

In addition to domestic political considerations, there was the broader strategic question of where Japan eventually would fit into the new world order. Although various schemes were considered for finding ways of permanently pacifying Japan (including one proposal from an anthropologist at the Smithsonian Institution for cross breeding the Japanese with supposedly less bellicose Pacific islanders[42]), in the long run it became increasingly clear that Japan would eventually reemerge as an independent nation with the greatest industrial and potential military power in Asia. To prevent Japan from becoming once again a threat to peace and stability, U.S. policy makers concluded – as they had with respect to Germany – that it would be necessary to remake Japan and remove those elements that were believed to have inclined it toward aggression.

This grand enterprise, often described as one of the greatest attempts at social engineering in human history, entailed not only eliminating the Japanese army and navy as institutions, but fundamentally changing Japanese attitudes and political and social institutions as well. Its ultimate aim was to transform once bellicose Japan into a peaceful, democratic nation fully integrated into the world community. An essential component of this bold undertaking was to convince the Japanese people that theirs had not only been a military defeat, but a moral one as well. To this end the occupation authorities reached for the same panoply of instruments that had been employed in Germany and Austria, including war crimes trials, purges, and an extensive effort to reeducate the Japanese through the press, media, and educational establishment.

In the end, the occupation succeeded magnificently in its larger goal of turning Japan into a peaceful, democratic nation. The effort to convince the Japanese of their moral culpability, however, was by and large a failure. Although by the end of the occupation, Japan would formally acknowledge its guilt, its official historical narrative remained resolutely impenitent, and although there was some general awareness of the horrors that had been committed, on the whole the Japanese public and political elites exhibited few signs of contrition.

---

[41] Gwen and Meirion Harries, *Sheathing the Sword*, p. 99, 103.

[42] In 1942, Roosevelt had asked the prominent anthropologist Ales Hrdlicka, well known for his strong eugenicist views, to investigate the issue. See Rudolf V. A. Jannssens, *"What Future for Japan?" US Wartime Planning for the Postwar Era, 1942–1945* (Amsterdam and Atlanta, GA: Rodopoi B.V., 1995), pp. 52–53.

At the time, however, it did not seem a foregone conclusion that the campaign to convince Japan of their guilt would fail. There were masses of evidence available regarding Japanese war crimes and the brutalization of occupied areas – in the form of photographic evidence and eyewitness accounts. Moreover, the occupation authorities enjoyed tremendous leverage at the end of the war and had unimpeded access to the Japanese people and political elites. The Japanese empire was utterly defeated, the economy had collapsed, and the Japanese people were dependent on the United States for their very survival. The Soviet Union, which had swept through Northern China, Korea, and the Kurile islands, was at Japan's door step and demanded a direct role in the occupation of Japan, much as they had in Austria and Germany in Europe. Without U.S. support, famine, partition, and possibly worse seemed very real possibilities. In addition, unlike Germany and Austria, where the United States had to share control with the other occupying powers – including the Soviet Union – the United States was de facto solely in control of occupation policy in Japan.[43] In short, occupation policy making in Japan was relatively untrammeled by international or Japanese domestic political considerations.

Just as importantly, in the wake of the catastrophic defeat there was a great ground swell of popular anger within Japan aimed at the Imperial government and the "militarist clique."[44] Fears that such sentiments could translate into a revolutionary movement that could topple the government and transform the existing social, political, and economic order – much as defeat in 1918 had paved the way for the Bolshevik Revolution in Russia – had been the primary motive behind the decision to surrender in August 1945.[45] Popular discontent did not end with surrender, and in the midst of the pain and suffering of the defeat there swelled up a fierce debate over who should be held responsible for the war – the question of *Sensōsekinin*, or responsibility for the war, as it was referred to at the time. On August 28, only a few days after the surrender, the opening salvo in this debate began when the new prime minister of Japan, Prince Higashikuni Naruhiko, called on the nation to engage in what he called the "general contrition of the nation" (*Ichiokunin no sōzange* – literally repentance of 100 million) and blamed defeat in the war on the material superiority of the Allies.[46] By implication, the prime minister was arguing that the defeat

---

[43] There was a joint Far Eastern Commission that oversaw the Allied Council for Japan, both bodies which included representatives from all the victorious Allied powers including (nationalist) China and the Soviet Union. For the most part, however, it merely rubber stamped the decisions taken by SCAP (the Supreme Commander Allied Powers) in Japan.

[44] Yoshida Yutaka, *Nihonjin Sensōkan*, (Tokyo: Iwanami, 1995), pp. 27–29; Dower, *Embracing Defeat*.

[45] On the thinking of the Japanese elite at the time of the defeat, see John Dower, *Empire and Aftermath: Yoshida Shigeru and the Japanese Experience, 1875–1954* (Cambridge, MA: Harvard University Press, 1979). On the mood of the Japanese people, see Dower, *Embracing Defeat: Japan in the Wake of World War II* (New York: W.W. Norton, 1999).

[46] A case could be made that this argument was already prefigured in the Emperor's address to the Japanese people on August 15 in which he announced the end of the war and de facto

had been the shared responsibility of the nation and was not the fault of the leadership and the Emperor. Higashikuni's efforts to deflect criticism, however, were not successful, and even centrist politicians such as Ashida Hitoshi, founder of the Liberal Party, pushed for a more far-reaching inquiry.[47] Leaders further to the Left were even more insistent that the issue of war responsibility should be pursued. As shocking revelations of Japanese atrocities were made public, major Japanese newspapers such the *Asahi* came out in favor of prosecuting war criminals.[48]

At the same time, the occupation faced formidable obstacles in its efforts to create a narrative of Japanese guilt. Although the Japanese population had been thoroughly disillusioned by their defeat, there was considerable evidence that many of the basic beliefs and attitudes that had helped support the expansion of the old Imperial order had survived the defeat. According to the first opinion survey taken by the occupation authorities in December 1945, 45 percent (vs. 42 percent) of those surveyed believed that Japan had to annex Manchuria in 1931 to survive; 59 percent (vs. 39 percent) believed that China was not a nation, but a collection of various people without political unity; 69 percent (vs. 22 percent) believed that if Chinese agitators had not created confusion, the Sino-Japanese war could have been averted in 1937; 61 percent (vs. 30 percent) believed that if the Chinese people had understood Japan's true intentions, the Japanese army would probably have won the war; and finally a full 86 percent (vs. 9 percent) thought that the Japanese people were superior to the other peoples of East Asia.[49] Although minds could be changed, clearly the Allies faced an uphill battle.

At the elite level, the occupation was handicapped by the way in which Japan had been defeated and by the chaotic character of Japanese politics in the immediate postwar period. Although in theory Japan had suffered a total defeat, its defeat was much less total than that of Germany or Austria. Unlike the Nazi regime, which had fought to the bitter end, Japan had surrendered, and the Japanese state never ceased to operate. Not only did this mean that the Japanese government had time to destroy or conceal much of the documentation that could have been used to demonstrate its involvement in the most atrocious aspects of the war, it also meant that by and large the very same people who had been in charge of the Japanese empire before the surrender remained in charge at the start of the occupation. Since the U.S.-led occupation did not have the resources to govern Japan on their own – given the critical shortage of personnel with the requisite language skills – they were heavily dependent on the old bureaucracy for the day-to-day running of the country.

surrendered. In that address, he blamed the defeat on "a most cruel and inhuman weapon," the atomic bomb.

47  Yoshida Yutaka, *Nihonjin Sensōkan*, op. cit., pp. 26–27; James Orr, *The Victim as Hero*, op. cit., pp. 25–27.
48  John Dower, *Embracing Defeat*, op. cit., pp. 474–476.
49  Yoshida Yutaka, *Nihonjin no Sensōkan*, op. cit., p. 53.

This gave the old Japanese ruling class considerable leverage over their occupiers, and naturally they sought to use their influence to hold onto power and to insulate themselves from prosecution.

Even more importantly, the United States faced serious difficulties in finding elites to work with who were both untainted by their connections with the old regime and willing to support the objectives of the American occupation. Most Japanese, including the majority of those on the Left, had been successfully co-opted by the Imperial system, far more so than was true in either of the far more short-lived regimes of Nazi Germany or Austria under the Third Reich. There was no substantial group of political exiles who came back to Japan to restart their careers after the collapse of the empire – political leaders such as Herbert Wehner or Willy Brandt in Germany or Bruno Kreisky in Austria, or intellectuals such as Carl Friedrichs and Karl Jaspers. Nor was there a large pool of stalwart opponents of the militarist regime who could be called upon to serve as the leaders of a new Japan.

There had been those who were opposed to the military clique that had gradually gained control of policy making in the 1930s and 1940s. For the most part, however, even these opponents of the military had been far more implicated in the running of the empire. For instance, Yoshida Shigeru, who was to become the most influential Japanese prime minister in the early post-1945 period, had been a member of a group of leaders who opposed the war and was briefly imprisoned by the police for his activities. However, Yoshida had also been a protégé of Prince Konoe Fumimaro – prime minister at the outbreak of the Second Sino-Japanese in 1937 and creator of the quasi-fascist Imperial Rule Assistance Association – and had spent much of his professional life as a diplomat supporting Imperial policy in China.[50] Naturally Yoshida, given his personal ties and experiences, was far more sympathetic to the old regime than Adenauer or Leopold Figl (the first postwar Austrian chancellor).[51] Yoshida and other conservative leaders at all costs wished to confine the blame for the war with the United States to the senior military leadership and were unwilling to raise the broader issue to what degree Imperial policies in general – which they had supported – had been wrong or immoral.

[50] See John Dower, *Yoshida Shigeru*, op. cit. For a revealing comparison of Yoshida and Konrad Adenauer, which underlines the extent to which Yoshida was far more deeply implicated in the pre-1945 regime, while Adenauer had been an active opponent, see Ōtake Hideo, *Yoshida to Adenauaa* (Tokyo: Chūōkōronsha, 1986).

[51] Figl had survived both Dachau and Mauthausen; however, his successor, Julius Raab, although ousted from political office after the Anschluss, had also been a member of the archconservative *Heimwehr* and enjoyed the protection of important figures in the Nazi administration of Austria. In contrast, Yoshida had been particularly close to Hirota Koki, the only Japanese civilian class A war criminal executed by the allies for his part in the events leading up to the Sino-Japanese War and his involvement in sealing the Tripartite Pact allying Japan with Nazi Germany and Fascist Italy. Richard Finn speculates that it was only by accident that Yoshida had not become a member of the Hirota cabinet and thus potentially a class A war criminal himself. See Richard B. Finn, *Winners in Peace: MacArthur, Yoshida and Postwar Japan* (Berkeley and Los Angeles: University of California Press, 1992), p. 20.

Other leading political figures on the Right were even more deeply implicated in the old regime. For instance, Kishi Nobusuke, who was a senior faction leader in the ruling conservative party, the Liberal Democratic Party (LDP), and prime minister from 1957 to 1960, had been a former senior official in the colonial administration of Manchuria and then munitions minister in the Tojo Cabinet. As such, he had been one of the signatories of the declaration of war on the United States in 1941. Shigemitsu Mamoru, another leading conservative politician, had been the foreign minister who signed the instrument of surrender at the end of the war in the Pacific. After the war, Shigemitsu was convicted as a class A war criminal and sentenced to seven years in prison. Nonetheless, he came to serve as foreign minister again from 1954 to 1956. Kaya Okinori was another high-level official in the occupation of China and finance minister in the Konoe cabinet who was sentenced by the Allies to life imprisonment for his role in, among other things, raising revenue through the sale of opium to the Chinese. Ironically enough, the former drug dealer Kaya would become a minister of justice in the 1960s. Although there were important figures in postwar Germany with a past tainted by association with the Nazis – most notably Adenauer's chief of staff, Hans Globke – there was no one even close to the prominence of Shigemitsu or Kaya, much less Kishi. Even in the case of Austria, where former Nazis played an influential political role, the Far Right was integrated into the system as a separate political movement, first as the VdU and then as the FPÖ. They did not permeate the power structure the way their counterparts did in Japan. Naturally, men such as Kishi, Shigemitsu, and Kaya were even less interested than Yoshida in promoting a historical narrative that would have undermined their legitimacy.[52]

Those Japanese who had been truly opposed to Japan's Imperial policies were for the most part on the Left (and even many leftists, as was mentioned earlier, had been supporters of the empire). Many on the Left vigorously supported pursuing the issue of Japan's responsibility for the war (*Sensō Sekinin*), partly out of genuine moral outrage and partly as a means of attacking their opponents on the Right. At the same time, however, the Left chose to focus not so much on the crimes Japan had committed in Asia (which they openly acknowledged), but rather on the suffering the war had brought to the Japanese people. They calculated that by doing so, they would be better able to mobilize popular sympathies against their primary political target after 1945 – the emerging security relationship with the United States.[53] In addition, the Japanese Left was far more closely aligned with the Soviet Union and the People's Republic of China than was true of their counterparts in Austria and Germany. Nonaka Sanzō, for example, was a hero of the Left and later longtime chairman of the Japanese Communist Party who had spent much of the war with Mao Zedong. After the cold war had ended, it was revealed that even after the war he had been working for the Soviet Union. Although Nonaka may

[52] See Wakafumi Yoshibumi, *The Postwar Conservative View of Asia*, op. cit., pp. 126–134.
[53] See Orr, *The Victim as Hero*, chapter 3; and Dower, "The Bombed."

have been extreme in terms of his being directly beholden to the Communist powers, much of the Japanese Left was remarkably ideological in its world view and ready to accept Soviet or Chinese propaganda at face value until well into the cold war.[54]

The contrast with Willy Brandt and Herbert Wehner of the German Social Democratic Party, or their counterparts in the Austrian Socialist party, could not be greater. Although Brandt and Wehner were committed socialists, they were also harshly critical of the "real existing Socialism" that they saw in the Soviet Union and Eastern Europe. The same could be said of Bruno Kreisky and the Austrian socialists. As a result, the German and Austrian leftists were far more willing than their Japanese counterparts to seek common ground with their conservative opponents and far more favorable to maintaining good relations with the United States.

The political situation in Japan was thus far more polarized than was the case in Austria and Germany. The more moderate elements on the Right and Center of the Japanese political spectrum were more closely tied to the wartime regime; the Japanese Left was more bitterly critical of U.S. strategic designs and potentially more susceptible to Communist influence. For the Left, the conservatives were unreformed fascists. In the eyes of the Right, the progressives were Communist agents or dupes. The polarized nature of Japanese politics had a self-reinforcing character. The conservatism of the Right increased suspicions on the Left, while the Communist sympathies of the Left deepened the conservatism of the Right and alienated genuinely centrist leaders. These political realities would greatly complicate almost every element in the U.S. campaign to instill a contrite historical narrative in Japan, including the war crimes tribunals, the purges, public reeducation, and reparations.

## The Trials

As in Europe, the Allied powers conducted an extensive series of war crimes tribunals in Asia. These were broken down into three categories – class A war crimes (the senior Japanese political and military leadership, charged with crimes against Peace), class B (crimes against the laws of war), and class C (crimes against humanity). Of these, the twenty-eight indicted class A war criminals were by far of the greatest symbolic importance, and their trial before the International Military Tribunal in the Far East (IMFTE) in Tokyo, the Asian counterpart to the Nuremberg trials in Europe, was intended to serve as a showcase in which the Allied version of history would be presented and impressed upon the Japanese people. In addition to the IMFTE trials in Tokyo, the U.S. occupation tried 1,334 Japanese as class B and C criminals inside of

---

[54] Kojima Ryō, *Hangarii Jiken to Nihon: 1956 Nen Shisōshiteki Kōsatsu* (Tokyo: Chūōkōronsha, 1987).

Japan, and at least 5,357 more were tried in national tribunals throughout the rest of Asia.[55]

From the beginning, however, Allied efforts to pursue the issue of criminal responsibility for the war were severely compromised on multiple fronts. To begin with, the Tokyo tribunal suffered from the same major shortcomings that hampered the Nuremberg Trials in Europe: The defendants were prosecuted for actions that were not clearly defined as crimes under international law at the time they were committed thus opening up the tribunal to the charge of post hoc, or victor's justice. Moreover, those who were sitting in judgment were guilty of many of the same crimes as the accused, including the indiscriminate slaughter of noncombatants (the fire bombings and the use of the atomic bombs by the United States), the systematic and unchecked brutalization of civilians in conquered regions (especially by the Soviets), and the waging of aggressive wars resulting in the subjugation of foreign peoples (the Western Imperial powers – Britain, France, and Holland).

In addition to these already serious flaws, the IMFTE suffered from a host of additional problems. The conduct of the prosecution was distinctly sloppy compared to Nuremberg. The primary victims of Japanese aggression – the Chinese and the Koreans – were not represented on the bench or the prosecution, and as a result, crimes against Westerners took the center stage, whereas the much wider and more serious abuses involving Asians were relatively neglected. In addition, Allied efforts to prove intent on the part of the defendants were hopelessly complicated by the lack of adequate documentation and by the diffuse and drawn-out character of the decision making that led Japan to launch the Pacific War.[56]

Perhaps most crippling, however, was the decision to exempt the Japanese emperor from prosecution, even though he had been head of state during the war and his approval was required for the implementation of all major policy decisions. The decision to exempt him was made on pragmatic grounds, to avoid the risk of sparking a resistance movement and to place pressure on the Japanese government to accept the reforms being imposed on them by the United States, especially a draft constitution that had been written by General Douglas MacArthur's legal staff. The decision to exclude the emperor clearly underlined the political nature of the trials, and in the eyes of many observers – including two of the justices presiding over the court, Henri Bernard and William Webb – fatally undermined the proceedings and thus permanently frustrated Allied efforts to instill in the Japanese people a sense that they and their nation had done anything wrong in the war.[57]

[55] Philip R. Piccigallo, *The Japanese on Trial: Allied War Crimes Operations in the East, 1945–1951* (Austin: University of Texas Press, 1979), p. xiv; Finn, *Winners in Peace*, pp. 184–185.

[56] On the problems of the IMFTE, and in particular the argument that its highly Western orientation encouraged Japan to ignore its responsibility for atrocities in Asia, see Yoshida Yutaka, *Shōwa Tennō no Shūsenshi* (Tokyo: Iwanami Shoten, 1992).

[57] See Richard Minear, *Victor's Justice: The Tokyo War Crimes Tribunal* (Princeton, NJ: Princeton University Press, 1971); Arnold C. Brackman, *The Other Nuremberg: The Untold Story of*

Not surprisingly in light of these shortcomings, the Japanese public response to the trials was lukewarm at best. Although there had been considerable animosity toward General Tojo Hideki and the other defendants at the start of the trials, once the trials began and the many flaws of the proceedings became evident, popular opinion increasingly turned in a negative direction. In many quarters, anger even turned to sympathy as the perception spread that Tojo and the other defendants were not even trying to mount a serious defense to protect the emperor.[58] According to a 1955 poll, only 19 percent of those surveyed felt that it was appropriate that the trials were held; 66 percent thought they had been unfortunate, but unavoidable (*shikata ga nai*); 63 percent thought that the verdicts had been too harsh versus 31 percent who felt that they had been just.[59]

By the early 1950s, a broad-based movement emerged calling for the release of Japanese prisoners held by the Allied powers. In 1952, an umbrella organization was formed, the People's Movement for the Complete Release of Prisoners of War and Pardoning of War Criminals, to actively lobby on the prisoners' behalf. In a mammoth letter-signing campaign, the organization collected the signatures of over 30 million people.[60]

Although trials continued outside of Japan into the 1950s, the Yokohama trials of class B and C war criminals came to an end in 1948. As Japan moved toward independence, and as the pressures of the cold war began to mount, the United States began to bow to Japanese opinion and reverse its policy on war criminals, much as it had done in Europe. Already by March 1950 General MacArthur ordered that sentences be reduced by one-third for good behavior, and he authorized the parole of those who had been sentenced to life imprisonment after they served fifteen years. Once the Japanese regained full sovereignty in 1952, unlike in Germany and Austria, the trials were not only halted but eventually their results would be reversed entirely.

## The Purges

In addition to the war crimes tribunals, the U.S. occupation also implemented a vast purge of the political system, dismantling various organizations associated with the militarists and removing hundreds of thousands of individuals from public life who were deemed potentially harmful to the establishment of democracy. Most importantly, the Japanese Imperial Navy and Navy were disbanded, and steps were taken to ensure that they never be reconstituted. The new Japanese constitution included a clause – Article 9 – in which Japan

---

the *Tokyo War Crimes Trials* (New York: Morrow, 1987); and Gwen and Merion Harries, *Sheathing the Sword: The Demilitarization of Japan* (New York: MacMillan, 1987). For a short overview of the trial, see Dower, *Embracing Defeat*, op. cit., chapter 15.

[58] Yoshida, *Nihonjin no Sensōkan*, op. cit., pp. 38–41.
[59] Cabinet office poll, quoted in Yoshida, *Nihonjin no Sensōkan*, op. cit., p. 41.
[60] Yoshida Yutaka, *Nihonjin no Sensōkan*, op. cit., pp. 82–83.

gave up the right to the use of force and pledged not to maintain air, sea, or ground forces.[61] The Japanese police forces were decentralized, and the fearsome Internal Affairs Ministry, the *Naimusho*, which in the prewar period had been responsible for maintaining domestic order and ideological purity, was disbanded. Various auxiliary associations associated with the military regime, over 200 in all, were also dissolved.[62]

As in Germany and Austria, the U.S. occupation authorities distributed a survey to all members of the Japanese government exploring their role in wartime policy making. Altogether over 2.3 million such surveys were distributed. On the basis of the survey results, 220,000 people were removed from positions of authority.[63] This was approximately half of 418,000 who were purged by the United States and the Western allies in Germany.[64] The vast majority of those purged were military officers, because unlike Austria or Germany, there was no organization comparable to the Nazi party that could be assigned political responsibility for the former regime's criminal acts.[65] However, many politicians and officials were also affected, at least temporarily, and the purges were far-reaching and quite severe in their initial effects: Over 80 percent of the 1945 Diet and 50 percent of the cabinet of Prime Minister Shidehara were removed by the start of 1946.[66]

The purges in Japan suffered from many of the same deficiencies as the purges in Germany and Austria. Many of the organizations that were dismantled provided valuable social services. Veterans groups, for instance, helped provide support for millions of demobilized soldiers and their families. The weakening of the police was associated with a sharp deterioration in domestic political order.[67] In addition, the purges were often quite unjust in their effects. Some of the individuals who had been purged – most prominently Ishibashi Tanzan and Hatoyama Ichirō (both of whom were to become prime minister in the late 1950s) – were well-known critics of the militarist regime who had fallen afoul of the vagaries of the purge process. Others who were not tried or purged were arguably as guilty – or more so – than those who were. The most egregious example was Lieutenant General Ishii Shirō and other members of Unit 731,

---

[61] There was considerable controversy from the start regarding the exact meaning of Article 9.

[62] Harries, *Sheathing the Sword*, pp. 44–45.

[63] Kazuo Kawai, *Japan's American Interlude* (Chicago: University of Chicago Press, 1964), p. 94. See also Hans H. Baerwald, *The Purge of Japanese Leaders under the Occupation* (Berkeley, CA: University of California Press, 1959); and Masuda Hiroshi, *Seijika Tsuihō* (Tokyo: Chūōkōronsha, 2001).

[64] Finn, *Winners in Peace*, pp. 82–86; Harries, *Sheathing the Sword*, pp. 44–49.

[65] Baerwald, *The Purge of Japanese Leaders*, op. cit.

[66] Finn, *Winners in Peace*, op. cit., p. 85.

[67] Of particular concern in this context was the rise of the militant Left and the related problem of Korean and other foreign laborers – many of whom were attracted to left-wing unions and other organizations. The police were seen as being helpless in dealing with this problem, leading to an increased reliance on nonofficial forms of control, including the use of the Yakuza. See David Kaplan and Alec Dubro, *Yakuza: Japan's Criminal Underworld* (Berkeley: University of California Press, 2003), chapter 2.

who had killed thousands in gruesome medical experiments in China, but who were not indicted in return for granting the Americans access to their research data.[68] Although Ishii's case was not publicly known at the time, others – such as that of Kishi Nobusuke – were.

In addition to the capricious and often unjust character of the purges, there was the problem that – much as in Europe – the skills and talents of the purgees were desperately needed to assist with the economic and political reconstruction of Japan. As the occupation continued, and as American policy makers increasingly became concerned with reducing the cost of the occupation to the U.S. taxpayer and speedily strengthening Japan as a bulwark against Communism in East Asia, pressures to reverse the purges increased. After visiting Japan in March 1948, George Kennan wrote disapprovingly of the purges as bearing a "sickening resemblance to the concepts of certain totalitarian governments." He was equally scathing in his assessment of the trials and efforts at extracting reparations from Japan.[69]

General MacArthur was able to resist pressures emanating from Washington to reverse the purges for a few more years; however, in 1951, MacArthur was dismissed by President Truman because of policy disagreements over how to respond to the Chinese intervention in the Korean War. MacArthur's successor, General Matthew Ridgeway, speedily de-purged over 200,000 of the accused in 1951, many of whom immediately resumed playing an active role in Japanese political life.[70] Among those who returned to prominent positions in the Japanese political world at that time were three future prime ministers: Hatoyama Ichirō, Ishibashi Tanzan, and Kishi Nobusuke. In the October 1952 Diet elections, fully 42 percent of those elected were former purgees.[71] Although comparable trends were observable in Germany and even more so in Austria, Japan went far further than they did in rehabilitating its old elite. Given the nature of Japan's postwar elites and the pressures of the cold war, such a result was perhaps all but inevitable.

The only important group that was not restored to a prominent role in postwar Japan was the military. Although Japan did create a new military institution – the Self Defense Forces – to help defend against a possible attack and to appease a United States eager to get Japan to share the burden of defending East Asia – Japanese leaders from Yoshida Shigeru on were careful to limit its power and influence. Former military officers who were ready and eager to help rebuild the military institution were deliberately prevented from doing so until the basic foundation for a limited defense force was set. The business

---

[68] Recently uncovered documents suggest that the United States not only pardoned Ishii and company for their cooperation but even paid them. See "U.S. Paid Unit 731 Members for Data," *Japan Times*, August 15, 2005, at http://www.japantimes.co.jp/print/news/nn08-2005/nn20050815a1.htm (accessed May 29, 2006).

[69] Finn, *Winners in Peace*, op. cit., pp. 201–209.

[70] Harries, *Sheathing the Sword*, op. cit., pp. 196–197.

[71] Finn, *Winners in Peace*, op. cit., p. 296.

community, initially eager to get back into arms manufacturing, was discouraged from doing so and instead looked for growth opportunities elsewhere. Although a handful of former military men, such as Admiral Nomura Kichisaburō, who was elected to the Japanese Upper House after the war, would become influential in postwar politics, theirs was the exception rather than the rule. This "silent purge" of the military from Japanese politics, however, was accomplished almost entirely by the Japanese themselves – after receiving the critical initial impetus from the United States – relying on unofficial means. Ironically, from the mid-1950s on the United States would find itself frustrated by the antimilitary bias it had helped create as it repeatedly turned to Japan for assistance in fighting the cold war in Asia.[72]

## Reeducation

Compared with the disastrous experiences with war crimes tribunals and purges, the U.S. effort to reeducate the Japanese people and to promote a new historical narrative through the media and the educational establishment enjoyed some measure of success, especially in the early years of the occupation. In this, the Allies benefited from a strong constituency within Japan that wished to challenge the conservative historical narrative. Progressive (i.e., more contrite) views on Japanese history naturally were more strongly represented on the left end of the political spectrum, but were shared also by many more centrist, establishment figures.

Setting the stage for reform was a far-reaching purge of the educational establishment that was by and large conducted by the Japanese themselves with relatively little need for additional support from the occupation authorities. Even before the occupation began, 115,778 teachers and officials resigned from their posts. An additional 6,000 more were removed by the occupation by April 1949, after over 700,000 had been screened. In all, 22 percent of all teachers and officials from the prewar period were either removed or resigned.[73] Many of the teachers who remained were either leftists or became sympathetic to the Left. The powerful Japan Teachers Union (JTU, or *Nikkyosō*) would become one of the bastions of the Socialist and Communist parties.

Existing textbooks were carefully edited to remove propagandistic references to the empire and the war effort before being replaced with new textbooks in 1946. The new textbooks portrayed the Japanese people as dupes of the militarists, who they blamed for manipulating the nation into embarking on a destructive and misguided quest to dominate Asia from the time of the Manchurian incident on.[74] Military drill, along with martial arts training, was abolished, as were traditional classes on "moral education" (*shushin*) that had been designed to instill attitudes of obedience and self-sacrifice in children.

[72] Thomas Berger, *Cultures of Antimilitarism*, op. cit.
[73] Finn, *Winners in Peace*, op. cit., p. 60.
[74] Orr, *The Victim as Hero*, op. cit., pp. 75–78.

In their place was a new emphasis on American-inspired notions of democracy and individual freedom. Efforts were also made to weaken the influence of the Ministry of Education over the curriculum and to decentralize educational policy making. These measures would have only limited success, as the Japanese bureaucracy fought a stubborn rearguard battle to retain control and to contain or reverse the occupation's impact. Conservative politicians in the Democratic Party (which later joined with Yoshida's Liberals to form the Liberal Democratic Party in 1955) sided with the Ministry in its battle against the Teachers' Union, fighting hard to limit the influence of the Left on the nation's youth.

A central concern of the occupation was to reeducate the adult population using the press and media. Films and radio broadcasts detailing Japanese atrocities at Nanjing and elsewhere were released, and the major Japanese newspapers were directed to publish a series of articles on Japanese war crimes. Some newspapers, notably the Communist *Akahata*, went out of their way to publish accounts of Imperial atrocities, including reports on the abuse of slave laborers inside Japan and on the medical experiments conducted on prisoners.[75] As a result, knowledge of Japanese wrongdoing was widespread inside of Japan after the war, even if many Japanese tended to relativize their guilt through reference to Allied atrocities or to attribute responsibility for them to a relatively small militarist clique.

With the onset of the cold war, however, these policies were increasingly reversed. By 1951, the conservative controlled Ministry of Education began to reimpose some measure of ideological controls through the introduction of a system of screening textbooks for "factual" errors.[76] After the occupation ended, the system was used to discourage references to Japanese Imperial atrocities. In 1956, many of the draft textbooks submitted to the screening committees were rejected, most of them as a result of disputes between the Ministry and the textbook writers over the history issue.[77] By the late 1950s, even references to Allied atrocities such as the atomic and fire bombings of Japanese cities – which had become a focal point of the political debate over Japanese history – began to be de-emphasized.[78]

Whereas the Teachers' Union and the Japanese Left were concerned with familiarizing young people with the horrors of the war – and in particular with the enormous suffering that it had caused Japan's civilian population – so as to encourage them to oppose the remilitarization of Japan, conservatives wanted to de-emphasize them and encourage instead the development of a healthy sense of patriotism, one that would support – or at least not oppose – the government's policies of rearmament and alliance with the United States.

---

[75] Frederick Dickinson, "Biohazard: Unit 731," p. 2.

[76] Dower, *Embracing Defeat*, op. cit., p. 351.

[77] Mikyoung Kim, "Myths, Milieu and Facts: History Textbook Controversies," in Hasegawa and Togo, *East Asia's Haunted Present*, op. cit., p. 87–98.

[78] Benjamin Duke, "The Textbook Controversy" *Japan Quarterly* 19 (1972), pp. 337–352; Orr, *The Victim as Hero*, op. cit., pp. 89–97.

Neither the Left nor the Right was interested in focusing on the atrocities committed by Imperial forces or to begin to grapple with the question of the moral responsibility the Japanese people bore for them. The depiction of history in textbooks became one of the central ideological battlefields in postwar Japan, and in the end neither side could claim political victory or defeat. Lost in the interstices were vital historical issues – in particular regarding the suffering of Asian people – that would reemerge to plague Japan at a later date.

A similar trend could be observed in other domains of the new official narrative. After 1945, the occupation had quickly taken down monuments that were associated with militarism and the empire. Although after some debate the occupation authorities decided not to dismantle the Yasukuni shrine dedicated to the spirits of the soldiers and sailors that had given their lives in the service of the Empire, the shrine was turned into a private entity run by an independent association. Officially, the government was no longer involved in the running of the shrine. Secretly, however, the Ministry of Health cooperated with the shrine authorities in gathering the names of some 2 million Japanese soldiers who had died during the war to inscribe their names on the list of spirits housed at the shrine.[79] Not until 1951 did a Japanese prime minister (Yoshida Shigeru) visit the shrine, and then only in an unofficial capacity. The emperor visited for the first time in 1952, and again avoided reference to the past. There were no new official museums dealing with the war or the empire. Although the cities of Hiroshima and Nagasaki opened local museums and "peace parks" commemorating the atomic bombings in 1955, these were dedicated almost exclusively to the memory of the victims of the bombings and did not deal with the broader context of the war and the empire. As in the textbooks, the issue of atrocities in Asia was largely avoided.

### Reparations

One of the thorniest issues Japan had to deal with after the war was the question of reparations. The economic consequences of Allied demands for reparations were potentially enormous. At Potsdam, the Allied powers had agreed that Japan would be allowed to "maintain such industries as will sustain her economy and permit the exaction of just reparations in kind."[80] Although what kind of action this would translate into was left vague, there were powerful constituencies who looked to reparations both as a way of crippling Japanese military capabilities and as a means of reconstructing other parts of Asia that had been devastated by the war. In addition, there were the many thousands of

---

[79] Among those enshrined were thousands of Koreans and Taiwanese who died in Japanese military service and who, at the time they had fallen, had been citizens of the Empire. The enshrinement of these non-Japanese would later become a significant political issue in Japan's relations to its neighbors.

[80] As specified in article 11 of the declaration. The full text is available at http://www.ndl.go.jp/constitution/e/etc/c06.html, accessed January 20, 2012.

Allied prisoners of war, not to mention the citizens of Western aligned countries or colonies such as the Philippines, Malaysia, and Singapore, who had been brutalized by the Japanese and now expected compensation.

From the beginning, however, the United States was concerned that reparations not cripple the Japanese economy and destabilize it politically, as they had done in Germany after World War I. Early U.S. thinking about reparations, however, envisioned quite draconian measures, with the extraction of resources to be limited only by Japan's ability to pay. The Edwin Pauley Commission was charged with looking into the issue and, in December 1945, recommended to President Truman that the occupation remove all of Japan's war industries – including the aircraft industry – and enforce drastic reductions in its capacity to produce iron, steel, ships, and machine tools.[81]

By 1947, however, the United States became increasingly concerned with reviving the still moribund Japanese economy. A series of follow-up commissions– the Strikes and Johnson commissions – recommended writing off the properties the Japanese Empire had lost in Asia (estimated at $50 billion in value) and sharply reducing the reparations exacted from the Japanese home islands to 25 percent of what had been originally planned for by the Pauley Commission.[82] Many of America's Asian allies – especially the Republic of China and the Philippines – were fiercely opposed to this change in occupation policy.[83] The United States, however, was able to brush off their protests and pushed through a generous reparations settlement under the terms of the Treaty of San Francisco, the formal peace treaty that ended the state of war between Japan and the Western Allied powers.[84]

Under Article 14 of the treaty, all Japanese overseas assets (valued at approximately $25 billion in 1945) – private and public – were seized as reparations by the countries in which they were located.[85] The Japanese government agreed to pay an additional $1 billion to the countries it had occupied between 1941 and 1945 (Burma, Indonesia, the Philippines, and Vietnam) and promised to negotiate with the countries that it had occupied "with a view to assisting to compensate those countries for the cost of repairing the damage done, by making available the services of the Japanese people in production, salvaging and other work." The United States and other Western powers would

---

[81] Finn, *Winners in Peace*, op. cit., pp. 70–71.

[82] Finn, *Winners in Peace*, op. cit., pp. 197–199.

[83] The Taiwanese government was estimating the economic cost of the Japanese invasion of China at $31.3 billion, the Philippines government was asking for $8 billion. See Caroline Rose, *Sino-Japanese Relations: Facing the Past, Looking to the Future?* (New York and London: Routledge, 2005), pp. 41–43.

[84] India and Burma refused to attend the conference, and Indonesia attended but did not ratify it. China was excluded because of a disagreement between the United States and Britain over who should represent China. The United States wished to invite the Nationalist government in Taipei; Britain insisted on the Communist government in Beijing. In the end, it was agreed that Japan should sign a separate treaty with whatever country it chose to.

[85] Korea and eventually China were covered under Article 21 of the treaty.

supply the needed raw materials for such operations.[86] In addition, under Article 16 of the treaty, the Japanese government agreed to pay $16 million to the International Committee of the Red Cross to help compensate former Allied prisoners of war who had "suffered undue hardship" during their captivity.[87] This sum was duly paid, using funds that de facto were provided by the United States. In return, the Western powers, led by the United States, agreed to forgo demanding any further reparations, both for themselves and by their citizens.[88]

Measured against the size of the loss and suffering inflicted by the war and Japan's history of colonial exploitation, these sums seemed paltry indeed. They were far inferior to the large-scale program of compensation the Federal Republic of Germany initiated around the same time. The victims of Japanese aggression and abuse – the veterans and the Asian peoples who had been occupied by the empire – had good reason to feel that their interests had been ignored for the sake of Western strategic interests in the cold war.

Instead of paying compensation to other countries, Japan became increasingly concerned with compensating its own citizens for the suffering inflicted by the war. Of particular concern was providing for the millions of veterans, wounded soldiers, and the family members of fallen soldiers. After the surrender, the occupation had eliminated all special benefits for these groups on the grounds that in a peaceful, democratic society, all citizens, regardless of whether they had some connection to the military or not, should receive equal access to the welfare system. Once the occupation was ended in 1952, however, veteran pensions and other special benefits for the wounded and the bereaved were quickly reinstated. Special provisions also were made available to the millions of refugees who had returned to the main islands from abroad (*Hikiagesha* – also referred to as the "repatriated" in English) as well as for landlords and other groups who could claim to have been negatively affected by occupation reforms.[89]

Powerful societal interests motivated the extension of benefits to these various groups. The Japan Association of the War-bereaved (or *Izokukai*) had over 8 million members in the 1950s,[90] and there were close to 6 million veterans. These groups had a strong material interest in pushing for compensation for their suffering, and winning their electoral support through policies such as the 1952 Wounded Veteran and Bereaved Family Assistance Act was of critical importance to the conservative parties.[91] These policies, however, were

---

[86] Finn, *Winners in Peace*, op. cit., p. 199.

[87] See *Asahi*, November 13, 1993 and Kiyomizu Masayoshi, "Sengo Hoshō no Kokusaihikaku," *Sekai* (February 1994).

[88] Yoshida Yutaka, *Nihonjin no Sensōkan*, op. cit., p. 70.

[89] For a discussion of the compensation of domestic groups after the war, see Orr, *The Victim as Hero*, op. cit., chapter 6.

[90] Daiki Shibuchi, "The Yasukuni Shrine Dispute," p. 215. For an excellent overview of the development of the *Izokukai* see Seraphim, *War Memory and Social Politics*, op. cit., chapter 2.

[91] Takenaka, "Enshrinement Politics," op. cit., pp. 5–6.

predicated on a historical narrative that treated veterans and other groups as victims worthy of societal support.

Just as important as who was compensated was who was not. The victims of atomic bombings (*Hibakusha*) were long denied special benefits because the Left had turned them into potent symbols of civilian suffering in their campaign against the U.S.-Japanese security relationship and rearmament.[92] Similarly, Koreans, Chinese, and Taiwanese who before 1945 had been citizens of the Japanese Empire were systematically excluded from any form of compensation on the grounds that they were no longer Japanese citizens.[93] Even Koreans and Taiwanese who had served in the Imperial Army were declared ineligible for pension benefits, although they could be – and often were – involuntarily enshrined at the Yasukuni shrine in Tokyo. Apparently, the obligation of the Japanese nation to those former subjects who had once served it extended only into the hereafter.

Former slave laborers, including the hundreds of thousands of Koreans and Chinese who had been forcibly brought to labor under atrocious conditions in Japan, were entirely ignored, despite efforts by some Japanese leftists to publicize their plight. The Ministry of Health and Welfare, concerned that the former slave laborers might mount a campaign demanding compensation, systematically sought to suppress all information regarding their history.[94] As with Germany, which during the cold war offered only limited compensation to its victims in Communist Eastern Europe, such disregard could be justified with respect to the victims of Japanese Imperialism in Communist China and North Korea. However, unlike Germany, which offered substantial aid and compensation to Israel and the victims of Nazism in Western countries, Japan did not help the victims of Imperialism even in staunchly pro-Western, anti-Communist South Korea and Taiwan.

Japanese reparations policy was a reflection of a historical narrative that assigned to the postwar state only a highly attenuated degree of responsibility for the material destruction and suffering wrought by the war. Japan had become what one might call a "rice bowl penitent," dutifully mouthing a ritualistic formula of contrition in return for the forgiveness of the Western powers and integration into the newly emerging international economic and political order created by the United States. The Japanese state did extend

---

[92] Orr, *The Victim as Hero*, op. cit., pp. 140–148.

[93] After the collapse of the Empire, Japanese citizenship was withdrawn from all Koreans, Taiwanese, and Chinese who did not re-naturalize as Japanese citizens. Subsequently, clauses were inserted into all Japanese laws governing the provision of welfare benefits – including the national pensions law and national health insurance – restricting them to Japanese citizens. The only benefit that the foreign residents of Japan were eligible for was emergency medical treatment. See Tanaka Hiroshi, *Zainichi Gagokujin: Hō no Kabe, Kokoro no Mizo Shinpan*, 2nd edition (Tokyo: Iwanami Shoten, 1995).

[94] William Underwood, "Chinese Forced Labor, the Japanese Government and the Prospects for Redress," *Japan Focus*, available at http://www.japanfocus.org/article.asp?id=326 (accessed November 18, 2005).

significant levels of support to the domestic victims of the war, but only to those who were politically favored by the dominant Japanese conservatives.

## Summary

Japan emerged from the American-led occupation an economically vibrant, peaceful, and by and large, democratic nation closely aligned with the West. Many of the same leaders, who before 1945 had led their nation into authoritarian dictatorship and war against the Western powers, now reappeared on the political stage as staunch defenders of freedom and solidly behind the United States in the struggle against Communism. When it came to its history, however, Japan's leaders held views starkly at odds with those of its new allies. Under the terms of the Treaty of San Francisco, Japan agreed to accept the verdict of the IMFTE and other Allied war crimes tribunals. Beyond this, however, it paid only lip service to the notion that postwar Japan bore any guilt or responsibility for the suffering inflicted by the war and the empire. The official narrative portrayed the war as the fault of a small clique of military leaders and their followers. Now that they had been successfully removed from power, as far as the Japanese government was concerned, the issue of war responsibility had been closed. This relatively impenitent official narrative served the interests of the Japanese state and of the moderate to conservative elites who dominated Japanese politics in the post-1945 era. It also enjoyed the backing of significant segments of the broader Japanese population and was supported by large and politically powerful interests – most notably those representing the war veterans and their families.

The official narrative was challenged vigorously by the Japanese Left, who wished to focus on Japanese civilian suffering to promote the ideal of Japan as a "peace nation" (*Heiwa Kokka*), a country that had suffered the most terrible ravages of modern warfare – including nuclear war – and thus could serve as a warning to the rest of the world in urgent need to disarm and embrace pacifism. To a lesser degree, it was also challenged by those on the Right who felt that Japan had little or nothing to be penitent about, although at this point in time their voices were drowned out in the din of the main political struggle between the Left and the basically centrist or right-of-center government.[95] Their ability, however, to substantively alter government policy was decidedly limited given the realities of Japanese politics in the early postwar period.

For the next three decades, the politics of history in Japan would largely revolve around the issue of how to remember Japanese civilian suffering, an

---

[95] These voices became louder in the early 1960s as writers such as Yukio Mishima, Etō Jun, and Kōsaka Masaaki began producing novels and histories reflecting a more affirmative view of Imperial Japan. A landmark in this process was the publication of Hayashi Fusao's *Daitōasensō Kōteiron* (Affirming the Great East Asian War) (Tokyo: Banchō-Shobō, 1964). See Andrew Barshay, "Postwar Social and Political Thought 1945–1990," in Bod Tadashi Wakabayashi, *Modern Japanese Thought* (Cambridge and New York; Cambridge University Press, 1998), pp. 329–337.

issue that was formed by the larger debate over which national security policy would best serve Japanese national interests – alliance with the United States (as preferred by the Center Right and the LDP) – or unarmed neutrality (as advocated by the Japanese Socialist Party and the peace movement on the Left). Largely forgotten were the millions of non-Japanese who had suffered during the war or under Japanese Imperial Rule.

### A Guilty Innocence – 1952–1982

Similar to Austria, Japan ended its status as an occupied nation while at the same time managing to avoid taking official responsibility for the horrors of its recent history to a remarkable degree, and, in large part, Japan was able to do so as a result of a permissive international environment. Japan's permissive environment, however, differed greatly from that of Austria's. Austria benefited from its status as a small, neutral state in the center of cold war Europe – freely interacting with both sides but aligned with none. In contrast, Japan found itself in almost the opposite position. Although it was aligned with the United States militarily, it was a large and powerful island nation in Asia, relatively insulated from the pressures of the East-West confrontation and comparatively isolated from its neighbors. This had significant geostrategic as well as geoeconomic consequences.

On a strategic level, unlike West Germany, Japan was not integrated into a tightly woven, multilateral military alliance. Although the United States had tried to build an East Asian equivalent to NATO, its efforts had foundered because of the sheer size and diversity of the region.[96] Even if such an attempt had succeeded, Japan had little motive to join. Japan did not face a direct Soviet military threat (unlike Germany, which had to contend with well over 300,000 Soviet troops inside East Germany alone), and it could be reasonably sure that the United States would provide the basic level of strategic security (nuclear deterrence and protection for its vital sea lanes of communication), if for no other reason than that the United States could not afford to allow Japan's industrial and technological resources to fall into the hands of the Soviet Union. During the cold war, Japan was the lynch pin for U.S. strategy in Asia, and the bases it provided were critical for the U.S. campaign to contain Communism. In addition, the first half of the cold war in Asia was in fact quite hot, with numerous savage local wars – including the immensely destructive Korean and Vietnam wars. Throughout the period, there were very real fears in Japan that it could be dragged into a bloody regional conflict in which none of its own vital strategic interests were at stake. As a result, Japan had relatively little

---

[96] In 1954, the United States had encouraged the creation of a multilateral security framework, the Manila Pact, which included many of its regional allies – but not Japan. Moreover, from the beginning, the members of the alliance had extreme difficulty coordinating their policies, and it finally disintegrated altogether in 1977. See Leszek Buszynski, *SEATO: Failure of an Alliance Strategy* (Singapore: Singapore University Press, 1983).

incentive to develop close security ties with its neighbors and good reason to be wary of becoming overly entangled in U.S. strategic designs for the region.[97]

Economically as well, Japan was far more isolated in Asia than either Germany or Austria was in Europe. After 1945, the leading industrial powers in Western Europe soon realized that they needed to cooperate with one another economically and created first the European Coal and Steel Community in 1952, which was subsequently upgraded into the broader European Economic Community in 1957.[98] In Asia, on the other hand, the situation was far more fractious and complex. Initially, Japan was very interested in restoring commercial relations with Asia that had been disrupted by the war and the collapse of the empire. The United States as well was convinced that Japan's economic destiny lay in Asia and sought to promote regional economic cooperation, partly because of the in retrospect almost comically mistaken belief that Japanese products could never be competitive in Western markets.[99] However, the triumph of Communism, first in China and North Korea and then in parts of South East Asia, effectively closed off or at least severely restricted Japanese access to vast swathes of the Asian market. The strong preference in most of non-Communist Asia for import substitution development strategies and sluggish growth rates helped further reduce the region's economic appeal. As a result, Japanese industry chose to focus its energies on cracking the more open and lucrative markets of the West instead.

In the 1960s, Japan made a number of efforts to promote regional institution building. These initiatives, however, foundered on, among other things, residual fears of Japanese economic domination and historically rooted memories of the "Greater East Asian Coprosperity Sphere" it had created during the Pacific War.[100] While the nations of South East Asia did come together to create the Association of South East Asian Nations (ASEAN), Japan did not participate in ASEAN and, at the time, had only a relatively limited interest in doing so.[101]

---

[97] In the parlance of international relations, Japan had a relatively low fear of abandonment and a quite high fear of entanglement. For an excellent exploration of these issues, see Jitsuo Tsuchiyama, "The End of the Alliance? Dilemmas in the U.S.-Japan Relationship," in Peter Gourevitch, et al., eds., *United States-Japan Relations and International Institutions after the Cold War* (San Diego: Graduate School of International Relations and Pacific Studies, 1995).

[98] See Alan S. Milward, *The European Rescue of the Nation State* (Berkeley: University of California Press, 1992).

[99] For the motivations behind the growing U.S. involvement in South East Asian security in the 1950s, see Gustav Schmidt and Charles F. Doran, eds., *Amerikas Option für Deutschland und Japan: Die Position und Rolle Deutschlands und Japans in regionalen und internationalen Strukturen, Die 1950er und 1990er Jahre im Vergleich* (Bochum: Brockmeyer, 1996) and John Welfield, *An Empire in Eclipse: Japan in the Postwar American Alliance System* (London: Athlone Press, 1988), chapter 4.

[100] For a detailed account of the failure of Japan's regional initiatives at the time, see Pekka Korhonen, *Japan and Pacific Asia Free Trade Area* (New York: Routledge, 1994).

[101] On the slow and difficult Japanese reintegration with south East Asia, see Akira Suehiro, "The Road to Economic Re-entry: Japan's Policy Towards Southeast Asian Development in the 1950s-1960s," *Social Science Japan* 2:1 (1999), pp. 85–105.

Just as there was no Asian equivalent of NATO, there was no equivalent of the European Economic Community either.

As a result – compared with the enormous influence that countries such as Britain, France, or even the much smaller Netherlands wielded over the Federal Republic – the other Asian countries had only a very limited influence over Japan. Japan was not dependent on its Asian neighbors for its security, nor did it rely on them for its prosperity. Moreover, whereas the European region was characterized by a spirit of multilateralism, by and large diplomatic relations in Asia was conducted primarily on a bilateral basis. Although Japan had strong strategic and economic interests in the region, it held the upper hand in almost every bilateral relationship it had with its Asian neighbors. In contrast to Germany, which had to be sensitive to the desires of every one of its Western neighbors, Japan could afford to be concerned only with its relationship with the United States.[102] From the U.S. perspective, the minimal level of contrition offered by Japan was perfectly satisfactory. As long as the aggressive nationalism of the prewar period did not resurface (a perennial source of concern to policy makers in Washington),[103] the United States was more concerned with getting Japan to provide more support for its East Asian strategic designs.[104]

Some Asian leaders, notably Chiang Kai Shek of Taiwan and Synghman Rhee of South Korea, did try to pressure Japan on historical issues. Their failures, however, underlined their relative powerlessness. After severely punishing those Japanese war criminals who had fallen into its hands and initially demanding that Japan pay large sums in reparations, the Nationalist government found itself under growing pressure from the United States to abandon its claims. In the negotiations leading up to the 1952 Peace Treaty between Japan and the Nationalist Chinese, Taipei stubbornly continued to demand reparations. However, faced with Japanese intransigence (Japan insisted that that the former Imperial properties that had been seized by the Nationalists in Taiwan were worth "many tens of billions of dollars") and U.S. pressure, the

[102] Austria, it should be pointed out, was also very heavily dependent on its neighbors for its economic well-being, even though it was not integrated into the EU until the 1990s. However, in the 1940s, 1950s, and 1960s, its most important economic partner by far was the Federal Republic, which was not pursuing claims against Austria on historical issues (although the two countries did squabble over who bore responsibility for claims pressed by other parties).

[103] Such concerns would reemerge with remarkable regularity throughout the cold war era and beyond. See Thomas Berger, "Waiting for the Rising Sun," in Berger, Hollifield, and Newton, eds., *Japan's New Nationalism* (forthcoming). Such concerns would often peak when conservative politicians such as Nakasone Yasuhiro became prime minister. The author is indebted to observations on this point made by Professor Nat Thayer of Johns Hopkins, who was attached to the U.S. embassy in the 1960s and was closely involved in U.S.-Japanese relations throughout the cold war era.

[104] On Japan in America's strategic calculations at the time, see Michael Schaller, *The American Occupation of Japan: The Origins of the Cold War in East Asia* (Oxford and New York: Oxford University Press, 1985); John Welfield, *An Empire in Eclipse*, op. cit.; and Walter LaFeber, *The Clash: U.S.-Japan Relations Throughout History* (New York: Norton, 1997).

Chiang regime was forced to renounce its claims. Although Tokyo provided valuable diplomatic support and foreign aid (including military trainers for the Taiwanese air forces), the issue of Japanese moral responsibility for atrocities in China was avoided entirely.[105]

A similar pattern was established when Japan normalized its relations with its other Asian neighbors, beginning with Burma in 1954 and the Philippines in 1956. Despite strong, often emotional demands, Japanese diplomats were able to fend off demands for apologies and compensation, offering instead substantial foreign aid packages in return for a settlement of claims. When they visited countries in the region, Japanese leaders, such as Kishi in the late 1950s, would offer some general words of regret over the past but studiously avoided making an apology or acknowledging Japanese responsibility.[106]

South Korea proved to be a partial exception to this pattern. After China, Koreans arguably had suffered the most for the longest period of time at the hands of the Japanese Empire. Anti-Japanese nationalist sentiments ran deep in post-1945 Korea,[107] and the South Korean leader, the irascible Syngman Rhee, harbored strong, personal feelings of animosity toward Japan. During the Korean War, the United States had managed to arrange a meeting between Rhee and Yoshida Shigeru in Tokyo, hoping to foster a closer security relationship between its two main East Asian allies. Reportedly, the two men sat in stoic silence for a while before Yoshida, hoping to break the ice, mentioned that he had heard that there were tigers in Korea. Rhee responded, yes, there used to be, and then the Japanese had killed them all. In short, the meeting was not a success.[108]

Despite their differences, the two countries also had powerful common interests, including the desire to contain Communism, to retain a U.S. commitment to East Asian security, and to revitalize the strong economic and social ties that

[105] Yinan He, *The Search for Reconciliation: Sino-Japanese and German-Polish Relations since World War II* (Cambridge and New York; Cambridge University Press, 2009), pp. 148–151; Rose, *Sino-Japanese Relations*, op. cit., pp. 43–47.

[106] On reparations to Asian countries, see Kiyomizu Masayoshi, "Sengo Hoshō no Kokusai-hikaku," *Sekai* February 1994. In Australia, for instance, Kishi laid a wreath at the National War memorial and said, "It is my official duty, and my personal desire, to express to the people of Australia our heartfelt sorrow for what occurred during the war." The Australian prime minister Robert Menzies accepted Kishi's words, responding, "That we have reached the wise conclusion, that it is better to hope than to always remember," and adding that Australia and Japan should "concentrate our minds on peace." Press coverage on the whole positive, and Australian Veterans organizations helped squelch internal dissension in the interest of Australian-Japanese reconciliation. See Jennifer Lind, *Sorry States*, op. cit., p. 168. Kishi made similar statements while touring South East Asia. On the importance of south East Asia to Japan's (and the United States') plans in the 1950s, see Hiroyuki Hoshiro, "Coprosperity Sphere Again? United States Foreign Policy and Japan's 'First' Regionalism in the 1950s," *Pacific Affairs* 82:3 (Fall 2009), pp. 385–406.

[107] See Sung Hwa Cheong, *The Politics of Anti-Japanese Sentiment in Korea: Japanese-South Korean Relations under American Occupation* (New York: Greenwood Press, 1991).

[108] This is a well-known anecdote related by, among others, John Welfield, *An Empire in Eclipse*, op. cit., pp. 92–93.

historically had existed between their two countries.[109] Nonetheless, nation-alism trumped geostrategic and material interests as, time and again, negoti-ations between the two countries collapsed over differences in how the two sides viewed history. In 1953, the leader of the Japanese delegation Kubota Kenichirō claimed that if Japan had not taken over Korea, either China or Rus-sia would have done so. He went on to suggest that any harm Japan may have inflicted on Korea was outweighed by the enormous investment it had made to Korean development and that this should cancel out any Korean claims for reparations or compensation. Kubota's comments, which were backed by Foreign Minister Okazaki Katsuo, triggered an outpouring of outrage in the Korean press and led to a complete breakdown in negotiations until 1958.[110] When negotiations resumed, Japan retracted the Kubota statement and Prime Minister Kishi, using a back channel, sent Syngman Rhee a private apology. When Kishi's comments were made public, however, he was forced to retract them because of political pressures from the Right.[111] Disagreements broke out as well over of the repatriation of Korean residents in Japan to North Korea and over the status of the Dokdo/Takeshima islands in the Sea of Japan. As a result, once again talks between the two nations stalled.

It was not until 1961, after General Park Chung Hee took power in a coup d'etat, that the negotiations with Korea finally began to make progress. Given his personal history, Park was naturally disinclined to reexamining the past: During the war, he had been an officer in the Japanese Imperial Army assigned to hunting down Communist guerillas (many of whom were Korean) in North-ern China. In the early 1960s, Park's overriding concern was to strengthen the South Korean economy and increase Korea's ability to counter the continued menace of North Korea.[112]

Korean domestic opinion, however, remained strongly committed to ques-tions of historical justice, and the opposition parties demanded at least $2.7 billion in reparations, paid both to the Korean government as well as to indi-viduals who had suffered under Japanese rule.[113] Although the Japanese gov-ernment showed some flexibility on historical issues, it insisted on defining the money it offered the Korean government as foreign aid, not reparations. The Korean government dropped the right to pursue reparations claims, both

---

[109] See Victor Cha, *Alignment Despite Antagonism: The United States-Korea-Japan Security Tri-angle* (Stanford, CA: Stanford University Press, 1999).

[110] Wakamiya Yoshibumi, *The Postwar Conservative View of Asia, How the Political Right has Delayed Japan's Coming to Terms with its History of Aggression in Asia* (Tokyo: LTCB International Library Foundation, 1998), pp. 186–188.

[111] See Wakamiya, *The Postwar Conservative View of Asia*, op. cit., pp. 33–48.

[112] Victor Cha, "Bridging the Gap: The Strategic Context of the 1965 Korea-Japan Normalization Treaty," *Korean Studies* 20 (1996), pp. 123–160; Kimiya Tadashi, "1960 Nendai Kankoku ni okeru reisen gaikō no san ruikei: Nikkan Seijoka, Betnomau happei, ASPAC," in Okonogi Masa and Moon Chung-In, eds., *Shijo, Kokka, Kokusai Taisei* (Tokyo: Keio Daigaku Shup-pankai, 2001), pp. 96–105; Alexis Dudden, *Troubled Apologies*, op. cit., pp. 42–45.

[113] Wakamiya, *The Postwar Conservative Views of Asia*, op. cit., p. 193.

by the government and by Korean citizens (although this latter part of the agreement was kept secret for several decades).[114] In February 1965, Japanese Foreign Minister Shiina Etsusaburō visited South Korea and expressed "sincere regret" and "deep remorse" for the "difficult period in the two countries' past." Although his words were received very positively by the Korean press, it was not clear whether he had spoken in an official capacity, nor was his statement followed up with any further changes in Japan's official narrative. Once again, despite over a decade of sustained pressure from Korea, Japan had managed to avoid making a clear apology for the past.[115]

The one regional power that conceivably could have exerted more leverage on the history issue was the People's Republic of China. China had been the principal victim of Japanese aggression in the prewar period, and although many Japanese believed that the war had been justifiable or at least unavoidable, there was also a widespread awareness of the scale of the atrocities in China, especially among members of the older generation.[116] And unlike the Soviet Union, China was not viewed as a serious security threat by Japan at this point in time. Thus, Japanese feelings of remorse over their actions in China during the war were not constrained by a sense of threat in the way that German feelings of guilt toward Russia were during the cold war. In addition, there was strong sentiment inside Japan in favor of better relations on the basis of both pragmatic grounds (the lure of China's potentially huge market and as a counterbalance to both the United States and the Soviet Union) and ideological ones (China as a fellow Asian nation).[117] Later, after Sino-U.S. relations thawed in the early 1970s and China became a de facto ally in the struggle against the Soviet Union, Chinese influence increased even further. However, for a variety of reasons, China chose not to exercise its influence to pursue the issue of historical justice. In fact, if anything, it aided and abetted Japan's effort to avoid facing up to its past.

During the early part of the cold war, the People's Republic of China (PRC) adopted a remarkably lenient stance on the issue of Japanese guilt and war responsibility. Although the Communists had taken a large number of Japanese prisoners and put over 1,000 of them on trial in Nanjing, it executed only forty-five and allowed the rest to return home in 1946. China also helped repatriate a large number of Japanese stranded on the mainland, around 29,000 by 1955,

[114] Japan had also been willing to pay individual compensation to former slave laborers, but it balked when the Korean side insisted that any such monies be paid into a central, government-controlled fund. Francesca Seraphim, *War Memory and Social Politics*, op. cit., pp. 202–205.

[115] Wakamiya, *The Postwar Conservative View of Asia*, pp. 194, 235–240. Originally, the Korean government had hoped for an official statement of apology by Prime Minister Sato, but the Japanese side, mindful of Kishi's negative experience and fearful of a domestic political backlash, demurred and sent Foreign Minister Shiina instead.

[116] This is a point the author has heard many times from Japanese interlocutors over the years, including ones who were decidedly centrist or even conservative in their political views.

[117] See in particular John Welfield, *An Empire in Eclipse: Japan in the American Alliance System*, op. cit.; John Dower, *Yoshida Shigeru*, op. cit.; see also Tanaka Akihiko and Yoshihide Soeya.

and – in marked contrast to the Chiang Kai Shek regime in Taiwan – it showed little interest in pursuing the reparations issue.[118]

Behind Beijing's generosity was the calculation that Japan could be lured away from the U.S. embrace through "people's diplomacy," reaching out to nongovernmental actors and popular opinion to indirectly reshape Japan's political agenda in the long term. To this end, China at that time espoused a historical narrative that downplayed Japanese atrocities in China and diminished its feelings of guilt. It was the militarists and imperialism that was China's enemy, the architect of Chinese foreign policy, Zhou En Lai insisted, not the Japanese people. The Japanese people were themselves the victims of imperialism, and it was the aim of the Chinese government to form a united front with them and other independent nations to counter the United States' baneful influence in the region.[119] This position dovetailed with the historical narrative promoted by the Japanese Left and the peace movement and may have reinforced the Japanese Socialists' preference to focus on the Japanese people as victims rather than victimizers.

One consequence of this strategy was that, although there was a massive, antigovernment student movement in Japan during the 1960s and 1970s, unlike their counterparts in France and Germany at the time, young people in Japan did not seize on the history issue to criticize the older generation. Instead, they protested the Mutual Security Treaty, the Vietnam War, and what they perceived as the government's insensitivity to public concerns on a broad range of issues, including the environment. Japan's history of aggression and atrocities in Asia was not a central issue. The U.S. bombing of North Vietnam evoked widespread popular sympathy and revived memories of the savage bombing campaigns against Japan during the war, memories that were exploited by the Left in their campaign opposing the U.S.-Japanese alliance. They did not stir the memory of the Japanese bombing of Shanghai or other comparable events during the Imperial era.[120]

In the later part of the cold war, China chose not to pursue the history issue because of Japan's strategic value as an ally against the Soviet Union. Although the PRC rejected the argument that it was obliged to drop the right to claim reparations because Taiwan had already done so, China agreed to do so as a gesture of friendship to the Japanese people. When Prime Minister Tanaka visited Beijing in September 1972, Zhou Enlai greeted him saying, "We know the crippling hardships of war reparations. We do not want the Japanese people to suffer these hardships."[121] In effect, China joined the Western powers and other Asian nations (with the exception of North Korea) in giving up its

---

[118] Yinan He, *The Search for Reconciliation*, op. cit., pp. 151–153.

[119] Yinan He, ibid., pp. 119, 134–136, 153–156.

[120] Thomas Havens, *Fire Across the Sea: the Vietnam War and Japan, 1965–1975* (Princeton: Princeton University Press, 1987).

[121] Cited in Wakamiya, *The Postwar Conservative View of Asia*, p. 251. This was a subtle dig at Japan because the Chinese experience Zhou was referring to was the reparations that Japan imposed on Qing dynasty China after the Sino-Japanese war in 1895. Once again, Zhou

right to demand reparations. Similarly, China did not insist on an apology for the war from Japan, even though Prime Minister Tanaka had publicly acknowledged that a contrite stance on history would be necessary.[122] Again, on this issue Zhou Enlai chose to adopt a generous position. In the official banquet greeting Tanaka, Zhou referred to the 2,000-year history of relations between the two countries, and although he blamed Japanese militarists for the war and suffering caused between 1895 and 1945, he did not raise the issue of apology. For his part, Tanaka spoke of "an unfortunate period over dozens of years in the past" and said that he would like to express "deep remorse for the huge trouble (*meiwaku*) which Japan caused to the Chinese people."[123] Although one could describe the prime minister's words as an apology, they were vague in form and content.

In sum, although operating in a very different international setting and with a very different domestic political system (Left-Right polarization in Japan as opposed to Left-Right collusion in Austria), similar to the Austrians, Japan was successful in establishing and maintaining through the 1950s, 1960s, and 1970s an official historical narrative that by and large bypassed the more unpleasant chapters in its modern history. On the level of public discourse, however, the issue never disappeared. Beginning in the 1960s, debates and controversies over this topic increased, as conservative historians and opinion makers tried to promote an exculpatory narrative regarding the war in China and the Pacific,[124] and liberal commentators, bolstered by increased contact with the East Asia region, published long descriptions of Japanese atrocities, especially on mainland Asia. This public debate was reflected in Japanese textbook policies, which after 1972 began to include increased references to Japanese aggression and atrocities in Asia.[125]

---

was underlining China's moral superiority to Japan. See also Zhu Jianrong, *Gaikō Foramu* (October, 1992).

[122] In March 1972, before he became prime minister, Tanaka had said in the Diet that, "In my opinion, the first precondition for the normalization of diplomatic relations with China is our understanding that Japan caused China tremendous trouble (*meiwaku*) and that we truly want to offer an apology from the bottom of our heart." According to his memoirs, however, Tanaka did not necessarily believe that it was a war of aggression, but he wanted to send a signal to China. Wakamiya, *The Postwar Conservative View of Asia*, op. cit., p. 250.

[123] Wakamiya, *The Postwar Conservative View of Asia*, op. cit., pp. 251–252.

[124] The key work here was Haysahi Fusao's *Daitōasensō Kōteiron*, op. cit.

[125] Orr, *The Victim as Hero*, chapter 4, op. cit.; Takashi Yoshida, "The Battle over History: The Nanjing Massacre in Kapan," in Joshua Fogel, ed., *The Nanjing Massacre in History and Historiography* (Berkeley and Los Angeles, CA; University of California Press, 2000); Nozaki Yoshiko and Inokuchi Hiromitsu, "Japanese Education, Nationalism and Ienaga Saburō's Textbook Lawsuits," in Laura Hein and Mark Selden, *Censoring History: Citizenship and Memory in Japan, Germany and the United States* (Armonk, NY: M.E. Sharpe, 2000); Mitani Hiroshi, *Rekishi Kyokashō Mondai* (Tokyo: Nihon Tosho Sentaa, 2007), esp. p. 175 ff. For a quantitative content analysis of Japanese textbooks, see Tomochiko Okamoto, *The Distortion and Revision of Postwar Japanese History Textbooks, 1945–1998*, available at http://homepage3.nifty.com/ubiquitous/MA/index.htm (accessed March 2006).

Japanese public opinion data as well pointed toward the development of a more critical view of the past. According to a 1967 Cabinet office poll, when asked "What do you think of the Sino-Japanese war?" 17.1 percent of those surveyed said, "We did a bad thing." By 1972, the number of those who believed Japan had done wrong had increased to 26.4 percent, and the percentage who felt that it had been a war of self-defense declined from 9.7 to 8.4 percent – a substantial increase in the number of those with a clearly penitent view of Japanese history relative to those with a clearly impenitent one. Nevertheless, the percentage of those who felt that the war had been unavoidable increased from 35.9 to 46.6 percent, reflecting the continued ambiguity that much of the Japanese public felt about the war.[126]

There was also a great increase in public interest in the war, including in atrocities such as the Nanjing massacre and Unit 731. Reflecting this increase in public interest was a publishing boom of books on the subject, beginning with the best-selling series by Asahi correspondent Honda Tatsukichi in which he revisited the sites of wartime atrocities by Imperial forces.[127] During the same period, regional governments and nongovernmental organizations – typically of a left-wing political orientation – began gathering and publicizing accounts of civilian suffering on a local level.[128] Instead of receding with the passage of time, the memory of the war and the debate over its horrors and who was responsible for them in certain respects was intensifying.

Whereas the international environment of the 1950s through the 1970s allowed Japan to maintain an official narrative that, on the whole, was only minimally contrite, as in Austria on a societal level, the overall trend in the discourse on history was in a decidedly more contrite direction. The Japanese government professed an official stance of innocence, but in reality it was an increasingly guilty innocence. Developments in the international sphere in the 1980s would accelerate that trend.

## Getting to Be Sorry: Japan's Discovery of Guilt 1982–1993

As in Europe, the 1980s was a decade when history returned with a vengeance to the diplomatic agenda in Asia. After having apparently worked out a *modus vivendi* on historical justice issues with all of its major partners, the Japanese were shocked when Japan's official narrative was challenged not only by its traditional opponents on the Left but also by many of the countries that in the past had acquiesced to Japan's ritual professions of regret, but not repentance. A number of factors drove the reemergence of history on the international stage,

---

[126] Yoshida Yutaka, *Nihonjin no Sensōkan*, op. cit., p. 125.

[127] Honda Tatsukichi, *Chūgoku no Tabi* (Tokyo: Asahi Shimbunsha, 1972) followed by *Chūgoku no Nihongun* (Tokyo: Sōjusha, 1972). On the debate that this triggered, see Takashi Yoshida, *The Making of the "Rape of Nanking": History and Memory in Japan, China and the United States* (Oxford and New York: Oxford University Press, 2006), pp. 82–89.

[128] Yoshida Yutaka, *Nihonjin Sensōkan*, op. cit., pp. 154–156.

including changes in the domestic politics of neighboring countries (particularly south Korea and the PRC), shifts in the character of the Asian region, and finally, international political trends.

On the level of domestic politics, the pluralization of politics inside South Korea and China opened up the political discourse of both countries. Whereas the dictatorial Park Chung Hee regime could afford to ignore popular protests during the normalization negotiations in 1965, Park's successors became increasingly sensitive to public opinion on a range of issues, including the question of pursuing historical justice in the context of Korean relations with Japan. Once Korea democratized after 1988, these pressures gained strength and fueled the emergence of political groups who sought to place pressures on Japan to apologize. The most notable of these were the various nongovernmental associations (NGOs) supporting the cause of Korean Comfort Women.[129]

In the case of China, beginning in the early 1980s, students and other critics of the Chinese regime increasingly used the history issue to indirectly criticize their own government. Although it remained difficult to directly challenge the authority of the Chinese Communist Party (CCP), it was relatively safe to criticize the policies of the party toward relations with Japan. This pattern of protest, which could already be seen in 1982, followed a long tradition in Chinese history, dating back to the May Fourth Movement of 1919 when masses of demonstrators took to protest the Nationalist government's acceptance of the award of German colonial interests to Japan at the Paris Peace Treaty. This tendency grew stronger as the Communist party increasingly turned to Chinese nationalism as a substitute for the discredited Maoist ideology that had helped legitimate the regime in the past.[130] In both countries, Japan's unwillingness to pursue historical justice became symbols of the previous regime's disregard of the interests of the people.

On a regional level, the growing economic power of the rest of Asia – and the concomitant growth in regional trade, investment, and political interaction – helped transform the terms under which historical issues were negotiated. Whereas in the 1970s Japan was still by far the most advanced and powerful economy in the region, by the 1980s other Asian countries were beginning to

---

[129] On the development of the comfort women movement, see Chunghee Sarah Soh, "Korean Comfort Women: The Movement for Redress," *Asian Survey* 36:12 (1996), pp. 1227–1240.

[130] See in particular Yinan He, *The Search for Reconciliation*, op. cit., especially pp. 214–215. The argument that bottom-up nationalism plays an important role in feeding Chinese anti-Japanese sentiment is made by a number of other experts on China: Peter Hays Gries, "Nationalism, Indignation and China's Japan Policy," *SAIS Review* 25:2 (Summer-Fall, 2005), pp. 105–114; and James Reilly, "China's History Activists and the War of Resistance against Japan," *Asian Survey* 44:2 (March/April 2004), pp. 276–294. Suisheng Zhao argues that there are several, different nationalist currents in China – nativists, anti-traditionalists, and Liberal nationalists – all of whom are critical of the state and the more pragmatic nationalism of the state. One of the prime concerns of China's leaders in recent years has been to keep control of China's nationalist discourse and to prevent it from being used to undermine the rule of the Chinese Communist Party. Suisheng Zhao, "China's Pragmatic Nationalism: Is It Manageable?" *The Washington Quarterly* 29:1 (Winter 2005–06), pp. 131–144.

catch up. South Korea and Taiwan, which had been engaged largely in light manufacturing into the 1970s, were emerging as industrial powerhouses in their own right, competing with Japan in such fields as consumer electronics, ship building, steel, and even automobiles. After 1978, China, which had been for decades crippled by Communist ideology and the stifling hand of state economic controls, began to progressively liberalize its economy, triggering an economic boom that would last well into the twenty-first century. In Southeast Asia as well, economic growth began to take off – much of it fueled at first by Japanese investment but increasingly driven by the rise of a large and prosperous domestic middle class. Japan was naturally keen to tap Asia's vast economic potential, especially as the more mature markets of Europe and the United States were turning increasingly protectionist. Already in the 1970s, Japanese firms had started to invest huge amounts of moneys in the rest of Asia, and by the late 1980s, Japanese commentators were proudly declaring that the twenty-first century would be "the Asian century" (with the underlying assumption that it would be an Asia led by Japan).[131] Japan's growing economic interests in East Asia made it increasingly sensitive to pressures coming from the region. Whereas in the 1950s or 1960s Japanese elites could be relatively indifferent to Chinese or Korean public opinion, by the 1980s this was no longer the case.

The third and final factor that fueled the development of the history issue in the 1980s was a factor that we already saw at play in Europe during the same period: the emergence of a nascent global historical justice regime. Stemming from the development of the international human rights regime, there emerged a worldwide movement of activists, internationally active NGOs, and last, but not least, lawyers promoting the cause of historical justice.[132] Buttressed by a growing body of international treaties and conventions and buoyed by a highly globalized media, these groups put considerable pressures on countries to apologize for their past transgressions. The human rights discourse helped legitimate Chinese and Korean demands for apologies and compensation from Japan. Beginning in the 1980s, this new international movement supported demands for justice and compensation on the behalf of various victim groups, such as former prisoners of war, forced laborers, and the comfort women. Often they pointed to West Germany as a model for the type of policies that they wished Japan should adopt.

In sum, by the 1980s, the international parameters within which the history issue had been handled in the past had been transformed. As in Europe, the tenor of the times favored a marked increase in demands for historical justice. The pluralization of politics in China and South Korea allowed the long

---

[131] The literature on the economic rise of East Asia is vast. A good overview is offered by Jose Edgardo Campos, *The Key to the East Asian Miracle* (Washington, DC: Brookings, 1995). On Japanese investment in the region, see Warren Hatch, *Asia in Japan's Embrace: Building a Regional Production Alliance* (Cambridge and New York: Cambridge University Press 1996).

[132] For a fascinating examination of the role of lawyers, see Eizenstat, *Imperfect Justice*, op. cit.

stifled voices of former victims to be heard. Increased regional economic and political interdependence gave those voices greater international political weight, while the spread of human rights norms gave them enhanced legitimacy.

The triggering event for the reemergence of the history issue came in 1982, against the backdrop of a sharp renewal of cold war tensions. Following the Soviet invasion of Afghanistan and the expansion of its influence in the developing world, détente between the two superpowers had collapsed. At the same time, the Soviet military buildup – including its air and sea forces in the Asia Pacific region – increased Japan's sense of threat. For the first time since World War II, Soviet conventional forces could conceivably threaten Japan itself as well as its strategic sea-lanes on which its economic prosperity rested. The Soviet buildup of nuclear missiles – including a new generation of intermediate nuclear weapons stationed in Asia as well as Europe – raised difficult questions about the credibility of the "nuclear umbrella" the United States had extended over Japan. In response, Japanese conservatives led by the hawkish Prime Minister Nakasone Yasuhirō sought to rally domestic political support for a significant strengthening of the U.S.-Japanese alliance and a large-scale expansion of Japan's international military role.

From the perspective of conservative politicians such as Nakasone – much like his German counterpart Chancellor Helmut Kohl – this meant not only making the intellectual case for increasing Japan's military efforts but also a spiritual one. Japan needed to develop once again a healthy sense of patriotism, based on an affirmative view of Japan's past.[133] Already in the early 1980s, LDP heavy-weight Okunō Sosuke and other members of the "education tribe" (LDP members specializing in educational policy) turned their sights on textbooks and pushed for a more positive portrayal of the Japanese Empire and its expansion into Asia in the belief that Japan had to counter the debilitating effects of the liberal educational establishment.[134]

In June 1982, the liberal *Asahi* newspaper published a series of articles criticizing government pressures on textbook writers to change the wording of their manuscripts in ways that would downplay Japan's history of aggression in Asia. For instance, instead of "invading" (*shinryaku*) China in 1937, Japanese forces were described as "advancing" (*shinshutsu*) into China. These media reports were only partly accurate, and they drew a swift rebuttal from the Japanese government. Nonetheless, they sparked a wave of controversy throughout Asia and beyond. Formal protests were issued by the governments of China, Taiwan, and South Korea. Asian newspapers were scathing in their criticism of the move and warned that it was a potential harbinger of the revival of Japanese militarism. Labor Unions in Hong Kong delivered a note of protest

[133] The author is indebted in particular to the late Satō Seizaburō, professor at Tokyo University and advisor to Prime Minister Nakasone, for his insight and guidance on this issue.

[134] See Ōtake Hideo, *Sengo Nihon no Ideorogii tairitsu* (Tokyo: Sanichi Shobo, 1996), chapters 2 and 3.

to the Japanese consulate. In Geneva, the British representative to the UN High Commission on refugees criticized Japan for distorting history.[135]

Japanese public opinion as well tended to be critical of government efforts to whitewash history. According to a *Mainichi* newspaper poll taken that year, only 6 percent supported the position that the "darker sides of the past should not be taught in the classroom," whereas 92 percent took the position that all aspects of the wartime past should be taught.[136] With respect to the specific historical questions that were at issue, however, Japanese public opinion was somewhat more ambiguous. According to a *Yomiuri* poll, only 27.6 percent thought that the textbooks were historically mistaken, whereas 18.3 percent felt that they were accurate at least from a Japanese perspective, and 3.7 percent felt that they were historically correct. A further 28.5 percent felt that regardless whether they were accurate or not, they showed inadequate sensitivity toward China and Korea.[137] Despite these uncertainties about the historical facts (and even about the nature of "facts"), these data suggest that a clear majority (56.1–27.6 percent who felt they were inaccurate plus 28.5 percent who felt they were insensitive) were critical of the Ministry's proposals on either factual or practical grounds.

A subsequent survey conducted by the Japanese cabinet office in 1984 provides further evidence that the public's views on history were complex and ambiguous. According to the data, over 50 percent of those surveyed believed that Japan's history from the Meiji period on had been one of aggression, and 82.5 percent believed that the Japanese people should reflect deeply and critically ((*kokoro kara fukaku hanseisubeki da*) on the oppression and massacres that were suffered by the people of China and Korea. However, 44.8 percent also felt that Japan's military expansion had been inevitable (versus 38.7 percent who did not), and 45.5 percent believed that the war had hastened the liberation of Asian people's from Western colonial domination. When asked whether the Japanese people had been victims or victimizers, 36.1 percent felt that the Japanese themselves had been deceived by the militarists and were thus themselves victims, as against 29.5 percent who felt that the large majority of the people at the time had cooperated with the militarists and could, therefore, be counted as victimizers, at least with respect to other Asian countries.[138] In short, there persisted a widespread feeling that the Japanese people had been victims of the war and that the conflict had been inevitable. At the same time, there was considerable agreement that Japan had behaved reprehensibly and should try to face up to the dark side of its history to the best of its ability.

---

[135] See Takashi Yoshida, *The Making of the "Rape of Nanking,"* op. cit., pp. 89–91.
[136] Sven Saaler, *Politics, Memory and Public Opinion: The History Textbook Controversy and Japanese Society* (Munich: Ludicum, 2005), op. cit., p. 131.
[137] Yoshida Yutaka, *Nihonjin no Sensōkan*, op. cit., p. 199.
[138] Yoshida Yutaka, *Nihonjin no Sensōkan*, op. cit., p. 12. Only 17 percent subscribed to the solidly impenitent view that the war had been about defending Japan and bringing peace to Asia.

Faced with sharp international and domestic political criticism, the Japanese government quickly revised its position. After defending the Education Ministry's policies, the Minister of Education Ogawa Heji described the invasion of China in 1937 as an invasion, the first time a cabinet-level official had done so.[139] Soon thereafter, Cabinet Minister Miyazawa Kiichi announced that the texts would be revised to reflect that Japan had indeed been guilty of aggression and that henceforth the opinions of Japan's neighbors should be one of the criteria for evaluating textbooks.[140] In short, instead of shifting Japanese opinion to the right, the conservative campaign to promote a more affirmative view of Japanese history had the opposite effect: It underlined and reinforced the trend toward greater contrition.

In 1985, an even bigger controversy erupted when on August 15 – the fortieth anniversary of Japan's surrender – Nakasone visited the Yasukuni shrine dedicated to the spirits of the 2.5 million soldiers and sailors who had fallen in Japan's wars since the Meiji restoration. Only a few months earlier, Chancellor Kohl and President Reagan had visited the military cemetery at Bitburg in Germany. Nakasone made a point of visiting the shrine in a public capacity and linked his move to a general "settlement of Japanese politics" (*Nihon Seiji no Sōkessan*) aimed at reversing what he and other conservatives saw as Japan's lack of a sense of patriotism. Nakasone also linked his visit to a significant shift in defense policy, namely breaking a self-imposed limit of 1 percent of gross national product (GNP) on defense spending.[141] While Japanese prime ministers had visited the shrine many times since the 1950s, none had done so in an official capacity since 1978[142] when the shrine authorities had decided to inscribe the names of the men who had been convicted as class A war criminals in the rolls of those honored at the shrine.

This time around, Japanese public opinion was relatively supportive of the prime minister's visit. According to an *Asahi* poll from October 1985, 50 percent of those surveyed thought it was good that the prime minister had officially visited the shrine, while only 23 percent thought it problematic.[143] Nonetheless, there was sharp criticism from the left end of the political spectrum, including

---

[139] Wakamiya, *The Postwar Conservative View of Asia*, op. cit., p. 197.

[140] Roger B. Jeans, *Victims or Victimizers?* Op. cit., p. 185; Yoshimasa Irie, "The History of the Textbook Controversy," *Japan Echo* 24:3 (August 1997), pp. 34–38.

[141] See Berger, *Culture's of Antimilitarism*, op. cit.; Kamanishi, *GNP 1% Waku*, op. cit., especially, pp. 21–22.

[142] Nakasone's predecessors, prime ministers Ohira and Suzuki had both visited the shrine but had declined to specify whether they were doing so in an official capacity or as private citizens.

[143] Cited in Daiki Shibuchi, "The Yasukuni Shrine Dispute," op. cit., p. 212, footnote 51. The *Asahi* figures jibed with other polls conducted at the time. A *Yomiuri* poll found 52 percent approved of the visit, against 25 percent who disapproved (23 percent gave no answer). When asked why they approved, 72 percent said that "regardless of constitutional provisions, it is appropriate to honor those who died for the sake of the country." *Yomiuri*, September 1985, cited in Elizabeth Hahn Hastings and Philip K. Hastings, eds., *Index to International Public Opinion, 1985–1986* (Westport, CT: Greenwood Press, 1987), pp. 333–334.

the *Asahi* and *Mainichi* newspapers.[144] More importantly, the international political response was overwhelmingly negative. Large-scale protests erupted all across China and South Korea, leading their governments to issue strongly worded protests to the Japanese government. Of particular concern to Nakasone were the repercussions of his visit in China. Communist Party General Secretary Hu Yaobang, who had good personal relations to Nakasone and had been a strong advocate of improved ties with Japan, warned him that the visit was having a devastating impact on the Sino-Japanese relationship and was being used by conservatives within the PRC government to attack the work of Hu and other reformers.[145]

To avoid further damage to Japan's international image, Nakasone foreswore making any further trips to the shrine, despite strong pressures from the right wing of his party and the Association of Bereaved Families (*Izokukai*). When in the following year conservatives pushed Nakasone to make another visit, he declined, saying that he was sure that the honored spirits of the war dead would not wish him to do anything that would harm the national interest – a delightfully ingenious combination of Shinto theology and Realpolitik.[146] In taking this strong stand against the conservatives, Nakasone was backed by his powerful cabinet secretary Gotoda Masaharu and other pragmatically minded LDP leaders.[147]

Subsequently, despite his archconservative background, Nakasone went further in moving Japan's official narrative in a more contrite direction. In September 1986, Nakasone made a series of official statements in which he underlined that the invasion of China had been a war of aggression, and he instructed the Ministry of Education to force the revision of new textbooks produced by conservative authors who wished to downplay the Nanjing massacre and other wartime atrocities.[148] A few weeks later, when the conservative Minister of Education Fujio Masayuki published an article in which he justified the annexation of Korea in 1910 as having been a mutually agreed upon arrangement, Nakasone forced him to resign.[149]

In the late 1980s and early 1990s, as the cold war slowly wound down, conservative forces continued to agitate for a more positive view of Japanese history. Nakasone and his successors, however, did not succumb to these

[144] Daiki Shibuchi, "The Yasukuni Shrine Dispute," op. cit., pp. 206–207.
[145] Akihiko Tanaka, "The Yasukuni Issue and Japan's International Relations," in Hasegawa and Togo, *East Asia's Haunted Present*, op. cit., pp. 125–127. Hu's fears were in fact well founded, and it is believed that the anti-Japanese demonstrations in 1985 contributed to Hu's eventual downfall in 1987. See Yinan He, *Shadows of the Past*, op. cit., pp. 273–274.
[146] See interview with Nakasone, "Watakushi ga Yasukuni Jinja Koshiki Sanpai o dannen Shita Ryu," in *Seiron* (September 2001); and Wakamiya, *The Postwar Conservative View of Asia*, op. cit., pp. 176–177.
[147] Tanaka, "The Yasukuni Issue and Japan's International Relations," in Hasegawa and Togo, *East Asia's Haunted Present*, op. cit., p. 128.
[148] Wakamiya, *The Postwar Conservative View of Asia*, op. cit., pp. 177–178.
[149] Wakamiya, *The Postwar Conservative View of Asia*, op. cit., pp. 199–201.

pressures.[150] As the Soviet threat receded, the economic and political importance of Asia increased and so too the external pressures for Japan to address
the unresolved issues from its past.[151] Japanese business leaders were particularly sensitive to these pressures, and beginning in the 1980s, they began to
urge their government to find ways of reconciling Japan with its neighbors.[152]

In May 1991, Japanese Prime Minister Kaifu Toshiki made a landmark
speech in Singapore in which he outlined his vision for the creation of a new
Asian-Pacific community. In his speech, Kaifu stressed that understanding the
past and critically reflecting (*kibishiku hansei suru*) upon the harm that Japan
had inflicted on its neighbors was key to Japan's playing a more active role in
the region. Speaking on behalf of the Japanese people, he added, "I express our
sincere contrition for past Japanese actions which inflicted unbearable suffering
and sorrow upon a great many people of the Asia-Pacific region."[153] While the
prime minister's speech was criticized for not going far enough, it underlined a
general trend toward contrition that was continuing and even accelerating as
the cold war ended.

### Conclusions

Japan's experience with the politics of history during the cold war differed from
that of Europe's on many levels. From a Historical Determinist perspective,
Japan's history of Imperial expansion and aggression was fundamentally different from the European experience with Nazism, despite some broad parallels
and direct linkages. Japanese militarism was proportionately less destructive,
had emerged more slowly over time, and within an international political context that was more complex and ambiguous than that of Nazism or Fascism
in Europe. Similarly, the sociocultural prism through which these experiences
were filtered was quite different, and the terms used to discuss the war had

---

[150] Another challenge came in 1988, when director general of the National Land Agency Okuno
Seisuke was ousted for justifying Japan's actions in World War II. Okuno argued that it had
been "the white race" that colonized Asia and been an aggressor, and that it was therefore
nonsense to call Japan the aggressor militaristic. *Asahi*, April 26, 1988. Like Fujio, Okuno was
forced to resign.

[151] Australia in particular was voluble in pushing Japan to adopt a more penitent stance on the
past, with both prime ministers Keating (in 1991) and Hawke (in 1992) pushing Japan to
acknowledge responsibility for wartime horrors. Lind, *Sorry States*, op. cit., p. 169. Historical
issues also inserted themselves on the political agenda in relations with China and North Korea.
On China, see for instance Yinan He, "The Emerging Sino-Japanese Conflict," pp. 11–12. On
the intrusion of history on negotiations with North Korea in 1990, see Wakamiya, *The Postwar
Conservative View of Asia*, op. cit., p. 249. There was considerable activity on an NGO level
as well, particularly in South Korea, where issues that had long been neglected – such as the
fate of the comfort women – were brought to national attention. Soh, "The Comfort Woman
Movement," op. cit., Hicks, *Comfort Women*, op. cit., p. 173.

[152] *Gekkan Keidanren* (April 1992), cited in Yoshida, *Nihonjin no Sensōkan*, op. cit., p. 175.

[153] The text of the speech is available at http://www.mofa.go.jp/policy/other/bluebook/1991/
1991-appendix-2.htm (accessed May 30, 2006).

very different nuances and connotations than the ones used in the German and Austrian contexts. Instead of "guilt" (*Schuld* in German), in Japan the debate focused on "responsibility" (*sekinin*), and while the churches were active political actors in the German and Austrian debates and would eventually push for expressing repentance for the horrors of the past, in Japan religious organizations by and large played a much more passive role. When they did engage in the political debate, the focus was more on appeasing the spirits of the dead than on acknowledging moral culpability.

These historical and cultural differences, however, did not rule out the expression of remorse in the Japanese context. Already during the occupation, many individual Japanese were horrified by the immensity of the suffering that had been inflicted on the rest of Asia, and there was considerable popular sentiment favoring some sort of punishment for those responsible for the disasters of the war. To be sure, the Japanese public's sense of mortification was outweighed by their preoccupation with their own sense of victimization. Much the same, however, could be said of Austrians and Germans during the same period. In addition, as in Austria and Germany, with the passage of time and the establishment of greater temporal distance from the Imperial past, the Japanese public exhibited a growing sense of remorse for the actions of the past, as reflected in public opinion surveys and the general tone of public discourse.

The critical factor that prevented, or at least slowed, the emergence of a more penitent Japanese official narrative during the cold war was Instrumental calculations of interest, in particular the character of the dominant political elites in the immediate postwar era and to the nature of the international system in Asia. Far more so than in Austria or Germany, the political elites in post-1945 Japan were deeply implicated in the crimes of the Imperial era. Men such as Kishi Nobosuke, Shigemitsu Mamoru, or Kaya Okinori had every reason to resist supporting a historical narrative that would undermine their own legitimacy. They preferred either to avoid the issue or to blame the war on a small militarist clique. In this they were aided by the Left, which preferred to focus on Japanese civilian suffering to mobilize popular sentiment as part of their campaign against rearmament and the U.S.-Japanese military alliance.

Japan's international environment, like Austria's, allowed it to largely dissipate international pressures for a more systematic confrontation with the moral consequences of its history. Already before the cold war began in earnest, the United States had abandoned its initial zealous efforts to pursue the cause of historical justice in favor of a speedy reconstruction of Japan. Once containing the threat of Communism became the central objective of American foreign policy, what little enthusiasm that was left for punishing Japan's wartime elite evaporated. Other Western powers, including Britain, Australia, and the Netherlands, followed the American lead, whereas Japan's Asian neighbors had relatively little economic or political leverage to pursue the issue on their own. In the case of the PRC, calculations of interest even led the Chinese government under Mao Zedong to effectively aid and abet the conspiracy of silence about Imperial Japanese atrocities.

The contrast with the Federal Republic in this respect is instructive. As we have seen, similar to Japan – and Austria – the German political class's appetite for confronting its recent history was quite limited in the 1940s and 1950s. Although the German leadership was far more critical of the wartime regime than was true of their Japanese counterparts, like the Japanese and the Austrians, the overwhelming pressures to reintegrate the old elite and concentrate on national reconstruction made the active pursuit of historical justice not only impractical but even dangerous. Nonetheless, the Federal Republic's extreme vulnerability to pressures from countries that had been victimized by the Third Reich, forced it to adopt an official narrative that was far more contrite than was true of the other two cases in terms of the types of statements its political leaders made, the reparations that it offered, and the continued prosecution of those who had been responsible for the worst crimes of the wartime period.[154] Even in the case of the Federal Republic, however, the German expression of contrition into the 1960s continued to be diluted by the emphasis on the "Hitlerite clique" who had committed terrible crimes "in Germany's name."

As the cold war progressed, however, the international pressure on Japan to adopt a more contrite stance increased. Diplomatic pressures, particularly from China and Korea grew, while grass roots activists in neighboring countries began to revive the memory of Imperial Japanese atrocities (a topic we will return to in Chapter 5). The Japanese public discourse on the past also began to change, and increasing attention was paid not only to Japanese civilian suffering (which had long been an obsession of the Left) but also on civilian suffering in the rest of Asia. Spurred on by the belief that Japan had an opportunity to play a leadership role in Asia that was contingent on its ability to reconcile with its neighbors on historical issues, by the 1980s even deeply conservative political leaders such as Nakasone Yasuhirō were offering apologies for the misdeeds of Imperial Japan. Austria, in contrast, was entirely free of any comparable ambitions. As a result, Instrumentalist calculations of national interest led Japan to adopt, at least on the level of political rhetoric, a more penitent official narrative almost a decade before Austria began to do so.

The shift toward greater contrition in the Japanese official narrative, as was true in Germany in the 1960s to 1980s and in Austria in the 1990s, was far from easy. Japanese public opinion remained mixed on the issue, and there were powerful conservative elites – in the LDP, in interest groups such as the Association of Bereaved Families (*Izokukai*) and the Yasukuni shrine, and in major media outlets such as *Bungeishunjū* and *Sankei* – who promoted an impenitent historical narrative. They were motivated in part by the belief that Japan had

---

[154] A fact overlooked by some analysts who suggest that Japan today adopt an "Adenauerian approach" to the problem of history – that is pursuing reconciliation without contrition. See Jennifer Lind, "The Perils of Apology," *Foreign Affairs* 5:88 (September/October 2009). Even in the 1950s, the Federal Republic's official was far more contrite than Japan is today, and it is doubtful that it could have achieved as high level of cooperation as it did with France and the other Western powers in the 1950s if it had been less so.

nothing to be sorry about and in part because they feared that contrition would inhibit the development of a healthy sense of patriotism. Precisely as the Historical Realist perspective suggests, instrumental calculations of interest alone cannot explain the evolution of the historical narrative. Not only did the powerful emotional attachment that many people had placed in the existing official narrative make change difficult but the way in which many Japanese interpreted history shaped the way in which they understood the national interest. For a conservative politician such as Nakasone, an unburdened view of the Imperial past served Japanese national interest insofar as it strengthened the nation's capacity to defend itself and to pursue a more independent foreign policy. As many so-called constructivist scholars in the field of International Relations have argued, countries' perceptions of their interests are decisively shaped by their definition of national identity. Indeed, the protection and promotion of that identity is itself a vital national interest, for without it the nation's unity and its ability to mobilize for collective action are bound to collapse.[155]

As we saw earlier, similar factors had hindered the shift to a more contrite official narrative in Austria and the Federal Republic. Over time, however, the pressures of the international discourse on human rights combined with the practical interest in improving relations with neighboring countries had overcome resistance in Europe. As the cold war came to an end, similar dynamics seemed to be at work in Asia as well, and there were numerous signs that the Japanese government was ready to embark on a campaign of reconciliation with the rest of the region. As Japanese business and political leaders – quite correctly, as it would turn out – foresaw, in a region increasingly characterized by economic interdependence, increased political pluralism, and growing respect for human rights, it would be dangerous, if not impossible, to ignore strongly rooted demands for historical justice. Japan's efforts to act on this insight, however, were destined to be far less successful.

---

[155] Alexander Wendt, *Social Theory and International Relations*, op. cit.

# 5

## The Geopolitics of Remembering and Forgetting in Asia, 1991–2010

### Toward an Expanded Analytical Model

As Chapter 4 has shown, by the early 1990s Japan was in the process of redefining its official historical narrative in a more penitent direction. International pressures were pushing Japan toward greater contrition. Japanese public opinion had shifted significantly toward recognizing the suffering the empire had inflicted on other Asian countries. Powerful interest groups, in particular the business community, were pushing for a more conciliatory stance, and Japanese political leaders – even very conservative ones like Nakasone – were progressively adopting a more contrite rhetoric when speaking about the past. Within a decade, however, Japan was embroiled in a diplomatic crisis over history that was far more severe and more protracted than anything it had experienced before. Chinese and Korean resentment over aspects of the Japanese official narrative – in particular Prime Minister Koizumi's trips to the Yasukuni and the Ministry of Education's approval for the adoption of revisionist textbooks – boiled over into sometimes violent street demonstrations and mass letter-writing campaigns. High-level diplomatic contacts between Japan and its two main Asian neighbors – China and South Korea – were severely disrupted for nearly five years, and disputes that previously had been manageable – in particular the territorial disputes with China over the Senkaku/Diaoyutai islands and with Korea over the Dokdo/Takeshima islands[1] – intensified to an alarming and potentially dangerous degree.

While a complete breakdown in relations was avoided, the 2001–2007 war over history was an unusually turbulent and politically costly one. The bright hopes for building stronger regional structures that had characterized regional

---

[1] As is typical in such disputes, each side asserts its ownership by giving its own name to the territory. The cluster of small, uninhabited islands in the East China Sea that Japan refers to as the Senkaku, China calls Diaoyutai. The U.S. State Department prefers the name the Liancourt rocks. The two small islands in the Sea of Japan that Japan calls Takeshima, the Koreans insist should be named Dokdo. Because Korea is in de facto control of Dokdo/Takeshima, the Korean name is given preference here. On the same principle, because Japan occupies the Senkaku/Diaoytai islands, the Japanese name is given priority.

dialogue in the early 1990s were drowned out in a rising tide of nationalist recrimination.[2] Sharply growing threat perceptions between the major Northeast Asian powers helped to fuel a significant military buildup,[3] and new flashpoints for conflict between Japan and its neighbors emerged in the shape of an array of territorial disputes that would continue to fester well after the 2001–2007 diplomatic crisis was over.

In this respect, the evolution of the Japanese official narrative and its impact on the East Asian region differs sharply from the politics of history in Europe during the same period. In Europe previously impenitent Austria successfully – if fitfully – forged a domestic political consensus in favor of a more contrite official narrative. Other West European countries – most notably France – also began to wrestle with their past and began to offer apologies and restitution for past misdeeds. In contrast, Japanese efforts to move in a similar direction in Asia led to domestic political controversy and international diplomatic conflict. The examination of the politics of history in Japan during the cold war period in Chapter 4 has shown that neither Japan's alleged "historical amnesia" nor the power of conservatives with revisionist views alone can explain this outcome. Nor do the particulars of Japanese Imperial history or the peculiarities of Japanese culture provide an adequate explanation. Clearly, in this sense, the Asian experience confounds any teleological worldview that holds that there is a general trend toward increased acknowledgement of historical injustices – perhaps as a result of the emergence of some nascent international justice regime as has been suggested by some[4] or as a result of a universal crisis of the nation state as prophesized by others.[5] What then does account for Japan's inability to successfully pursue reconciliation with its Asian neighbors and for the extraordinary degree of contention that resulted?

To answer this question, we will need to widen the scope of our analysis beyond the range of factors we have looked at in the earlier chapters and examine the broader international and regional context within which they occurred.[6]

---

[2] For a detailed analysis of the disruptive impact of nationalism on efforts to build regional institutions, see especially Gilbert Rozman, *Northeast Asia's Stunted Regionalism: Bilateral Distrust in the Shadow of Globalism* (Cambridge and New York: Cambridge University Press, 2004); and Takehiko Kamo, "Globalism, Regionalism and Nationalism: Asia in Search of its Role in the Twenty-first Century," in Yoshinobu Yamamoto, ed., *Globalism, Regionalism and Nationalism: Asia in Search of its Role in the Twenty-first Century* (London: Blackwell, 1999).

[3] On the impact of Japanese impenitence on threat perceptions, see Thomas Christensen, "China, The U.S.-Japan Alliance and the Security Dilemma in East Asia," op. cit.; and Jennifer Lind, *Sorry States*, op. cit. On the buildup in arms in the Asian region, see Desmond Ball, "Arms and Influence: Military Acquisitions in the Asia-Pacific Region," *International Security* 18:3 (Winter 1993/1994), pp. 78–112. For a more sanguine look a decade later, see Ball, "Security Trends in the Asia-Pacific Region: An Emerging Complex Arms Race," Australian National University, Strategic and Defense Studies Centre, 2003, Working Paper No. 380.

[4] See Barkan, *The Guilt of Nations*, op. cit.

[5] See Jeffrey Olick and Brenda Coughlin, "The Politics of Regret," op. cit.

[6] Ideally, such an analysis would have been undertaken for all of the cases over time, and a number of recent excellent studies of the politics of history adopt precisely such an approach. See Yinan

This analytical expansion is necessary because if one looks at the international impact of the historical narrative solely within the context of a single country, there is a natural tendency to attribute the blame for any problem – or conversely, the credit for any success – to that particular country's action, without taking into account that the domestic dynamics of other countries may have an equally important impact on whether countries reconcile or not. One could refer to this omission as the problem "listening to the sound of one hand slapping."

The following three sections examine the evolution of the official narrative in Japan in the 1990s, the era of what I call "ah so sorry diplomacy" during which Japan made an abortive attempt to mend relations with its neighbors. The first of these three sections examines the changing domestic and international context of the Japanese debate; the second, the changes that they engendered in the Japanese official historical narrative; and the third, on how the history issue affected relations with neighboring countries. The next two sections then focus in some detail on the politics of history in South Korea and the PRC; focusing on the role of societal memory, calculations of interest, and the influence of the pattern of cultural discourse on the past will be considered in all three. The final section then focuses in on the diplomatic crisis that emerged between 2001 and 2007 following Koizumi's trips to Yasukuni and the approval for adoption of revisionist textbooks in Japan. The main concern here will be on how the intersection of historical memory and political interests produced a "war over history" of unprecedented dimensions.

## Japan and the Era of "Ah So Sorry Diplomacy": The Domestic and International Political Context

The end of the cold war and the changes in the international and East Asian regional system described in the previous chapters translated into a growing perception in Japan that more needed to be done on the history issue. Shifts in Japan's domestic political environment – some of which were indirectly encouraged by changes in the international system – further worked to increase the political saliency of the history issue. However, although both domestic and international forces were pushing Japan in the direction of expressing greater contrition regarding the war, the international system also created powerful incentives to promote a sense of patriotism to win greater public acceptance of the military and the use of force in foreign policy in general. In the end, there was significant movement toward greater contrition, but the Japanese official

He, *The Search for Reconciliation* op. cit.; Jennifer Lind, *Sorry States*, op. cit.; and Alexis Dudden, *Troubled Apologies among Japan, Korea and the United States* (New York: Columbia University Press, 2008). However, such an examination using the approach adopted here for the range of cases under consideration here would go well beyond what could be managed within the framework of a single volume. Fortunately, it is possible to come to some important conclusions regarding our central question – what are the determinants of the official narrative of states? – even using the more truncated approach adopted here.

narrative did not move as far or as fast as its counterparts did in Europe, and the gains that were made would soon prove reversible.

The effect of external pressures were most obvious and straight forward on the economic front, where burgeoning Japanese interests in Asian markets seemed to dictate increased responsiveness to the concerns of neighboring countries. Already in the early 1990s Japanese business leaders had begun to urge their government to tackle unresolved issues regarding the past. Over the next two decades, the business community would consistently be one of the leading voices for moderation on historical issues.[7]

Geostrategic considerations as well suggested that Japan needed to make greater efforts to seek reconciliation over history. The demise of the old Soviet military threat implied that originally compelling reasons for the U.S. military commitment to the region was gone, and there was considerable evidence that the United States was losing its interest in playing the role of guardian of the free world. President George H. Bush, whose administration had managed the collapse of Communism and successfully driven Iraq out of Kuwait, was defeated in a campaign whose most memorable line was "It's the economy stupid." At the same time, new security threats soon emerged in Asia, beginning with renewed tensions on the Korean peninsula over Pyongyang's atomic weapons program, followed by evidence of increased Chinese assertiveness in the shape of a series of incidents involving nuclear tests, disputed territories, and Taiwan.[8]

The initial response of Japanese policy makers to the new security environment was to bolster regional and global security institutions, starting in 1991 with the creation of the ASEAN Regional Forum (ARF) – an expanded regional security dialog centered on the nations of South East Asia, but including participation by China, Russia, the United States, and eventually both North and South Korea. Soon thereafter, in 1992, Japan for the first time dispatched Japanese military forces as part of UN sponsored peacekeeping operations. Institution building alone, however, soon proved inadequate for dealing with the new security challenges. As evidence mounted that the U.S.-Japanese alliance was foundering over burden-sharing issues,[9] Japanese leaders – beginning with Prime Minister Hashimoto Ryūtarō – reinvigorated the security relationship with the United States by turning it from an arrangement

---

[7] On business concerns, see *Gekkan Keidanren* (April 1992) cited in Yoshida, *Nihonjin no Sensōkan*, p. 175. See also Koike Hirotsugu, *Ajia Taiheiyō Shinron: Sekai o Kawaeru Keizai Dainamizumu* (Tokyo: Nihon Keizai Shimbunsha, 1993), especially pp. 306–307. The book as a whole reflects the great expectations that Japanese business leaders had at the time for a Japanese leadership role in the region.

[8] See Michael, J. Greene, *Japan's Reluctant Realism*, op. cit., as well as Michael J. Green and Benjamin L. Self, "Japan's Changing China Policy: From Commercial Liberalism to Reluctant Realism," *Survival* 38:2 (1996), pp. 35–58.

[9] For an excellent summary of the problems faced by the alliance in the first half of the 1990s, see Yoichi Funabashi, *Alliance Adrift* (New York: Council on Foreign Relations Press, 1999).

focused solely on defending Japan into one in which Japan would more actively support regional and (after 9/11) global U.S. security efforts.

However, Japan knew that its new efforts in the security field would be viewed with suspicion by the rest of Asia, in no small measure because of the widespread perception that Japan had not done enough in terms of facing up to its past. Lee Kwan Yew, the highly regarded prime minister of Singapore, was perhaps the most visible and eloquent spokesman for such fears, famously remarking that encouraging Japan to join in peacekeeping operations was like offering chocolate liqueurs to a reformed alcoholic: One taste and they were likely to keep on going. Similarly, at a public symposium in 1994, Lee warned that Japan – unlike Germany – was not entirely trustworthy because elements of the old militarist order had managed to "creep back into the mainstream."[10] Lee's concerns were echoed by Australian prime ministers Bob Hawke and his successor Paul Keating – both key allies of Japan in the creation of the ARF – who on repeated occasions urged Japan to apologize for the horrors of the past.[11] In short, as Paul Midford put it, Japan suffered from a bad reputation in the region. If it were to play a larger security role without starting a regional arms race, it needed to find ways of reassuring its neighbors.[12] Japan's official stance on history seemed the obvious and necessary place to start doing so.

Within the context of Japan's politics, where the armed forces were viewed with considerable distrust and there was a widespread reluctance to rely on military means for pursuing national interests, conservatives felt compelled to build public support for the armed forces by promoting a more positive public perception of the them. The need to reassure Japan's neighbors thus clashed with the need to mobilize domestic support for the military – a tension that Japanese policy makers would find particularly difficult to negotiate. Although Germany faced similar pressures to do so, especially as NATO became increasingly involved in the former Yugoslavia, it was fortunate that it could do so in a multilateral context in which military intervention could be justified on the grounds of defending human rights and living up to the expectations of the broader international community. Japanese policy makers, on the other hand, had only the narrower bilateral framework of the Mutual Security Treaty to work with.

Japan's domestic political climate as well was shifting in ways that encouraged a rethinking of the official narrative. In this connection, three developments were of particular importance. First, the death of Emperor Hirohito in 1989 marked the passing of an era and prompted a renewed discussion

---

[10] Wakamiya Yoshibumi, *The Postwar Conservative View of Asia*, op. cit., p. 49, 222. The author would also like to express his thanks to conversations with Kishore Mahubani on this point.

[11] Jennifer Lind, *Sorry States*, op. cit., p.169.

[12] See Paul Midford, "Making the Best of a bad Reputation: Reassurance Strategies in Japan's Security Policy," *Social Science Japan* 11 (November 1997); and Christopher W. Hughes and Akiko Fukushima, "U.S.-Japan Security Relations – Toward Bilateralsim Plus?" in Ells Krauss and T.J. Pempel, eds., *Beyond Bilateralism U.S.-Japan Relations in the New Asia-Pacific* (Stanford, CA; Stanford Press, 2004).

of Japan's pre-1945 past, both inside Japan as well as internationally. Many topics that had been taboo for decades now could be discussed without fear of embarrassing the emperor personally, including such sensitive issues as the emperor's – and Japan's – responsibility for Imperial expansionism and wartime atrocities. An explosion of publications on the war, the emperor, and Japan's responsibility for the war soon followed.[13]

Second, the end of the cold war triggered a dramatic reordering of the Japanese party political system. The LDP had always been fractious and faction ridden, but during the cold war, it had largely been held together by the fear that if the Socialists came into power, they would abrogate the Mutual Security Treaty with the United States. The demise of the Soviet threat thus weakened the bonds that held the party together and was one of the key background factors behind the LDP to split in 1993. Although the LDP was able to come back into power the following year, henceforth, it would be able to do so only in coalition with other parties – beginning with its old adversaries, the Socialists, followed by the Buddhist Kōmeitō. Both the Socialists and Kōmeitō had views on history that differed sharply from those of the majority of the LDP. For the Socialists in particular, changing the official narrative was an important part of their political agenda. To enter into coalition with the LDP, the Socialists had been forced to abandon many of the pacifist principles that had defined their party, including their opposition to the Self Defense Forces and the alliance with the United States. Socialist leaders saw changing the official narrative and improving relations with Asia as vital to maintaining their credibility with their rank-and-file members on the Left.[14]

Third and finally, Japanese civil society continued to gain in strength in the 1990s, and groups concerned with issues of history and historical justice grew apace – both on the left and right ends of the political spectrum. On the Left, groups such as Peace Osaka, with support from local government, opened museums and promoted exhibitions that moved beyond the Left's traditional focus on the Japanese people as victims of the war and placed new emphasis on Japan as the perpetrator of atrocities such as the Nanjing Massacre. Other groups, such as the Violence against Women in War network (VAWW) took up the cause of Chinese and Korean victims groups – most importantly the former comfort women and slave laborers – promoted their views through the media, and helped them to file law suits demanding compensation and apologies from the Japanese government.[15]

---

[13] Seraphim, *War Memory and Social Politics*, op. cit., pp. 272–275, and more generally Laura Fields, *In the Realm of the Dying Emperor* (New York: Vintage, 1993).

[14] Asano Atsushi, *Renritsu Seiken: Nihon no Seiji* (Tokyo: Bungeishunjū, 1999), Part II, chapter 3; Ryuji Mukae, "Japan's Diet Resolution on World War II: Keeping History at Bay," *Asian Survey* 36:10 (October 1996), pp. 1013–1014, 1017–1019.

[15] On NGO efforts on the behalf of the comfort women, see Hideko Mistsui, "The Resignification of the 'Comfort Women' through NGO Trials," in Gi-wook Shin, Soon-Won Park and Daqing Yang, *Rethinking Historical Injustice and Reconciliation in Northeast Asia: The Korean Experience* (New York: Routledge, 2007), pp. 36–54; and Carol Gluck, "Operations of Memory:

At the same time, groups on the Right redoubled their efforts to challenge what they saw as the shift to a "self-flagellatory" (*jigyaku*) view of history. These included both old groups such as the *Izokukai* (the Association of War Bereaved Families), which despite its declining membership remained a potent force in Japanese politics, as well as new groups such as the Society for Textbook Reform (*Atarashii Rekishi Kyōkasho o Tsukurukai*) – a politically well-connected and media-savvy group of writers and intellectuals who promoted the adoption of texts with a starkly unapologetic view of modern Japanese history.[16]

### Changes in Japan's Official Historical Narrative

This combination of changes in Japan's international and domestic political contest led to a sharp intensification of the debate over history. On the balance, the outcome of this debate in the 1990s was a shift toward greater contrition in the official narrative, especially on the rhetorical level. The shift was less pronounced, however, in other dimensions of the official narrative. Moreover, the fierce polemical battles that were sparked by efforts to change the official narrative seriously undercut – but did not entirely negate – efforts to promote reconciliation with Japan's neighbors.

The most controversial aspect of the new historical narrative was a sustained diplomatic campaign to apologize to its neighbors for the suffering that Japan had inflicted on the region in the pre-1945 era. The opening shot in this "apology offensive" came in Prime Minister Kaifu's 1991 speech in Singapore referenced at the end of Chapter 4. Kaifu's speech was widely criticized for evading the issue of Japanese responsibility for the war and colonial oppression. Nonetheless, it marked a significant turn in Japanese political rhetoric in the direction of greater contrition, and subsequently, other Japanese prime ministers would expand on Kaifu's remarks. In August 1993, in Diet interpellation Prime Minister Hosokawa Morihiro – the first non-LDP prime minister since 1955 – went further, saying that he believed that the "previous war" (*saki no sensō*) had been one of aggression and a mistake. Because his comments could be interpreted as applying not just to the war with the United States but might also apply more broadly to the history of Japanese Imperial expansion, it became an immediate source of controversy, and Hosokawa was much criticized not only by the LDP (which was then in the opposition) but also by voices from within his own coalition.[17] Hosokawa's stance on the issue, however, enjoyed broad public support. According to one poll taken soon after

Comfort Women and the World," in Sheila Miyoshi Jager and Rana Mitter, *Ruptured Histories: War, Memory and the Post-Cold War in Asia* (Cambridge: Harvard University Press, 2007), pp. 47–77.

[16] On the Tsukurukai, see Sven Saaler, *Politic, Memory and Public Opinion*, op. cit., especially chapter 1, and Tawara Yoshifumi, *Abunai Kyōkasho: 'Sensō o Dekiru Kuni o Mezasu 'Tsukurukai' no Jittai* (Tokyo: Gakushū no Tomosha, 2001).

[17] *Asahi* August 11, 2003.

Hosokawa's comments, fully 67 percent of the Japanese public approved of his comments, whereas only 15 percent did not.[18]

When the LDP returned to power in June 1994, it did so in coalition with its former rivals, the Japanese Socialists. The new prime minister Murayama Tomiichi of the Socialist Party was eager to use the history issue to demonstrate to his party's constituents that the Socialists had not simply sold out to the conservatives for the sake of gaining office.[19] He was therefore determined to go beyond Hosokawa and offer the most complete and forthright apology yet for both the war and Japan's history of colonial oppression. On August 15, the fiftieth anniversary of the end of the war, Murayama offered the following apology for Japan's actions before 1945:

During a certain period in the not too distant past, Japan, following a mistaken national policy, advanced along the road to war, only to ensnare the Japanese people in a fateful crisis, and, through its colonial rule and aggression, caused tremendous damage and suffering to the people of many countries, particularly to those of Asian nations. In the hope that no such mistake be made in the future, I regard, in a spirit of humility, these irrefutable facts of history, and express here once again my feelings of deep remorse and state my heartfelt apology (*kokoro kara owabi o hyōmei itashimasu*). Allow me also to express my feelings of profound mourning for all victims, both at home and abroad, of that history.[20]

Murayama's statement represented a watershed in the Japanese debate that bears comparison with the speech Friedrich von Weizsäcker, the president of the German Federal Republic, had given a decade before and the speech made by Franz Vranitzky in Austria three years earlier. Despite certain ambiguities,[21] it was the most far-reaching official acknowledgement of Japanese responsibility for the war and colonial domination to date. Moreover, the statement was approved unanimously by the full cabinet (*kakugi kettei*), giving the statement legal status as government policy as well as underlining its bipartisan character (half of the cabinet was composed of LDP members).

As with Hosokawa's comments a few years earlier, Japanese public opinion was generally supportive of the prime minister's statement. According to a June 1995 NHK (the Japanese public broadcasting corporation) poll, only 7 percent of those surveyed felt that Japan had apologized enough for the war; 45 percent felt that it had apologized to some extent, and 35 percent felt that

---

[18] Cited in Sven Saaler, *Politics, Memory and Public Opinion*, op. cit., p. 137.

[19] On the political importance of the campaign to the Japanese Socialist Party, see Asano Atsushi, *Renritsu Seiken:* op. cit., Part II, chapter 3.

[20] The full text (in Japanese, English, Chinese and Korean versions) is available at http://www. mofa.go.jp/announce/press/pm/murayama/9508.html (accessed March 12, 2006).

[21] Critics pointed out that the prime minister used the word "I" (*watakushi*) in offering his apology, suggesting that this was a personal view of his own and his cabinet and not one that reflected the broader Japanese nation. An analysis of subsequent statements would suggest that these concerns were not unfounded. Beginning in the late 1990s, the phrase "on behalf of the Japanese people," was added to "I", thereafter the phrase "the Japanese side" was substituted for "I." It was not until 2005 that Prime Minister Koizumi unambiguously said that Japan was making the apology.

it had not apologized enough.[22] Another NHK survey from that same year showed that fully 57 percent of the respondents felt that Japan had committed acts for which it should apologize.[23]

This shift toward a more penitent stance, however, was not uncontested, especially on the elite level. On the same day that Murayama made his apology, no fewer than eight members of his own cabinet visited the Yasukuni shrine. Time and again, senior political leaders – including members of the Hosokawa and Murayama cabinets – expressed revisionist views on history. In May 1994, Nagano Shigeto, former chief of staff of the Ground Self-Defense Forces and justice minister in the Hosokawa Cabinet, told newspaper reporters that Japan had been forced into the war for its own survival and that the Nanjing massacre had been a fabrication.[24] A few months later, in August, the director general of the Environmental Protection Agency in the Murayama cabinet, Sakurai Shin, similarly claimed that Japan had had "no aggressive intent" when it invaded Asia and emphasized that the Empire had an overall positive impact on the region.[25]

Both Nagano and Sakurai were forced to resign as a result of their outspoken revisionist stance on history. Nonetheless, they represented only the tip of an iceberg of opposition. Whenever a Japanese prime minister sought to adopt a more penitent stance on history, prominent members of the government gave voice to a solidly impenitent view of history, undermining and diluting the impact of the prime minister's statements.

The most dramatic example of this pattern came in June 1995, just a few weeks before Maruyama's landmark apology, when his government attempted to pass through the Diet a resolution marking the fiftieth anniversary of the end of World War II. Originally, the resolution was to include both a renunciation of war and a general recognition of the historical injustices perpetrated by Japan. However, a powerful coalition of LDP lawmakers, the Parliamentarian League on the Fiftieth Anniversary of the End of World War II, formed to block the measure. Headed by the ultraconservative Okuno Seisuke, this group counted altogether 143 of the upper and lower houses representatives among its members.[26] Another group – the Parliamentarians League to Bequeath Correct History – consisting of 28 lawmakers from the *Shinshintō* party, likewise attacked the proposal from the ranks of the opposition.[27] Behind both groups stood an alliance of ideologically conservative interest groups – including the *Izokukai* and the Shinto Shrines Headquarters (*Jinja Honcho*).[28] In the end,

[22] Cited in Mikyoung Kim, "Myths, Milieu, and Facts: History Textbook Controversies," in Hasegawa and Togo, eds., *East Asia's Haunted Present*, op. cit., p. 102.

[23] Sven Saaler, *Politics, Memory and Public Opinion*, op. cit., p. 150.

[24] *Mainichi* May 5, 1994.

[25] *Asahi* August 13, 1994.

[26] Mukae, "Japan's Diet Resolution on the End of World War II," op. cit., p. 115.

[27] Mukae, "Japan's Diet Resolution on the End of World War II," ibid., p. 116.

[28] These groups were believed to wield greater political power than ever as a result of the introduction of a new electoral law. Mukae, "Japan's Diet Resolution on the End of World War II," ibid.

the greatly diluted language of the resolution avoided making a direct apology and relativized Japanese actions through reference to the history of Western expansionism and colonialism. As a result, unlike the Weizsäcker statement in Germany, the No War Resolution had only limited impact on the official historical narrative in Japan and may actually have helped undermine the credibility of the prime ministers' apologies overseas.[29]

Other dimensions of Japan's official historical narrative reflected a similar pattern of a general trend toward greater contrition coupled with strong countervailing pressures coming from the Right. In the area of policies pertaining to commemoration, there was a proliferation of monuments and museums dealing with Japan's wartime past. Some of these provided extensive coverage of Japanese war atrocities and colonial oppression.[30] For instance, in 1995 museums in both Hiroshima and Nagasaki included exhibits on Japan's history of aggression even though they continued to condemn the atomic bombings and the suffering that had been inflicted on the Japanese people. When asked about the change in policy, the mayor of Hiroshima said, "We ourselves were overwhelmed by the terrible damage of the atomic bomb. But we found that people around the world were not necessarily sympathetic. We realized it was necessary to see ourselves not only as victims of war but also as perpetrators."[31]

The new museums presenting a more penitent view of Japan's modern history were supported exclusively by local as opposed to the national government. Moreover, they soon came under fierce attack from conservative groups and politicians, who questioned the accuracy of the new exhibits and demanded a more "balanced" view of Japanese history, that is, one that offered a more positive evaluation of the nation's past. In 1996, upper house LDP members set up a special investigatory committee that criticized Peace Osaka for disseminating what it labeled politically motivated propaganda.[32] The political pressure became so intense that in 2000 one progressive museum, Peace Osaka, was compelled to allow conservative groups to hold a starkly revisionist event on their premises entitled, "The Biggest Lie in the Twentieth Century: Complete Verification of the Massacre in Nanjing."[33]

Although the battle over history raged on the local level, still there was no national government sponsored memorial or museum dealing with Japanese

[29] See editorial in the *Asahi* satellite edition, June 23, 1995. For detailed analyses, Mukae, "Japan's Diet Resolution on the End of World War II," ibid., and John Dower, "Japan Addresses its Wartime Responsibility," *Journal of the International Institute: University of Michigan* 3:1 (Fall 1995), pp. 8–11.

[30] Yamabe Masahiko, "Chiiki ni nesazu Heiwa no Tame no Sensō Tenji," *Rekishi Hyōron* 556 (August 1996), pp. 12–22.

[31] Roger B. Jeans, "Victims or Victimizers?" op. cit., pp. 168–170. Left-wing activists had already petitioned the Hiroshima government in 1987 to set up an exhibit to be called the "Aggressor's corner" that would deal with Japanese wartime atrocities. However, after a right-wing rally, the petition was rejected. See Ian Buruma, *The Wages of Guilt* (New York: Farrar, Strau, Giroux, 1994), op. cit., pp. 106–108.

[32] Hein and Takenaka, "Exhibiting World War II," op. cit., p. 70.

[33] Roger B. Jeans, *Victims or Victimizers?* op. cit., pp. 176–177.

war crimes and oppression. After tremendous controversy and political infighting, the Showa Hall (*Showakan*) – which is a national (*kokuritsu*) museum sponsored by the Ministry of Health and Welfare – was opened in Tokyo in 1999. Unlike the openly revisionist Yushukan museum attached to the Yasukuni shrine, the Showakan did not attempt to defend pre-1945 policies. Instead, the museum's exhibitions focused on everyday life in wartime Japan – the types of clothing women wore during the war, posters exhorting the population to save money, or the kinds of boots worn by Japanese soldiers when they were dispatched to fight and die for the sake of the Empire. Insofar as the museum brought to light the immense suffering of the Japanese people during the war, it could be said to fit into the antimilitarist mainstream in Japanese public discourse. At the same time, the Showakan avoided entirely the larger political and international context that had brought the war about in the first place. It thus sparked considerable outrage both abroad and among progressive circles in Japan, who had hoped for a more serious engagement with the issue of Japanese responsibility for the war.[34] As one U.S. reporter sarcastically put it, the history of the war "is less about Japanese soldiers' footwear than about whom they stepped on."[35]

The 1990s also saw a progressive shift in Japanese educational policy as a growing number of textbooks approved for adoption by the Ministry of Education included references to wartime atrocities such as the Nanjing massacre, the savagery of the counter insurgency campaign in North China, Unit 731, and, most controversially, the comfort women.[36] Lending further impetus to the trend was a 1993 Supreme Court ruling in favor of a lawsuit brought by Ienaga Saburo, a liberal historian at Chuo University who had repeatedly challenged the Ministry's textbook screening system. While the court ruled that the system of textbook screening was constitutional insofar as it corrected factual errors and inaccuracies, it found that Ministry of Education's efforts to censor

---

[34] Roger B. Jeans, "Victims or Victimizers?" op. cit., p. 157. The museum had been proposed already in the late 1970s, but the project had been repeatedly delayed as a result of bitter fighting between various ideological groups. Conservatives and veterans groups wanted the museum to pay tribute to those who had lost their lives in the war and avoid criticizing the war and the motives of those who fought it. Centrists and progressives were opposed to whitewashing history. The focus on civilian suffering represented the lowest common denominator on which all the parties could agree. For more on the background to the controversy, see Ellen Hammond, "Politics of the War and Public History: Japan's Own Museum Controversy," *Bulletin of Concerned Asian Scholars* 27:2 (1995), pp. 56–60; Hosoya Chirhiro and Ide Magoroku, "Sensō o kioku suro to iu koto, Rekishi o kioku suru to iu koto," *Sekai* 607 (1995), pp. 22–37; Fujiwara Kiichi, *Sensō o kioku suru: Hiroshima, Horokoosto to Gendai* (Tokyo: Kōdanhsa, 2001); and Tanaka Nobumasa, "Sensō no Kioku Sono Impei no Kozō: Kokuritsu Sensō Memoriaru o Tōshite* (Tokyo: Midori Kaze Shuppan, 1997).

[35] Jeans, "Victims or Victimizers," op. cit., p. 38.

[36] After 1997, the Ministry of Education even approved mention of the comfort women in textbooks for middle school students, a move that provoked considerable outrage not only among conservatives but also more mainstream Japanese who were concerned that such material might not be appropriate for adolescents.

references to sexual assaults by Japanese forces at Nanjing and the activities of Unit 731 constituted undue government interference in the textbook writing and ruled that 400,000 yen should be paid to Ienaga in compensation. Although previous rulings by the courts had come to a similar position, this was the clearest expression yet of judicial support for a more progressive stance on textbook writing.[37]

It should be pointed out that this shift in educational policy – unlike the changes in Austria around the same time – were not the product of explicit government policies to promote a more contrite historical narrative through the educational system. Rather, it was the result of trends in public and elite opinion, which took advantage of openings in the institutional structure of Japan's educational system – that is, the fact that textbooks were written by independent scholars and published by private companies. That the ministry approved of such textbooks, however, reflected the changed political atmosphere.

This new trend in textbook writing provoked a powerful counterreaction. Already in the 1980s, following the first textbook controversy of 1982, a network of conservative groups had formed under the aegis of an umbrella organization, the National Conference to Defend Japan (*Nihon o Mamoru Kaigi*). With close links to conservative politicians and government officials (especially in the Ministry of Education), the conference had become best known in the 1980s for its sponsorship of resolutions in various local assemblies that registered support for the Self Defense Forces. The conference was also active in promoting a conservative view of modern Japanese history, with a particular emphasis on textbook writing. One offshoot of this movement was the Society for the Creation of New History Textbooks (*Shinkyokashō o Tsukurukai*, commonly referred to as the *Tsukurukai*), which was formed in 1996 by several prominent conservative scholars.[38]

As its name suggests, the *Tsukurukai*'s main objective was to produce textbooks with a more positive historical narrative, but its members soon produced a wave of historical revisionist literature as well. Their output included not only scholarly treatises and polemics for a well-educated public[39] but also works aimed at a mass audience. Particularly successful in this connection

---

37 Nozaki Yoshiko and Inokuchi Hiromitsu, "Japanese Education, Nationalism and Ienaga Saburō's Textbook Lawsuits," in Laura Hein and Mark Selden, *Censoring History: Citizenship and Memory in Japan, Germany and the United States* (Armonk, NY: M.E. Sharpe, 2000).

38 Yoshida Takashi, "A Battle over History," op. cit., pp. 96–99; Saaler, op. cit.; Daiki Shibuichi, "Japan's History Textbook Controversy: Social Movements and Governments in East Asia, 1982–2006" Discussion Paper 4, *Electronic Journal of Contemporary Japanese Studies* (March 2008), available at http://www.japanesestudies.org.uk/discussionpapers/2008/Shibuichi.html (accessed November 13, 2009). For a more detailed look at the development of the Tsukurukai and its grassroots organizations, see Oguma Eiji and Ueno Yoko, *Iyashi Nashionarizumu: Kusa no Ne Hoshu Undō no Jishhō* (Tokyo: Keiō Gijuku Daigaku Shuppankai, 2003).

39 See for instance, Etō Jun, *Wasureta Koto to wasuresaserareta Koto* (Tokyo: Bunshun Bunko, 1996); Fujioka Nobukatsu, *Kingendaishi Kyoiku no Kaikaku: Zendama Akudama Shikan o koete* (Tokyo: Meiji Tosho, 1996); and Fujioka Nobukatsu, *"Jigyakushikan" no Byōri* (Tokyo: Bungeishunjū, 2001).

were the works of the popular *manga* author, Kobayashi Yoshinoro's, whose best-selling works *Sensōron* parts I and II, offered starry-eyed depictions of Japanese troops valiantly fighting against treacherous Chinese guerillas and brutal American invaders, images of demure comfort women bravely doing their best to assist in the war effort, and progressive intellectuals as agents of foreign powers who were trying to brainwash the Japanese people for their own nefarious purposes.[40]

The *Tsukurukai* evolved out of the traditional right-wing intellectual milieu, and many of its members – such as Etō Jun – had been prominent polemicists already in the early 1980s. What was new was the organization's adeptness at repackaging the traditional conservative-nationalist message to suit the tastes of a new generation. Its activities were soon to have international reverberations.

The final dimension of the official historical narrative that saw some change after the cold war was in the area of compensation and restitution. The most notable came with respect to the comfort women. The issue of the comfort women had been publicized in Japan beginning in the late 1970s, and the first suit by a former comfort woman demanding compensation was filed in Japanese courts in 1990. The Japanese government, however, adamantly denied that there had been any official involvement in the comfort women system, insisting that it had been organized entirely by private contractors. In 1992, however, the discovery of new documentary evidence in the archives of the National Defense Agency[41] compelled Prime Minister Hosokawa Morihirō to acknowledge that the Imperial government had in fact been involved in the forcible recruiting of comfort women. A special fund, the Asian Women's Fund (AWF), intended to identify surviving comfort women and to offer them financial assistance was subsequently established in 1995 under joint Japanese government and Japanese nongovernmental organization auspices. Two formal apologies were offered to each comfort woman, one on behalf of the Japanese government, the other on behalf of the Japanese people as represented by NGOs, along with 2 million yen (slightly under $20,000 at the time) in financial support, the bulk coming from the government. Unfortunately, the complicated structure of the AWF caused considerable confusion and gave rise to the impression that no apology or compensation was being offered by the Japanese government. Moreover, campaigns developed in Korea and other parts of Asia that rejected Japanese actions as insufficient and insulting. As a result, only a handful of comfort women came forward, and in the end, Japanese efforts on this front, instead of promoting reconciliation, arguably succeeded only in prompting a fresh round of criticism.[42]

---

[40] See Kobayashi Yoshinori, *Sensōron Sōsen* (Tokyo: Bunkasha 1999). On Kobayashi's nationalist views, see Kobayashi Yoshinori, "Rekishi o mamoru Kigai o ima koso torimadose," *Seiron* (September 2007).

[41] The author is especially grateful to the insights of Professor Onuma Yasuaki of Tokyo University, who was intimately involved in helping organize the AWF, on this issue.

[42] The author is indebted to the comments of Professor Onuma Yasuaki on this point. See also *Japan Times* August 13, 1998. There is some uncertainty over why only a handful of comfort

On the issue of individual compensation for other victims of Japanese actions prior to 1945 – including the large numbers of former forced laborers who filed suits in Japanese courts demanding apologies and compensation – the government refused to budge, arguing that the issue had been legally solved at the signing of the various bilateral treaties normalizing relations between Japan and other nations. Despite legal challenges, the Japanese courts, in the main, supported this government's position.[43]

In sum, although there was a significant shift toward greater contrition across the main dimensions of the Japanese historical narrative, compared with the European cases examined earlier, the shift was smaller, more uneven, and more deeply contested. The shift was far more pronounced in the area of official rhetoric and educational policies than was true with respect to commemoration. In the area of victim compensation, there was hardly any shift at all – in sharp contrast with both Austria and Germany, who saw compensating the victims of Nazism as central to their efforts to pursue reconciliation with their neighbors. In addition, unlike in Austria and Germany (and a number of other European countries at the time, including France[44]), there was no movement to punish the perpetrators of wartime atrocities or to clamp down on the expression of revisionist views. Although Japanese political leaders were convinced of the need to improve ties with their neighbors, their ability or willingness to implement an integrated political program to change the official narrative was decidedly limited by the weight of the political and social forces arrayed behind the existing, more impenitent stance on history. Instrumental calculations of interest thus clashed with an entrenched cultural discourse on history, producing considerable social and political friction, precisely as a Historical Realist perspective would suggest it would.

### The History Issue and Japan's Foreign Relations in the 1990s

Despite these shortcomings, Japan's efforts to achieve reconciliation with its neighbors had some success. In particular, considerable progress was made in improving the relationship between Japan and South Korea. President Kim Dae Jung's pivotal summit meeting with Japanese Prime Minister Ōbuchi Keizo in 1998 marked a high point in the relations between Seoul and Tokyo with

---

women have come forward. Some, such as Professor Onuma, blame it on the ambiguities of apology. Others point out that the considerable social stigma attached to being a former comfort woman discourages women from coming forward. Many Japanese conservatives not surprisingly claim it was because the problem has been much exaggerated if not wholly invented.

43 William Underwood, "Chinese Forced Labor, the Japanese Government and the Prospects for Redress," *Japan Focus*, available at http://www.japanfocus.org/article.asp?id=326 (accessed November 18, 2005); and Underwood, "Mitsubishi, Historical Revisionism and Japanese Corporate Resistance to Chinese Forced Labor Redress," *Japan Focus*, February 6, 2006, available at http://japanfocus.org/article.asp?id=513 (accessed March 21, 2005).

44 During the 1990s, there was a general movement toward adopting anti-Holocaust denial laws in Europe.

Ōbuchi offering an apology, and Kim Dae Jung accepting it on behalf of the Korean people.[45] Thereafter, agreements were reached on lifting the ban on the import of Japanese cultural products to Korea, on fishing in disputed waters in the Sea of Japan, and on the joint hosting of the World Cup soccer games. Following the successful conclusion of the soccer games in 2002, there was considerable evidence of a marked improvement in Japanese and South Korean public perceptions of each other, as reflected in both public opinion polls and increased popular interest in each other's culture.

Similar progress could be detected in Japanese relations with South East Asia, where anti-Japanese sentiment had been quite strong in the past – as reflected by the anti-Japanese riots that greeted Prime Minister Tanaka Kakuei when he toured the region in 1974 – and where the memory of the brutality of the Japanese occupation during the Pacific War could at least potentially have made history a major diplomatic issue. However, despite occasional expressions of historically based misgivings, South East Asian perceptions became increasingly positive throughout the decade.[46]

Despite burgeoning economic ties and substantive cooperation in other policy areas, there were no signs of any substantive movement toward reconciliation on the history issue in Sino-Japanese relations. This lack of progress is attributable in part to rising tensions between the two countries over a range of other issues, notably in the area of national security. Chinese nuclear tests in 1995 provoked considerable consternation in Japan, as did Chinese challenges to Japan's control over the Senkaku/Diaoyutai islands claimed by both countries. Even more disturbing to Japan were the PRC's 1986 efforts to intimidate pro-independence forces on Taiwan by firing barrages of missiles. As a result, a growing number of Japanese defense and foreign policy analysts began to openly talk of China as a potential security threat.[47]

Chinese demands for further apologies tended to be viewed by Japanese conservatives as the blatant efforts of a Communist regime to manipulate public

---

[45] For the text of the statement and initial press reactions, see *Asahi Shimbun* and *Yomiuri Shimbun*, October 8, 1998, p. 1. A cynic might observe that Kim did not go unrewarded for his tact. In return for softening his demands for an apology, Korea received an additional $3 billion in aid from Japan, thus continuing a pattern of Japanese money in return for Korean circumspection that dates back to 1965.

[46] See Bhubinhindar Singh, "ASEAN's Perceptions of Japan: Change and Continuity," *Asian Survey* 42:2 (March/April 2002), pp. 276–296. Diane Wong makes the argument that in Southeast Asian countries, unlike China and Korea, the focus of national passions is on the former colonial powers of the West. See Diana Wong, "Memory Suppression and Memory Production: The Japanese Occupation of Singapore," in Takashi Fujitani and Lisa Yoneyama, eds., *Perilous Memories: The Asia-Pacific War(s)* (Durham and London: Duke University Press, 2001), pp. 218–228.

[47] On the evolution of Sino-Japanese relations through the 1990s, see Michael Green, *Japan's Reluctant Realism* (New York: Palgrave, 2001), chapter 3; Mike Mochizuki, "Terms of Engagement: The U.S.-Japan Alliance and the Rise of China," in TJ Pempel, et al., *Beyond Bilateralism*, op. cit.; and Thomas Christensen, "China, The U.S.-Japan Alliance and the Security Dilemma in East Asia," *International Security*, op. cit.

opinion to bolster its own domestic legitimacy and to win diplomatic concessions. What made the PRC's actions all the more galling in their eyes was the
fact that the Chinese Communists themselves were guilty of appalling human
rights abuses that had occurred far more recently than Japanese misdeeds. As
a result, when Chinese leader Jiang Zemin visited Tokyo in the summer of
1998 – only a few weeks after Korea's Kim Dae Jung had – there was no comparable breakthrough on the history issue. Instead, Jiang's efforts to lecture his
Japanese hosts on the need to draw the correct lessons from the past were met
with a decidedly cool response. On the level of political symbolism, the trip
could only be viewed as a failure.[48] A year later, differences over history were
paved over when Obuchi visited China, and the two sides came to significant
agreements on economic and other issues; however, whereas Japan could make
some progress with Korea on the history issue, with China the best that could
be done was to maintain an uneasy peace.

At the start of the twenty-first century, Japan appeared to have taken the
first steps toward achieving a new equilibrium on the history issue, one that
was widely hoped to herald a new age of regional amity and cooperation.
Resistance from the conservative end of the political spectrum in Japan was
fierce; however, it should be recalled that there had been considerable right-
wing opposition in Europe as well when those countries had made their turn
toward a more contrite historical narrative. In the case of Austria, over 26
percent of the electorate had voted for Haider and the FPÖ in 1999, a party
widely known for its revisionist historical view. At the time of Weizsäcker's
1985 speech in Germany, Chancellor Kohl himself spearheaded a campaign to
promote a "healthy concept of patriotism," sparking international controversy
with his visit to the military cemetery at Bitburg. Politically powerful conservative backlashes against a more apologetic stance, however, did not prevent
the consolidation of a new official historical narrative in the German or Austrian cases, even though (as in Japan), their governments were dominated by
conservative parties.[49]

Japan failed to go further for a variety of reasons. One important factor was
the fractured nature of the Japanese political system and the inability of political elites to stymie initiatives that could not muster a consensus. As a result,
changes to the official historical narrative tended to be made in a haphazard
fashion. Japanese prime ministers such as Murayama and Obuchi might offer

---

[48] For a comparison of the Japanese reaction to the two visits, see Wakaiyama Yoshibumi, *The
Postwar Conservative View of Asia* (Tokyo: LTCB Library Foundation, 1998), pp. 256–261;
and Michael Green, *Japan's Reluctant Realism*, op. cit., pp. 96–98. Jiang Zemin's aggressive
stance on the history issue contributed to the failure of the trip and can be explained in part as
the product of the need to reach out to the military in the context of Chinese succession politics
at the time. See Caroline Rose, "The Yasukuni Shrine Problem in Sino-Japanese Relations,"
in John Breen, ed., *Yasukuni, the War Dead and the Struggle for Japan's Past* (New York:
Columbia University Press, 2010), p. 37.

[49] On this point, the analysis here disagrees fundamentally with the position taken by Jennifer
Lind, "Perils of Apology," op. cit.

apologies, only to have their impact undercut almost immediately by contradictory statements offered by senior conservative politicians. Progressive scholars might produce textbooks that covered Japanese misdeeds, but conservative scholars could counter mobilize and produce revisionist texts that attracted far more attention. In some areas, such as compensation and commemoration, there was no movement at all.

In addition to these domestic political factors, however, international political variables played a role as well. Unlike Germany and Austria, Japan received relatively little positive reinforcement from its neighbors for its efforts at reconciliation. Even in the case of South Korea, the overall Korean response was relatively muted, and there were no grand gestures of reconciliation comparable to Kohl and Mitterand's walk through Verdun (or earlier, de Gaulle and Adenauer's meeting at the Cathedral in Rheims). In the case of China, there was even less response. To understand the reasons why Japanese efforts evoked such tepid reactions, and why Asia – in contrast to Europe – would soon become mired in controversy over history, we need to explore how the Japanese official historical narrative intersected with the politics of history in its two closest and most important neighbors, South Korea and China.

## South Korea: History, Democracy, and the Endurance of Enmity

In many respects, South Korea and Japan should be natural partners and allies.[50] They face common security threats in the form of a belligerent North Korea and a rapidly growing and unpredictable Communist China. They rely heavily on a common ally – the United States – for their security, especially in terms of nuclear deterrence as well as for the defense of their vital sea lines of communication. The Korean and Japanese economies are intimately tied together on multiple levels (Japan regularly ranks as Korea's second most important trading partner, and Korea is Japan's third largest). Both nations have been among the prime beneficiaries of the global free-trade regime, and both have broadly similar interests in supporting open world markets. Finally, the two countries share many deep social, cultural, and historical links. Japanese is – along with English and Chinese- the language that most young Korean college students choose to study. Korean singers and television stars are immensely popular in Japan, and Japanese authors such as Haruki Murakami are best sellers in Korea. The cultural impact of Korea on Japan is widely acknowledged. Even that most quintessential of Japanese institutions – the Imperial household – can trace its roots to the Korean peninsula.[51] However,

---

[50] Numerous authors and commentators have emphasized the anomalous character of Korean-Japanese relations. The author is especially indebted to early conversations that he had on this point with General (then Colonel) Noboru Yamaguchi of the Japan Self-Defense Forces (JSDF) and Professor Chung-In Moon of Seoul University.

[51] In December 2001, Emperor Akihito stunned many when, during a public conference marking his sixty-eighth birthday, he referred to the Korean connections of the Imperial household.

despite the many factors that tie the two nations together and appear to favor cooperation between them, the best Korea and Japan have been able to achieve over most of the post-1945 period is a precarious partnership – one that is constantly challenged and undermined by an enduring deep-seated, emotional enmity.

The most obvious source of this enmity is the memory of Japan's forty-year[52] colonial domination of the Korean peninsula, an era marked by numerous atrocities and brutal suppressions. Of course, it can be argued that Japan contributed greatly to the economic and social development of Korea[53] and that many Koreans benefited from Imperial rule; however, these facts do little to mitigate the terrible suffering of millions of other Koreans who were tortured and killed as rebels, conscripted as soldiers or slave laborers, or found themselves the target of subtle and not so subtle forms of discrimination on an everyday basis.

Beyond the physical and emotional suffering inflicted on Koreans on an individual basis, there was the psychic anguish inflicted by Japan's efforts to impose its culture on the Korean nation – including such measures as the forced adoption of Japanese names and restrictions on the use of the Korean language – to assimilate Koreans as the "children of the Emperor." Whereas many Koreans adjusted themselves to Imperial rule and were successfully assimilated as citizens of the Empire, others clung fiercely to their own Korean identity. In this sense, modern Korean nationalism was founded in opposition to Japanese rule, and the first expression of Korean nationalism on a mass basis – the March 1st Movement of 1919, when hundreds of thousands of protestors took to the streets in Korea demanding better treatment and independence – was colored by powerful anti-Japanese sentiments.

The anti-Japanese character of Korean nationalism was reinforced in the postindependence period by a variety of factors. As in Austria after 1945, the active repudiation of the occupier's culture and identity became a paramount task in the newly founded Korean Republic in 1945. The very fact that Japan had successfully assimilated many Koreans during the colonial period made it all the more important for Korean nationalists that every last vestige of the old Imperial identity be extirpated. Synghman Rhee, the first post-1945 president of the new Korean Republic, was particularly outspoken in his anti-Japanese views, stating repeatedly that the promotion of Korean ethnic national identity

---

[52] Dating from Japan's final consolidation of control over the peninsula following the Russo-Japanese War of 1904–1905. Japan had been ruthlessly expanding its influence in Korea for decades well before then.

[53] This is an issue that has been much debated in recent decades both inside and outside of Korea. For an overview of the Korean debate, see Yonson An, "The Colonial Past in Post-Colonial Korea: Colonialism, Modernity and Gender," in Steffi Richter, ed., *Contested Views of a Common Past: Revisions of History in Contemporary East Asia* (Frankfurt/New York: Campus Verlag, 2008). For an American perspective, see Atuhl Kohli. For a critique, see Stepehen Haggard, Chung-In Moon, and David Kang, "Japanese Colonialism and Korean Development: A Critique," *World Development* 25:6 (June 1997), pp. 867–881.

and the opposition to Japan, together with anti-Communism, were the two main ideological pillars of his regime.[54]

These already powerful anti-nationalist sentiments were exacerbated greatly by what has been described as the "original sin" of South Korean politics, the uncomfortable fact that most of the postindependence political and economic elites had enjoyed privileged positions under colonial rule.[55] Much as in the other countries we have examined, there existed considerable popular anger against collaborators in the immediate postwar period. At the same time, the new government was in desperate need of skilled and capable people who could help restore order and restart the economy. Inevitably, the requisite human resources could be found only among the ranks of those who had supported the old regime. This tendency of turning to the old elites was reinforced by the United States Military Government in Korea (USAMIGIK), which was concerned with containing the influence of pro-Communist forces – fears that were reinforced as the Communists solidified their control over the Soviet controlled northern part of the country.

As a result, although many of the leading political figures in Korean politics after 1945 – including Synghman Rhee – had been in exile during the colonial period, on a day-to-day level, Korea continued to be run by many of the same people who had run the country under Japanese rule and who now had to demonstrate their distance from Japan. In particular, the South Korean military and police forces, the two most powerful institutions in post-1945 Korea, were frequently led by officers, judges, and officials who had willingly served the Japanese colonial authorities and had often worked against and even persecuted the pro-independence forces whose cause they now espoused.[56] While the new Korean government made some token efforts to cleanse the collaborators from public life, its efforts were, on the whole, rather feeble. In the end, only a handful of people were prosecuted or removed from office.[57]

To make matters worse, the Communist regime in Pyongyang – with its roots in the anti-Japanese guerilla movement operating in Northern Korea and China before 1945 – claimed that it represented the true forces of nationalist liberation in Korea, whereas the government in Seoul was the pawn of Imperialist forces. In light of the collaborationist past of many leading South Koreans, this claim

---

[54] On Rhee's use of ethnic nationalism and his appeal to anti-Japanese and anti-Communist sentiments, see Gi-Wook Shin, *Ethnic Nationalism in Korea* (Stanford, CA: Stanford University Press, 2006), pp. 97–103.

[55] See Koen de Ceuster, "The Nation Exorcised: the Historiography of Collaboration in South Korea," *Korean Studies* 25:2 (June 2001), p. 27. See also Chung Youn-tae, "Refracted Modernity and the Issue of Pro-Japan Collaboration in Korea," available at http://www.ekoreajournal. ent/upload/html_20030820.org/html4231 (accessed December 15, 2009).

[56] For a detailed study of the social and political background of the South Korean Regime, Bruce Cummings, *Origins of the Korean War Volume 2 The Raging of the Cataract, 1947–1950* (Ithaca, NY: Cornell University Press, 2004), especially chapters 6, 7, and 8.

[57] Only thirty-eight former collaborators were ultimately referred to court for trial. Only twelve were found guilty and sentenced, and of these, five ultimately had their sentences suspended. See De Ceuster, "The Nation Exorcised," op. cit., p. 213.

had a certain degree of plausibility.[58] As a result, those South Korean politicians who vociferously pursued colonial era collaborators ran the risk of appearing to undermine national unity and supporting the North.[59]

The international circumstances of the early cold war period served to further dampen any incentives that might have existed for cooperation between Seoul and Tokyo. For both nations, the United States was by far their most important economic and political partner at the time. There was, thus, no compelling reason for either side to pursue reconciliation, unlike in Europe where France and Germany were both countries compelled to find a modus vivendi for economic and geostrategic reasons.[60] If anything, the reverse was true in East Asia. Japanese leaders, beginning with Yoshida Shigeru, feared that moving closer to South Korea could drag Japan into a military confrontation on the Korean peninsula, an outcome that went very much against Yoshida's preferred strategy to focus on Japan's economic reconstruction while relying on the United States to take care of external security relations.[61] In addition, conservative Japanese viewed the country's sizable resident Korean population as a latent security threat (Yoshida famously referred to the resident Koreans as "ants within the stomach of the lion," with the implication that they could devour Japan from within), and Japanese government policy encouraged their repatriation to the peninsula.[62] For its part, the Korean government saw the United States as its chief patron and protector. Any benefits that might have come from deepening ties with Japan were outweighed by the potential loss of legitimacy that would result if the Korean public perceived its government as caving in to the hated former colonial oppressor.[63]

---

[58] Hahm Chaibong and Kim Seog-gun, "Remembering Japan and North Korea," in Gerrit W. Gong, *Memory and History in East and South East Asia. Issues of Identity and International Relations* (Washington, DC: Center for Strategic and International Studies, 2001), pp. 106–108.

[59] De Ceuster, "The Nation Exorcised," op. cit., pp. 212–213.

[60] As has been argued by Sung-Hwa Cheong, *The Politics of Anti-Japanese Resentment in Korea: Japanese-South Korean Relations under American Occupation, 1945–1952* (Westport, CT: Greenwood Press, 1991). A similar dynamic may have been at work in Turkish-Greek relations. See Ronald Krebs, "Perverse Institutionalism: NATO and Greco-Turkish Conflict," *International Organization* 53:2 (Spring 1999), pp. 343–377.

[61] Ōtake Hideo, *Saigumbi to Nashionarizumu*, op. cit.

[62] By the end of World War II, nearly 2.5 million Koreans resided in Japan, about half of whom had been forcibly recruited as laborers during the war. After liberation, many Korean residents gravitated toward radical leftist groups who emerged with the collapse of the internal controls created by the Imperial Japanese state. Others turned to criminal activities, often taking advantage of the special protections that initially were afforded them by the American occupation. It is, thus, unsurprising that many Japanese viewed the Koreans as a security threat in the early postwar period, a position that the United States was eventually won around to when, after the outbreak of the Korean War, the American authorities allowed the Yoshida government to strip the Koreans of their Japanese citizenship. For more on the status of Koreans in Japan during this period, see Michael Weiner, *Race and Migration in Imperial Japan* (New York: Routledge, 1994). On the impact of Japanese anti-Korean sentiments on Republic of Korea (ROK)-Japan relations, the author is indebted in particular to the insights of John Swenson-Wright of Oxford University.

[63] The United States sought quietly to overcome the enmity between its chief Asian rivals but eschewed direct forms of intervention. There were strong anti-American feelings in both countries at the time, and the United States had good reason to fear that if it sought to mediate

This combination of a domestically driven anti-Japanese nationalism in Korea and anti-Korean chauvinism in Japan, together with permissive international political circumstances, created a witches brew of mutual recrimination and acrimony between the two countries in the 1940s and 1950s. Behind the scenes, however, ties between Korean and Japanese elites were often quite deep and mutually beneficial. American intelligence reports from the late 1950s, for instance, indicated that the Korean conservative party received a large proportion of its political funding from fellow anti-Communists in the LDP, and many Japanese and Korean businessmen continued to work together.[64] The general atmosphere, however, was poisonous, and on an official level the two governments adopted sharply confrontational stances vis-à-vis one another. As described in Chapter 4, in the 1950s efforts to normalize diplomatic ties broke down repeatedly as a result of comments by Japanese negotiators indicating a blatantly unrepentant view of Japan's colonial domination of Korea and a complete unwillingness to offer any form of apology or compensation for its past actions.

Tensions mounted over other issues as well. Of particular significance in this regard was the territorial dispute over the Dokdo/Takeshima islands located in the Sea of Japan (or East Sea, as the Koreans today prefer to call it). The islands – consisting of a few uninhabited outcroppings of rock – had been incorporated into Japan in 1905 in the aftermath of the Russo-Japanese war. After Japan's defeat in 1945, the U.S. occupation authorities had forbidden Japanese vessels from approaching within 12 kilometers of the islands as a part of the general limitations it imposed on Japanese fishing and navigation at the time. In 1949, as the U.S. occupation began to loosen these restrictions, the Rhee government made a great show of pressing Korea's claims to the islands in response to nationalist sentiment expressed in the Korean press.[65]

In 1953 and 1954 tensions between Tokyo and Seoul escalated to the point where armed clashes broke out between the Japanese coast guard and Korean forces that had been stationed on the island. Fishermen from both sides were arrested and imprisoned, and firefights broke out in which several people were killed. In 1954, the two sides de-escalated the conflict. An exchange of prisoners was arranged, and Japan tacitly accepted Seoul's de facto control over the islands. The Japanese government, however, did not abandon its claims, and

---

between Seoul and Tokyo, opponents of the alliances would accuse it of favoring the other side, and instead of achieving Japanese-Korean reconciliation, it would wind up fomenting anti-American feelings. See Mark Mobius, "The Japan-Korea Normalization Process and Korean Anti-Americanism," *Asian Survey* 6:4 (April 1966), pp, 241–248.

[64] Bruce Cummings, *Korea's Place in the Sun: A Modern History* (New York: W.W. Norton, 1998); and John Wlefield, *An Empire in Eclipse: Japan in the Postwar American Alliance* (London and New York: The Athlone Press, 1988).

[65] Sung-Hwa Cheong, *The Politics of Anti-Japanese Sentiment in Korea: Japanese-South Korean Relations under American Occupation* (New York: Greenwood Press, 1991) p. 138; Victor Cha, "Hypotheses on History and Hate in Asia: Japan and the Korean Peninsula," in Yoichi Funabashi, ed., *Reconciliation in the Asia-Pacific* (Washington, DC: Institute of Peace Press, 2003), p. 50.

the islands remained a focus of nationalist passions that would periodically flare up to trouble bilateral relations.[66] Although economic interests may have played a role in the conflict, nationalist sentiments appeared to have been the ultimate driving force (codfish and squid alone are not usually considered an adequate reason for major powers to engage in a military confrontation).

In the 1960s, the authoritarian Park Chung Hee government overrode domestic anti-Japanese sentiment to place Japanese-Korean relations on a more pragmatic footing. It did so in the face of intense domestic opposition – antigovernment riots rocked Korean cities, and Park was forced to deploy four divisions to Seoul to restore order. When the treaty normalizing diplomatic relations between the two countries was presented to the Korean National Assembly for ratification, the entire opposition walked out in protest. In the end, the treaty had to be rammed through by the ruling party in a secret session.[67] Although the vague apology offered by Japanese Foreign Minister Shiina Etsusaburō was favorably received at the time, the Korean opposition parties were sharply critical of the treaty's failure to pay direct reparations to both Korea and to Korean individuals who had suffered under colonial rule.[68]

In many respects, the 1965 Normalization Treaty represented a considerable step forward in Korean-Japanese relations. It opened the door for intensified Japanese-Korean economic ties and helped to set the stage for Korea's spectacular leap into steel and ship building in the 1970s and 1980s. On a more subtle level, however, the treaty also came at a substantial cost, a cost that would continue to be paid long after the controversy of 1965 had died down and been forgotten. By compromising on the history issue, the Korean government was widely perceived to have pursued state interests at the expense of the nation's honor and the interests of the many hundreds of thousands of ordinary Koreans who had been victimized under colonial rule. This willingness to disregard the interests of the people created a linkage in the popular mind between authoritarianism and the neglect of historical justice issues. That the politically dominant South Korean elites – beginning with Park Chung Hee himself – had come to the fore under Japanese rule and had now pushed this treaty through forcibly made this state of affairs all the more appalling.

The Park government's willingness to compromise with Japan on the history issue, thus, inadvertently helped to promote a critical historiography that saw the contemporary Korean authoritarianism as the product of a "colonial modernity" that had emerged under Japanese rule and that now warped the development of Korea as a nation after the Japanese had left. From this critical perspective, the same elite sectors of society that had benefited under Japanese rule had been allowed – with American compliance – to perpetuate an oppressive form of government that achieved prosperity through the ruthless exploitation of the people (*Minjung*) and that could maintain its control only

---

[66] Alexis Dudden, *Troubled Apologies*, op. cit., pp. 79–83.
[67] Jennifer Lind, *Sorry States*, op. cit., p. 48.
[68] Wakamiya, *The Postwar Conservative Views of Asia*, op. cit., p. 193.

through the ruthless exercise of state power. Many pro-democracy advocates consequently came to believe that true democracy could only be achieved by tackling this history of political and social injustice stretching all the way back to the colonial era.[69]

The identification of the authoritarian state with pro-Japanese sentiment was further reinforced by the way in which the two governments tried to respond to the 1982 outcry over proposed revisionist changes to Japanese school textbooks justifying Japan's colonial rule over Korea and the invasion of China. For Nakasone – as for the government of Ronald Reagan, which also warmly embraced President Chun Doo Hwan despite his deplorable human rights record – the Republic of Korea was a critical ally at a time when tensions with the Soviet Union were on the rise. It was, therefore, of considerable strategic importance that ties be restored. For South Korea as well, Japan was a vitally important partner, and the Chun government was looking to Tokyo to fund its ambitious industrial modernization plans. Thus, both sides had strong reasons to get the history issue back under control, and they proceeded to do so.

In 1983, Nakasone visited Seoul bringing $4 billion worth of aid as well as a raft of new initiatives on economic and political cooperation. In 1984, Chun visited Tokyo, where he was received with great pomp and met with the Japanese emperor, who offered an apology based on the 1965 Shiina apology. The new policy of contrition was further reinforced by Nakasone at a state banquet, where he said " . . . Japan caused great suffering to your country and your people during a certain period during this century. I would like to announce that the Japanese government and people express deep regret for the wrongs done to you and are determined to strictly caution themselves against repeating them in the future."[70]

As in 1965, the initial Korean public response to Nakasone's comments appeared positive. Opinion polls and newspaper editorials were strongly positive. However, as in 1965, it appeared to many in Korea that a brutal authoritarian Korean regime that only a few years earlier – in 1980 – had massacred hundreds of protestors in the city of Kwanju and routinely arrested and tortured students, labor leaders, and human rights activists to maintain its grip on power had once again allowed Japan to avoid a full accounting for its past misdeeds. The Japanese government had apologized, but look at who they apologized to! Moreover, the nature of the wrongs committed were not specified by Japan, nor did it offer any explicit compensation made for those wrongs, neither to the Korean nation as the whole (once again, Japan offered only foreign aid) nor to any of the individual Koreans who had been victimized. And once again,

---

[69] Koen de Ceuster, "The Nation Exorcised: Historiography of Collaboration in South Korea," *Korean Studies* 25:2 (2002), pp. 207–242; and Kenneth M. Wells, *South Korea's Minjung Movement: The Culture and Politics of Dissidence* (Honolulu: University of Hawaii, 1995).

[70] Wakamiya, *The Postwar Conservative View of Asia*, op. cit., pp. 198–199, 243–246. Quote on p. 246.

the Korean government had cynically tolerated this obvious injustice on the grounds of international security and political and economic expedience.[71]

After Korea began to democratize in the late 1980s, widespread popular discontent with how the question of historical justice had been handled began to bubble up. Much as the Historical Determinist school of thought would lead us to expect, once the political opportunity structure had shifted, suppressed societal level memory reemerged and reshaped the parameters within which the Korean official historical narrative was made. Various civil society groups that had helped drive the democratization process took up the issue of historical justice and pressed actively for confronting the crimes of the past and the compensation of victims. The most prominent of these were various groups who represented the long neglected comfort women. By 1990, the Korean Council for the Women Drafted for Military Sexual Slavery by Japan began to hold regular Wednesday Demonstrations in front of the Japanese Embassy in Seoul, and the cause of the comfort women began to draw worldwide attention, including in Japan, where, as pointed out earlier, various Japanese civil society activists helped the comfort women to file claims in Japanese courts.[72] Other groups, such as the Institute for Research on Collaborationist Activities, began to collect and disseminate information on the extent of collaboration during the colonial period as well as the degree to which former collaborationists continued to wield influence in contemporary Korea.[73]

This new focus on coming to terms with the colonial past was part of a larger trend of dealing with a whole gamut of issues, including the many crimes and atrocities that had occurred during the Korean War and the long period of rule by authoritarian governments. Although from an outsiders' point of view, the atrocities that occurred under Japanese rule and the crimes committed by post-1945 Korean governments might appear separate from the "colonial modernity" perspective, they were part and parcel of a single complex of unresolved issues. In this sense, the issue of seeking justice for the crimes of the colonial era had been reinforced and revalorized by the question of how to handle the misdeeds of the authoritarian era.

However, the linkage between colonial era atrocities and the crimes of the authoritarian past also made both issues more difficult to manage. When the Kim Young Sam government – the first genuinely democratic government to be elected in South Korea – came to power in 1992, it did so with the cooperation of conservatives led by Kim Jong Pil, former head of the Korean CIA (KCIA) and one of the chief pillars of the old authoritarian state. At the same

---

[71] Yangmo Ku, "International Reconciliation in the Postwar Era, 1945–2005: A Comparison of Japan-ROK and Franco-German Relations," *Asian Perspective* 32:3 (2008), p. 24.

[72] See George Hicks, *The Comfort Women*, op. cit., especially p. 173 ff; and Yangmo Ku, "International Reconciliation in the Postwar Era," p. 29, available at hptt://www.womenandwar.net/menu_02.php.

[73] Koen De Ceuster, "When History Matters: Reconstructing South Korea's National Memory in the Age of Democracy," in Steffi Richter, ed., *Contested Views of a Common Past: Revisions of History in Contemporary East Asia* (Frankfurt/New York: Campus Verlag, 2008), pp. 86–87.

time, the security climate on the Korean peninsula worsened as well. War was only narrowly averted during the first North Korean nuclear weapons crisis of 1992–1993, and throughout the 1990s, Pyongyang continued to build up its military forces, despite occasional diplomatic lulls when the political temperatures seemed to drop from subzero to merely freezing. Not surprisingly, the new government showed little enthusiasm for pursuing historical justice issues. Although Kim Young Sam had been a leading critic of the military Chun Doo Hwan and Roh Tae Woo governments and had fought and suffered for decades to promote democracy, once in office he called for national reconciliation and rejected a comprehensive purging or prosecuting of members of previous regimes. Investigations were launched of those individuals responsible for some of the most notorious incidents of the past – most importantly the Kwanju massacre of 1980. Chun Doo Hwan and his successor, Roh Tae Woo, were eventually prosecuted and found guilty for their roles in the massacre and the subversion of democracy. Investigations were suspended, however, for fear of "undermining the legal foundation of the state," and Chun and Roh were issued presidential pardons.[74]

Other efforts were made to recognize and correct the wrongs that had been committed during the era of authoritarian rule. So, for example, the police records of the approximately 40,000 people who had been arrested during the 1980 Kwanju uprising were expunged. Likewise, the Kim Young Sam government rather reluctantly took up the cause of the comfort women. It rejected as inadequate the Japanese government-sponsored attempts to compensate them through the Asian Women's Fund and proceeded to set up an alternative compensation scheme.[75]

The question of historical justice was thus still very much alive in 1998 when Kim Young Sam was succeeded by his archrival Kim Dae Jung. Similar to Kim Young Sam, Kim Dae Jung had been a staunch critic of the authoritarian Park Chung Hee, Chun Doo Hwan, and Roh Tae Woo governments, and even more than Kim Young Sam, he had suffered for his opposition. In 1972, Kim Dae Jung had even been kidnapped and almost executed by KCIA agents while he had been in exile in Tokyo. He thus was able to speak with considerable moral authority on issues of historical justice. Moreover, as a native of Jeolla (Cholla province) where the Kwanju massacre had taken place, Kim Dae Jung was viewed favorably by some of the most outspoken advocates of pursuing the crimes of the previous governments. Similar to his predecessor, however, Kim Dae Jung was a strong advocate of reconciliation and "restorative justice" – that is, of trying to rehabilitate the victims of past injustices rather than punishing

---

[74] For a brief overview, see Koen De Ceuster, "When History Matters: Reconstructing South Korea's National Memory in the Age of Democracy," in Steffi Richter, ed., *Contested Views of a Common Past: Revisions of History in Contemporary East Asia* (Frankfurt/New York: Campus Verlag, 2008), especially pp. 82–84.

[75] For a factual and useful overview of the issue at the time of Abe's comments, see Larry Niksch, *Japanese Military's "Comfort Women" System*, Congressional Research Service memorandum, April 3, 2007, especially p. 15.

TABLE 5.1. *Korean Views of Japan*

| Year | 1973 | 1978 | 1984 | 1988 | 1990 | 1995 | 1997 | 1999 | 2000 | 2001 | 2005 |
|---|---|---|---|---|---|---|---|---|---|---|---|
| Dislike | 58.6 | 69.9 | 38.9 | 50.6 | 66 | 68.9 | 65 | 42.6 | 42.2 | 56.6 | 63 |
| Like | 12.9 | 7.6 | 22.6 | 13.6 | 5.4 | 5.5 | 8 | 9.6 | 17.1 | 12.1 | 8 |

*Source: Jung Ang Daily* (1973, 1978); *Dong-A Daily* (1984–2005) cited in Yangmo Ku, "International Reconciliation in the Postwar Era," op. cit., p. 25.

the perpetrators to help society heal the wounds of the past. He extended this philosophy to South Korea's relations with its neighbors, seeking to engage North Korea economically and politically (the so-called Sunshine policy), as well as to Japan.[76]

It was against this background that Kim Dae Jung met with Japanese Prime Minister Keizō Obuchi in the summer of 1998. The symbolic success of the visit was made possible not only by the remarkably frank and forthright nature of Obuchi's apology for Japan's colonial oppression of Korea – presented both orally and in writing – but also by Kim Dae Jung's acceptance of that apology, an acceptance made possible by Kim's stature as a defender of human rights and as a democratically elected leader of the Korean nation. The visit was followed by a marked improvement in the character of Korean-Japanese relations after the visit. The ideologically sensitive issue of Dokdo/Takeshima was put aside to allow the two sides to renegotiate fishing rights in the disputed area between the two nations. The decades old South Korean ban on Japanese cultural products such as Japanese language films and traditional Japanese art forms such as *Kabuki* and *Bunraku* was lifted.[77] In addition, in 2002 the two countries were able to jointly host the World Cup soccer tournament and cheer each other's teams. Public opinion data showed a marked improvement in each country's perception of the other (see Tables 5.1 and 5.2). A new era in Korean-Japanese relations seemed to be dawning.

The shadow of history, however, had not been completely dispelled and continued to hover over the relations between the two countries. The question of compensation for the victims of Japanese past injustices remained unresolved, and the growing tide of revisionist views in parts of Japan's political system and civil society was viewed with alarm in Korea. In addition, both Japan's apology and South Korea's acceptance of that apology were not based purely on good will and broad philosophical principles. Japan had been prompted to pursue the issue in part because of growing concerns over the military threat emanating from North Korea, which had been exacerbated by North Korea's

---

[76] Kim Young Sam, in contrast, harbored a deep personal animosity towars Pyongyang that was rooted, it is believed, in the fact that his mother had been killed by North Korean commandos.

[77] In many ways, the ban had long been a sham, circumvented by a thriving black market for such products. Nonetheless, symbolically it had been of some significance given post-1945 Korea's historical desire to assert its national identity after Japan's efforts at cultural assimilation during the colonial era.

TABLE 5.2. *Japanese Views of Korea*

| Year | 1978 | 1985 | 1989 | 1993 | 1996 | 1999 | 2001 | 2003 | 2004 | 2005 |
|---|---|---|---|---|---|---|---|---|---|---|
| Feel No intimacy with Korea | 45.2 | 45.2 | 52.2 | 51.8 | 60.6 | 46.9 | 45.5 | 41.0 | 39.2 | 44.3 |
| Feel Intimacy | 40.1 | 45.2 | 40.7 | 43.4 | 35.8 | 48.3 | 50.3 | 55.0 | 56.7 | 51.1 |

*Source:* Japanese Cabinet Office, *Gaikō ni Kan suru Yoronchōsa* December 26, 2005, http://www8 .cao.go.jp/survey/h17/h17-gaikou/images/z07.gif.

test of a new generation of ballistic missiles – the *Taepodong* – earlier in 1998. Both Japan and the Republic of Korea were coming under increased pressure from the United States to improve trilateral coordination on the North Korean issue, and the history issue was viewed as a serious impediment in this regard. Moreover, the Asian Financial crisis of 1997–1998 had plunged South Korea into the most serious financial and economic crisis in decades. It desperately needed Japanese assistance in renegotiating its external debts and in channeling billions of dollars to struggling Korean firms and banks.[78] In the broader public, the suspicion lingered on that the Korean government had once again – as it had in 1965 under Park Chung Hee and again in 1984 under Chun Doo Hwan – been willing to forsake honor and justice for the sake of immediate political advantages.

In addition, the broader issue of colonial era collaboration as well as other historical justice issues not only continued but expanded during the Kim Dae Jung era. Increased evidence of authoritarian era atrocities was uncovered, and demands for the recognition of the suffering of victims of military and Synghman Rhee governments continued to escalate. These concerns with historical justice in general ensured that continued public attention was paid to the issue of Japanese wartime collaboration and created conditions in which the question of compensation for colonial atrocities could easily be revived.

To sum up, Korean and Japanese relations have long labored under the burden of history. During the early cold war period, that animosity based on the bitter memories of ordinary Koreans on a societal level was reinforced by the need of the newly independent Korean state to foster a strong sense of Korean national identity. Instrumental calculations of economic and strategic interest allowed the two sides to work out a practical modus vivendi. However, the two nations' alignment was constantly constrained – and often strained – by antagonism. In time, some of the barriers to cooperation wore off. Nonetheless, anti-Japanese sentiments became firmly woven into the Korean political culture. Initially encouraged by the Korean state, these sentiments were taken up by antistate critics in a new way that identified Korean authoritarianism with

---

[78] For more on the background to the 1998 summit written by a close advisor to the Kim Dae Jung government, see Chung-in Moon and Seung-won Suh, "Security, Economy and Identity Politics: Japan-South Korean Relations under the Kim-Dae Jung Government," *Korea Observer* 36:4 (Winter 2005), pp. 564–573.

the legacy of Japanese colonialism. As a result, even when the international and domestic political circumstances of Korea were dramatically altered by the end of the cold war and even as the proportion of the Korean population that had direct experiences of Japanese oppression dwindled, anti-Japanese sentiments remained a potent force in Korean politics. These sentiments had become embedded in a cultural discourse that was driven by more than calculations of material and political interest and were themselves a constitutive element in how Korean leaders understood those interests.

Democratic governments in the 1990s, much like their authoritarian predecessors, continued to find it in their interest to work with Japan, and they worked to overcome the cultural-ideological obstacles to doing so. Under Kim Dae Jung, significant progress was made in improving the character of relations between the two countries. Certain parallels can be seen here to the experience of German-Polish and German-Czech relations. Although already in the Communist period the German, Polish, and Czech governments agreed to put the past behind them in order to work together on issues of common interest (economic development and relieving the tensions of the cold war), not until democratization after the cold war did genuine changes in public opinion begin to become possible.

The progress that had been made in Japan-Korean relations, however, was far more fragile than was commonly realized – especially in Tokyo, where it was the common view that the issues of the past had finally been consigned to the past.[79] The underlying historically and culturally embedded roots of animosity remained, and in certain respects even intensified. As we saw earlier, this was true in the German-Polish context as well. However, in the European case the common political framework of the European Union helped dampen tensions by providing powerful material incentives for continued cooperation and creating an avenue in which other parties – France, Holland, Luxembourg, and so forth – were able to exert political leverage. In effect, the European Union helped resocialize both Germany and Poland, helping smooth over tensions over historical issues when they emerged. In the Asian context, there was no comparable mitigating force. As a result, conflict over history between Tokyo and Seoul could be easily reignited, and soon would be.

### China: Between Pragmatic Forgiveness and Useful Resentment

Like Korea, China's relationship with Japan is a long and tortured one. Before the 1890s, Japan occupied a relatively peripheral position in the Chinese view of the world and tended to be seen as a sometimes hostile, semicivilized kingdom that had to be handled with caution but, on the whole, did not represent a

---

[79] The author had the opportunity to speak to many well-placed Japanese officials and foreign policy intellectuals in Tokyo between 1998 and 2000, shortly after the successful Kim-Obuchi summit. At the time, the near unanimous view was that the history issue between South Korea and Japan had been resolved.

serious political or cultural rival. Japan's successful modernization and industrialization in the second half of the nineteenth century, however, allowed it to
upend what the Chinese had come to view as the natural Sino-Centric order in
Asia.[80]

The Japanese victory over the Qing dynasty in the Sino-Japanese War of
1894–1895 came as a great shock to the Chinese. Japan's subsequent ruthless
and relentless expansion of its sphere of interest at China's expense – first on
the Korean peninsula and then in China itself – represented a fundamental
challenge to China's sense of pride and power. The crushing burden of the
reparations Japan imposed on China after 1895 was a major factor behind
the collapse of the Qing dynasty and ushered in a period of weakness and
internal disunity that lasted for nearly half a century. In addition, when in
the aftermath of the first Sino-Japanese War Japan separated Taiwan from
the Chinese mainland, a problem was created that would endure well into the
twenty-first century.

Although Japan was hardly the first Imperial power to impose its will on
China – that distinction goes to Great Britain, which began China's "century of
humiliation" with the Opium Wars of 1839–1842 – it was arguably the most
dangerous and rapacious. Whereas other European powers chipped away at
Chinese sovereignty (imposing unequal treaties and creating special zones such
as the International Settlement in Shanghai), Japan sought wholesale control
over the Chinese government, first through its "twenty one demands" in 1915
and subsequently by seizing direct control over huge swathes of Chinese territory – Manchuria in 1931 and much of coastal China following the outbreak
of the Second Sino-Japanese War in 1937. The fact that the Japanese were
fellow Asians – ones who historically had been viewed as China's inferiors – if
anything, intensified Chinese feelings of humiliation.

Modern Chinese nationalism – like Korean nationalism – thus emerged
against the backdrop of Japanese Imperial expansionism and was profoundly
shaped by anti-Japanese sentiments. The first major expression of Chinese
national sentiment on a mass level – the May Fourth Movement of 1919 –
followed only a few weeks after the Korean March 1st Movement, and as its
Korean counterpart, was triggered by the Paris Peace Conference. Although
Republican China had joined the Western allies, at the conference the Chinese nationalist government was forced to transfer German interests in China,
including control over Shandong, to Japan. Thousands of students took to the

---

[80] As any number of prominent historians have pointed out, this vision of a benign Sino-Centric
order was very much debatable. For long periods of time, China was in fact the dominant
power in the region, but it had also been frequently challenged, divided, and even conquered.
Moreover, when it did enjoy hegemonic status, it had frequently used force ruthlessly and
with great brutality to serve its interests. These historical realities, however, did not prevent
Chinese intellectuals and leaders from believing that their nation was the natural and benevolent
hegemon in the region. For a perspective on China's position in the world, see Warren I. Cohen,
*East Asia at the Center: Four Thousand Years of Engagement with the World* (New York:
Columbia University Press, 2000).

streets in protest to what they viewed as a betrayal of the national interest. They were soon joined by workers, peasants, and merchants who all had various, separate grievances. A pattern – almost a cultural trope – was thus established of criticizing the government for failing to stand up for the nation, defined in this instance as challenging Japan. Anti-Japanese feelings were further intensified as the Chinese Nationalist government increasingly found itself at odds with Japan, culminating in the immensely destructive and bloody Second Sino-Japanese War of 1937–1945.[81]

Complicating matters further, the Sino-Japanese War was a three-sided affair, pitting not only the Japanese and their Chinese puppet allies against the Nationalists, but also the Nationalists under Chiang Kai-Shek against their Communist rivals led by Mao Zedong. Neither the Nationalists nor the Communists were very effective in warding off the Japanese Imperial forces. However, both during and the after the war, each side accused the other of cowardice and incompetence while claiming that it was they who had been the true defenders of the Chinese nation.[82]

After 1945, Sino-Japanese relations thus faced a tremendous burden of thickly layered resentment that had built up on the Chinese side over half a century. Chinese national identity – the core of its political culture – contained a strong anti-Japanese element creating a strong incentive for political elites to claim that they were opposed to Japan. This anti-Japanese resentment was further reinforced by the memories of the tremendous human suffering that had been inflicted on the Chinese people by the Japanese invasion. From both a Historical Determinist and a Culturalist perspective, there was ample reason to expect enmity. However, despite this dark legacy, over the next forty years, issues of historical justice surprisingly did not have the kind of disruptive impact that they had on the relations between Korea and Japan, although they certainly did exert a powerful influence behind the scenes and occasionally bubbled up on a number of occasions. A combination of historical, Chinese domestic political and international political factors worked together to contain the history issue for much of the cold war.

---

[81] Zhu Jiangrong, "Japan's Role in the Rise of Chinese Nationalism: History and Prospects," in Tsuyoshi Hasegawa and Kazuhiko Togo, *East Asia's Haunted Present*, op. cit., pp. 180–189.

[82] For the claim that Communists in fact had been more effective and the resulting legitimacy that they enjoyed had been a major factor behind the CCP's victory in the subsequent Chinese Civil War, see Chalmers Johnson, *Peasant Nationalism and Communist Power: The Emergence of Revolutionary China, 1937–1945* (Stanford, CA: Stanford University Press, 1962). Whether, in fact, the Communists really were more active in fighting against the Communists can be disputed. As Arthur Waldron has pointed out, with only one major exception, most of the battles pitting the Communists against the Japanese were small-scale affairs. The one exception, the Hundred Regiments campaign, ended in military defeat and triggered a brutal Japanese reprisal. To make matters worse, Mao had opposed taking on the Japanese before the Hundred Regiments campaign, and after the defeat, ensured that no similar operations were undertaken again. See Arthur Waldron, "China's New Remembering of World War II: The Case of Zhang Zizhong," *Modern Asian Studies* 30:4 (1996), pp. 945–978.

First, unlike Korea, China had not been conquered by Japan. Chinese leaders, both Nationalist and Communist, therefore could plausibly claim to have defeated Japan, at least in the end. Although there were undoubtedly many who thirsted for further vengeance, the national honor had in some sense been restored by victory. Moreover, while many hundreds of thousands of Chinese had actively collaborated with the Japanese occupation, an independent Chinese government had never ceased to exist, and the cultural impact of Japan on China, on the whole, had been relatively limited. Although there was an anti-Japanese element woven into modern Chinese national identity, it was not as central as in Korea. Although the material losses inflicted on China by Japan, measured in terms of the number of people killed and cities destroyed, was far greater than the losses imposed on Korea, the psychic wounds were less severe. Consequently, both the Nationalist and Chinese Communist governments had greater leeway to adopt a magnanimous stance on the past than was true of the postcolonial regime in Korea.

Second, both the Communist Chinese and their Nationalist rivals were harsh authoritarian regimes that could suppress any domestic political pressures for vigorously pursuing historical justice issues. Korea as well was authoritarian, but decidedly less so, with greater scope for freedom of speech and association than was true of either the PRC or Taiwan. Although many Chinese harbored bitter memories of their suffering at the hands of the Japanese Imperial Forces, they were in no position to express those views without the sanction of their government. This allowed the Chinese leadership to shape their official historical narrative based on Instrumental factors – that is, calculations of interest. Although potentially there was some possible benefit to be derived by elites from appealing to those sentiments on the ground level, there were even stronger domestic and international political reasons not to do so.

Domestically, because both the Nationalists and the Communists had not been terribly effective in the fight against Japan, neither government was terribly eager to dwell on a period that, if closely examined, might underline their failures. If anything, they wanted to emphasize the positive contribution their side had made to the victory over Japan while stressing the failure of the other. Thus, on the mainland, Nanjing was primarily recalled as an example of the failure of the Nationalists to defend the city, and the issue of the subsequent civilian suffering was raised primarily to demonstrate the callous indifference of foreign powers (especially Britain and the United States) to the plight of the Chinese people.[83] To make matters worse in the case of mainland China, one of the chief military leaders of the resistance against Japan, Marshall Peng Dehuai, also became one of the first senior Communist leaders purged by Mao

---

[83] Mark Eykholt, "Aggression, Victimization and Chinese Historiography," in Joshua A. Fogel, *The Nanjing Massacre in History and Historiography* (Berkeley: University of California Press, 2000), pp. 24–26.

in the late 1950s.[84] The Communist government, thus, had a strong, additional motive to avoid examining the anti-Japanese struggle too closely.

Internationally, both Taiwan and the PRC found themselves competing for influence in Japan after the war. For both governments, the history issue was an important instrument for gaining influence. Whereas the United States was the dominant power in Asia at the time, both Beijing and Taipei were well aware of Japan's strategic military and economic potential and sought to court favor with influential groups inside Japanese politics. Arguably, the Nationalists were the first to do so. In his initial broadcast after the Japanese surrender on August 15, 1945, Chiang Kai Shek cited both the Bible and the Chinese sages in calling on the Chinese people to forgo exacting revenge on the defeated Japanese. He added that it was Japanese militarism and not the Japanese people who had been the enemy of China and that indeed the people of Japan should even be pitied for having been deceived by their leaders.[85]

In keeping with this policy of "repaying violence with virtue," the Chinese Nationalist government arranged for the orderly surrender and repatriation of over 2 million Japanese soldiers and civilians. Moreover, Chiang Kai Shek's decision not to join the Allied occupation of Japan helped to legitimate Truman's decision to turn down Moscow's request for a Soviet zone of occupation on the Japanese home islands. There were limits to the Nationalists' compassion for their defeated foes. For instance, the Nationalist government did try to punish several hundred Japanese war criminals. Moreover, Chiang pushed hard for substantial reparations from Japan, only to be foiled by U.S. diplomatic pressure. Nonetheless, on balance, the Nationalist policy toward its former enemy was quite generous in light of the savagery of the war.

Although any hopes that the Nationalists might have harbored to turn Japan into a more active ally in the fight against Communism were disappointed, the Nationalist government's policy of leniency on the history issue was rewarded in a number of ways. First, it helped ease the process of taking control of the substantial portions of China that were still under Japanese control in August 1945.[86] Second, it created an influential network of pro-Taiwanese supporters on the right end of the Japanese political spectrum – especially in the Kishi faction – who would provide political support to Taiwan.[87] Finally, and most importantly, by helping the Japanese conservatives, the Taiwanese helped to

---

[84] Waldron, "China's New Remembering," op. cit.

[85] An English language version of the text of Chiang's speech can be found at http://www.ibiblio.org/pha/policy/1945/450815c.html (accessed February 22, 2010).

[86] On Japanese-Nationalist cooperation in the immediate wake of the war, see Ronald H. Spector, *In the Ruins of Empire: The Japanese Surrender and the Battle for Postwar Asia* (New York: Random House, 2007), pp. 38–42.

[87] John Welfield, *An Empire in Eclipse*, op. cit., pp. 229; Michael Schaller, *Altered States: The United States and Japan since the Occupation* (Oxford and New York: Oxford University Press, 1997), pp. 77–79. In general, see Yoshihide Soeya, *Nihon Gaikō to Chūgoku: 1968–1972* (Tokyo: Keiō Tsūshin, 1995), especially pp. 115–116 on the formation of the Taiwan lobby.

significantly bolster the containment of Communism in East Asia during the early stages of the cold war.

In certain respects, the Chinese Communists were even more generous in their stance toward Japan. Like the Nationalists, the Communists adopted a historical narrative that blamed the "militarist clique" for the war and defined both the Japanese and the Chinese peoples as victims of Imperialism. This narrative dovetailed neatly with the Japanese peace movement's efforts to rally popular support against the alliance with the United States on the basis of feelings of Japanese victimization.[88] The effort to use history as an instrument to influence Japanese domestic politics also lay behind Beijing's lenient stance toward the Japanese prisoners of war who had fallen into its hands, most of whom it released unpunished in the 1950s.[89] Moreover, it informed the Chinese decision not to press for compensation or a more far-reaching apology for Japanese actions after relations between the two countries began to be normalized in 1972. As Zhou En Lai put it, both the Japanese and the Chinese people had been victimized by the militarists, so how could victims demand compensation from other victims?[90]

As was true for Taiwan, this lenient stance on history yielded significant dividends for Beijing. Although the PRC was unable to lure Japan out of the alliance with the United States – as it hoped to do in the 1950s and 1960s – ultimately this proved to be in China's interest. As the Sino-Soviet rift deepened in the 1960s, Beijing came to view the U.S.-Japanese alliance as a useful counterbalance to the Soviet Union. In the meantime, its policies on historical justice issues generated considerable goodwill in Japan, first on the left end of the political spectrum and, after 1972, within the LDP as well – in particular within the then dominant Tanaka faction. The Japanese public as well formed quite favorable views of China, in part because of its supposedly generous stance toward history. Survey data from the 1970s and 1980s showed remarkably positive views of China, with over 78 percent of respondents expressing positive views of China in 1980. Although Japan did not directly pay any reparations to China, from 1978 on it provided $1 to $2 billion a year in foreign aid for over twenty years. At a time when China remained a desperately poor country with an underdeveloped infrastructure and limited foreign currency reserves (China's GDP was just $183 billion in 1980), this represented a highly useful sum of money.

In short, for much of the cold war, international politics gave Beijing (and Taipei) a strong motive *not* to pursue the question of historical justice. At the same time, historical realities as well as the totalitarian nature of their regime

---

[88] Orr, *The Victim as Hero*, op. cit.

[89] Yinan He, *The Search for Reconciliation*, op. cit.

[90] The Chinese Communists had initially taken a harder stance on both reparations and war criminals. At the time of the Treaty of San Francisco, Beijing had offered an estimate of 10 million war deaths and property damages valued at $50 billion. See Rose, *Sino-Japanese Relations*, op. cit., p. 42.

gave Chinese leaders – unlike their Korean counterparts – the capacity to be magnanimous about the past. In the early 1980s, however, international and domestic circumstances began to change in ways that would allow latent anti-Japanese sentiments to come to the fore on the mainland (but not on Taiwan, where Japan was viewed as a useful balance to China) and to make history a more problematic issue in Sino-Japanese relations.

On the international level, China was becoming increasingly worried about Japan's growing economic and military might. These concerns were amplified in the 1980s as Japan under Nakasone began to build up the Self Defense Forces as part of a general strengthening of the alliance with the United States. In this context, Nakasone's tendencies toward historical revisionism – most notably when he undertook his 1985 trip to Yasukuni – alarmed many Chinese observers and encouraged them to sound the alarm about a potential remilitarization of Japan.

Moreover, the PRC's victory in displacing Taiwan at the United Nations and winning U.S. and Japanese recognition as the representative of the Chinese nation greatly reduced its need to seek influence in Japan. At the same time, hopes were raised that it might be possible to reunify Taiwan with the mainland in the relatively near future. As a result, in the early 1980s a marked shift in Chinese historiography of the Sino-Japanese War can be observed. Whereas previously the Nationalist side was disparaged for its incompetence and cowardice, in the 1980s, textbooks and museums on the mainland began to depict the Nationalist side in more positive terms, as allies in the fight against the Japanese invaders. Inadvertently, this more positive evaluation of the Nationalists implied a more negative one of Japan and helped to open the door for paying greater attention to the long suppressed issue of Chinese civilian suffering at the hands of the Japanese.

These international developments were reinforced by changes in Chinese domestic politics. The end of the Maoist period allowed a far-reaching reevaluation of Chinese history and a readiness to admit the failings of the past, and of Maoism. Former enemies of Mao, such as Marshall Peng Dehuai, were rehabilitated. As the lure of Maoist ideology faded, new emphasis was placed on nationalism as the legitimating principle of the Chinese state. The struggle against Japan became soon a central element in the new official narrative. In 1985, a museum was opened in Nanjing that had the figure "300,000" – the official number of victims who are said to have died in the Japanese massacre – inscribed on the front wall of the Museum.[91] That same year, the Chinese Ministry of Education launched the Five Loves Education (love the motherland, the people, work, science, and public property), which emphasized the history of China as resisting successive waves of foreign invasions, the most recent of which was the Japanese invasion of 1937–1945.[92]

---

[91] Yinan He, *Shadows of the Past*, op. cit., p. 207.

[92] Yinan He, ibid., chapter 7; Zheng Wang, "National Humiliation, History Education and the Politics of Historical Memory: Patriotic Education Campaign in China," *International Studies Quarterly* 52 (2008), pp. 783–806; and Zhao Suisheng, "State Led Nationalism: The Patriotic

At the same time, the loosening of the Maoist era system of domestic political controls allowed for a wider expression of views inside Chinese society.
Although the PRC remained a harshly authoritarian system, and the instruments of totalitarian control remained firmly in place, a new atmosphere of
relatively open discussion across a broad range of issues – including history –
set in. In this more relaxed climate, a new generation emerged of what James
Reilly has termed "history activists," a group of people intent on recovering
a past that had been suppressed during the Maoist period.[93] The forgotten
history of civilian suffering during the war against Japan now became one of
their chief concerns. In many cases, these history activists were primarily concerned with history for its own sake. In other cases, however, they saw history –
and in particular the state's failure to take up the cause of victims of Japanese
aggression – as a way of indirectly criticizing their own government. One still
could not challenge the rule of the CCP, but it was legitimate to criticize a
government who supported a generous stance on Japan for being insufficiently
patriotic – much in the tradition of the student protestors of the 1919 May
Fourth Movement.

Under these conditions, history, and in particular the history of the Sino-
Japanese War, became a political issue in a new way in China. During the
1980s Chinese leaders began to appeal to anti-Japanese sentiments as a way of
mobilizing political support or for attacking the legitimacy of their rivals. For
instance, Yinan He speculates that one of the reasons why the Chinese government took up the Japanese textbook issue in 1982 was that Deng Xiaoping
wanted to win the backing of conservative leaders like Chen Yun and General
Ye Jianying for his program of liberal economic reforms.[94] At the same time,
failure to appear patriotic by being soft on Japan could become a significant
political liability. Hu Yaobang, the general secretary of the Chinese Communist Party, highly regarded as one of Japan's friends in senior Chinese political
leadership circles, was significantly weakened by protests that erupted in China
after Nakasone's visit to the Yasukuni shrine in 1985, despite efforts by the
senior leadership to shield him.[95] Whereas in the past instrumental calculations
of elite interest had led to the suppression of societally based anti-Japanese feeling, under the changed structure of discourse, elites found it increasingly in their
interest to take advantage of anti-Japanese sentiments, or at least to make sure
that they did not fall victim to them.

These trends, apparent already in the 1980s, deepened in the 1990s. The
emphasis on nationalism in Chinese education increased after the suppression
of pro-democracy activists in Tiananmen, and textbooks after 1989 expanded

Education Campaign in Post-Tiananmen China," *Communist and Post-Communist Studies*
31:3 (1998), pp. 287–302.

[93] ² See James Reilly, "China's History Activists and Sino-Japanese Relations," *China: An International Journal* 4:2 (2006), pp. 189–216.

[94] Yinan He, *The Search for Reconciliation*, op. cit., pp. 212–214, 230–232.

[95] Susan Shirk, *China: Fragile Superpower: How China's Internal Politics Could Derail its Peaceful
Rise* (Oxford and New York: Oxford University Press, 2007), pp. 160–166; Yinan He, "The
Emerging Sino-Japanese Conflict," op. cit., pp. 12–13.

their coverage of Japanese wartime atrocities, with little corresponding treatment of the positive aspects of Sino-Japanese relations.[96] However, although direct criticism of the Communist government became more difficult after Tiananmen, Chinese civil society continued to develop and grow, taking on new forms and dimensions with the advent of the Internet and the rapid growth of the Chinese blogosphere.[97]

The new generation of Chinese leaders who came to the fore during this period was by and large relatively weak and colorless, devoid of the charisma and authority of Mao, Deng, and the other founders of the Communist state. Lacking the legitimacy of their predecessors, they became more sensitive to public opinion. In particular, when there were splits in the leadership, leaders were now more inclined to take a hard-line stance on ideological issues, especially the history issue with Japan, lest they be outflanked ideologically by their rivals.[98]

At the same time, on the international level, the balance of power shifted increasingly in China's favor, both strategically and economically. Strategically, with the end of the cold war, China no longer relied on the U.S.-Japanese alliance to counterbalance the Soviet threat to the West. As the Chinese economy continued to grow at a blistering pace, its dependence on Japan decreased commensurably. In the early 1990s, Sino-Japanese relations continued to be excellent – so much so that Japan was roundly criticized when it became the first nation to lift sanctions on China following the Tiananmen massacre.[99] By the middle of the decade, however, China and Japan began to clash over a growing range of issues, including China's continued rapid military buildup, the intensification of U.S.-Japanese military relations – which China feared was aimed at containing it much as the United States had contained the Soviet Union during the cold war – and a growing number of trade disputes. Most ominously, Sino-Japanese tensions grew over two issues that were particularly laden with historical implications: the Senkaku/Diaoyutai islands and Taiwan.

---

[96] It is important, however, not to exaggerate the extent of the shift. Zhu Jiangrong, "Japan's Role in the Rise of Chinese Nationalism: History and Prospects," in Tsuyoshi Hasegawa and Kazuhiko Togo, *East Asia's Haunted Present*, op. cit., p. 183.

[97] Shirk, *China: Fragile Superpower*, op. cit., chapter 4.

[98] Susan Shirk, *China: the Fragile Superpower*, op. cit., p. 176. This is a point that has also been made to the author by veteran China watchers Joe Fewsmith of Boston University and Ezra Vogel of Harvard.

[99] Japanese public opinion became sharply negative of China after Tiananmen, and some Japanese politicians wished to pressure China on human rights issues after the massacre. China was able to defuse such critics through a number of means, including through the use of the history issue. One of the leading critics of China was former Foreign Minister Itō Masayoshi. When Itō rushed to China to pressure China to take a more lenient stance, Chinese Premier Li Peng arranged to meet him at the site of an infamous massacre in North East China. See Jing Zhao, "The Betrayal of Democracy: Tiananmen's Shadow over Japan," *Haol* 4 (Spring 2004), pp. 75–82. More generally on the Japanese reaction to Tiananmen, see Tanaka Akihiko, *NiChū Kankei 1945–1990* (Tokyo: Tokyo Daigakushuppankai, 1991) chapter 7.

The Senkaku/Diaoyutai are an uninhabited group of islands that had been incorporated into Japan after the first Sino-Japanese War in 1895. Both the Republic of China and the PRC claimed that they had been part of Chinese territory since the fifteenth century. After 1945, the islands had been administered by the United States and returned to Japan in 1972 as part of the reversion of Okinawa to Japan.[100] In the early 1990s at the time of Sino-Japanese diplomatic normalization, Zhou En Lai suggested that settlement of the issue be postponed, and the two sides agreed to the joint economic development of the islands – including its potentially rich natural gas resources. The economic and strategic stakes of the disputes grew dramatically in the 1990s, however, as China went from being an exporter to an importer of energy and when the UN Law of the Seas went into effect giving control over vast swathes of ocean to the country that could claim ownership of the islands.[101] As with Dokdo/Takeshima, the Senkaku/Diaoyutai islands were lightning rods for nationalist sentiments because Japan's claims to the islands had been established during the colonial period. Whereas in the past, Beijing and Tokyo had worked to dampen the ideological dimensions of the dispute, under the new conditions of the 1990s, they took on a dangerous new symbolic significance.

Even more worrying were developments on Taiwan. By the mid-1990s, it became clear that Chinese hopes for an early reunification with the mainland were dashed, and Taiwanese public opinion seemed increasingly to drift in favor of declaring independence from the mainland. Pro-independence forces on the island promoted a historical narrative that stressed that over the past century. They pointed out that Taiwan had been governed for only approximately two years by Beijing. The rest of the time it had been either under Imperial Japanese control or had been de facto self-administered. During this period, pro-independence forces argued that Taiwan had evolved into a separate society distinct from that of the mainland.[102] The democratization of Taiwan beginning in the 1980s increased the political influence of these forces so that by the 1990s even the Kuomintang – which historically had been committed to reunification with the Mainland – began to emphasize a uniquely Taiwanese identity. For many Taiwanese, democracy became equated with abandoning

[100] As a result, when tensions over the islands developed in the mid-1990s, the United States found itself committed to a definition of Japanese territory that included the Senkaku/Diaoyutai islands.

[101] For a useful overview, see Reinhard Drifte, "Japanese-Chinese Territorial Disputes in the East China Sea: Between Military Confrontation and Economic Cooperation," *LSE Asia Research Centre* Working Paper No. 24, (April 24, 2008), available at http://www.lse.ac .uk/asiaResearchCentre/pdf/WorkingPaper/ARCWorkingPaper24Drifte2008.pdf. The author would like to thank Professor Drifte for passing a copy along. For a very interesting, if also controversial, discussion of the background behind the Senkaku and other island disputes, see Hara Kimie, *Cold War Frontiers in the Asia-Pacific: Divided Territories in the San Francisco System* (London and New York: Routledge, 2007). See also Downs and Saunders, "Legitimacy and the Limits of Nationalism," pp. 129–131.

[102] Alan Wachman, *Taiwan: National Identity and Democratization* (Armonk, NY: M.E. Sharpe, 1997).

the idea of reunification with the mainland, while embracing Taiwan's colonial heritage was associated with freedom and independence.[103] A new generation of Taiwanese leaders – beginning with President Lee Teng Hui – emerged with little or no personal connection to the mainland. Lee, whose family was of Taiwanese origin, had been educated at Kyoto University and reportedly spoke better Japanese than Mandarin. Lee's personal connections to Japan and his efforts to increase Taiwan's diplomatic profile was viewed by many in China as part of a plot on the part of Tokyo and Washington to permanently separate the island from the mainland.[104]

Against this background, the new Chinese government led by Jiang Zemin began to adopt an increasingly harsh tone in its dealings with Japan. In 1994, Japanese proposals for joint historical research were shot down by the Chinese government, which stated that the only purpose of such research would be to encourage deeper Japanese "self-reflection."[105] In 1995, Chinese Foreign Minister Qian Qichen reopened the reparations issue, stating that although the Chinese government had forgone the right to raise state-to-state claims, it would still be possible for individuals to demand compensation.[106] Qian's statements were soon followed by legal claims pressed against Japan by various victim groups, including former Chinese comfort women, slave laborers, victims of germ warfare experiments, and people who had been injured by Japanese chemical weapons. As in Korea, these long-suppressed voices were making themselves heard now that the political situation had changed.

The Chinese government also began to frame other issues in terms of China's history as a victim of Japanese aggression. In 1995, when former Prime Minister Kaifu asked Jiang Zemin for Chinese support for a Japanese bid for a permanent seat on the UN Security Council, Jiang responded that Japan's views on history made it difficult for China to do so.[107] When Japan protested Chinese nuclear tests that same year, the Chinese foreign ministry dismissed its complaints, commenting, "In Japan there are still recalcitrant elements who do all they can to distort history and glorify invasion."[108] In August 1996, shortly after Prime Minister Hashimoto made his visit to the Yasukuni shrine, tensions heated up over the Senkaku/Diaoyutai islands as activists from both sides tried to reaffirm their countries' claims to the islands. Japanese right wingers landed on one of

---

[103] For an interesting discussion of how these issues played out the Taiwanese educational system, see Hsin-Huang Michael, Hsiao, "One Colonialism, Two Memories: Representing Japanese Colonialism in Taiwan and South Korea," in Gi-Wook Shin and Daniel C. Sneider, eds., *History Textbooks and Wars in Asia: Divided Memories* (London: Routledge, 2010), pp. 173–190.

[104] See Qingxin Ken Wang, "Taiwan in Japan's Relations with China and the United States after the Cold War," *Pacific Affairs* 73:3 (2001), pp. 353–373.

[105] Yinan He, "The Emerging Sino-Japanese Conflict," op. cit., p. 24.

[106] He, ibid., p. 10.

[107] Wakamiya, *The Postwar Conservative View of Asia*, op. cit., p. 26.

[108] Chinese foreign ministry press secretary quoted in Wakamiya Yoshuibumi, *The Postwar Conservative View of Asia*, op. cit., p. 26; see also He, *Shadows of the Past*, op. cit., pp. 271–272.

the islands and built a crude lighthouse, and Chinese activists tried to swim to the islands after being denied permission to visit. The Chinese press was blistering in its criticism of the Japanese stance on the islands, warning that China would never renounce its sovereign rights to the islands and vowing there would be no more Li Hongzhangs – the Chinese official who had signed the Peace Treaty ending the Sino-Japanese War of 1895 under which Japan had won control over the islands.[109]

Jiang Zemin's disastrous trip to Tokyo in 1998 represented the high point of the 1990s tensions over history. Various factors contributed to making Jiang's visit an exceptionally difficult one. Earlier that year, Beijing had managed to extract an unusually strong statement from President Bill Clinton that seemed to support the PRC's position on Taiwan. Jiang may well have hoped to win a similarly favorable statement from Japan. The Japanese government, however, was aware that Clinton had been heavily criticized inside the United States for leaning too far in favor of Beijing and was unwilling to comply with Jiang's wishes.[110] Lack of adequate preparation for the trip may also have played a role. Jiang, having seen that Kim Dae Jung had received a written apology, wanted the same, even though it had not been on the original agenda for the visit.[111] The most important reasons for failure, however, were the domestic political dynamics at play. Jiang, who only recently had taken charge in Beijing, was still insecure in his position and felt that he needed to take a strong line on history to court conservative political forces in the Chinese military.[112] As a result, although Jiang demanded an apology from Japan, unlike Kim Dae Jung, he did not offer any language that suggested that the apology would be accepted. The Japanese side, therefore, felt that it was getting nothing in return for meeting Jiang's demands and that the Chinese would continue to bludgeon it with the history issue in the future as well. As a result, the meeting in Tokyo ended in a diplomatic impasse.[113]

In the subsequent months, the two sides worked to paper over their differences. When Obuchi visited China the next year, the main focus of his trip was on economic issues, and the history issue was largely sidelined. Likewise, when Premier Zhu Rongji visited Japan in 2000, he neatly sidestepped reporters' questions about the past by noting that both the Chinese and the Japanese peoples had suffered during the war. During the same period, both sides seemed to work together to deepen their political ties, especially through the

---

[109] Yinan He, *Shadows of the Past*, op. cit., p. 280.

[110] Jin Linbo, "Japan's Neonationalism and China's Response," in Tsuyoshi Hasegawa and Kazuhiko Tog, eds., *East Asia's Haunted Present*, op. cit., p. 176.

[111] Susan Shirk, *China: Fragile Superpower*, op. cit., pp. 166–167.

[112] Caroline Rose, "The Yasukuni Shrine Problem in Sino-Japanese relations," in John Breen, ed., *Yasukuni*, op. cit., p. 37.

[113] See Wakaiyama Yoshibumi, *The Postwar Conservative View of Asia*, op. cit., pp. 256–261; Yinan He, *Shadows of the Past*, pp. 248–249; and Michael Green, *Japan's Reluctant Realism: Foreign Policy Changes in a Era of Uncertain Power* (New York: St. Martin's Press, 2001), pp. 96–98.

development of regional institutions such as the ASEAN plus Three Ini-tiative.[114] Thus the two nations – for instrumental reasons – were able to contain the very significant tensions over history that had developed between them. Beneath the surface, however, deeper structural changes in the domestic and international politics of the region had taken place that made any morato-rium on dealing with the history of Japanese atrocities inherently fragile. The Chinese political system had changed in ways that allowed the long suppressed voices of the victims of Japanese atrocities to be heard. The international system had changed in ways that weakened the case for circumspection on history for the sake of concern with larger Chinese national history. Perhaps most impor-tantly, the Chinese discourse on the nation and its history had fundamentally changed since the 1980s so that Chinese political elites were encouraged rather then discouraged from taking up the history issue. To put it more colorfully, China's leaders had unleashed the tiger of an aggrieved nationalism. Now they had the unenviable task of having to try to ride it.

## The Storm over History 2001–2007

In 2001, whatever progress had been made in dealing with the history issue between Japan and its closest neighbors began to unravel. Over the next six years, Japan's relations with its two closest neighbors underwent an unusually severe diplomatic crisis, one that threatened to undermine regional harmony and raised tensions over other issues – in particular territorial disputes – to dangerous levels.

Two developments served as a catalyst for the rapid deterioration of rela-tions. First, there was the Japanese Ministry of Education's approval for adop-tion of a controversial new series of textbooks drafted by the revisionist *Tsuku-rukai*. The first book was adopted by only a handful of schools (less than .01 percent of the total number of schools in 2001 – including, ironically, a voca-tional school for the blind) and was immediately criticized not only by the left end of the Japanese political spectrum but by many centrists as well, includ-ing eight associations representing professional historians. Nonetheless, the decision of the ministry to approve for adoption the 2001 textbook and its successors suggested continuing support within the Japanese government for revisionist views and sparked waves of protest in China and Korea.[115]

Even more disruptive was the decision by the newly nominated prime minis-ter Koizumi Junichirō to visit the Yasukuni shrine. In his campaign to win the LDP nomination for prime minister, Koizumi reached out to the *Izokukai* and

---

[114] Susan Shirk, *China: Fragile Superpower*, op. cit., pp. 167–168.
[115] On general background to the 2001 textbook dispute, see Mitani Hiroshi, *Rekishi Kyōkasho Mondai* Part II. On some of the diplomatic consequences, see Alexander Bukh, "Japan's History Textbook Debate." For a conservative Japanese perspective, see Komori Yōichi, Sakamoto Yoshikazu, and Yasumaru Yoshio, eds., *Rekishi Kyōkasho Nani ga Mondai ka: tettei Kensho Q&A* (Tokyo: Iwanami, 2001).

the powerful Mori faction – descendant of the Kishi faction and traditionally associated with the ideological right wing of the LDP – by promising to visit the Yasukuni shrine every year in his official capacity as prime minister.[116] Despite repeated and sharp warnings from Beijing and Seoul, as well as from several senior Japanese political figures, Koizumi made good on his promise, paying his first visit to the Shrine on August 13, 2001.[117]

Koizumi tried various ways of softening the diplomatic ramifications of his visits. For instance, in 2001 he went to the shrine two days before the anniversary of the Japanese surrender in 1945, instead of on the day of surrender itself, and he repeatedly stressed that his visit was only meant to mourn the dead and by no means was to deny that Japan had been guilty of inflicting great pain on the peoples of Asia through its policies of aggression and colonization.[118] Despite these efforts, however, Koizumi's visit prompted an avalanche of condemnation. In response, Beijing suspended direct, bilateral meetings between the two heads of state, relying on lower level meetings and contacts in such multilateral settings as the meetings of the Asian Pacific Economic Cooperation (APEC). The Korean response was even sharper. Seoul suspended military talks between Japan and Korea, reimposed the ban on Japanese cultural items, and temporarily recalled the South Korean ambassador for "consultations" to Seoul.[119]

Spurred by the need to coordinate policies in response to 9/11 and the war on terror – especially with respect to North Korea – China, Japan, and South Korea tried to find ways after Koizumi's first visit to Yasukuni to patch their differences over history. In October 2001, Koizumi visited China and placed a wreath on the statue of a Chinese soldier at the Marco Polo Bridge, where the second Sino-Japanese War had broken out in 1937.[120] Likewise, joint historical research commissions were set up both with Korea and China.[121] In 2001, Beijing and Seoul hoped that after Nakasone's trip in 1985 and Hashimoto's in 1996 that the Japanese government would suspend further visits and the problem would soon blow over. Against the backdrop of "apology fatigue" in Japan, Tokyo, for its part, seemed to believe that it could put history behind it again. A more fatal combination of views would be difficult to imagine.

---

[116] Shino Watanabe, "Foreign Aid and Influence: Paradoxical Power Dynamics in Japan's Official Development Assistance to China" (Dissertation in Politics at the University of Virginia, 2007), p. 176. The author would like to thank Len Schoppa for bringing this source to his attention.
[117] *Asahi* August 4, 2001, pp. 1 and 4; Daiki Shibuchi, "The Yasukuni Shrine Dispute," op. cit., p. 211.
[118] Tanaka Akihiko, "The Yasukuni Issue in Japan's Foreign Relations," in Hasegawa and Togo, *East Asia's Haunted Present*, op. cit., pp. 134–135.
[119] See *The Korean Herald*, August 15, 2001.
[120] Akihiko, "The Yasukuni Issue in Japan's Foreign Relations," in Hasegawa and Togo, *East Asia's Haunted Present*, pp. 135–136; Shirk, *China: Fragile Superpower*, op. cit., p. 169.
[121] NiChūkan Sangoku Kyōtsu *Rekishi* Kyōzai Iinkai, ed., *Mirai o hiraku Rekishi: Higashi Ajia Sangoku no Kingendaishi* (Tokyo: Kobunken, 2005); Mitani Hiroshi, "The History Textbook Issue in Japan and East Asia," in Hasegawa and Tokyo, *East Asia's Haunted Present*, op. cit., pp. 89–90.

Japan's readiness for compromise over the history issue was severely limited by its own domestic political dynamics. A commission to consider possible alternatives to commemorating Japan's war dead at Yasukuni – established by Koizumi and directed by his very able Chief Cabinet Secretary Fukuda Yasuo – ran into heavy opposition from the *Izokukai* and conservative LDP parliamentarians. In June 2002, a group of 125 LDP Diet members, led by former General Secretary Koga Makoto, gathered in Tokyo and warned that the Fukuda commission should not ignore the sentiments of the war bereaved or damage Yasukuni's unique role as the place where the spirits of the dead could be appeased. The idea that an alternative commemorative site could be found was strongly rejected. As conservative Japanese pointed out, when Japan's soldiers had marched off to war, they had typically vowed to "meet again at Yasukuni." From this perspective, choosing another site would be tantamount to betraying the spirits of the dead.[122]

Political positions in both China and South Korea hardened as well. In 2003, the new leadership team of Hu Jintao and Wen Jiabao took over from the Jiang Zemin. Hu and Wen essentially were technocrats, and they came into office stressing that they wished for closer, forward-looking relations with Japan. Nonetheless, they soon exhibited the same need to consolidate their support on the right end of the Chinese political spectrum that Jiang Zemin had, and they were doing so at a time when popular nationalist passions were on the rise. Commentators such as the liberal journalist Ma Licheng and international relations expert Shi Yinhong, who called for an end to attacking Japan over its stance on history, were soon silenced, and the new leadership adopted a tolerant attitude toward various anti-Japanese nationalist groups.[123]

Meanwhile, in 2003, Roh Moo-Hyun took over the presidency from the ailing Kim Dae Jung in South Korea. Roh came into office intent on continuing his predecessor's policy to seek reconciliation with Japan. His efforts to do so, however, were frustrated by the textbook issue and Koizumi's decision to visit Yasukuni despite Roh's repeated entreaties to not do so. As Roh's political fortunes declined because of controversies over his handling of the economy and other issues, Roh increasingly became inclined to appeal to Korean nationalist sentiments to bolster his own public opinion ratings.

As a result, Japan's relations with its two most important Asian neighbors went on a downward spiral over the next few years. Increasingly, popular anger began to turn into sporadic action at the grassroots level. In 2003, a series of anti-Japanese incidents began to break out in China. Many of the incidents appeared quite trivial. For instance, in October 2003 riots broke out in the western city of Xian after two Japanese exchange students put on a sexually

---

[122] The author is indebted to his conversations with a number of Japanese on this point, in particular, former Ambassador Togo Kazuhiko and Tokyo University Professor Tanaka Akihiko.

[123] See Peter Hays Gries, "China's 'New Thinking' on Japan," *The China Quarterly* 184 (December 2005); and Susan Shirk, *China: Fragile Superpower*, op. cit., pp. 172–173, 177.

inappropriate skit in the local university, which their Chinese compatriots interpreted as an insult to China's national honor.[124] Others were more serious, such as the public uproar that was generated after a worker was killed and four others were injured by abandoned Japanese poison gas munitions that were unearthed during construction in Qihar.[125]

These incidents escalated steadily. A high point came in early April 2005 when an Internet campaign to collect signatures opposing Japan's bid for a permanent seat on the United Nation's Security Council (reportedly well over 30 million were collected within a year) sparked countrywide riots. Over a period of two weeks, Japanese shops and diplomatic outposts were pelted with stones and garbage, and several Japanese were injured by mobs of Chinese demonstrators.[126] The Japanese diplomatic response became increasingly tough as the violence continued, and even usually pro-Chinese groups and commentators, such as the liberal *Asahi* newspaper, began to become highly critical of the Chinese government's unwillingness to clamp down on the protestors.

At this point, the Chinese leadership became concerned that the tensions were getting out of hand. They feared that if the protests continued, they could damage Chinese diplomatic interests and potentially might mutate into a broader critique of the Chinese Communist government. Although the Chinese authorities had adopted a lenient stance to the protestors in the beginning – possibly believing that they were just letting off steam – in late April they took forceful measure to contain the unrest. At an April 17 meeting of the CCP Propaganda Department, Foreign Minister Li Zhaoxiang called on the cadres to contain the violence in the name of "maintaining social order."[127] Chinese officials fanned across the country to explain why boycotts were ineffective and good relations should be maintained with Japan. Restrictions were placed on the use of cell phones and the Internet, which had been used to organize the protests, and the Chinese media launched a full-court press on the need for social stability.[128] The government's measures proved effective, and the unrest soon ended.

The Japanese side as well did what it could to bring the crisis under control. At a conference to mark the fiftieth anniversary of the Asian-African Nonaligned Movement in Bandung, Koizumi delivered a keynote speech in which he repeated Murayama's 1995 apology for Japan's historical role as an

---

[124] During a school performance, the two students appeared on stage semi-nude with heart-shaped signs over their privates with the words "We love China" written on them.

[125] "Relic of War Adds Strain to Beijing ties," *New York Times*, August 12, 2003; He, "History, Chinese Nationalism and the Emerging Sino-Japanese Conflict," op. cit., p. 2.

[126] *Asahi* satellite edition, April 9, 10, 11, 17, 18, and 21, 2005, p. 1.

[127] Joseph Kahn, "Chinese Official Orders End to Anti-Japanese Demonstrations," *New York Times*, April 20, 2005, available at http://www.nytimes.com/2005/04/20/international/asia/ 20china.html?ex=1271649600&en=d539df61c78c523a&ei=5090&partner=rssuserland& emc=rss (accessed May 17, 2006).

[128] Susan Shirk, *China: The Fragile Superpower*, op. cit., p. 175.

aggressor and colonizer. Whereas Murayama had made his speech in Japan, Koizumi's speech was at an international event well attended by regional leaders.[129]

Japanese public opinion as well showed signs of increased concern about the political impact of Japan's official narrative on the country's relations with its neighbors. According to a poll taken by *Asahi* in March, still 54 percent of those surveyed approved of the visits to the Yasukuni, whereas only 28 percent opposed them. However, according to a follow-up poll taken by *Asahi* in April, as the crisis with China developed, only 36 percent approved of the visits, whereas 46 percent were opposed.[130] Although the Japanese public wished to honor their dead, like Nakasone twenty years earlier, they did not want to do so in a way that would harm Japan's broader international interests.

Although the violence had ended, relations between Beijing and Tokyo remained poisonous for the duration of the Koizumi administration. When Vice Premier Wu Yi visited Japan in May 2005, she abruptly ended her visit reportedly because she was offended by conservatives in the LDP who continued to insist that Yasukuni was an internal matter.[131] High-level contacts between Beijing and Tokyo remained impaired,[132] and tensions were evident at high-level multilateral meetings as well. For instance, at the East Asian summit in 2006, little was accomplished by regional leaders after China joined South Korea in criticizing Japan over its stand on the history issue.[133]

In September 2005, after the riots in China had ended, tensions rose to even more dangerous levels when a group of five Chinese military vessels were spotted in the disputed waters around the Senkaku/Diaoyutai islands. One warship even "locked" its radar on a Japanese coast guard plane, a step that could indicate it is preparing to fire.[134] The possibility that the dispute could escalate to the military level suddenly seemed quite real. Similar maneuvers in 2001 had led to the downing of a U.S. reconnaissance plane by a Chinese fighter near Hainan Island and had severely tested Sino-U.S. relations.

---

[129] For the text of the speech, see http://www.mofa.go.jp/region/asia-paci/meet0504/speech.html (accessed May 26, 2006).

[130] *Asahi Shimbun*, April 25, 2005, pp. 1 and 3.

[131] "Wuu Fukushusho no Kikoku – 'Yasukuni ga Genin' Chukoku Setsumei," (China explains "Yasukuni's the Cause' of Vice Prime Wu's Return to China," *Asahi* satellite edition, May 25, 2005, p. 1.

[132] "APEC Meeting Sees Splits over Trade, Japan's Past," *AFP*, November 15, 2005, at http://asia.news.yahoo.com/051115/afp/051115085837.business.html (accessed November 15, 2005); "China Kills Summit with Japan, Korea," *Japan Times*, December 5, 2005, at http://www.japantimes.co.jp/cgi-bin/makeprfy.pl5?nn20051205a1.htm (accessed December 5, 2005).

[133] "NiChuKan Gikushaku: Yasukuni kennen, takoku ni mo Kakudai," (The Awkwardness between China and Japan: Worries over Yasukuni Spreads to other Countries as well") *Asahi* satellite edition, December 15, 2005, p. 4.

[134] "Chinese Warships Make a Show of Force at Protested Gas Rig," *Japan Times*, September 10, 2005; "Chinese Warship Pointed Gun at MSDF Plane," *Japan Times*, October 2, 2005.

A similar deterioration was to be observed in Japanese-Korean relations. Soon after Kim Dae Jung's successor, Roh Moo Hyun, entered office he found himself confronted first with an escalating war of words between the two countries over the Japanese Ministry of Education's approval of revisionist textbooks and then over the Dokdo/Takeshima islands in the Sea of Japan. Like Beijing, Seoul had been incensed by Koizumi's repeated visits to Yasukuni. However, even more than Yasukuni, the central issue on the Korean side revolved around territorial disputes. From 2002 to 2003, the two sides maneuvered to underline their claim to the islands. The Korean government's campaign to rename the Sea of Japan the East Sea intensified, and when Korea issued a postage stamp commemorating the islands, nationalist sentiment on the Japanese side were inflamed. Tokyo, for its part, continued to insist that the islands belonged to Japan.

In March 2005 a major diplomatic crisis ensued after the Shimane prefectural government declared February 22 to be Takeshima Day. President Roh stressed that from the Korean standpoint, Dokdo had been the start of the annexation of Korea and, therefore, had a symbolic and historical significance that far outweighed its economic or strategic importance. Japan's stance, he claimed, was an effort to legitimate its policies of expansion and colonialism in Asia. Roh went on to declare the "diplomatic equivalent of war."[135] In a rare show of unity, the Korean National Assembly backed Roh, voting 241 to 1 that Dokdo belongs to Korea and that Japan's claims were part of an unacceptable political movement that sought to whitewash Japan's Imperial past.[136]

As with the Senkaku/Diaoyutai dispute a year earlier, the competing claims to Dokdo/Takeshima began to escalate to a potentially dangerous level. In April 2006, after Korea threatened to give oceanographic features around the island Korean names, Japan announced that it would send survey ships from the Japanese Maritime Safety Agency to the islands to present its own naming counter proposals at an upcoming international oceanographic conference in Berlin. In response, South Korea then dispatched a flotilla of military vessels to the islands and threatened to use force if Japan sent the survey ships. In a televised speech, President Roh accused Japan of denying Korean independence and once again declared diplomatic war on Japan.[137] In response, conservative politicians in Japan advocated sending an armed coast guard escort for the survey ships. Thanks to last minute diplomatic efforts – with quiet, behind the scenes support from the United States – the crisis was eventually contained. Japan chose not to dispatch the survey vessels, and the Korean government chose largely symbolic measures to underline Korean sovereignty

---

[135] "Kankoku Daitoryo: 'Nihon, Shinryaku o Seitōka' Takeshima Kyōkashohihan no Danwa" (Korean President Criticizes Takeshima and Japanese Textbooks as Legitimating Japan's Invasion), *Ashai* satellite edition, March 24, 2005, pages 1, 2 and 7.

[136] Michael Weinstein, "South Korea-Japan Dokdo Takeshim Dispute: Towards Confrontation," *Japan Focus*, May 10, 2006, p. 4, available at http://japanfocus.org/article.asp?id=596.

[137] "Takeshima wa 'Rekshininshikimondai,'" *Asahi* satellite edition, March 26, 2006, p. 1.

over the islands.[138] Nationalist sentiment on both sides, however, remained unappeased, and public opinion data showed a sharp rise in negative attitudes toward the other country. By 2005, according to a *Dong-A* survey, 63 percent of Korean respondents had a negative view of Japan, up from 42.2 percent in 2000.[139] Meanwhile in Japan, nationalists embarked on an anti-Korean propaganda campaign, producing a stream of critical press commentary on Korea and publishing best-selling *manga* with titles such as "Hating the Korean Wave" – a repudiation of the era of warm feelings that followed the Kim-Obuchi summit of 1998.[140]

The downward trend in Japan's relations with its Asian neighbors began to provoke growing concern in a variety of quarters. Naturally, the Japanese Foreign Ministry was concerned over the Japan's growing diplomatic isolation in the region.[141] The Japanese business community, worried about the potential damage to Japan's rapidly growing economic interests in the region (China had become Japan's number one trading partner, outstripping the United States, and by some estimates as much as of half of the increase in Japan's economic growth since 2002 can be attributed to exports to Asia), took the unusual steps of making independent overtures to the Chinese leadership and to publicly admonish the LDP against continuing official prime ministerial visits to Yasukuni.[142] Meanwhile, mainstream Japanese opinion leaders, both right-of-center and left-of-center, together to tried to forge a new consensus on history that could diffuse the tensions that were threatening to overwhelm Japan's relations with its neighbors. The most visible reflection of this trend was a highly unusual joint historical research enterprise launched by the liberal *Asahi* and conservative *Yomiuri* newspapers. Their efforts culminated in the publishing of a two-volume history of modern Japan that was strikingly moderate in tone and quite critical of the views of the *Tsukurukai* and other revisionist groups.[143]

---

[138] For an overview of the crisis over Dokdo/Takeshima, see Michael Weinstein, "South Korea-Japan Dokdo-Takeshim Dispute: Towards Confrontation," *Japan Focus* May 10, 2006, pp. 2–3, available at http://japanfocus.org/article.asp?id=596.

[139] *Dong-A Daily* (1984–2005) cited in Yangmo Ku, "International Reconciliation in the Postwar Era," op. cit., p. 25.

[140] See Rumi Sakamoto and Matthew Allen, "Hating 'The Korean Wave' Comic Books: A Sign of New Nationalism in Japan," *Japan Focus* (October 4, 2007), available at http://www .japanfocus.org/-Rumi-SAKAMOTO/2535 (accessed July 3, 2011).

[141] Ajia Gaiko Yuzuranu Shusho ("The Prime Minister Refuses to Back Down on Asian Diplomacy"), *Asahi* satellite edition, November 15, 2005, p. 2.

[142] See the critical comments on Yasukuni made by the Japanese Business Federation, Keizaidōyūkai, *Asahi* satellite edition, May 10, 2006, p. 2. On the Japanese Federation of Business (Keidanren) diplomatic overtures to China, see "Keidanren Made Covert Trip to China Last Month," *Japan Times*, October 23, 2005, available at http://www.japntimes.co.jp/ cgi-bin/makeprfy.pl15?nn20051023a1.htm.

[143] The effort began in 2006, after the editors of the two newspapers Watanabe Tsuneo and Wakamiya Yoshibumi participated in a public seminar and found themselves surprisingly in agreement on many of the central issues in the history dispute. See "Yomiuri and Asahi Editors Call for a National Memorial to Replace Yasukuni," *Japan Focus*, February 14, 2006, at http://www.japanfocus.org/products/topdf/2124. Abridged version of article appearing in

Even the *Izokukai* began to strike a more measured tone on history after it was revealed that the late Emperor Hirohito had chosen to no longer visit Yasukuni after class A war criminals had been enshrined there in 1978. Because many Izokukai members longed for Imperial participation in rites to mourn the dead, and because there was no prospect that the new emperor or his likely successor would visit the shrine under current circumstances, support grew within the organization for either de-enshrining the class A war criminals from the shrine (by removing them from the list of names of the spirits who have been admitted to the shrine) or perhaps even creating an alternative commemorative site.[144]

U.S. political policy makers, traditionally hesitant to interfere in what they see as an issue that should be left to the Asian nations to settle, became increasingly vocal in their efforts to persuade Japan and the other governments to adopt a more moderate stance.[145] Although the United States continued to avoid trying to mediate between the different sides for fear of becoming the target of criticism itself, senior U.S. policy makers grew concerned that the territorial disputes between Japan and Korea as well as with China could escalate to the level of military clashes in which case the United States would find itself automatically involved because of its alliances with Japan and South Korea.[146]

Whereas Koizumi continued to visit Yasukuni right until he left office in 2006, his immediate successor Abe Shinzo, the grandson of Kishi Nobusuke, took a more measured stance on history. Before running for prime minister, Abe had been viewed as a leading hawk who had visited Yasukuni many times in the past and had close ties to the *Izokukai* and other groups known for their conservative views on history. Nonetheless, during the race to succeed Koizumi, Abe along with the other leading candidates, suggested that he would avoid going to the Shrine, at least publicly, to improve relations with Japan's Asian neighbors.[147] After taking office, Abe immediately visited Beijing even before he went to Washington, signaling the increased importance of China to Japan. During his time as prime minister, Abe sought to avoid the history issue as much as possible, although it occasionally bubbled up, as it did in late 2006

*Ronza,* February 9, 2006. The author is also very grateful for the insights on the process provided by a number of Japanese journalists, in particular Miura Toshiaki of the *Asahi.*

[144] "Kogashi A-Kyū Sempan Bunshi Kentō o Teigen," *Asahi* satellite edition, May 19, 2006, p. 4. For a useful summary, see John Breen, "Introduction: A Yasukuni Geneaology," pp. 1–5, in John Breen, ed., *Yasukuni,* op. cit.

[145] "U.S. Lawmaker Wants Koizumi's Guarantee that He Won't Visit Yasukuni," May 16, 2006, at http://asia.news.yahoo.com/060516/Kyodo/d8hkji981.html (accessed May 25, 2006). See also "Yasukuni'Nichibei ni mo Eikyo," *Asahi* satellite edition, April 30, 2006, p. 1. On the U.S. position on the history issue in general, see David Straub, "The United States and Reconciliation in East Asia," in Hasegawa and Togo, *East Asia's Haunted Past,* op. cit.

[146] The author is indebted to several high-level U.S. policy makers based both in Washington and in the U.S. embassy in Tokyo for their insight on this issue.

[147] *Asahi* "Sampai Shuh wa Kotaisho," (Favorable Contrast in how to visit the Shrine) *Asahi* satellite edition, August 5, 2006, p. 2.

when he made remarks that suggested the Imperial government had not been directly involved in the forcible recruitment of comfort women.[148]

The Democratic Party of Japan (DPJ), which took power from the LDP in 2009, went further and tried to actively reach out to China and Korea in an effort to reconcile over the history issue. As the party prepared to take office, senior DPJ leaders sent signals that improved relations with Asia would be at the top of their diplomatic agenda. Soon after taking power, they took concrete steps to promote reconciliation by releasing records on forced laborers and preparing to pay them compensation for their suffering.[149]

## Aftermath

In closing, there are three questions that need to be addressed. First, how serious was the 2001–2006 dispute over history? Second, was it an aberration, a one time "perfect storm" of historically contingent factors coming together to create an unusual degree of turbulence, or could it reoccur? And finally, why were Japan and it neighbors in Asian unable to attain a degree of reconciliation on historical issues comparable to what Germany and Austria managed to achieve in Europe?

With regard to the first question, it is important not to exaggerate the extent of the crisis. The violence that was triggered was relatively constrained, and no deaths or serious injuries resulted. Diplomatic contacts between Japan and its two neighbors never ceased, and although high-level contacts were restricted to regional multilateral meetings, there continued to be dialogue on a range of pressing issues, such as trade, managing the regional economy, dealing with North Korea, or responding to the U.S. war on terror. Likewise, despite fears of an economic embargo and the politically motivated cancellation of contracts,[150] trade between Japan and its Asian neighbors continued to grow steadily throughout the period. Chinese and Korean consumers and companies continued to eagerly buy high-quality Japanese goods despite their differences over history, and Japanese corporations continued to be happy to make profits by selling to them. It might be tempting, therefore, to conclude that the whole thing had been a rhetorical tempest in an Asian teapot.

---

[148] For a review of the controversy over Abe's comments regarding the comfort women, see Larry Niksch, *The Japanese Military's "Comfort Women" System*, op. cit. For the text of the speech in which Abe originally made his comments, see http://www.fmprc.gov.cn/eng/zxxx/t311544 .htm#.

[149] Koizumi's immediate successor, Abe, reached out to China and was rewarded by a highly successful visit by Chinese Premier Wen Jiabao in April 2007. The incoming DPJ made addressing history an important issue and saw it as part of a new, more Asia-oriented foreign policy. See "Ozawa in his own Words," interview by Dan Sneider, *The Oriental Economist*, June 2009, pp. 5–6. See also Sneider, "A Japan That Can Say Maybe," same issue, pp. 7–8.

[150] Of particular concern was the possibility that Japan would lose its bid to participate in the construction of a high speed, multibillion dollar rail project linking Beijing and Shanghai. In 2004, the Chinese vice foreign minister even warned visiting Japanese officials that anti-Japanese popular sentiment made it difficult awarding the contract to Japanese firms. He, "The Emerging Sino-Japanese Conflict," op. cit., pp. 19–20.

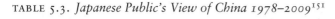

TABLE 5.3. *Japanese Public's View of China 1978–2009*[151]

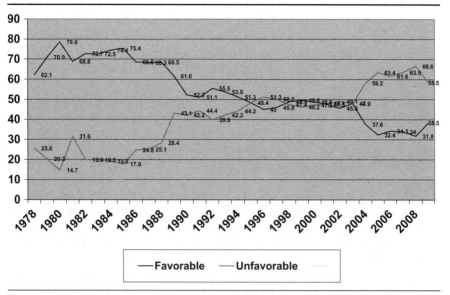

A more careful look at the events, however, would suggest that a less sanguine view of the crisis is in order. Certainly from the point of view of the governments involved, the dispute over history had been enormously costly. Senior political leaders spent huge amounts of time on managing the crisis, and there were extended periods when the battle over history had gone to the top of the domestic and international political agenda. Managing relations with Japan's Asian neighbors became a central issue in the LDP presidential election of 2006. It was clearly of similar importance to the Roh Moo Hyun government and perhaps only slightly less important to the Hu Jintao regime in China.

The crisis also had a distinctly negative impact on public opinion. Japanese popular perceptions of China, which had turned negative after the Tiananmen crisis, turned even more negative after the start of the history crisis, peaking in 2006 with surveys showing that 66.6 percent said that they had little or no feeling of liking (*shitashimi*) for China. Although there was some improvement in popular views after the crisis peaked, with over 58 percent expressing negative views in 2009, popular antipathy toward China remained higher than it had been at any point before the crisis began (see Table 5.3).

Public opinion data from China is harder to come by and is not as systematic as the data available from Japan and Korea in that the same question is asked repeatedly over the space of years. Sporadic public polls began to be conducted in China only from the late 1980s on. The available data nonetheless suggest an ever-deteriorating Chinese popular image of Japan. Whereas a joint Sino-Japanese poll in 1988 showed 53.6 percent of Chinese respondents felt close to Japan, 38.6 percent felt not close; the two joint polls conducted by the *Asahi* and Chinese People's University in 1997 shows only 10 percent of Chinese liked Japan, whereas 34 percent disliked it. By 2002, a survey revealed that only 10 percent liked Japan, whereas those who disliked Japan increased to 53 percent.[152]

Korean views of Japan showed a similar negative trend. Whereas in 2000, before the onset of the crisis, 42.2 percent of those surveyed by the *Dong-A Ilbo* newspaper had a negative view of Japan, by 2001 that percentage had climbed to 56.6 percent before rising to 63 percent in 2005.[153]

Not coincidentally, the Japanese public's perception of threat also grew during this time period. When asked, What is the danger that Japan will be dragged into a war (*makikomareru*) by 2006?, 46 percent of those surveyed said that there was considerable danger, and 32 percent said there was some level of danger, and only 16.5 percent said that there was no danger. This was a far greater perception of threat than had existed at any point during the cold war, when thousands of Soviet nuclear missiles were pointed at Japan, and the Soviet Union was building military bases on the disputed Northern islands just off the shore of Hokkaido. Much of the public's perception of threat was driven by the enormous media attention that was focused on North Korea, the international crisis over its nuclear weapons program and the revelations that North Korean agents had kidnapped possibly dozens of Japanese citizens over the space of several decades. Nonetheless, there could be little doubt that public apprehensions were sharpened greatly by the perception that Japan was hated by its two closest neighbors. In 2009, after the crisis over history had ended, the percentage of those who said that there was a danger of entanglement had dropped to 26.6 percent, even though little concrete progress on the North Korean nuclear weapons program had been made (see Table 5.4).

Of course, it is impossible to say what the impact on regional relations would have been if the tensions over history had escalated any further. It is quite possible that if a violent incident of some sort had occurred – say, if Japanese citizens had been killed by Chinese rioters, if right wingers had assaulted Chinese students, or if a firefight had broken out between Japanese and Chinese or Korean naval forces maneuvering around the disputed territories – it would have had a sobering effect on the political leadership in the countries involved and that some way would have been found to paper over their differences. However, given the domestic political realities described above – that is, the unfortunate interplay of the Chinese, Japanese, and Korean official narratives and public discourses on history and the resultant deepening of negative public and elite attitudes – it is almost certain that the animosity between the countries

---

[152] Yinan He, *The Search for Reconciliation*, op. cit., p. 261.
[153] Data cited in Yangmo Ku, "International Reconciliation in the Postwar Era," op. cit., p. 25.

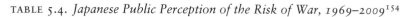

TABLE 5.4. *Japanese Public Perception of the Risk of War, 1969–2009*[154]

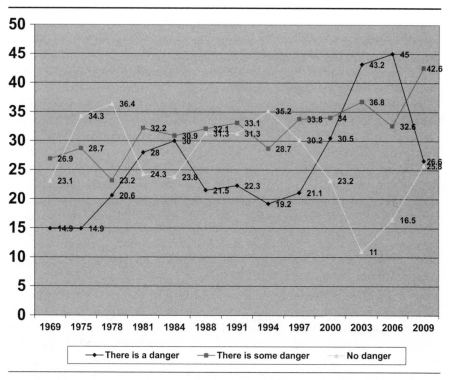

in the region would have deepened further and led to the adoption of policies that would have made regional cooperation less likely and regional confrontation more probable. As it was, Japanese and Korean diplomatic and security cooperation broke down almost completely during the crisis. Sino-Japanese relations deteriorated even further, and increasingly both governments began to openly plan and equip their forces for the possibility of a military confrontation between them.

In short, although it is highly unlikely (but not impossible) that the dispute over history would have led directly to war between Japan and its neighbors, it did poison the relationship between them and set the stage for a possible militarized confrontation between them at a later date. A possible analogy can be seen in the historical impact of U.S.-Japanese relations over immigration before World War II. Although growing discrimination against Asian immigrants in the United States did not directly lead to the attack on Pearl Harbor, it strongly reinforced the sense in Japan that it would never be accepted as an equal by the

---

[154] *Jietai Bōeimondai ni Kan suru Yoron Chōsa* Chief Cabinet Secretary's Office, May 1, 2006, updated with data from 2009 survey. Available at http://www8.cao.go.jp/survey/h17/h17-bouei/images/z24.gif.

racist Western powers. This greatly undermined those in the Japanese political system – internationalists like Foreign Minister Shidehara Kijuro and many members of the Japanese business community – who wanted to maintain better relations with the West and strengthened those who believed that Japan would have to carve out its own, autonomous sphere of influence in Asia.[155]

Was the 2001–2006 crisis a unique event, an unfortunate confluence of factors that made for a sort of perfect storm of controversy over history? Certainly accident and personality played an important role in shaping the course of events. Koizumi, who began his term in office as a weak prime minister lacking an effective power base inside the party, had a strong incentive to find a way to rally ideological support. Visiting Yasukuni was a readily available and convenient option for him. Having made this a signature issue, one that helped reinforce his image as a politician who acted on the basis of conviction rather than convenience, Koizumi continued to visit the shrine despite growing domestic and international political opposition. Similar points could be made about Roh Moo Hyun in Korea and – to a lesser extent – about Hu Jintao in China.

In addition, it is clear that none of the players at the start of the crisis could envision that the crisis would take on the kind of amplitude it did. Certainly there was little international political incentive for them to allow it to do so, either from the Realist or Liberal international relations perspective. If they had, it is quite possible that they would have taken steps to avoid it. The crisis was in many ways a new phenomenon, born of miscalculation and inexperience on the part of the leaders.

However, if the 2001–2006 clash was an accident, it was an accident waiting to happen. Similar, although less virulent, disputes had developed in the early 1980s, and they had increased in intensity over time. Long-term developments in the domestic discourses of the countries involved as well as shifts in the broader international parameters within which the history issue played itself out fed this trend. Growing weariness over history ("apology fatigue") and the mobilization of grassroots history activists in Japan clashed directly with the pluralization of public discourse in South Korea and China and the efforts of both countries to come to terms with the unfortunate aspects of their own political history both before and after 1945. In this sense, although one could attribute these developments to the interests of different political actors in China, Korea, and Japan, reducing the crisis to a rational calculation of interest on part of elite actors offers only a partial explanation. The problem with such a reductionist account is that the definition of elite interests and their association with particular interpretations of history were themselves the product of a discursive evolution in the political cultures of the three countries that developed over time and was beyond the control of any individual or group of individuals, however influential.

[155] For a useful, general discussion, *U.S.-Japanese Relations throughout History* (New York: W.W. Norton, 1997), pp. 88–89, 104–106, 120, 123–124, and 144–146.

For instance, as we have seen, the link in South Korea between the Japanese colonial past and post-1945 authoritarianism emerged out of Korean political and intellectual debates over the space of several decades. Certainly, the Korean government would have preferred to avoid such an association; however, the authoritarian government had only incomplete control over the cultural discourse in Korea, allowing the theory to take root in the Korean academy and inspired a generation of Korean political activists to view a facing up to the country's colonial past as being inextricably intertwined with their project of establishing democracy in Korea. Likewise, the parallels between the May 4 demonstrators in China and anti-Japanese protestors in the late twentieth and early twenty-first centuries was a contextual feature of Chinese politics that had not been manufactured by manipulative elites. Individuals, such as Roh Moo Hyun or the Chinese critics of Hu Yaobang, may have been acting rationally when they chose to try to utilize anti-Japanese sentiments to pursue their own, instrumental objectives (in Roh's case, to bolster his flagging popularity, in the case of Hu's critics to strengthen their own political faction's influence). The existence of these sentiments, however, was a feature of the Chinese and Korean political cultures that could not be ignored or wished away. History alone did not create these dynamics, nor did the concrete material interests of political actors. As the Historical Realist position would predict, interest and historical memory combine to create a cultural discourse that is difficult for any actor to control.

These trends came together in the early years of the twenty-first century and created a severe crisis over history between 2001 and 2007. They did not, however, disappear after the crisis was over. In all three countries, very different views of history continued to persist and were propagated, sometimes with feverish intensity, by a broad array of societal actors such as the history activists in China, groups pursuing historical justice in South Korea, or the *Tsukurukai* and other similar organizations seeking to promote a "healthy sense of patriotism" in Japan. Each of these groups understood these projects as being linked to other key objectives. The history activists in China saw it as a way of opening public discourse and indirectly criticizing the CCP. The Korean history activists used it to promote democracy. Taiwanese nationalists saw it as a way of underlining their independence from the mainland. The Japanese right wing sought to strengthen Japan and prepare the population for a more assertive foreign policy and for assuming a greater defense role, and so on. Although after 2007 political leaders in the region understood these dynamics better and sought to reign them in, the underlying social and political cultural trends remained. Under the right circumstances, it is easy to imagine that these forces could be reignited. Indeed, in certain respects they never really died out, and instead found a new, and more dangerous, outlet in the simmering territorial disputes between all three nations.

The answer to the third question, Why has history been so much more problematic in Asia than in Europe? now becomes answerable. Clearly, no single feature of the Asian international environment made history especially contentious there. Conversely, a variety of factors pushed Europe toward reconciliation. As the Historical Realist position would lead us to expect, a combination of historical, practical, and cultural factors were at play. The international environment in Europe forced Germany to be more penitent than was true of Japan. As a divided, ruined nation on the front lines of the cold war, Germany desperately needed not only U.S. support but also that of the other major European powers. For their part, the West European countries needed Germany for much the same reason, as a bastion against Communism and as an engine for economic growth and reconstruction. Austria, which stood outside of the cold war system, was not subject to similar pressures and inducements. Japan, which was aligned with the anti-Communist block, was much more loosely integrated and, therefore, as Austria, could afford to ignore the history issue. History was a contentious issue in Japan but primarily for domestic political reasons.

Germany's rapprochement with its Western neighbors over history – however incomplete – helped it create a network of multilateral institutional ties – the most important of which were NATO and the European Union, which helped to lock in the benefits of a penitent official historical narrative. At the same time, however, it also led to the development of a culture of contrition that slowly spread and solidified over the courses of the 1990s. In time, the attractive power of Germany's network of institutions, together with the growing costs of a non-contrite historical narrative in an increasingly interdependent world, led previously impenitent Austria to reconsider its stance on history. Closely following the German model, Austria embarked on a full-scale campaign of reconciling itself on history with its neighbors, including not only making official apologies but offering compensation to the victims of Nazism and fostering its own culture of contrition through museums, monuments ,and the state-controlled school system. And like Germany, it was rewarded for its efforts by membership in the new European Union.

In Asia, in contrast, no similar network of institutions came into existence, and relatively little effort was made by Japan or its neighbors to foster reconciliation on historical issues. Instead, there was a piecemeal approach of defusing particular historical issues as they emerged. Although over time Japan did grow more penitent, both on a societal level and in terms of its official historical narrative, it was a highly incomplete contrition. Japan's partial penance was further complicated by the factionalized nature of Japanese politics and the lack of strong leadership on the history issue, on the one hand, and by domestic political cultural dynamics in China and South Korea, where national identity, democratization, and anti-Japanese feelings had come together to form a potent and highly toxic brew, on the other. A catch-22 situation emerged in which Japan failed to apologize in part because it felt that its apologies would not be accepted, and such apologies as it did – grudgingly – offer tended to be viewed with suspicion because Chinese and Koreans tended to view them as insincere. Without the mitigating impact of strong international institutions like the EU, tensions over history would continue to flare up, leaving regional governments lurching from one crisis to another with no final resolution in sight.

Eventually, it can be hoped that domestic and international conditions will fall into place that will allow for a more stable solution (although, as the German tensions with Poland in 2003–2007 demonstrated, there always remains the possibility for new flare-ups even when such structures are in place). Strong leadership will be required, as well as a better understanding of the dynamics of the international politics of history. In Chapter 6, we will offer some thoughts as to what kind of solutions may be possible.

# 6

## Conclusions

### *Varieties of Penance*

The forgoing chapters have told the story of how the governments of Austria, Germany, and Japan have struggled for over half a century to deal with the consequences of terrible histories that continue to haunt them to this day. The evolution of their official historical narratives, along with the changes in their collective memories and the domestic and international tensions that have arisen over historical issues have been traced in some detail. Now, in conclusion, it is appropriate to step back from the particulars of the empirical cases and ask what their stories have told us about the dynamics of the politics of history in general.

Five sets of conclusions stand out. First, with respect to the determinants of the official narrative, we can see that no one theoretical approach alone – be it of the Historical Determinist, Instrumentalist, or Culturalist variety – can provide an adequate explanation for any particular case. Instead, as the Historical Realist perspective developed in this book suggests, a combination of the explanatory factors emphasized by the different theoretical schools is needed to understand the evolution of the official narrative and the politics of history over time.

Second, with regard to the causes and consequences of tensions over history, the evidence suggests that tensions over history are not only the product of material interests but that differences in historical views themselves can be a significant determinant of conflict. Although countries do not fight wars directly over history, the tensions generated by different interpretations of historical issues can degrade the quality of interstate relations in ways that make conflict over other issues – such as disputed territorial boundaries – more likely.

Third, the three cases suggest that there are certain common problems associated with the pursuit of historical justice in the aftermath of regime change. Whereas to some extent such problems were the product of the missteps of the American occupation and the pressures of the cold war, they were rooted in more fundamental dilemmas associated with trying to deal with past transgressions in the context of societies struggling to come to terms with the political and economic challenges of reconstruction. These problems constitute a syndrome that can be fairly described as the "tragedy of transitional justice."

Fourth, the cases also suggest that there are powerful new forces making history and official narratives increasingly contentious and difficult to avoid. Although the effects of these forces are unfolding at different rates in different parts of the world, they appear to be global in scope and suggest that governments around the world are likely to be confronted with these types of issues for some time to come.

Fifth and finally, the Historical Realist perspective on the history problem suggests that policy makers confronted with conflicts over the establishment of an official historical narrative would do well to adopt a hard-nosed approach that correctly assesses the costs as well as the benefits of attempting to achieve reconciliation.

In what follows, each of these five points will be elaborated upon in turn.

## Historical Realism: The Eclectic Determinants of the Official Historical Narrative

This book started out with a synopsis of three approaches to this topic: Historical Determinism in which the narrative emerges from the actual facts of the particular history ("what really happened"); Instrumentalism in which the outcome is determined by the political interests (domestic and/or international) of the narrators; and Cultural Determinism in which the outcome is to a considerable degree influenced by the general culture of the society to which the narrators belong. This distinction is useful; however, in light of the empirical record reviewed here, it should be clear that any explanation based on only one of these approaches will fail to explain the formation of the official narrative.

The Historical Determinist position is correct in emphasizing the lasting impact that the historical experience of World War II had on Germans, Austrians, and Japanese as well as on the nations that fell victim to German and Japanese aggression – such as China, South Korea, and Poland. More than sixty years after the end of World War II, groups of survivors and their supporters continue to push for the recognition of their suffering and for compensation, even if they had been ignored for decades, as in the case of the Korean comfort women. The same can be said for groups that represent the perpetrators of atrocities themselves – such as veteran groups in Austria or the bereaved families of fallen soldiers in Japan. The historian Carol Gluck has described such groups as the "energizer bunnies" of the politics of history – they keep on going and going. Especially in democratic societies, such groups cannot be ignored, and they can have a decisive impact on the formation of the official historical narrative, both in terms of pushing it in a more contrite direction, or conversely, in suppressing contrition.

At the same time, Historical Determinism by itself cannot provide an adequate account of the development of the official narrative. This can best be demonstrated through comparison. Take the cases of West Germany and

Austria. The same facts about Nazi crimes prevailed in both countries after 1938 (when Austria became an integral part of the Third Reich); however, vastly different official narratives were constructed by the two governments after the war and sustained for decades to come. The differences between the two countries' official narratives can be readily explained through reference to Instrumental factors: From the outset of its existence, the Federal Republic was subject to overwhelming external pressures to apologize and make restitution – external pressures that overcame the powerful sense of victimization existing in German society at the time. Austria – and to a lesser extent Japan – were relatively insulated from such pressures and, consequently, developed less penitent official narratives. In the 1980s and 1990s, however, when external pressures for Austria and Japan to apologize began to build, their governments too began to adopt more contrite narratives.

Instrumentalism thus can explain a great deal about why states develop the kind of official narrative that they do. It is particularly useful for explaining shifts in the official narrative. In every instance examined in this volume, calculations of national or partisan interests informed the government's policies on history. This is as true of the Federal Republic, which usually (and deservedly) is praised for its sincere efforts to come to terms with the past, as it is of Austria and Japan. However, the West German decision to pay compensation to the victims of Nazism in the West, but not in Eastern Europe, can only be understood against the background of the cold war. President Willy Brandt's decision to offer apologies to the East was motivated by the exigencies of Ostpolitik and detente as well as by domestic German politics and the Social Democratic Party's need to reach out to the new generation of student activists emerging at the time. The long-delayed payment of compensation to former slave laborers in Eastern Europe was a product of the end of the cold war as well as by Germany's interest in forging closer relations with the post-Communist nations on its Eastern borders. Although German contrition may have been sincere, it was clearly a calculated sincerity. Instrumental calculations were, if anything, even more prominent in shaping the development of the Austrian and Japanese official narratives.

There are clearly limitations to the Instrumental approach as well. Even the most imaginative and repeated retelling of the past cannot deny certain facts completely, whatever political interests might suggest. The former inmate of a concentration camp will be disinclined to ignore what happened to him or her regardless of what the official narrative contends; a veteran will continue to remember the self-sacrifice of his comrades who lost their lives fighting bravely against what they saw to be a vicious and implacable foe. Cultural factors can trump calculations of interest as well. This can be seen particularly clearly in the case of Japanese–South Korean relations. Rarely have there been two nations that have so much to gain from cooperation. Rarely, however, have efforts to cooperate been as difficult to achieve and maintain as between Korea and Japan because of the deep-rooted biases and animosities that continue to color their relations.

Cultural factors as well played an important, if often subtle, role in the cases under examination, although not necessarily culture as it is often thought of – that is, as a set of deep-rooted, unchanging cultural traits. Despite the many very real cultural similarities between them, West Germany and Austria developed strikingly different official narratives during the cold war: the Germans a relatively contrite one, the Austrians an impenitent one. Despite the supposed differences between Japanese "shame" versus Western "guilt" cultures, the Austrian historical narrative in its blithe impenitence was closer to that of Japan than to that of their cultural kinsmen, the Germans.[1]

This does not mean, however, that cultural forces have played no role. The cases we have looked at underline the importance of understanding that culture is not an inert constant. Cultures change. Specifically, cultures are shaped and reshaped as different narratives come to be widely accepted. The changed culture then becomes sedimented in the politics and broader culture of a given society and consequently hard to change. This is part of the paradox of the "sincerity of insincerity": Even though historical narratives are a social construct and are often adopted for instrumental reasons, they can have a very real, powerful emotional impact once they are commonly accepted.

Over the course of the cold war a *culture of contrition* came to be established in Germany. German guilt was continually reaffirmed in public rhetoric and ritual and widely diffused in the population both through state-controlled and private media. This does not mean that given changed circumstances a different, much less contrite culture, might not come into being; however, this will not be easy – the culture of contrition will resist a revisionist narrative. President Weizsäcker's 1985 speech had greater resonance with broad swathes of the German public than the arguments of conservative historians like Andreas Hillgruber because it was more consistent with the nearly forty-year general trend of contrition and its correspondingly political rhetoric. Conversely, in Japan there formed a *culture of incomplete contrition* in which gestures of contrition by the political leadership had to contend with widespread passive resistance and even open opposition by right-wing groups.

As we have seen in the case of Austria, however, it is possible to change the cultural discourse on history. Austria's discourse on history was even more impenitent than Japan's. However, over the course of the 1990s, it came to display German levels of guilt. Such a dramatic change, however, requires a major sustained effort and is likely to generate resistance. The Austrian government

---

[1] This is not to say that deep-rooted cultural tendencies have played no role in the shaping of the Austrian, German, and Japanese historical narratives. The terms in which issues of responsibility are spoken of are deeply shaded by cultural meaning and nuance. Instead of guilt (*kokai* in Japanese), the Japanese have been inclined to talk of "war responsibility" (*sensōsekinin*), which does not have the strongly moral and religious connotations of the German word for guilt (*Schuld*). The German churches have played a particular role in the debates over war guilt that no Japanese religious institution has, whereas Shinto theology has deeply colored the way in which Yasukuni is debated and understood. Their role, however, is not as central as an earlier generation of scholars – beginning with Ruth Benedict – once believed.

began to adopt a more penitent official narrative already in the early 1990s, but in so doing, it helped to feed the rise of the blatantly revisionist Jörg Haider and the FPÖ. It took nearly a decade of international pressure and fierce domestic debate before a societal consensus in favor of a penitent stance on history could be forged. In the case of Japan, where the international environment provided fewer positive reinforcements for the adoption of a penitent narrative, the shift has been more difficult, and it has been more arduous to overcome entrenched resistance.

More broadly, and this is a point to which we will return to later in this chapter, there exists considerable evidence that beyond the specific culture of discourse on history that develops in a given country, there is a broader global culture that has a very real and significant impact on the politics of history on the national level. This global discourse on history developed over the course of the cold war and has been diffused across national boundaries through a broad variety of mechanisms. In some cases, they are cultural artifacts, such as the American-made TV miniseries *Shoah*, which was broadcast in both Austria and Germany in the late 1970s. In other cases, they are the work of scholars, such as Iris Chang's *Rape of Nanjing*, which inspired history activists in China to redouble their criticisms of Japan.

Transnational networks of activists, such as those that sprang up espousing the cause of the comfort women in Japan and Korea or the slave laborers in Europe, have also played a role, as has the international media, which has helped spread their message to a far wider audience than they could ever have reached on their own.

In the case of Germany, the politics of history evolved in tandem with the development of the global culture of contrition, and therefore, the impact of global trends are more difficult to discern. The influence of the international discourse can be seen more clearly in Austria and Japan, where public views of their respective histories began to shift in the late 1970s and 1980s toward a greater receptiveness to contrition in a way that an interest based, an Instrumentalist approach, would have difficulty accounting for. For instance, in 1970, after the Austrian Freedom Party member Karl Öllinger was forced to resign over revelations concerning his past in the Waffen SS, Socialist Prime Minister Bruno Kreisky's decision to appoint another former Nazi in his place was met with little public protest. In contrast, in 1986, after Kurt Waldheim was elected federal president, the outcry was so great that Socialist leader Fred Sinowatz was forced to resign and his successor, Franz Vranitzky, tolerated Waldheim only because of the exigencies of coalitional politics. Between 1970 and 1986 something important had shifted in public attitudes toward the past, especially on the Left, that could not be attributed simply to changes in Austria's geostrategic landscape or the electoral calculations of the Socialist party.

Clearly, there are limits to the power of this global cultural discourse. For one, countries can resist the global discourse. Austria, for instance, was out of step on the issue of Nazism for many, many years. Likewise, it is clear that not all historical injustices are treated equally in the global discourse. Allied transgressions during the war, beginning with the atomic bombings, have not been the object of global opprobrium. Beyond the legacy of World War II, there are many historical injustices that have been ignored or only partially addressed. For instance, the former European Imperial powers have by and large evaded the issue of the responsibility they may bear for colonialism. The darker sides of the history of Communism remain much disputed. The same Chinese history activists who focus on Japanese wartime atrocities often blithely ignore the much more recent misdeeds of the Chinese Communist Party. Indeed, as the Chinese example underlines, local elites frequently seize on the global discourse and use it to pursue their own interests – be it to protect or indirectly criticize Chinese communism. The list could be extended almost ad infinitum. There is a lot of potential guilt in the world. Despite these caveats, however, the evidence here strongly suggests that such a global discourse exists and that it has effects.

The forgoing observations have both practical and analytical implications. We will return to those relevant to policy later in this chapter. For analytical purposes, however, it is important to recognize that any account of the development of any specific country's official historical narrative will by necessity be eclectic in character. Simple but common explanations, such as "The Japanese show little contrition because of the atomic bombings" or "Germans are inclined toward guilt because of the immensity of the Holocaust" are both inadequate and misleading. However, although the determinants of the official historical narrative may be eclectic, this does not imply that there cannot be a systematic division of labor between the different approaches in analyzing the development of the official historical narrative. The following four-step schema is a first cut effort to develop such a systematic approach on the basis of Historical Realism.

1) The analyst should begin with the historical events themselves and recount how they were remembered on a societal level in the time period immediately after those events occurred.

2) With the next step the analyst should focus on the instrumental calculations that political elites make in choosing the kind of official narrative they adopted in the period immediately following when the events occurred. Of particular interest in this context is to show how conflicting pressures – between material calculations of interest and the different ways in which the recent past are regarded on a societal level – are resolved. The way in which specific versions of history are linked to other policy objectives – such as integration in the West, internal reconciliation and rebuilding, and so forth – deserve special attention because such linkages can have a lasting impact and may serve to anchor a particular historical narrative in the political system.

3) The analyst must then trace the development of the official narrative over time and look at the extent to which the views it espouses win – or fails to win – broader acceptance among elites and the society at large. Over time, certain views are likely to become embedded in the political

culture – e.g., Germany's culture of contrition or the trope of China's century of humiliation.

4) Finally, the analyst must note and analyze the implications of changes in the international system and domestic politics – for instance, the rise of a new generation, the coming to power of a new political party, the development of new issues (such as the pressures of reintegrating East Germany into the Federal Republic or adopting military missions going beyond territorial defense) – that have the potential to generate new pressures for change. Such critical junctures in a nation's history allow the analyst to gauge the degree to which official narrative has become institutionalized in the political system and the broader collective memory of the society. At the same time, it is in such periods that the historical narrative evolves and changes in potentially new ways.

## The Domestic and International Impact of History and Contentions over Historical Issues From a Historical Realist Perspective

Beyond sorting out the determinants of any given official historical narrative, the other central question that has motivated this study has been to investigate the conditions under which history becomes the object of political contention and to gauge the broader impact of such tensions over the past when they do emerge. Here again, the data support a Historical Realist approach, namely that a multiplicity of variables – Instrumental but also Historical Determinist and Culturalist – feed conflict over history. In many instances, battles over history are simply reflections of clashes of interest over other issues. To the extent that countries are in conflict over resources, territory, or other concrete interests, it may be only natural that they invest their animosity with extra emotional depth by citing differences over history.

To the extent, however, that particular understandings of history are embedded in the memory of individuals and the political culture of a society drive the kind of official narratives that they adopt, the official narrative itself may have a causal effect on conflict that goes beyond what other considerations would suggest. To put it another way, the more people believe in a particular historical narrative, the more it can itself be a source of conflict. Although states and groups of people may not fight wars directly because of differences over history, the evidence reviewed here strongly suggests that because people are attached – for personal as well as cultural reasons – to particular historical narratives, historical issues can have a disruptive impact on domestic politics and interstate relations that can set the stage for conflict later on.

The independent impact of the historical narrative is perhaps most visible on the level of domestic politics. One of the best examples comes from a comparison of the German and the Austrian cases. In the Federal Republic, the stigma attached to the Nazi past made it impossible for any mainstream political party to openly appeal to any organization or political group that was associated with Nazism. In contrast, for the better part of half a century, the

Freedom Party in Austria effectively held the political balance of power and both the left-wing Socialists and the more conservative People's Party actively tried to court its support despite its roots in the prewar Nazi movement. There is no obvious structural reason for this discrepancy. The proportion of ex-Nazis was not any greater in Austria than in Germany, and the issues that the Freedom Party capitalized on – such as anti-immigrant sentiments and populist dissatisfaction with the clientalism of the major parties – existed just as much in the Federal Republic as in Austria. Nonetheless, politicians in Germany went to great lengths to prevent the emergence of a political force resembling the Freedom Party, and when on occasion such formations did emerge in the Federal Republic, they were isolated and soon withered away. The most obvious difference between the two countries lies in their very different conceptions of history and in the very different moral as well as practical lessons that they drew from the past.[2]

The influence of historical memory and the official historical narrative on international politics may be most clearly observed in the enormous difficulties that continue to beset relations between Japan and South Korea. Despite the many common interests the two countries share and despite the many social and economic ties that bind them together, historical issues have time and again had an amazingly disruptive effect on their ability to cooperate. Of course, there are also instances in which their objective interests clash. A Realist might point out that South Korea, as a continental power, is far more exposed to the military threat posed by China and North Korea than Japan is. Thus, South Korea is likely to be more sensitive to any changes in Chinese or North Korean behavior than Japan is, and this fact alone should generate tensions between Seoul and Tokyo. Likewise, a liberal might be inclined to argue that Japanese and Korean firms are fierce competitors on global markets and that that competition could be expected to translate into sharp pressures on their governments to seek advantage for their own country's producers at the expense of the other. Nonetheless, similar differences have characterized the strategic relationship between Germany and France, however, these differences have not translated into intractable territorial disputes or prevented the two sides from forging one of the strongest and most enduring partnerships between any two major powers. Although, obviously, various factors make the relationship between Germany and France different from the one between South Korea and Japan, it is almost impossible to overlook the role of historical memory and the official narrative in ameliorating tensions in the case of Europe and exacerbating them in the case of Asia.

In these and other instances, the argument here is not that historical memory rooted in actual historical experience and embedded in evolving cultural discourse shaped outcomes entirely independent of instrumental calculations of interest. Political leaders and elites were generally aware of the possible costs

---

[2] This is a point that has been made with great persuasiveness by David Art, *The Politics of the Nazi Past*, op. cit.

and benefits of conflicting or reconciling over history and acted accordingly. Nonetheless, the existence of these broader societal trends crucially shaped the way in which leaders and nations calculate their interests and their ability to implement their plans. Of course, President Roh Moo Hyun exploited anti-Japanese sentiment to bolster his sagging poll numbers; however, he was only able to do so because there already existed powerful anti-Japanese sentiments deeply embedded in the Korean national identity waiting to be tapped.

On a very general level, it is possible to view the official narrative as resting on a more or less stable equilibrium of interests and beliefs about history (be they grounded in historical experiences or in the cultural discourse on history). To the degree that there exists a disjuncture between official narratives and either interests or historical memory, there are likely to be tensions over history. When a shift occurs in the constellation of interests and/or the societal discourse on history, these tensions may increase, creating the possibility for domestic or international political conflict. The rise of the student movement in Germany in the 1960s, for example, created a powerful incentive for the Left and the Social Democratic Party to reopen the issue of German responsibility for the Holocaust. There then followed a powerful and vitriolic controversy over history that led to demonstrations, bitter parliamentary debates over issues such as the extension of the statute of limitations, and the destruction of political careers. In Asia, the pluralization of Korean and Chinese politics in the 1980s, as well as the PRC's new emphasis on a more nationalist version of history, increased regional sensitivity to the Japanese official historical narrative, setting the stage for first the 1982 textbook controversy and subsequently the 1985 crisis over Nakasone's trip to the Yasukuni shrine.

Although in both Europe and Asia governments were ultimately able to reign in the passions that were unleashed by disputes over history, those disputes were often costly and disruptive. In Europe, Austria found itself at least twice diplomatically isolated, first during the Waldheim affair between 1986 and 1991 and then again – more briefly but more dramatically – after the Freedom Party joined the governing coalition in 2000. Germany as well found itself embroiled in a protracted diplomatic dispute with Poland, which spilled over into EU-level diplomacy during the Brussels conference of 2008. Both Germany and Austria benefited from being embedded in a regional system of institutions that provided powerful incentives to harmonize their official narratives with international political expectations and offered an effective forum for resolving disputes when they did emerge.

In the case of Asia, there were no institutional structures comparable to NATO or the European Union. Thus, there was less incentive for Asian countries to harmonize their official narratives and historically grounded disputes. Moreover, when such tensions did emerge in Asia, they were potentially bigger and more difficult to manage. Issues that in principle should have been manageable – and had been manageable in the past – such as the Dokdo/Takeshima and Senkaku/Diaoyutai island disputes took on a magnitude far beyond any of the European cases that we examined and potentially could have escalated to the level of militarized conflict.

## The Tragedy of Transitional Justice

A third set of conclusions that emerges from the cases we have looked at concerns the great difficulties involved in pursuing historical justice in the aftermath of wrenching systemic changes. Despite the considerable differences between the Austrian, German, and Japanese experiences in the immediate postwar period, the problems that were encountered in trying to deal with the legacy of the past were broadly similar. This suggests that the difficulties they faced were inherent to the situation they found themselves in.

There is, today, an international movement demanding that the horrors of the past be seriously confronted. The movement has become a central component of the larger campaign in support of international human rights and is actively promoted by a plethora of international nongovernment organizations as well as by important elements in the media, the churches, and academia. All over the world this international movement has led to conferences, truth commissions, redress movements, and even trials (the latter sometimes resulting from claims of "universal jurisdiction" by courts in Spain, Belgium, and elsewhere). The call is for a public accounting for all past atrocities, followed by solemn acts of apology, the incorporation of the victims' perspectives in the official narrative of the state, and the payment of compensation.[3] The Nuremberg trials and, to a lesser extent, the IMFTE are often pointed to as important precedents by the advocates of this movement. The successful reintegration of Germany and Japan into the international community after World War II and the establishment of democratic systems in what once had been brutal authoritarian systems are frequently advertised as proof that such forthright transitional justice policies can offer practical benefits.

The problem with this argument is that the empirical facts do not fit this tidy version of German, Japanese, and Austrian history. In the three cases analyzed in detail in the preceding chapters, transitional justice was at first imposed by the victorious Allies. The Nuremberg trials and those of the major Japanese war criminals are paradigmatic; however, all three cases underline the limits of this type of formal jurisprudence. There emerged powerful domestic political resistance against "victors' justice," with public sympathy for at least some of the defendants. There were also serious criticisms of the courts in question: Just what kind of law was being applied? Were some laws invented ad hoc

---

[3] Barkan, *The Guilt of Nations*, op. cit.; Robertson, *Crimes against Humanity*, op. cit. See also Thomas Risse, Stephen Roppe, and Kathryn Sikkink, eds., *The Power of Human Rights International Norms and Domestic Change* (Cambridge, 1999); and Margaret Keck and Kathryn Sikkink, *Activists Beyond Borders: Advocacy Networks in International Politics* (Ithaca, NY: Cornell University Press, 1998).

to convict the defendants singled out for trial (thus violating the venerable principle of *nulla poena sine lege* – "no punishment without law")? Why were possible crimes committed by the Allies excluded from consideration? Was it legitimate that Soviet judges could sit in judgment on these trials, condemning defendants for crimes that the Soviet Union was committing at the very time these trials were staged? Although there had been some support in all three countries for punishing the leaders of the old regime at the start of the trials, that support largely evaporated as the judicial proceedings dragged on and their various shortcomings became apparent.

Other aspects of the transitional justice programs proved equally problematic. The mechanics of purging officials and persons closely connected with the old regime turned out to be overwhelming and riddled with inconsistencies and injustices. Moreover, in all three cases there existed a desperate need to reintegrate the old elite to rebuild their economies and to restore equilibrium to their political systems. The exigencies of the cold war added to these pressures, although they were evident well before the task of fighting Communism became a paramount concern. Likewise, given the widespread sense of victimization that was prevalent in the countries at the time, it proved difficult to institute a contrite historical narrative in their educational and cultural establishments. Probably the most that could be done was to decry – as in West Germany – the evils that had been done "in Germany's name" and to avoid the wrenching question of the guilt of ordinary German individuals and of the German nation as a whole. Even in the German case, after a relatively brief period of trying to wrestle with these questions, by the early 1950s there followed a period of relative quiescence (what German President Hermann Lübbe called "eine gewisse Stille"). In Austria and Japan as well, the question of who bore moral responsibility for the war and its horrors largely disappeared around the same time or even earlier.

Victim compensation is the one area in which the historical justice movement can rightly claim success in the immediate aftermath of the war. While Austria and Japan paid relatively little, the Federal Republic began to pay significant sums early on without putting an unsustainable burden on its economy. However, it took immense international pressure to produce the necessary German political will to take this step, and even then it demanded all of Adenauer's political energies to win final approval from the German legislature.

In short, although the pursuit of historical justice may be desirable on moral grounds, it failed on its own terms in post-1945 Austria, Germany, and Japan. The noble goals espoused at the start of the Allied program to grapple with the legacy of the past were largely abandoned within the space of only a few years. This is not to say that the pursuit of justice may not be desirable for other reasons. The threat of trials and purges undoubtedly helped to make German and Japanese society more pliable and may have eased the task of reintegrating the old elites. In Japan, for instance, the threat of putting the Emperor on trial enabled General McArthur to win acceptance of the American-written new Japanese constitution. The removal of large numbers of military men and former Nazi officials in Germany may well have strengthened an ideological rupture with the authoritarian traditions of the past, easing the adoption of new and more democratic ideals and practices. Moreover, a case can be made that if there had not been an effort made to punish the former Axis powers, the public outcry in the countries of the Western Allies would have been such that it would have been difficult to reintegrate them into the international system (although on this score we are dealing in counterfactuals). In terms of bringing the perpetrators to justice and providing moral and material succor to their victims, however, it is hard not to be dubious about the merits of the Allied-sponsored programs. Moreover, it must be noted that despite these shortcomings, all three nations became peaceful democratic societies in a relatively brief period of time.

In the discussions over confrontation with past crimes, almost inevitably, reference is made to the statement by George Santayana to the effect that those who forget history are doomed to repeat it. It has become a kind of mantra, assumed to be obviously true and therefore not in need of further argument. The Austrian case in particular suggests that the assumption may be false.

The so-called Moscow Declaration, which listed the goals of the Allies, stated as one of these the restoration of the independence of Austria, described as Hitler's first victim. Not surprisingly, this phrase was seized upon by the postwar Austrian government. It distanced Austria from Germany, and in the role of victim, it allowed Austria to disclaim responsibility for all the crimes of the Nazi regime. Thus, Austria was very niggardly in compensating Jewish survivors of the Holocaust. Nor did Austria feel any need to apologize – crimes had been committed *against* Austria, not *by* it. The Austrian state did not exist between 1938 and 1945. It was in no way a successor state to Nazi Germany. With independence restored, it reemerged in a sort of Immaculate Conception. This was the official Austrian narrative, elevated to the status of state doctrine, reiterated in political rhetoric and ritual, in school textbooks, and very widely in public opinion. It persisted, with little challenge, for several decades – until the Waldheim affair seriously undermined its plausibility.

At best, this narrative rested on the basis of a half-truth. Technically, it is correct that Austria was the first country to be forcefully incorporated into the Third Reich and thus the latter's first victim. However, this narrative overlooks the fact that many Austrians, possibly a majority, enthusiastically welcomed the *Anschluß*, which was accompanied by an outbreak of anti-Semitic violence far worse than anything that had previously happened in Germany. Austrians were represented on the staffs administering the Holocaust, from Eichmann on down, well beyond their proportion in the population of Greater Germany. These empirical realities were suppressed in the narrative, whereas the scope of Austrian resistance to Nazism was greatly exaggerated. It should be emphasized that the political leadership, in both major parties, mainly consisted of people with impeccable anti-Nazi credentials. Several of them had been in Nazi concentration camps. Their endorsement of the official "victimology" did not come out of hidden Nazi sympathies; however, its instrumental value was overwhelming. Internationally, it legitimated Austria as a morally respectable country. Domestically, it provided cover for the reentry into politics of parties representing the old German nationalist sentiments, which could now parade as Austrian nationalists and avoid the legal strictures against "renewal of Nazi activities." Among other things, this made possible anti-Semitic rhetoric in Austria that would not have been tolerated in Germany.

Austria would furnish an ideal case for Santayana's famous dictum; however, what actually happened during the decades of the victim narrative hardly supports Santayana's view. A stable liberal democracy had been established, as had a robust market economy – in a country that after 1918 had been widely viewed as being politically and economically unsustainable. For the first time in history, there developed a strong sense of Austrian national identity (as against the old identity of being German in a multinational empire). For example, in European value surveys more Austrians said that they were "proud to be Austrian" than Germans confessing pride at being German – a remarkable historical reversal. A Jew – Bruno Kreisky – was elected to head the government and was widely popular. Austria reacted courageously to the events following the Hungarian revolution of 1956 (only a year after the departure of Soviet troops from Austria) and again to the 1968 events in Czechoslovakia, both times risking Soviet wrath by accepting large numbers of Hungarian and Czech refugees. And in the 1970s, it became a major gateway allowing the exit of Soviet Jews to the West. Austria may have forgotten the dark chapters of its past, but it certainly did not repeat it.

Other cases may be added to an anti-Santayana argument. Japan, newly redefined as a peace nation, succeeded in getting along with its Asian neighbors by emphasizing its peaceful and democratic features (though in recent years it proved to be less successful in smoothing over the horrors of the war). France rebuilt its national pride by exaggerating the scope of the resistance and minimizing the extent of collaboration with the Nazi occupation (including the collaboration of French authorities in the deportation of Jews from France).[4] The list could be easily extended. In sum, Santayana's famous dictum may well apply to individuals – a restatement of Freud's notion of the "return of the repressed" – but there are good reasons to be skeptical of its applicability to collectivities such as nations and states. It is possible that Machiavelli's idea of the useful lie may serve better in understanding the behavior of such collectivities.

Of course, one would need to look at a broader range of cases to determine how robust these findings really are; however, even a cursory examination of other cases suggests that similar problems seem to be endemic to the transitional

---

4 See Henry Rousso, *The Vichy Syndrome: History and Memory in France Since 1944* (Cambridge: Harvard University Press, 1991); and Eric Conan, Henry Rousso, Nathan Bracher, trans., *Vichy: An Ever-Present Past* (Hannover, NH: Dartmouth Press, 1998). For a useful overview, see Richard Goslan, "The Legacy of WW II in France," in Richard N. Lebow, ed., *The Politics of Memory in Postwar Europe* (Durham, NC: Duke University Press, 2006).

justice enterprise. For instance, the Truth and Reconciliation Commission that dealt with the crimes of the apartheid regime in South Africa has been widely hailed as a successful case of transitional justice; however, it too has exhibited some of the same problems that beset the Austrian, German, and Japanese cases. Its *modus operandi* had features reminiscent of a Protestant revival meeting – confession of the crime, expression of repentance, followed by an act of forgiveness. (Perhaps one should not be surprised by this: On the Commission sat an Anglican bishop and a prominent Calvinist theologian.) The accused had to recite the details of their crime, demonstrate that the motive was political rather than personal, and express regret. If these conditions were met, amnesty could follow (although the granting was at the discretion of the judges – in some cases the apology was judged as insincere or the crimes so egregious that a trial followed anyway).

Some of these procedures had a farcical character. Thus, in an effort at even-handedness, the Commission held hearings about crimes committed by the anti-apartheid forces as well as those committed by the supporters of the old regime. In the course of one of these, Winnie Mandela was examined about a murder committed by her bodyguards, presumably with her knowledge if not by her command. She was quite willing to acknowledge the act, but she explained it as an unavoidable side effect of the struggle. She would not express regret. This created a dilemma for the Commission: Unless she showed a willingness to repent, there could be no amnesty – and there might be the politically untenable spectacle of Nelson Mandela's ex-wife on trial for murder. In addition, Winnie Mandela had a large following on the left-wing of the African National Congress who might have been alienated by a conviction. So Bishop Desmond Tutu, who was chairing the hearing, kept pressing her to express contrition for her role in the affair. Finally, with obvious reluctance, Winnie Mandela agreed that she was sorry (though it stayed unclear whether this was an admission of guilt on her part). The bishop was visibly relieved, and amnesty could be pronounced. One positive result of these hearings was generally conceded: They provided a public recognition of the suffering of the victims, providing a very therapeutic catharsis. Was this justice? The accused walked out of the hearings as free citizens, without having to fear any further steps against them. Some of the victims would have preferred prosecutions.[5]

As in Germany, post-apartheid Africa made a serious attempt to confront the moral implications of the past; however, as in the post-1945 cases that have been examined here, the South African effort to confront the past soon ran afoul of the practical need to reintegrate society. Not only was Winnie Mandela spared, so was Chief Buthelezi of the Zulus, whose followers were responsible for large-scale massacres in the last years of the apartheid regime. Likewise,

---

[5] For a devastating account of the Mandela trial, see Martin Meredith, *Coming to Terms: South Africa's Search for the Truth* (New York: Perseus Books, 1999). For a broader look at the politics of the historical justice issue in South Africa, see Wilson, *The Politics of Truth and Reconciliation* (New York and Cambridge: Cambridge University Press, 2001).

some of the senior Afrikaans leadership – most notably former South African President Pik Botha[6] – refused to cooperate with the Commission but were left unpunished. Instrumental calculations of political expediency repeatedly trumped the quest for justice.

Similar dynamics can be observed in many other cases – in Latin America or in post-Communist Europe. Either amnesty was declared during the transitional period– as in Spain after Franco or Chile after Pinochet – or what efforts that were made soon ran into serious difficulties – as in East Germany after the fall of the Berlin Wall or Rwanda after the Rwandan genocide.[7] In many of these cases, years later efforts were made to come to terms with the past. Spain today, for instance, is in the throes of a painful reexamination of the horrors of the Spanish Civil War and the authoritarian period.[8] In each case, there are significant differences stemming from the unique histories and the varying political circumstances within which these debates over the past unfold. In each case, however, broadly similar problems soon emerge: The complexities of history and human psychology dwarf the capacities of the judicial system; the practical necessity of reintegrating the old elite tends to trump the desire for a reckoning; deeply rooted popular resistance to accepting any moral responsibility makes the implementation of contrite historical narratives – especially in the immediate wake of a political transition – extremely difficult. Only with the passage of time do societies seem to have the capacity (or perhaps the luxury) to reengage with the moral implications of the past. In this sense, transitional justice seems very much a tragic enterprise – a noble project, often pursued with great courage and vigor at its outset but destined by its very nature to failure – at least in the short term.

## The Rise of Discord over History – Sooner or Later We Will All Be Sorry!

Whatever difficulties may be attendant upon every effort to come to terms with the past, the cases we have looked at also suggest that the past is becoming increasingly salient on a global level. The quest for historical justice is not purely a European or Western phenomenon but is very much present in Asia (and Africa, Latin America, and the Middle East) as well. Although it may be possible to put off questions of historical justice in the short term – as in Austria and Japan after World War II, in Spain or Chile in the 1970s, or in

---

6 Botha was fined and given a suspended sentence by the Truth Commission, but the sentence later was overturned on technical grounds by the South African High Court.

7 On some of the problems afflicting transitional justice efforts in Rwanda, see Helen Hintjens, "Reconstructing Political Identities in Rwanda," and Susanne Buckley-Zistel, "We are Pretending Peace; Local Memory and the Absence of Social Transformation and Reconciliation in Rwanda," both in Phil Clark and Zachary D. Kaufman, eds., *After Genocide: Post-Conflict Reconstruction and Reconciliation in Rwanda and Beyond* (New York: Columbia University Press, 2009).

8 Carolyn P. Boyd, "The Politics of History and Memory in Democratic Spain," *Annals of the American Academy of Political and Social Science* 617:1 (May 2008), pp. 133–148.

Russia and the PRC today – in the longer run the spreading global culture of contrition seems to make apologies for past injustice almost inevitable.

What drives this increased salience of history on a worldwide scale? Of course, as we have seen, the particulars of each country's domestic politics and international setting will have a critical impact. However, beyond case-specific factors, on the basis of the cases we have looked at here, it is possible to identify at least key critical elements that help generate powerful pressures to critically engage with issues of historical justice: the spread of international human rights norms; rising levels of economic, social, and political interdependence (what Robert Keohane and Joseph Nye have referred to as "complex interdependence"); and the spread of democracy.[9]

Time and again have we seen how international networks have played a vital role in putting issues of historical justice on the diplomatic agenda. The Jewish Claims Conference, which began its campaign to win support for compensation and restitution for the Jewish victims of Nazism already in 1951, is prototypical of the many organizations that followed. Backed by a sympathetic media and employing the increasingly refined and widely accepted language of international human rights, such organizations have been able to win public attention and political legitimacy for their demands around the world – particularly in democratic societies. The growing organizational capacity and density of these networks have increasingly become a factor in international politics, one that governments can ignore only at a cost.

However, although such groups may be able to focus attention on historical justice issues and make legitimate demands for apologies and compensation, the cases we have looked at suggest that by themselves they cannot generate sufficient pressure to bring about a shift in government policy. The second set of forces that has played a critical role in this connection is the increased interdependence of nations today. Japan's desire to improve its relations with its Asian neighbors was an important factor behind its decision to adopt – at least on a rhetorical level – a more contrite official historical narrative already in the 1960s when it set out to normalize economic relations with South Korea. Japan's increased economic stake in Asia led to further revisions in its official narrative in the 1980s and even more so after the cold war as Japanese officials sought to promote the creation of Asian regional institutions that would lock in patterns of cooperation.

Similarly, it was not until Austria began to prepare for becoming a full member of the European Union that the Austrian government finally began to make the switch to a contrite official historical narrative. The spread of human rights norms may have helped legitimate historical justice claims; the rise of complex interdependence gave those claims teeth.

The third and final factor that has made for the increased salience of historical justice internationally is the spread of democracy. Groups demanding

---

[9] Robert O. Keohane and Joseph S. Nye, *Power and Interdependence: World Politics in Transition* (Boston: Little Brown, 1977).

justice find it easier making their voices heard in democratic or democratizing regimes than in nondemocratic ones. When China, Poland, and South Korea were authoritarian dictatorships, it was possible for the ruling elites to squelch their voices in the name of the national interest. When they democratized (or, in the case of China, loosened their control over the public discourse), various groups representing the victims of past injustices emerged to press their claims. Moreover, such claims tend to be viewed with greater sympathy in democratic societies when they are seen as emanating from genuine currents in the other countries' societies than when they are advanced on behalf of an authoritarian government. Chinese criticism regarding Japan's supposed impenitence tended to be dismissed when made by Jiang Zemin, the head of a Chinese Communist Party that maintained its hold on power through the ruthless application of force. Kim Dae Jung, on the other hand, with his background as a human rights activist and his status as a democratically elected leader, was in a better position to gain an audience for his views in Japan. Although the messy nature of democratic politics can make it difficult for leaders to respond to external pressures regarding historical justice issues because such demands are likely to trigger societal resistance, the spread of democracy also makes the increased occurrence of such demands almost inevitable.

To the extent that other countries become subject to similar pressures, we can expect a continued proliferation of demands for apologies and compensation. To the extent that dealing with such issues is difficult, such demands are likely to generate considerable controversy. As we have seen in the previous section, posttransitional societies are likely to find such demands especially difficult to satisfy. Even in nontransitional societies the complexities of history, the multiple instrumental calculations of interest that underlie the existing official narrative, as well as the inertia created by the extant historical political culture, are likely to make it difficult for governments to respond effectively to the growing international discord over the past. Sooner or later, it seems, we are all going to be sorry.

## Policy Implications

How can governments best respond to conflict over the historical narrative when they emerge? Generally speaking, there are two very different strategies that can be pursued. The first is the strategy of damage control. This means making a few gestures to appease hostility, without making any fundamental changes in the narrative. This strategy was followed by Japan from the 1950s to the 1980s by using highly ambiguous apologies coupled with development assistance to demonstrate Japan's benevolent character. The above-mentioned pressures have made this strategy more difficult since then both for Japan and for other countries in general. Instead of being appeased by such token efforts, many Koreans and Chinese were incensed.

Although there may be reasons to want to go beyond just damage control, nonetheless, the virtues of damage control should not be underestimated. First, it is arguably a major philosophical error to think that gratitude is much of a factor in international relations. One may recall the exclamation of an Austrian foreign minister of the nineteenth century when asked whether Austria was not grateful to Russia for support against the Hungarian revolution of 1848 – "Austria will astound the world by its ingratitude!" Even countries that have pursued historical reconciliation for decades can find that when political circumstances change, gratitude is swept away, and the past can become once again a controversial issue – as the Federal Republic discovered to its cost when the Kaczynski government took power in Poland in 2005. Second, in many cases it may not be possible to pursue a more ambitious strategy of reconciliation. The requirements for pursuing a successful reconciliation strategy are stringent, and the potential pitfalls many. Most importantly, as the Austrian as well as Japanese cases have shown, it is possible for countries to work with one another for decades by papering over deep-seated differences in their official narratives. Palliatives are better than nothing.

The second strategy is the active pursuit of reconciliation. This strategy was pursued by West Germany from the beginnings of the Federal Republic – first with the countries of Western Europe and with Israel and the world Jewish community and then with Eastern Europe. Despite occasional setbacks, it has been very successful on the whole. Although against the background of the cold war it may appear that the nations of Western Europe had no choice but to work together to rebuild their war-shattered economies and face up to the Communist threat from the East, in actuality cooperation was difficult to achieve because of deep-rooted tensions over territorial and other issues and lingering fears of possible German revanchism. German apologies and compensation helped make the project of ever-deepening European integration possible and allowed it to forge a lasting partnership first with France and the nations of Western Europe and, after the cold war, with the countries of Eastern Europe as well.[10] As a result, other European countries rallied to Germany's defense in 2007 when the Polish government demanded the Federal Republic make far-reaching concessions on the grounds of its history of aggression in World War II.[11] Even in Poland public opinion data from around the same period indicated

---

[10] Jennifer Lind has argued that Germany managed to cooperate with France already in the 1950s, before it began to adopt a more sincerely penitent stance on the past. Although this is partially true, it is also an exaggeration. Germany had already begun to pay large sums in compensation to the victims of the Third Reich, and it continued trials of war criminals even after the Allied occupation had ended. If it had not made such penitent gestures – incomplete as that penance may have been – it is quite plausible, even likely, that the European integration process that began in the early 1950s and in earnest after the signing of the Treaties of Rome in 1957 would never have been able to get off the ground. Jennifer Lind, "The Perils of Apology: What Japan Shouldn't Learn from Germany," *Foreign Affairs* 88:3 (May/June 2009), pp. 132–146.

[11] "Der Stete Blick zurück im Zorn," *Süddeutsche Zeitung*, June 23/24, 2007, p. 2.

relatively benign views of the Federal Republic, despite the tensions that existed between the two governments.[12] In contrast, Korean public opinion data from the 2001–2007 period showed that the average Korean developed a sharply more negative image of Japan as a result of their dispute over historical issues. Nearly three decades of sustained German efforts to improve relations with its Eastern neighbors had not been in vain.

The conditions that have to be met for a successful reconciliation strategy are quite stringent, however. There are at least five basic points:

1) There must be a powerful interest in seeking reconciliation on the part of the political leadership. The pursuit of reconciliation is bound to generate considerable political resistance, especially if it means adopting a more contrite historical stance and if it runs counter to the existing historical narratives that may exist on a societal level. Political leaders have to believe that reconciliation is in their own and the nation's interest. Only then will there be a willingness to override the political and emotional costs of the strategy, not to mention the willingness to invest the necessary time and energy. Put simply, reconciliation does not come cheaply.

2) There must be a degree of reciprocity – that is, a willingness by the designated victims to accept the apology. The Japanese case offers two very different outcomes of reconciliation moves. Kim Dae Jung, the democratically elected leader of South Korea, visited Japan in 1998. The Japanese government chose the occasion to issue a formal apology for Japanese crimes against Korea. The apology was formally accepted. There then followed a real improvement in relations between the two countries. In the same year, the Chinese leader Jiang Zemin visited Japan. He also put the history issue on the diplomatic agenda, albeit in very stark terms. However, not only did Jiang give no signal of his willingness to reconcile, but he also lacked the democratic legitimacy of his Korean counterpart. The Japanese believed that apology or no apology, nothing much would be changed. Thus, no formal apology was forthcoming.

3) There must be consistency across the various domains of the official narrative. Thus, rhetorical apologies will not convince if history textbooks in government-controlled schools continue to feature a narrative sharply at odds with the rhetoric – a chronic problem in Japan. Similarly, the rhetoric of contrition loses plausibility when leading Japanese politicians continue to make formal visits to the Yasukuni shrine (which, along with many other soldiers who died in battle for Japan, also contains the souls of several convicted class A war criminals). In other words, it is very unhelpful if a government is seen as speaking out of two sides of the mouth. More importantly, if a lasting political consensus is to be built in

---

12 Mateusz Falkowski, *Meinungen der Polen über die deutsch-polnischen Beziehungen nach dem Regierungswechsel in beidern Länder* November 2005, available at http://www.isp.org.pl/files/20442810390940702001134394938.pdf (accessed April 20, 2007).

favor of a contrite political narrative, it is necessary that the government does what it can to reshape the historical narrative as it exists on the societal level. Changes in educational policy and in the ways in which the society commemorates the past are prerequisites for such a successful transformation.

4) There must be a degree of coherence between government and grassroots actions, at least in a democracy. Put differently, the reconciliation effort must be bottom-up as well as top-down. Of course, in a democracy, government does not control the public manifestations of views divergent from its own. A reconciliation strategy will be helped if it is supported by significant actions of civil society – conferences, media programs, public diplomacy. Such actions will not be very effective, however, unless it is clear that the government supports them. Conversely, government efforts will have only limited plausibility unless it is clear that they have support from civil society.

5) A successful reconciliation strategy takes time. This follows directly from the preceding condition. The necessary coordination between government actions and public opinion cannot be orchestrated overnight. In 1951, when the Federal Republic signed the Luxembourg agreement on compensations for Jewish victims of Nazism, it accepted the rather humiliating stipulation that the agreement only settled the material claims against Germany. In the language of the text, it said specifically that no reconciliation between the two peoples was achieved by the signing of the treaty only that they could now begin "to walk the path of reconciliation together." It was a long walk, but in time German-Israeli relations improved dramatically. Just as importantly, the Federal Republic's efforts to reconcile with Jews around the world underlined its penitent stance and helped it to improve its relations with its neighbors in Europe.

Not all countries at all times can pursue reconciliation strategies. Arguably, democratic countries are better positioned than nondemocratic ones because once a consensus in favor of confronting the past has been built, it enjoys greater legitimacy. Likewise, there needs to be a favorable alignment of international and domestic political interests to make such efforts successful. However, there is no reason to believe that reconciliation is a uniquely European or Western phenomena. There are signs that such a strategy could be implemented between Japan and Korea, for instance. When the basic conditions are met and leaders understand the dynamics of the history problem, it is possible – even probable – that other countries as well will "begin to walk the path to reconciliation together."

# Index